CRITICAL PERSPECTIVES
IN MANAGEMENT CONTROL

Also by Wai Fong Chua

MANAGERIAL ACCOUNTING: METHOD AND MEANING
(*with R. M. S. Wilson*)

Also by Tony Lowe

*NEW PERSPECTIVES IN MANAGEMENT CONTROL
(*editor with John L. J. Machin*)

Also by Tony Puxty

NEW DIRECTIONS IN FINANCIAL CONTROL (*editor*)
REDUCTIONISM AD ABSURDUM: Critiques of Agency Theory in Accountancy (*editor*)
ORGANIZATION AND MANAGEMENT: An Accountant's Perspective
*MULTINATIONAL ENTERPRISE: An Encyclopaedic Dictionary of Concepts and Terms (*with Ankie M. M. Hoogvelt*)
FINANCIAL MANAGEMENT: METHOD AND MEANING
(*with J. C. Dodds*)

* *Also published by Macmillan*

Critical Perspectives in Management Control

Edited by

Wai Fong Chua
Senior Lecturer in Accounting
University of New South Wales

Tony Lowe
Emeritus Professor of Accounting and Financial Management
University of Sheffield

and

Tony Puxty
Professor of Accounting and Finance
University of Strathclyde

© Wai Fong Chua, Tony Lowe and Tony Puxty 1989

All rights reserved. No reproduction, copy or transmission of this publication may be made without written permission.

No paragraph of this publication may be reproduced, copied or transmitted save with written permission or in accordance with the provisions of the Copyright, Designs and Patents Act 1988, or under the terms of any licence permitting limited copying issued by the Copyright Licensing Agency, 90 Tottenham Court Road, London W1T 4LP.

Any person who does any unauthorised act in relation to this publication may be liable to criminal prosecution and civil claims for damages.

The authors have asserted their rights to be identified as the authors of this work in accordance with the Copyright, Designs and Patents Act 1988.

Published by
PALGRAVE
Houndmills, Basingstoke, Hampshire RG21 6XS and
175 Fifth Avenue, New York, N.Y. 10010
Companies and representatives throughout the world

PALGRAVE is the new global academic imprint of
St. Martin's Press LLC Scholarly and Reference Division and
Palgrave Publishers Ltd (formerly Macmillan Press Ltd).

ISBN 978-0-333-38355-1

This book is printed on paper suitable for recycling and made from fully managed and sustained forest sources.

A catalogue record for this book is available from the British Library.

Transferred to digital printing 2001

We dedicate this book to the memory of **David Rosenberg,** whose critical qualities and boundless enthusiasm will be long remembered by all who knew him.

Contents

Notes on the Contributors   ix

PART I CRITIQUE IN CONCEPT

1 Introduction
 Wai Fong Chua, Tony Lowe and Tony Puxty   3

2 The Problems of a Paradigm: A Critique of the Prevailing Orthodoxy in Management Control
 Tony Lowe and Tony Puxty   9

3 A Strategy for the Development of Theories in Management Control
 David Otley   27

4 Accounting as Social Science: Abstract Versus Concrete Sources of Accounting Change
 Tony Lowe and Tony Tinker   47

5 Authority, Accountability and Accounting
 Tony Berry   63

6 Power and Management Control
 Keith Robson and David J. Cooper   79

7 Ideology, Rationality and the Management Control Process
 Tony Puxty and Wai Fong Chua   115

8 Accounting and the Pursuit of Social Interests
 Anthony Hopwood   141

PART II CRITIQUE IN ACTION

9 Labour and Deskilling: A Critique of Managerial Control in the Glass Industry
   John Black and Fiona Neathey 161

10 The Management and Control of Experts and Expertise: The Case of the Nurse
    Wai Fong Chua 189

11 Accounting in the Production and Reproduction of Culture
    Teresa Capps, Trevor Hopper, Jan Mouritsen, David Cooper and Tony Lowe 217

12 The Accounting Profession, Corporatism and the State
    David Cooper, Tony Puxty, Tony Lowe and Hugh Willmott 245

13 Authority or Domination: Alternative Possibilities for the Practice of Control
    John Roberts 271

14 Professional Authority and Resource Allocation: Treasurers and Politics in UK Local Governments
    David Rosenberg 293

PART III AUTOCRITIQUES

15 Autocritique I
    Keith Maunders 325

16 Autocritique II
    Hugh Willmott 331

Index 341

Notes on the Contributors

Tony Berry is Senior Lecturer in Management Control at the Manchester Business School.

John Black is Principal Lecturer in Manpower Studies, The Wolverhampton Business School, Polytechnic of Wolverhampton.

Teresa Capps is an accountant with a major company.

Wai Fong Chua is Senior Lecturer in Accounting at the University of New South Wales.

David Cooper is Price Waterhouse Professor of Accounting and Finance at the University of Manchester Institute of Science and Technology.

Trever Hopper is Senior Lecturer in the Department of Accounting and Finance at the University of Manchester.

Anthony Hopwood is Arthur Young Professor of International Accounting and Financial Management at the London School of Economics and Political Science.

Tony Lowe is Emeritus Professor of Accounting and Financial Management at the University of Sheffield and after retirement has been attached to the University of Manchester Institute of Science and Technology. He is also serving as a Visiting Professor at the Universities of East Anglia and Southampton and at Trent Polytechnic.

Keith Maunders is Professor of Business Finance and Accounting at the University of Leeds.

Jan Mouritsen is Lektor at the Copenhagen School of Business Administration.

Fiona Neathey is Research Officer with the Civil and Public Services Association.

David Otley is Professor of Management Control in the Department of Accounting and Finance at the University of Lancaster.

Tony Puxty is Professor of Accounting and Finance at the University of Strathclyde.

John Roberts is Senior Research Fellow in Organisational Development at the University of Cambridge.

Keith Robson is a lecturer in accounting at the University of Manchester Institute of Science and Technology.

David Rosenberg has been a research fellow at the University of Manchester.

Tony Tinker is Professor of Accounting at Baruch College, City University of New York.

Hugh Willmott is a Lecturer in the School of Management at the University of Manchester Institute of Science and Technology.

Part I
Critique in Concept

1 Introduction
Wai Fong Chua, Tony Lowe and Tony Puxty

This is the second volume of papers to be produced by the Management Control Workshop Group, and follows from New Perspectives in Management Control which was edited by Tony Lowe and John Machin. The first volume was intended to survey the existing literature in management control, since it was felt that insufficient work had been published in this area.

The purpose of this second volume is different. Although some critical comment was inevitable and necessary in the first volume, it was not its primary purpose: but it is central to the purpose of the current collection. The development of management control generally in the literature and in management practice, as well as in the summary provided in the first volume, has been a positivistic one. It has developed quite narrowly. It has developed with little discussion of the social and/or moral conditions under which it does, can or should take place. It has tended to the furtherance of technical control. In short, management control as an area of study has not taken itself reflectively as a subject of discussion: the need for management control has been taken to be unproblematic, and writings in the area have then tended to be problem-solving discussions of how to achieve what managers are supposed to want. In this sense, therefore, management control has had an ideological bias in favour of those in positions of power and authority who seek more effective ways of controlling others. This need not however form the limits of the notion of management control: a critical approach is perfectly possible and, it is believed, thoroughly desirable. To make this clear it is necessary to discuss in some detail two terms in the title of this book: *management control* and *critique*.

As the first paper in this collection shows, the whole phrase management control – at least, as an area of study – arose from a broadening of management accounting. There is however no reason why the idea should be restricted in this way. A whole range of devices are available to control organisations – for example, personnel selection, Muzak for production workers, company pension schemes – and to restrict the useful phrase 'management control' to accounting is to distort the whole range which the idea of control implies.

There are moreover three clearly distinct meanings of control: one, as a means of steering or regulation, which is the classical cybernetic meaning: a second as a means of domination of one or more people or groups of people by other people or groups, which has more sociological and political overtones: and a third, as a process of the management of control and power.[1] Some, such as the cyberneticians themselves, have sought to distance 'control' from the idea of domination – the control by mutual veto idea of Ashby (1956) was particularly important in this regard – but study of the papers in this book suggests that perhaps regulation and domination are not so distinct as this suggests.

The second matter which needs discussion is the term *critique*. The idea of critique comes from German idealist philosophy, and is not the same as criticism – although clearly the two are closely related. In the development of knowledge, Popper, who seems to have been awarded paradigmatic status by many writers in economics and accounting whose familiarity with methodology is cursory at best, takes criticism of theories about the nature of reality to be essential to knowledge development. Criticism, in other words, is part of the process which examines theories that purport to explain reality, and declines to take them on trust: rather, it tries to find fault with them.

Critique goes beyond this. It takes criticism of previous knowledge to be fundamental to the development of new knowledge. In particular, dialectical and reflective criticism of ideas – and social structures themselves in some cases – is taken to be the natural way in which valid new knowledge can come about. Through the very nature of criticism of others' ideas a more valid set of propositions is believed to be attainable. Granting the value of previous work in the area concerned with which the writer does not agree in full, (s)he believes that it is through a dialogue with those ideas that a refining or even a complete revolution in thought can take place. This is a natural method therefore for those who do not believe in value-free observation; who believe in the intrinsic value of reflection and dialogue rather than assertion: and who hence take the human sciences (*Geisteswissenschaften*) to be different in nature from the physical sciences. Moreover the ultimate purpose of critique is different: unlike positivism, it does not take the purpose of inquiry to be 'discovery of facts' but much more. As Giddens (1977) has written of critical theory (see Puxty and Chua in this volume for a further discussion of management control in the context of critical theory)

> If there is a single dominating element... it is the defence of Reason (*Vernunft*) understood in the sense of Hegel and classical German philosophy: as the critical faculty which reconciles knowledge with the transformation of the world so as to further human fulfilment and freedom.[2]

This may be contrasted with a positivist conception of knowledge development. Taking the natural sciences as the model, positivism works within a framework and, taking the previous work within that framework as its starting point, it builds upon that. It does not see critique of other schools of thought to be important. Because of its immanent faith in the value of theory-free observation, it supposes that the truth of propositions can be found unproblematically in observation of the world. Hence acknowledgement of alternative views through critique is viewed as a fruitless task.

All writers in this volume do not take an approach based upon this notion of critique – indeed, diversity of view is a cornerstone of the volume – but the configuration of this diversity within an intention to be critical is taken as basic to the construction of the volume itself. It is also the reason for the closing autocritiques, in which the editors practice what they preach.

Mention of the autocritiques brings us to the structure of the volume. There are three sections in the book, entitled Critique in Concept, Critique in Action, and Autocritiques. These headings are not accidental: to have headed the first two (for instance) 'Theory' and 'Evidence' would have violated the spirit of epistemology which we as editors support. It would have incorporated at least two errors: first, the error of implying that theories and evidence are separate methodological stages and second, the error of implying that evidence is theory-free. We propose that the empirical situations analysed should be considered by the reader in the light of the methodological matters discussed above. In a similar way, to omit the appellation 'empirical' from the first section is to imply, wrongly, that theoretical issues are separate from the world of affairs. This is also mistaken: theory should always relate closely to the world. This is not to suggest that theoretical issues might not extend to highly abstract discussion: but the ultimate subject-matter of the discussion is the world-as-it-is (albeit frequently in the light of a theoretical framework based on the world-as-it-might-be).

Given that the intention of the book is critique rather than mere criticism, then, we have been careful to include a final section, the autocritique, in which the contents of the book itself are exposed to criticism. To have omitted such a section would have left us open to charges of didacticism, which must clearly be avoided.

A word is perhaps necessary at this point about the importance of the methodological and philosophical foundations of a subject. It has been suggested at times that such discussion is fruitless and smacks of scholasticism: that, in effect, what is proposed as the 'proper' method of investigation or of testing theories (for instance) has no real effect on empirical science itself. This is incorrect: on the contrary, the spirit in which theory and evidence are taken can have far-reaching implications for the development of knowledge. We give an example as evidence of this: the tendency of journal referees to be more resistant to papers which purport to give results contrary to the conventional wisdom. There is some systematic evidence of this: a controlled experiment on referees of journals of psychology, for example, showed a much greater reluctance to accept articles whose results contradicted prevailing beliefs, holding every other aspect of the research constant (Mahoney, 1977). Similarly there is anecdotal evidence of the same behaviour in the field of finance (Hempel, 1983) where papers are rejected for casting doubt on market efficiency. This appears to be a barrier to truer knowledge: but it comes about precisely because of prevailing beliefs in the nature of empirical evidence and theory, and their separation. Were such work to be considered in the spirit of critique as discussed here, then it would not violate the expectations of the gatekeepers who see it as their duty to guard the fortress of 'established knowledge'.

A final comment is necessary on the papers. They do not show a consistency of approach or view. They are indeed critical perspectives and not one perspective. Neither we, nor the authors here, believe that we have (to quote Popper again) 'the truth in our pocket'. To have imposed a homogeneity of viewpoint would, in the same way as we have detailed above, have violated the spirit of critique. We do consider however that the papers constitute a valuable addition to the literature on management control. We have learned a great deal from the process of editing this volume: we hope the reader gains as much from his or her reading of it.

Notes

1. Some further discussion on different meanings of management control can be found in the paper by Roberts in this volume.
2. A. Giddens, *Studies in Social and Political Theory* (London, 1977) p. 65.

References

W. Ross Ashby, *An Introduction to Cybernetics* (Chapman and Hall, 1956).

A. Giddens, *Studies in Social and Political Theory* (Hutchinson, 1977).

G. H. Hempel, 'Teaching and Research in Finance: Perceptions, Conflicts and the Future', *Financial Management*, Winter 1983, pp. 5–10 (presidential address to the Financial Management Association).

M. J. Mahoney, 'Publication Prejudices: An Experimental Study of Confirmatory Bias in the Peer Review System', *Cognitive Therapy and Research*, vol. 1, 1977, pp. 161–75.

2 The Problems of a Paradigm: A Critique of the Prevailing Orthodoxy in Management Control

Tony Lowe and Tony Puxty

The genesis of management control is difficult to trace – perhaps because, in the manner of Humpty Dumpty, different writers use the term to mean what they want it to mean. Giglioni and Bedeian (1974) see the earliest writings in the area being those of Emerson, Church and Diemer, who were writing in 1912, 1914 and 1915 respectively. Already at that date, the link between accounting and the control of the enterprise was being forged: they emphasised the importance of adequate records, of comparison with standards, and with the adequacy of those standards. Giglioni and Bedeian quote Church as follows:

> [the comparison is based on] three elements: (a) recognition of what facts are truly significant; (b) accurate record and convenient presentation of these facts; (c) judicious action based on study of the facts.

The modern development of management control as a subject within the field of accounting must however be credited to Robert Anthony and his colleagues at the Harvard Business School. Management control was intended to be a broadening out of the more technical kinds of accounting which were then taught – the mechanics of costing and bookkeeping methods.[1] Through this, it was felt, one of the essential functions of accounting could be applied in its context, and at the same time be enriched by the findings of other management researchers where they impinged on accounting. Until then the sole link between accounting and other disciplines had been economics, and the development of income theory had already reached a considerable degree of sophistication. Law, of course, has also been important to accounting history because of the significance accorded to accounting information in corporate legislation. But by the early 1960s it was becoming evident that other disciplines could throw light on the relevance of accounting to the firm: and chief among these was social psychology.

The link between accounting and social psychology can probably be traced at its earliest to the pioneering work of Chris Argyris (1952) who researched the effects budgeting systems had on middle management and supervisory grades. Development of the link, of the evident enrichment which could come from the insights social psychology could add to the accounting process, were at first slow. But they gained momentum throughout the decade, and the 1960s academics could base their research on a growing body of knowledge at the level of the individual: in particular, the effects of budget systems on motivation.

This body of knowledge was of course known at Harvard: but they were also able to add insights from the rapidly growing area of organisation theory. This had been fragmented, the interest of a minority of sociologists and industrial psychologists: but perhaps the turning point may be traced to publication of March and Simon's classic book *Organisations* (1958).[2] Here, perhaps for the first time, the particular characteristics of the organisation were being looked at within a coherent framework of their own. No longer did the reader have to turn to the (fragmented) translations of Max Weber (whose orientation was in any case very different from his own, interested as Weber was essentially in the interrelation between organisation type and societal development) or the mechanical prognostications of Frederick Taylor, or the equally mechanical if broader writings of practical businessmen such as Fayol, Urwick and Brech. A basis now existed for a theoretical and rigorous approach to the analysis of organisations.

With these as sources, a body of knowledge known as 'management control' could be tentatively developed. It can be seen from the first edition of Anthony, Dearden and Vancil's *Management Control Systems* (1965) just how tentative they were at the time. The opening essay of the book laid down the essential differences between strategic planning and management control: in particular, the 'source disciplines' of these two topics were said to be 'economics' and 'social psychology' respectively. Little of social psychology is seen in the rest of the book, however: apart from some implicit social psychology in the discussion of ideas such as decentralisation and the expense centre/financial performance centre/investment centre distinction, the book turns out to be concerned in the main with information and financial assessment. This has changed to some extent by the fifth edition (Anthony, Dearden and Bedford, 1984). By now the readings have gone, to be replaced by a more integrated text: and the text itself includes a 28-page essay entitled 'Control and Organizational Behaviour'. The structure of the book is also more assured, being divided into four parts entitled 'An Overview', 'The Management Control Structure' (which includes the material on different types of accounting centre) 'The Management Control Process' and 'Special Management Control Situations'. It might be said, therefore, that in the Harvard perspective at least, management control has come of age, and its subject matter and the way in which it should be approached are agreed upon. The influence of the approach can be seen in later works such as those by Dermer (1977) and Euske (1984).

The approach taken by these writers (which we shall describe in more detail in the next section) might still be said to be the ruling paradigm of management control, both in the eyes of management teachers and in the eyes of practical businessmen. Yet the insights available from the disciplines marshalled – principally, as we have said, social psychology – are limited in their applicability. Other disciplines can add much (such as general systems theory, sociology and cybernetics) and we shall discuss ways in which we feel that the approach taken by the classic authors is now incomplete and thus, as a managerial prescription, misleading. In taking these authors as our touchstone we are not questioning the value of the orientation which they have given to accounting, in helping it to move from a technical perspective to a more useful organisational perspective:[3] rather, we are choosing the latest edition of Anthony and his colleagues' work as a subject for critique precisely because of its authority. We begin by outlining our understanding of its approach and subject-matter.

THE ARCHITECTURE OF A PARADIGM

The book opens by outlining the general nature of control as it is understood by the authors. This is done in terms of negative feedback: of a process, a comparison with standard, and an effector to change the process if necessary to maintain its performance as near as possible to the standard. It is, therefore, essentially cybernetic, although a very simple kind of cybernetics. On page 6 a reference is given to Norbert Wiener and his book *Cybernetics* (1961): the term does not appear in the index however, and we must assume that the science of cybernetics itself is not considered relevant to the authors' purposes. From this general discussion of control they then consider its nature specifically in the organisation and, after noting certain differences between other control processes and organisational control they move on to consider management control and its characteristics as contrasted with strategic planning and task control.

It is at this stage that they define management control in the context of strategic planning which they have defined immediately previously:

> management control is the process by which management assures that the organization carries out its strategies.
> (Anthony, Dearden and Bedford (1984) p. 10)

In this way they make the distinction between planning and control quite clear. Strategic planning sets the strategies: management control checks they are being pursued appropriately. Their distinction between management control and (on each conceptual side) strategic planning and task control is given considerable prominence at this stage, and is seemingly done to assure the reader of the precise subject-matter of the rest of the book. By means of their definition they explain who carries out these functions, their nature (in such terms as time horizon and appraisal of the function's proper execution) and, as already mentioned, the source disciplines used. It is important for our later discussion to appreciate the restrictions placed on the nature of management control in these pages: it is programmed (in Simon's terms), concerns line and top management, involves large numbers of people, is concerned with administrative procedures, which are effected by 'persuasion', tends to have a short time horizon and is rather easier (although not 'easy') than strategic planning to appraise when done. We should like to emphasise here that it is concerned essentially with the control of *people rather than events*.

To close the introductory chapter, the authors give their phases of the process of management control. These are

1. Programming
2. Budgeting
3. Operating and Measurement
4. Reporting and Analysis

These are explicated in detail in Part III of the book.

The rest of Part I of the book consists of three chapters. The first, entitled 'Control and Organization Behaviour' outlines some elementary ideas of corporate structure in terms of managerial hierarchies – in fact, in common with the literature of organisational behaviour, structure is considered to be synonymous with the hierarchy of the people in the organisation; it considers a few characteristics of the individual which are seen as relevant to management, in particular, motivation: and the chapter ends with some comments on the function of the controller in the organisation. The second looks at goals and strategies. The third considers quite briefly some characteristics of information transmission in organisations.

Part II, which concerns structure (which, as we have already explained, means managerial structure), centres around the idea of reporting centres: and the characteristics of revenue and expense centres, and profit centres are explored in one chapter each, a separate chapter being devoted to transfer pricing. It is of course true that the organisation of the enterprise is being made congruent with the organisation of the management; the fact that a manager is responsible for a particular area of the enterprise has implications for the actual operation (as is shown by the classic case of Birch Paper Co.). Finally, there is a chapter on investment centres.

Some perhaps fairly obvious points should be mentioned at this stage about the implicit model of man presented here as a manager. He is, basically, expected to be in favour of the success of the total enterprise, although he is also self-interested, and will tend to put himself first when any conflict of interest arises. He is not expected to be wholly self-disciplined: procedures of accountability are intrinsic to the hierarchical structure of the responsibility-centre system, and externally imposed standards are there to ensure that he does not slip back. Despite these faults, he does not allow any matters extrinsic to the organisation to affect his orientation to his job: the control procedures of the firm take no account of his features other than as a 'managerial hand and mind'.

When we turn to Part III we find a discussion of the process of management control. This is based on the five headings of Programming; Budget Preparation; Analysing and Reporting Financial Performance; the Profit Budget in the Control Process; and Executive Compensation Plans. Each of these is the subject-matter of one chapter. The first two of these are heavily rationalistic, proposing procedures which are/should be gone through by management (the normative is not distinguished from the positive, so it is not always possible to tell to what extent the authors are describing what they believe to be business reality and the extent to which they are prescribing 'good' procedures). To the extent that social psychology is considered, it is only implicit, so that, for example, certain procedures are expected to motivate; other procedures recognise cognitive limits: and so on. There is no explicit discussion of human behaviour. The third chapter of this section is entirely devoted to variance analysis, and is similar to cost accounting textbooks.

The fourth chapter appears to reflect the philosophy of such management writers as Koontz, O'Donnell and Weihrich (1980) in its discussion of budget problems and performance appraisal. The fifth chapter, taking it for granted that bonus plans will 'encourage high performance by allowing managers to participate financially in the results of their accomplishments' (p. 585), discusses the different kinds of scheme available.

Part IV is concerned with special kinds of problems: multinational corporations, service organisations, non-profit organisations, and projects. Since it is essentially an application of the philosophy of the rest of the book to these areas it will not be considered further.

We have felt it necessary to go rapidly through the structure of Anthony, Dearden and Bedford's book despite the fact that this paper is not intended to be a book review but rather, as we stated earlier, because its very structure tells us the message behind its approach. We can now proceed to an evaluation.

AN EVALUATION

Before we consider our specific criticisms of this approach in detail, it is perhaps useful to clarify our contrasted approach to that of Anthony by means of diagrammatic representation. Anthony (1965) gives Figure 2.1 as a guide to his thinking. Anthony and Dearden (1976) give Figure 2.2. A better understanding of their approach as it now stands might however be depicted as in Figure 2.3. This

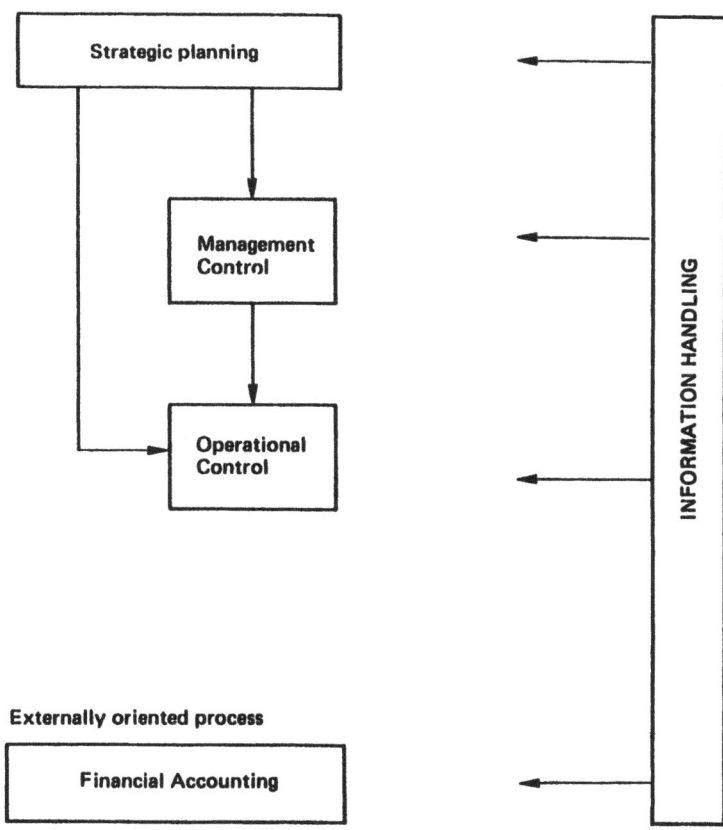

Figure 2.1

gives, specifically, a clarification of their ideas concerning the domain of strategic planning, management control, and task control.

We might suggest that a better approach is that shown in Figure 2.4. There is still a tripartite division; but it is now based specifically on an environmentally-founded typology. The environment is given prominence, as is the feedback loop which has effect coterminately with the environment. Above all, the difference between this approach and that of Anthony is that here, all decision functions are accommodated within the idea of management control, and contrasted with the subject matter of decisions made for control – namely financial funds and the physical subsystem.

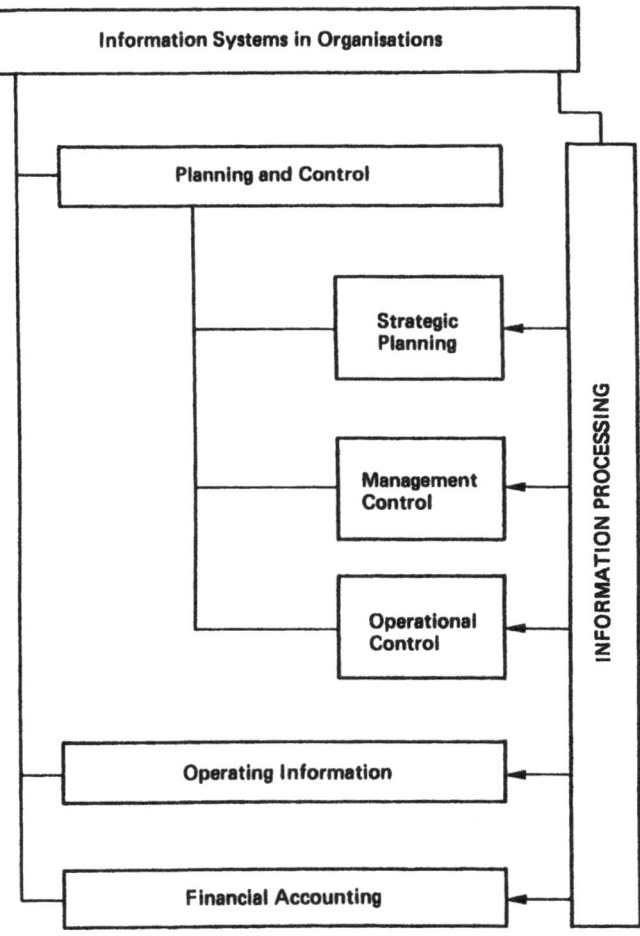

Figure 2.2

We now turn to an examination of the specific subject-matter of Anthony, Dearden and Bedford's book. We consider our objections to their scheme under seven headings.

The Environment and the Organisation

It is generally recognised in much recent literature that the environment of an organisation has a critical role in the determination of

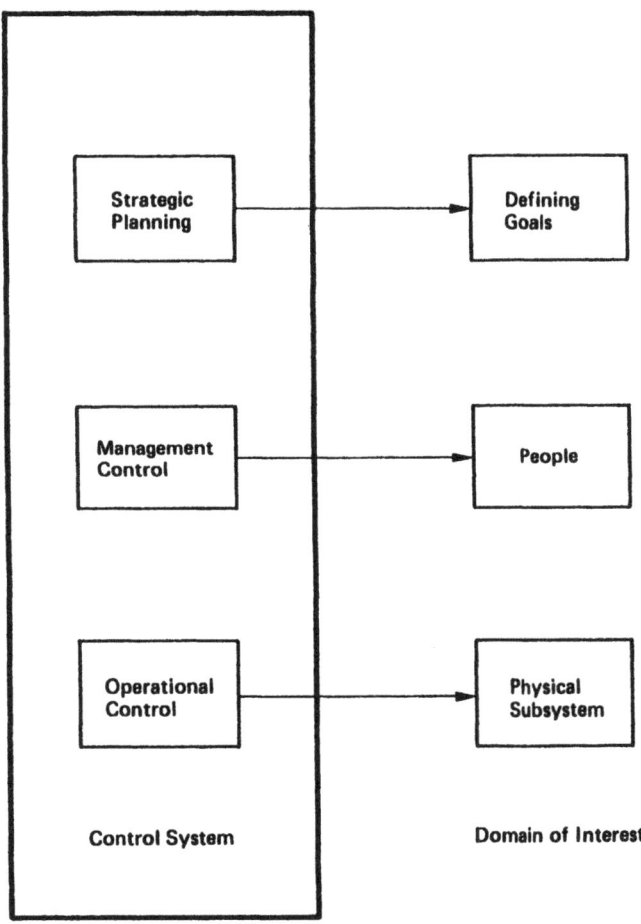

Figure 2.3

the organisation's success. The organisation exists because there is a need for it within the environment: and conversely, the organisation is dependent on its environment for resources. Much research has analysed this interdependence between the organisation and its environment (for example Rhenman, 1973; Lawrence and Lorsch, 1967; Duncan, 1972; Terreberry, 1968; Aldrich, 1979; Karpik, 1978; Pfeffer and Salancik, 1978). The most basic message of cybernetics and general systems theory is that control of an organisation is

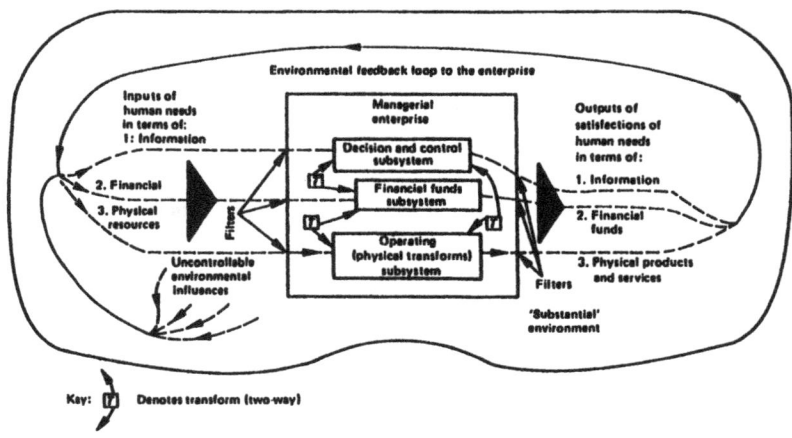

Figure 2.4

dependent on its being able to control its relationship with its environment (Lowe, 1971; Lowe and McInnes, 1971). Yet in the whole of the approach advocated by Anthony's paradigm, we find little acknowledgement of the environment.[4] Instead of relating control to the environment it is defined as

> (1) *planning* what the organization should do, (2) *co-ordinating* the activities of the several parts of the organization, (3) *communicating* information, (4) *evaluating* information and deciding what, if any, action should be taken, (5) *influencing* people to change their behaviour, and (6) *processing information* that is used in the other functions.
>
> (p. 6)[5]

The whole emphasis of this is on internal processes: on actions to be taken within the organisation. It is of course true that these actions will affect the relationship of the organisation to its environment, but this relationship is not made explicit and the specific ways in which it should be governed are not discussed. The result is an inward-looking philosophy of control which, by concentrating on a small part of the control process, ignores the most important part.

Control as Feedback

As a result, control is seen as a feedback process only. Just as Anthony, Dearden and Bedford take as their starting point for comparison the thermostat (a discrete regulator) and the body's homeostat (a continuous regulator) so they consider the control process as a feedback process only.

The result is that the reader is led to expect that control can only take place after the event. This is of course exemplified in the variance analysis of cost and budget statements. The understanding of the concept 'control' is thus imprisoned in the idea of the time-lagged regulator. Yet this is, in fact, the least effective and least efficient type of regulator. Consider Figure 2.5 (Lowe, Puxty and Tinker, 1979).

E = environmental variety
S = system
M = regulator
σ = effect upon system

Figure 2.5

In the first case, M forms a perfect regulator: it is able to sense the coming environmental variety and counter it in such a way that the state of the system S is preserved and there is no change in σ. In the second case the regulator is imperfect, and attempts to counter disturbances by sensing their immediate effects on the system. The third case is the error-controlled regulator: only after the system has been disturbed does it take remedial action. It is this third case that is exemplified by cost-variance analysis.

Now it is quite true that this traditional approach to management control recognises future control: it calls it planning. However, the very fact that planning is supposed to be *different* from control acts as a barrier to its integration into the total concept of the control system.

Planning and Control

Intuitively obvious, it is this dichotomy that appears to have hidden the true meaning of planning. Instead of the emphasis being placed on its role as a tool for controlling the future, emphasis is put on its relation to what orthodoxy restricts under the heading of control. *First* plans are made: *then* control takes over and ensures that plans are, so far as possible, adhered to. Now it cannot be denied that certain planning processes are discrete, and take place at specified intervals (such as a year) in a very formal way. Yet they are only a part of a much more general process which is taking place at all levels of the organisation all the time: the process of trying to foresee the next move in the organisation's relationship to its environment and take such action as will minimise disruption caused by any change.

Plans are formalisations of the process, and are useful in the total control process. Yet planning should be seen as a part of control rather than a prior but distinct process. As the framework stands, it seems to imply that if certain bureaucratic routines are kept to, control will result. This ignores the work of Burns and Stalker (1961) and Lawrence and Lorsch (1967) which suggest that in dynamic environments, the best organisation structures are those that are more prepared to adapt and which design their structure so as to facilitate this adaptation. Reliance on predesigned procedures will not do this: and as such, the emphasis we find here is positively misleading as a prescription, since environments are, in general, becoming more and more dynamic (cf. Emery and Trist, 1965). Remarkably, Anthony, Dearden and Bedford acknowledge contingency theory (pp. 46–7) while in most of the book continuing to put forward universal propositions.

A similar rigidity is to be seen in Anthony's distinction between strategic planning, management control and task control.

The Three-Way Distinction

As we have seen in our description of their framework, Anthony Dearden and Bedford consider this three-way distinction to be of great importance in defining their topic. Considerable detail is given to ensure that there is no confusion among the three levels. Despite the authors' assurance that 'we do not mean to imply that the three planning and control processes can be separated by sharply-defined boundaries; one shades into another' there is no disguising the fact that by designating the 'middle ground' of control as management control, and specifying that it is essentially psychologically-based, an opportunity is lost to emphasise the holistic nature of control. By creating this distinction they ensure that the general control problem – that which, in Beer's (1981) terminology would be systems 4 and 5 – is not to be confused with 'management control'. They ensure that the reader's attention is moved also from the more routine day-to-day control problems which are designated 'task control'. Of course, they do not deny that these are control processes: but the very act of shunting them off to a different world leaves one without an integrating framework to see how the three 'levels' fit in and interrelate in the achievement of control.

A particularly unfortunate result of this, then, is the lack of a holistic framework once again: a lack of recognition that the control problems interrelate in such a way that action to improve control in one area of the organisation will almost certainly have repercussions on other aspects of the organisation.

This causes another conceptual difficulty: because in defining the predictive function as the task of top management (that is, within the province of strategic planning) they fail to make it clear to the middle manager (supposedly particularly concerned with their concept of management control) that a predictive function as to future actions in his environment is essential to his effectiveness as a manager. Instead, there is an emphasis on the feedback function: on corrections of the past. Yet prediction, as part of the control process, is central to all kinds of control continuously at all levels of the organisation. It is particularly interesting that management control under Anthony's definition is claimed to be 'total control': because when it comes to a definition of that concept, the closed system nature of traditional thinking becomes plain:

> a management control system is a *total organizational system* in that it embraces all aspects of organization operations.
> (p. 13)

The Management Control Structure

When we turn to look at Part II of Anthony, Dearden and Bedford's book, we find that the structure of management control is concerned with responsibility centres of various kinds. Responsibility is a human concept: which brings us to the interesting observation that management control is being defined as control over people rather than control over or for an organisation as such. Control the people, the argument seems to suggest, and you have achieved control over the organisation. It will be seen how this links in to the social-psychological basis which, it is claimed, underlies management control.

Yet a proper understanding of control, as has already been suggested, is predicated on an understanding of the necessary relation between an organisation and its environment. Control over the people within the organisation in the very restricted sense is not control in a true sense. In the first place, it assumes a relation between the people 'controlled' and the actual operating system which interacts with the organisation's environment: and in the second place, it ignores one crucial feature of organisational control: the extent to which the organisation can dominate its environment (Rhenman). Being able to ensure that the managers controlled do as the plans require is a very different concept from being able to ensure that the organisation adapts, or dominates so as to reduce the need for adapting, to its environment. This match between the organisation's capabilities and the environment's demands is crucial: but a myopic insistence on profit-achievement will not ensure this in the long run.

Reification: Deification?

The nature of the relationship between the organisation and the society in which it is embedded has already been briefly discussed. The nature of the organisation's relation to its environment and of its goals cannot be understood except in the context of its relations with its wider social context. Equally, it is necessary to understand this context in order to understand the relation of the organisation to those who make it up: in particular, those who work for it.

In speaking of an organisation in this way, we are implicitly reifying it. To reify an organisation in isolation from its context however is a dangerous analytic approach.

Anthony, Dearden and Bedford do not analyse the social context of the organisation at all: and in such an omission they allow themselves to imply that, not only is the organisation a significant entity in itself (which is as may be) but it can do 'what it wishes': and it has 'goals' which appear from nowhere and then become imperatives upon the managers who must try to satisfy those goals.

A management control system ... is tailored to the particular goals of and the particular strategies of the organization ... the systems designer should insure that the control system is consistent with the organization's goals, whatever they are ... we use the term *goals* to mean broad, fairly timeless statements of what the organization wants to achieve.

'Wanting to achieve', we suggest, is simply not on. The goals of the organisation cannot be considered in isolation from the context in which it exists: and that context will constrain the organization – it will imbue the organisation through the fact that the members of the organisational coalition are also members of the environment – in such a way that, although not preordained, the goals cannot be considered as decidable 'by' the organisation. This is not achieved by the acknowledgement that 'goal changes may have to be made when the conditions of survival and growth imposed by a changed environment demand them' (p. 95) because there is still an unacceptable degree of voluntarism, rationality and intentionality implicit here.

Moreover, this approach distances the participants from the organisation. An organisational system is certainly more than the sum of its parts: but nevertheless it does consist of those parts, and it is misleading to treat it as some kind of deity that is to be served by those who happen to be its managers.

Structural Invariance

Finally, we must consider the way in which a school of thought such as this views organisational structure. Any organisation does indeed have a real structure but that structure is not the one which appears on organisation charts, or on the basis of which accounting systems are set up which allocate responsibility on the basis of responsibility centres. The true structure of an organisation is a renegotiation through a continuous process, and it is continually changing in subtle ways (see, for example, Murray and Puxty, 1981). The formal structure is a 'wish' by certain 'designers' of the organisation: it is in reality merely one more constraint on the way in which the real structure comes into being and changes over time.

This real structure is not considered by the traditional 'rationalist' school at all. Instead, the 'formal', planned structure is treated as if it were the real and only structure; and it is considered as *invariant*.[6]

Despite any evidence that organisations do change their structures (both real and formal) and despite the evidence of researchers that structure must be changed as other circumstances alter (see the considerable literature which treats structure in relation to environment, technology and size) no mention is made of changes, and in fact, the very treatment in the book we have been considering – in which various kinds of responsibility centre are treated in one chapter each, as if they were essential for all organisations at all times – gives an impression of such a narrow focus.

This is particularly dangerous when one considers the influence such a book has. It is intended as a manual to teach management control. It is concerned particularly with case studies, as a result of which the student is intended to come to conclusions as to the 'best' solution to adopt. If (s)he is constrained from adopting a solution of structural change, his or her mental set will become imbued with the notion that structure is and should be invariant: the structural change solution is not one that will even be considered (see Puxty and Chua, this volume).

CONCLUSION

It is particularly unfortunate that at a time of rapid change and development in our understanding of organisational processes (see, for example, the work of Hage, Aiken, Pennings, Aldrich, Weick and Karpik) a myopic approach to control can still be taught as legitimately useful: and indeed still considered the standard work on its topic. It is quite possible that in certain organisations in certain circumstances in certain cultural milieux the approach advocated by Anthony, Dearden and Bedford might be effective. But even in these circumstances it is being effective on the basis of a partial truth: one which, moreover, acknowledges no contingency of essential variables other than that implicit in those authors' last part (non-profit organisations and so on).

It is even more unfortunate when alternative schemas are becoming available. Despite Hofstede's (1975) misgivings, there is no poverty of management control philosophy. Open systems approaches to organisations are fruitful; cybernetics is not merely a matter of negative feedbacks (as Hofstede seems to imagine): and the understanding we already have of organisational processes, although certainly still fragmented, is sufficient to give a beginning to a new route that is still unmapped by Anthony, Dearden and Bedford.

Notes

1. This broadening out was also to be seen in other areas at the same time: see in particular the emergence of 'business policy' as a subject.
2. This is not to suggest that this work was a sudden efflorescence: its roots may be seen in the earlier work by Simon, *et al.* (1954).
3. Indeed, Anthony recognised early on the role of a preliminary framework: '... development of a framework or a conceptual scheme often has led to progress, *even though the framework turns out to be wrong*' (his emphasis) (Anthony, 1965).
4. One page of discussion is provided of 'Externally Oriented Organization Theory' (pp. 41–2). It mentions none of these authorities, however.
5. This succinct definition is taken from Anthony and Dearden (1976). The philosophy in the latest edition, though less tightly defined, is otherwise quite similar.
6. We are indebted to John Machin for pointing this out.

References

H. E. Aldrich, *Organizations and Environments* (Prentice-Hall, 1979).
R. N. Anthony, *Planning and Control Systems* (Harvard, 1965).
R. N. Anthony, J. Dearden and R. F. Vancil, *Management Control Systems* (Irwin, 1965).
R. N. Anthony and J. Dearden, *Management Control Systems* (3rd edn: Irwin, 1976).
R. N. Anthony, J. Dearden and N. Bedford, *Management Control Systems* (5th edn: Irwin, 1984).
C. Argyris, *The Impact of Budgets on People* (Controllership Foundation, 1952).
S. Beer, *Brain of the Firm* (2nd edn: Wiley, 1981).
T. Burns and G. M. Stalker, *The Management of Innovation* (Tavistock, 1961).
J. Dermer, *Management Planning and Control Systems* (Irwin, 1977).
R. B. Duncan, 'Characteristics of Organizational Environments and Perceived Environmental Uncertainty', *Administrative Science Quarterly* 17 (1972) pp. 313–27.
F. Emery and E. Trist, 'The Causal Texture of Organizational Environments', *Human Relations* 18 (1965) pp. 21–32.
K. J. Euske, *Management Control: Planning, Control, Measurement and Evaluation* (Addison-Wesley, 1984).

G. B. Giglioni and A. G. Bedeian, 'A Conspectus of Management Control Theory: 1900–1972', *Academy of Management Journal* (June 1974) pp. 292–305.

G. H. Hofstede, 'The Poverty of Management Control Philosophy', Working paper 75–44 (Dec. 1975); European Institute for Advanced Studies in Management.

L. Karpik, *Organization and Environment* (Sage, 1978).

H. Koontz, C. O'Donnell and H. Weihrich, *Management* (7th edn: McGraw-Hill, 1980).

P. R. Lawrence and J. W. Lorsch, *Organization and Environment* (Harvard, 1967).

E. A. Lowe, 'On the Idea of a Management Control System', *Journal of Management Studies* (Feb. 1971) pp. 1–12.

E. A. Lowe and J. M. McInnes, 'Control in Socio-Economic Organizations: A Rationale for the Design of Management Control Systems (Section 1)', *Journal of Management Studies* (May 1971) pp. 213–27.

E. A. Lowe, A. G. Puxty and A. M. Tinker, 'Improving the Accounting Function for Society: Proposals for a GST-Based Newcomer to Social Science', *Proceedings of the Silver Anniversary Meeting of the Society for General Systems Research* London (Aug. 1979).

J. G. March and H. A. Simon, *Organizations* (Wiley, 1958).

G. Murray and A. G. Puxty, 'An Action Approach to Control Systems', *Managerial Finance*, vol. 6, no. 1 (1981) pp. 9–19.

J. Pfeffer and G. Salancik, *The External Control of Organizations: A Resource Dependence Perspective* (New York: Harper and Row, 1978).

A. G. Puxty and W. F. Chua, 'Ideology, Rationality and the Management Control Process' this volume.

E. Rhenman, *Organization Theory for Long Range Planning* (Chichester: Wiley, 1973).

H. A. Simon, H. Guetzkow, G. Kozmetsky and G. Tyndall, *Centralization and Decentralization in Organizing the Controller's Department* (Controllership Foundation, 1954).

S. Terreberry, 'The Evolution of Organizational Environments', *Administrative Science Quarterly* (March 1968) vol. 12,4, pp. 540–613.

N. Wiener, *Cybernetics* (2nd edn: MIT Press, 1961).

3 A Strategy for the Development of Theories in Management Control
David Otley

There has been a tendency in recent years for management research to become polarised into two distinct streams, one predominately theoretical in approach, the other empirical. The first stream of work constructs overall theoretical frameworks, maybe drawn from a number of source disciplines, but having little empirical content. The second stream concerns itself with testing hypotheses, but hypotheses which often have only a tenuous connection with any coherent body of theory. Further, the results obtained from the two streams appear to have little impact on each other. Such a polarisation between what may be disparagingly described as the armchair generation of theory at the one extreme and mindless empiricism at the other is particularly unfortunate in a discipline having such immediate real-world application.

This paper begins by evaluating the contribution that can be made by paying greater attention to the integration of theoretical and empirical work in management research. Some examples from research in management accounting and organisation theory are given to illustrate the view that a polarisation in research approaches has occurred. A management control systems approach is then outlined, which has the advantage of providing an integrative theoretical focus combining both economic and behavioural approaches whilst covering a broad spectrum of management-related research. It is argued that a significant missing element in academic work on management control is the generation of theoretical structures soundly based on empirical observation. Such an approach, described by some sociologists as the generation of grounded theory, is then applied to the study of management control to demonstrate that it provides a means of integrating both approaches to management research. In particular, it is used to examine the neglected role of accounting data as a source of information for the management researcher.

APPROACHES TO MANAGEMENT RESEARCH

There are many different approaches to management research because many different issues and problems are being tackled. There can be no universally preferrred research methodology because a methodology can be assessed only in relationship to the problem it is attempting to tackle and the theoretical framework being adopted; it is a means rather than an end. However some fields of research do seem to have restricted themselves to a single methodology, with the rigorous and quantitative testing of hypotheses seemingly being regarded as the only valid approach. It will be argued here that other approaches are valid and necessary, with an example being given from the interface between management accounting and organisation theory.

Individuals seek patterns in their observations from which they form general explanations and make predictions. Scientific research can be regarded as a formalisation of these thought processes so that generalisations, perhaps raised to the status of theories, can be generated, tested and refined. This process is regarded as scientific to the extent that a correspondence is continually sought between the predicted consequences of theoretical generalisations and observed events. Thus a scientific theory represents a generalisation which explains or predicts outcomes in specific situations in a way that is open to refutation.

In many ways the verification stage of scientific research is the least problematic. The consequences of a given general theory applied to a specific situation are logically deduced and compared with observations made in some systematic manner. Discrepancies between predictions and observations are treated either as experimental error or as a stimulus to refine or reject the original theory (or perhaps most often, to question the process of deduction by which the specific hypotheses were deduced from the general theory). However the process of generating theory has received much less attention than the verification stage of research. Two processes are involved; deduction and induction. The deductive route derives a specific theory from some more general or higher level theory (incidentally raising the question of where the higher level theory itself came from). The inductive route generalises some specific results into a more complete or encompassing framework. Both processes are necessary, yet in management research most effort seems to have been devoted to the deduction of specific hypotheses and their empirical verification. Despite the fact that many of the results of this process are of low statistical significance, much less attention has been paid to the process of inducing and developing theory from observations, even when the data gathered has proved inconsistent with the prior hypotheses.

The inductive generation of theory still appears to be a controversial approach even in organisation theory where it has perhaps been most used. It has attracted criticism such as that by Hage (1980):

> The second error (when constructing theoretical models) is to fail to develop a number of general variables, that is, theoretical concepts, in these areas. Unfortunately, many sociologists have accepted the inductive model, relying on research as a method of generating ideas. Instead I would advocate that one should develop concepts and even hypotheses beforehand, and then use research to test them.

Yet such a criticism may be considered to be directed more at poorly performed inductive research than at the inductive model itself. What has been justly criticised as 'mindless empiricism' has been an over-concern with the collection of data with little concern for generating theoretical structures to explain it.

The distinction between deductive and inductive research has often been paralleled by that of quantitative and qualitative research. Deduction has been more prevalent in the quantitative desciplines such as economics; induction in the more qualitative behavioural sciences. There has also been a tendency to exalt quantitative research methodologies as being more scientific than their qualitative counterparts. This is unfortunate as both inductive and deductive processes are necessary in all research. As one cannot observe the real world without a prior conceptual framework, it is as well to make this as explicit as possible; nevertheless it is also possible to remain open to having one's prior categories and concepts modified by the research experience and to allow for the research design to be amended as information is collected and analysed. This inductive approach, referred to by some sociologists as the development of 'grounded theory' (Glaser and Strauss, 1967), seems to be underrepresented in much management research. However I will restrict myself to commenting on the interface between management accounting and organisation theory.

Management accounting is a widely occurring organisational process, yet one which has tended to be studied in isolation from its organisational context. Hopwood (1980) has characterised the situation as follows:

> Rather than delving into the complexities of accounting as it is practised, so often (accounting scholars of the behavioural) have preferred to rely on the possibilities of the psychological laboratory. Indeed it is difficult to name more than a handful of enquiries that have been undertaken within the factory gate – or even outside the college wall. The world of accounting as it is has been largely ignored. Seemingly questions of internal validity have been emphasised to the almost complete neglect of external validity. Almost invariably, emphasis has been placed on methodological rather than theoretical sophistication and on the rigours of hypothesis testing rather than theory generation.... Apparently it has been deemed sufficient to theorise in the armchair, to borrow a neat theory here and there and so to construct a basis for a tightly controlled excursion into a specifically constructed unknown. The net result of such a tradition of enquiry is a rather fragmented set of insights, however, many of which have a largely unknown and possibly equivocal relationship to accounting in action.

Although theoretical arguments for adopting a wider perspective have been advanced (for example by Burchell et al., 1980; and Banbury and Nahapiet, 1979) empirical studies are sparse. Although Hayes and Watson suggested in 1976 that management accounting would be integrated with organisation theory so that they would not be regarded as separate and distinct areas of knowledge, but as being reciprocally interdependent, this has shown little sign of occurring.

The uncritical use of general theories together with an undue stress on verification has been most apparent in the development of the so-called contingency theory of management accounting. Here theories were taken from the contingency theory of organisations and applied to management accounting. Unfortunately there was a tendency for researchers to take what were often tentative theories and to incorporate them uncritically into the accounting arena with little appreciation of their defects and weaknesses, even although organisational theorists themselves were becoming increasingly critical of their validity. This resulted in much of the work on hypothesis verification undertaken in the management accounting literature being of little value (see Otley (1980) for a review).

Observing the results of too much attention being paid to abstract theory generation and to verification of insubstantially based hypotheses led me to recommend a new emphasis in management accounting research (Otley, 1984). These recommendations included a stress on exploratory research using qualitative and interpretive methods where appropriate, the use of case studies as a research tool, the possibility of more action research and the greater use of contributions from other disciplines. Overall, an emphasis on the inductive generation of theory seems to offer more potential than the attempt to verify hypotheses of dubious parentage. The grounded theory approach offers one means of achieving greater emphasis on theory generation and development rather than the current preoccupation with verification.

Although the grounded theory approach was developed originally in sociology (Glaser and Strauss, 1967), it even then claimed to be the basis of a general method of comparative analysis especially well-suited to dealing with qualitative data. The approach is not, in itself, original but was explicitly propounded as a counter-weight to the trend towards quantification and verification that had developed in sociology during the 1950s and 1960s.

The essence of the grounded theory approach is that the researcher should continually be examining the data gathered during (rather than after) the research process, with a view to developing theoretical explanations for what is observed. Such tentative explanations will act as a guide to the next stage of the research. The researcher should also not be committed to a prior theoretical structure; rather it is necessary to be open to and actively explore alternative possibilities. Obviously no research approach can be theory-free; what is being suggested is the researcher should be open to having the prior theoretical structure brought to the data being challenged and amended in the light of observations. The inherent conflict between prior hypotheses and new theoretical ideas is well brought out in two quotations from the same page (p. 3) of Glaser's (1978) extension of the approach.

> The first step in gaining theoretical sensitivity is to enter the research setting with as few predetermined ideas as possible – especially logically deduced, a prior [sic] hypotheses. In this posture, the analyst is able to remain sensitive to the data by

being able to record events and detect happenings without first having them filtered through and squared with pre-existing hypotheses and biases. His mandate is to remain open to what is actually happening.

Sensitivity is necessarily increased by being steeped in the literature that deals with both the kinds of variables and the associated general ideas that will be used.

What is being recommended is that in exploratory research, aimed at the generation of theory, all steps of the research process should be undertaken by the researcher on the spot, with tentative findings guiding subsequent activity. Glaser concludes his book by stating:

> In sum, new uses and directions of grounded theory are just beginning to be proliferated. Grounded theory is a general methodology for generating theory. It is not wedded to Sociology or Social Science – let alone to any school or position in Sociology. It is useful in any field that wishes to generate inductive theory from systematically collected data, whether qualitative or quantitative. And generated theories which fit, work and are relevant have potentially many specific uses, for many fields.

I would argue that the grounded theory approach offers a way forward in management research that can aid in integrating theoretical and empirical approaches.

MANAGEMENT CONTROL SYSTEMS

It has been suggested that management is the profession of control (Beer, 1959). Certainly a great deal of management activity seems to be concerned with influencing the behaviour of others with the object of producing desired outcomes. Thus control, which is to do with keeping things on track, is one of the critical functions of management although it is necessary to question for whom and by whom control is exercised (Hopwood, in this book). It therefore appears sensible to explore the use that can be made of a management control systems (MCS) framework as a fundamental theoretical (or perhaps, meta-theoretical) approach to the study of managerial and organisational behaviour.

The MCS approach views an organisation as a controlled system, open to and interacting with a wider environment. In adapting to its environment it is directed, in part, by managers whose central role lies in ensuring that the organisation continues to exist as a viable entity. There is a broad stream of management literature which has followed this guiding framework, albeit in a variety of guises, but the core model on which it is based is drawn from cybernetics and general systems theory. For example, Beer (1972) has applied cybernetics, the science of control, to the management process, although his analogy between human nervous systems and organisational control systems is never justified theoretically. Tocher (1970) has also put forward a control model to be applied to managerial activity, but again it must be recognised that there are significant problems in transferring mechanical concepts of control into the organisational arena, as noted by Otley and Berry (1980).

General systems theory has been used as a framework for MCS seeking to explain observed behaviour by reference to open systems concepts of an organisation in an environment, the feedback and feedforward of information and by the application of holistic rather than reductionist thinking. Again it must be admitted that much systems theory is inappropriate to the analysis of human activity systems as it stems from the study of 'hard' systems where goals can be taken as given and system components engineered to fit into some overall design (Otley, 1983). The study of social systems requires a different approach such as the 'soft' systems approach pioneered by Checkland (1981). The systems approach has been categorised as sociological structural functionalism (Prévost, 1976) and subject to all the criticisms of that position, but although this may be true of some of its variants others seem able to deflect the charge. For example, Checkland claims that his methodology is more appropriately located within the *verstehen* and phenomenological traditions.

Systems ideas have been particularly prominent in the development of organisation theory, for example in the open systems and socio-technical systems approaches. The study of the impact of the environment on organisations led to a major change in the thrust of organisational research. Whereas nearly all previous work had been universalist in approach, seeking the one best organisational solution, much of the work conducted in the late fifties and early sixties noted that specific forms of organisation were best suited to particular environmental conditions, and laid the foundations for the development of contingency theories (Woodward, 1958; Burns and Stalker, 1961; Chandler, 1962; Lawrence and Lorsch, 1967). But it is important to recognise that whilst the contingency approach proved to be a necessary device for reconciling the results of a growing body of empirical work, there is little underlying consensus on its theoretical foundations. In its present state the contingency theory of organisations has been described by Burrell and Morgan (1979) as:

> A loosely organised set of propositions which in principle are committed to an open systems view of organisation, which are committed to some form of multi-variate analysis of the relationship between key organisational variables as a basis for organisational analysis, and which endorse the view that there are no universally valid rules of organisation and management.

The MCS approach combines a normative view of management as being concerned with 'initiating appropriate actions for the benefit of an organisation' (Rosenberg, 1979), a broad view of control as involving both the selection of ends to be attained and the choice of means to attain them, and an overall systemic view of an organisation interacting with and adapting to a wider environment. The study of management control systems in the context of economic organisations is thus concerned with the ways in which diverse activities are co-ordinated into coherent strategies and patterns of organisational behaviour so that they contribute to some overall desired result.

The area of study mapped out by such a definition of MCS is evidently very wide, encompassing most aspects of the management of organisational functioning. It also stands in some contrast to a classic definition of management control propounded in the management accounting literature by Anthony (1965) which distinguishes management control from strategic planning on the one hand and operational control on the other. This definition leads to a concentration upon the development of formal measurement systems to enable managers to better monitor and control organisational performance. By making these distinctions Anthony was able to avoid the fundamental issues involved in strategy formulation and of adaptation to environmental contingencies, and also the complexities of technological differences at operating level (Lowe and Puxty, p. 12). This permitted management control to become almost synonymous with management accounting. The concern expressed by Hofstede (1975) at the 'poverty of management control philosophy' was very much directed at the tradition developed and consolidated by Anthony and the Harvard school. The idea of MCS used here is a much wider concept than that put forward by Anthony. Provided that the concept of control is not interpreted too narrowly, or in a purely mechanical sense, the MCS approach provides a valuable (meta-) theoretical framework within which to study the management of organisations. Workers in the MCS tradition have progressively broadened their horizons to encompass a greater variety of academic subject disciplines, as exemplified by the recent collection of articles edited by Lowe and Machin (1983) which includes material deriving from cybernetics, general systems theory, psychology, sociology, organisation theory, operational research, economics and accounting. Although Anthony's concentration on management accounting has been criticised it nevertheless does draw attention to the function and contribution of an organisation's accounting system in attaining overall control. The study of the role of accounting information has been neglected by organisational and management researchers and will be returned to later.

At best the MCS approach is eclectic, taking relevant contributions from wherever they can be found; at worst, it may be argued, it has little theoretical structure and is dominated by a managerial ideology. However it is probably fair to say that it has brought an increasingly wide range of concepts to bear on the issues of management and organisational control; it is regrettable only that its theorising has not been accompanied by a similar amount of empirical study. By taking an overall perspective it provides a valuable counterweight to treating management as the province of a single academic discipline, whether it be economics, mathematics or sociology.

INTEGRATING QUANTITATIVE AND QUALITATIVE APPROACHES

There would seem to be great advantage in a research strategy that combines both quantitative and qualitative approaches within a grounded theory framework. Much managerial activity can be measured and assessed in quantitative terms although there is an equally significant amount that cannot. Similarly, where hypotheses can be derived from existing theories rigorous statistically-based testing is essential to scientific research. However where such theories do not exist or are highly tentative, exploratory research that seeks to generate theory is more appropriate and will tend to use more qualitative methods.

The grounded theory approach lays stress on the inductive generation of theory from data and on being open to the adaptation of research methods and aims as work progresses. It also is well-adapted to interpretive styles of research which lay stress on the interpretations and theories held by those actively participating in the situations being studied. Both theory generation and theory verification are important, but a weakness of current research is that it has become so specialised that the link between the two activities has become weakened. What is being suggested here is that both activities should be combined in individual research projects and that each researcher should hold himself responsible for both testing hypotheses and for generating theoretical explanations when his observations do not accord with accepted theory.

To illustrate how such an approach might be implemented in practice some recent work on the operation of systems of budgetary control will be outlined. This field of work has been selected for a number of reasons. Firstly I have been involved with much of the work described at first hand and am thus familiar with the research processes involved; the work of others is usually seen only in its final form without the details of the process by which it was generated being described. Secondly, budgeting is an interesting interface area involving both quantitative calculation of overall organisational performance and the qualitative assessment of the impact of many behavioural factors. Finally, it illustrates the way in which accounting data collected and stored by organisations themselves can be used in illuminating other aspects of organisational activity. However, it must be stressed that the work described here was not consciously designed to integrate the two approaches, nor was the grounded theory approach explicitly used at the time. Rather my advocacy of the approach has grown out of some of the experiences encountered in performing this type of research. With hindsight it is possible to see many lost opportunities for gathering data that would have enabled better and more comprehensive theories to be generated. Nevertheless I still hope that it is able to indicate the potential inherent in the approach.

The impact of the managerial use of budgets on the behaviour of subordinates was the subject of a study by Hopwood (1972). He investigated the differing ways in which senior managers made use of budgetary information in evaluating and rewarding the performance of their subordinates. In the organisation he studied he was able to distinguish between two major styles of budget use: a rigid style in which performance was evaluated primarily on the basis of budget variances with little or no opportunity for explanation and a more flexible style where, although budget variances were an important component of the evaluative process, other factors would be considered. The rigid style of evaluation was found to result in a variety of undesirable effects: managers working under this style experienced very high levels of job-related tension and anxiety; they had poor relationships with their peers and their subordinates; and they engaged in budgetary manipulation.

These results occurred because there was a poor fit between what the budget system measured and the actions which were necessary in order to achieve good overall performance. Because the system was operated in an organisation having sequential interdependence between successive departments it was not possible to evaluate the performance of a single department in isolation from what had occurred elsewhere. But the budget system purported to do this and it is hardly surprising that dysfunctional consequences followed from rigid budget use.

One of the more interesting results involved budgets for repairs and maintenance (R&M). In the company studied R&M budgets were set on a flexible basis, varying with production output, because experience had shown that there was a long-term relationship between required R&M expenditure and output. However monthly R&M budgets were flexed according to the same formula despite the fact that managers sensibly attempted to fit scheduled R&M into periods of low production. Thus an efficient manager might well have adverse spending variances in times of low activity (because he is heavily engaged in R&M) and favourable spending variances at times of peak production. Indeed this was the pattern Hopwood found when managers were evaluated using a flexible style. But managers evaluated in a rigid manner apparently fitted in with the budget as set, reporting only small variances at all times. However further investigation indicated that these apparently satisfactory variances concealed both overall under-spending on R&M and the diversion of the funds so released to other purposes.

This result opens up the way for exploratory research in the opposite direction. Budgetary data is routinely generated and stored by organisations and is usually easily available to the management researcher. Could not examination of budgets, actuals and reported variances give an insight into the areas of activity that might most repay further investigation? Different patterns of budgetary behaviour might well indicate contrasting areas of activity that could form the basis of a comparative study.

I must admit to having had a great deal of empathy with these results when I first read them. As an O.R. scientist I had spent several weeks labouring over a complex computerised simulation programme, attempting to discover the 'bugs' that were causing it to produce invalid results. Eventually I discovered the cause of the discrepancy between the model predictions and the actual reported results. Managers had been manipulating the reported actual results; in fact it was the model which was correct, and the data that was wrong!

The results of these and other studies led me to investigate the consequences of budget use in a situation where a rigid style of budgetary control might be appropriate – namely, where there were independent operating units for which the budget provided a valid basis for performance evaluation. In this situation Hopwood's results were not replicated; the rigid style appeared to lead to better rather than worse performance (Otley, 1978). Examination of my results led me to two major conclusions. Firstly, it was evident that the appropriate choice of evaluative style was dependent upon the situation in which it was being used. This result leads directly on to the contingency theory of management accounting which we will consider shortly. Secondly, it appeared that style of budget use was not an independent variable, selected at will by senior managers, but was itself affected by situational factors. In the organisation I studied, profitable operating units had their budgets set and were evaluated quite differently from unprofitable units. Again the choice of evaluative style was heavily inter-connected with other organisational and environmental variables.

The first finding was based on a prior theoretical model for which an empirical test had been designed, namely a comparison between organisations having independent and interdependent operating units. Although not based on contingency theory as such, for the term had not even been introduced into the management accounting literature at the time the research was designed, it provided some much needed empirical support to the discussion current in the literature at the time it was published. The second finding was quite unexpected and emerged in attempting to interpret a set of observed correlations in the light of conversations previously held with operating managers. The correlations were:

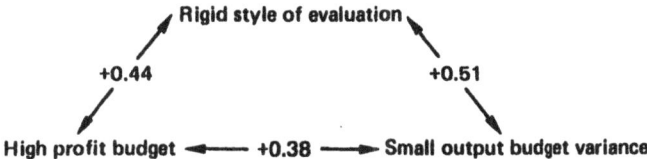

These results suggested a direction of causation the reverse of that originally considered. This changed the research problem from that of exploring the consequences of different styles of evaluation, originally assumed to be an independent variable, to that of discovering the reasons for their adoption. Such a re-appraisal changes the underlying theoretical model to a more systemic view of the relationships involving reciprocal causation. Also the level of analysis is redefined from an individual/group level to an organisational level.

These results led on to a study of the budgeting process in the organisation involved. It had been observed that managers were generally optimistic in setting their budget estimates; that is, they submitted figures that were only infrequently attained. As this observation was in contrast to the more frequently asserted concept of budgetary 'slack' (although falling within Lowe and Shaw's (1968) more general framework) it indicated a situation worthy of further study. The basic question to be answered was why, in this organisation, did managers submit optimistic budget estimates?

A number of possible reasons were discovered. A first level of explanation considered rewards and penalties. Perhaps there were rewards for promising good performance that were not outweighed by penalties for not actually achieving it. This was certainly partly true, and it was observed that managers evaluated under a rigid style were less optimistic than their more flexibly evaluated colleagues. In addition, it was noted that there was a time gap between the promise and the result; Lowe and Shaw's finding that currently insecure managers exploited this time gap by being more optimistic was supported. Finally, the notion that a budget had to be acceptable to one's superiors, even if it was unlikely to be fulfilled was also found to hold; this led directly to the discovery of cases of budgetary manipulation at the next higher level of management and an insight into the Head Office budgetary procedures.

Having observed that budget estimates were generally optimistic and having analysed some of the causes of this optimism it seemed sensible to explore some of the consequences of such biased estimates being used in the organisation's planning process. Budget estimates were aggregated through two levels of the organisational hierarchy and a statistical analysis of such an aggregation process indicated that budgets that are optimistic at one level of the hierarchy become very optimistic when aggregated at the next level (Otley and Berry, 1979). However, the organisation concerned avoided these extreme consequences by including what it termed 'relaxation' into the budget process; that is, the deduction of a contingency allowance at each stage of aggregation. The effect was quite marked; the monthly budget that had a 30 per cent chance of being achieved at unit level had a 44 per cent chance of being attained at group level and nearly 60 per cent chance of being achieved overall. It was of interest to observe how these probabilities, which were caused solely by the size of the deduction made by each level of management, were used to reinforce senior managers' views of themselves as better managers than their subordinates.

Once again, having considered some of the consequences of having optimistic budgets it seemed logical to re-consider their antecedents. The statistical analysis of budgetary aggregation had drawn attention to the statistical distribution underlying actual outcomes. Initially this had been assumed to be Normal, but a more refined analysis showed that this assumption was unnecessary. Discussion with unit managers had also indicated that outcomes might not be symmetric; there was a greater chance of doing very badly than there was of doing very well. What would be the consequences if the underlying distributions were not symmetric but skew? A brief analysis quickly indicated that if distributions of output were negatively skew, and managers made honest estimates centred on the most likely outcomes (that is, the mode of the distribution) then these estimates would, on average, be optimistic. As this optimism had been observed, attention was directed to ascertaining whether the underlying distribution of actual output was skew rather than symmetric. This study was conducted both in the original industry and in another single product industry. The results of this work indicate that distributions of output are indeed negatively skew at plant and machine level (Otley, 1985). However, the degree of skewness decreases when the data is aggregated as the organisational hierarchy is ascended, as one would expect from the Central Limit Theorem. It is not thought that this skewness is a major cause of budgetary optimism but it may well be a pre-disposing factor or one which makes optimism more justifiable. In any case it has implications for the design of budgetary control procedures and for the use of financial planning models.

The study of budgetary control can thus be seen to offer a fertile ground for the combination of quantitative and qualitative approaches. Moreover, it suggests that accounting data, which is collected and stored by most organisations can be an invaluable source of information about a wide range of organisational practices not directly connected with accounting and finance. There is a dearth of studies of the roles played by accounting information in organisations; certainly nothing akin to Pettigrew's (1973) study of the politics of organisational decision-making exists. Neither have relatively simple comparative studies been attempted, such as that of Bowey (1976) in organisation theory where observations of routine organisational situations were used to generate an improved theory of organisations that combined the best features of the systems and action approaches. This is not just a lapse on the part of accounting researchers for organisational theorists have not been active in this area as Goldner (1980) points out:

> All organizations have to obtain money to operate. Despite that awesome fact, sociologists and other students of organizations have not discussed or analysed the process of obtaining money or the consequences of those processes.

A complementary point of view is put forward by Boland and Pondy (1981) who argue that accounting is a focal point between rational and natural views of organisations:

> Accounting is a unique element in the experience of organizational life, and the study of accounting in its organizational context can do much to illuminate the interaction of rational and natural aspects of organizing.... Accounting thus both makes sense within and is used to make sense of the frames of reference that characterise an organization.

It is perhaps this nexus between the rational aspects of organisational life characterised by accounting and the natural aspects that feature in much current organisation theory that will provide a stimulus for innovative research. Accounting may be viewed as an attempt to deal with the control of a complex, interconnected human activity system by being *systematic*; approaches such as Checkland's (1981) 'soft systems thinking' offer the opportunity to be *systemic*. The grounded theory approach provides a methodology for generating much needed theory which allows for the combination of quantitative and qualitative approaches. It is an opportunity too good to be missed!

CONCLUSIONS

This paper has argued the case for a greater emphasis on theory generation in management research, and has proposed the use of the grounded theory approach as one means of achieving this end. The use of such a methodology would strengthen the links between theory verification and theory construction that often seem all too weak. As a side benefit it would also aid in encouraging research that balances the use of both quantitative and qualitative methods. A number of other issues have been raised in the examples given which suggest the following heuristics:

1. As all research is based upon theoretical assumptions and preconceptions, it is as well that the researcher makes the overall theoretical framework used as explicit as possible. This is both for his own benefit and for that of his readers, making it more likely that erroneous theoretical assumptions will be exposed and corrected. In this paper an MCS framework has been used to guide what is observed, but the observations made also challenge it. For example, the distinction made between rational and natural models of organisation suggests that the MCS approach may incline the researcher towards rational explanations. This should be guarded against by continually questioning how much observed behaviour is 'controlled' rather than 'naturally occurring', although even this distinction should itself be questioned. Essentially, progress is achieved by this process of dialectical questioning.

2. A diversified research strategy that involves both theory generation and theory verification has considerable merit. There is room in a single research project for both the rigorous testing of prior hypotheses and exploration of less well-specified ideas. If the researcher is open to new concepts and explanations as the work progresses, there is a greater chance of establishing fruitful theories.

The research design can then be modified as the work progresses, allowing new insights to be developed and perhaps tested.

3. There also seems to have been a neglect of interpretive methods in management research; that is, methods which tap the interpretations and explanations of the participants themselves. Using such information does not necessarily imply adopting a strict sociological interpretive position; only that such information can be useful in generating theoretical explanations.

4. A number of heuristics have been suggested that may assist in the development of grounded theory. These include:
   (a) consideration of different levels of analysis and their linkages.
   (b) exploration of the implications of different hypothesised directions of causation.
   (c) comparison of natural and rational explanations for observed behaviour.
   (d) consideration of both the antecedents and the consequences of observed phenomena.

However the overall message of this paper is not to advocate the use of any particular research methodology. Rather it is to indicate that a range of alternative methodologies are available, and that one should be chosen that best fits the objectives of a particular piece of research rather than expecting a standard off-the-shelf methodology to be appropriate. Theory, not methodology, should guide research.

References

R. N. Anthony, *Planning and Control Systems: A Framework for Analysis* (Harvard, 1965).
J. Banbury and J. E. Nahapiet, 'Towards a Framework for the Study of the Antecedents and Consequences of Information Systems in Organizations', *Accounting, Organizations and Society* (1979) pp. 163–77.
S. Beer, *Cybernetics and Management* (New York: Wiley, 1959).
S. Beer, *Brain of the Firm* (London: Allen Lane, 1972).
R. J. Boland and L. R. Pondy, 'Toward an Interactive Model of the Natural and Rational Aspects of Accounting in its Organisational Context' (Working Paper, May 1981).
A. M. Bowey, *The Sociology of Organisations* (London: Hodder & Stoughton, 1976).
S. Burchell, C. Clubb, A. Hopwood, J. Hughes and J. Nahapiet, 'The Roles of Accounting in Organizations and Society', *Accounting, Organizations and Society* (1980) pp. 5–27.

T. Burns and G. M. Stalker, *The Management of Innovation* (London: Tavistock, 1961).
G. Burrell and G. Morgan, *Sociological Paradigms and Organisational Analysis* (London: Heinemann, 1979).
A. Chandler, *Strategy and Structure* (MIT Press, 1962).
P. B. Checkland, *Systems Thinking, Systems Practice* (New York: Wiley, 1981).
B. G. Glaser, *Theoretical Sensitivity* (Mill Valley, Ca.: The Sociology Press, 1978).
B. G. Glaser and A. L. Strauss, *The Discovery of Grounded Theory: Strategies for Qualitative Research* (Aldine, 1967).
F. M. Goldner, 'The Future is Behind Us' in W. M. Evan (ed.), *Frontiers in Organization and Management* (Praeger, 1980).
J. Hage, 'Unresolved Problems in Organization Theory' in W. M. Evan (1980), op. cit.
D. C. Hayes and D. J. H. Watson, 'Modern Organization Theory and Accounting Research: An Interaction' (working paper, University of British Columbia, 1976).
G. Hofstede, 'The Poverty of Management Control Philosophy' (working paper 75-44, European Institute for Advanced Studies in Management, Brussels, December 1975).
A. G. Hopwood, 'An Empirical Study of the Role of Accounting Data in Performance Evaluation', *Empirical Research in Accounting: Selected Studies, Supplement to Journal of Accounting Research* (1972) pp. 156-93.
A. G. Hopwood, 'Discussion of "Some Inner Contradictions in Management Information Systems" and "Behavioral Implications of Planning and Control Systems"' in H. P. Holzer (ed.), *Management Accounting 1980* (Proceedings of the University of Illinois Management Accounting Symposium, University of Illinois, 1980).
A. G. Hopwood, 'Accounting and the Pursuit of Social Interests', this volume.
P. Lawrence and J. W. Lorsch, *Organization and Environment* (Harvard, 1967).
E. A. Lowe and J. L. J. Machin (eds), *New Perspectives in Management Control* (London: Macmillan, 1983).
E. A. Lowe and R. W. Shaw, 'An Analysis of Managerial Biasing: Evidence from a Company's Budgeting Process', *Journal of Management Studies* (Oct. 1968) pp. 304-15.
D. T. Otley, 'Budget Use and Managerial Performance', *Journal of Accounting Research* (Spring 1978) pp. 122-49.
D. T. Otley, 'The Contingency Theory of Management Accounting: Achievement and Prognosis', *Accounting, Organizations and Society* (1980) pp. 413-28.
D. T. Otley, 'Concepts of Control: The Contribution of Cybernetics and Systems Theory to Management Control' in E. A. Lowe and J. L. J. Machin (eds), op. cit. (1983).
D. T. Otley, 'Management Accounting and Organisation Theory: A Review of Their Interrelationship' in R. W. Scapens, D. T. Otley and R. J. Lister, *Management Accounting, Organizational Theory and Capital Budgeting* (London: Macmillan, 1984).

D. T. Otley, 'The Accuracy of Budgetary Estimates: Some Statistical Evidence', *Journal of Business Finance and Accounting* (1985) pp. 415–28.
D. T. Otley and A. J. Berry, 'Risk Distribution in the Budgetary Process', *Accounting and Business Research* (Autumn 1979) pp. 325–37.
D. T. Otley and A. J. Berry, 'Control, Organization and Accounting', *Accounting, Organizations and Society* (1980) pp. 231–44.
A. M. Pettigrew, *The Politics of Organizational Decision-Making* (London: Tavistock, 1973).
P. Prévost, '"Soft" Systems Methodology, Functionalism and the Social Sciences', *Journal of Applied Systems Analysis* (1976) pp. 65–73.
J. M. Rosenberg, *Dictionary of Business and Management* (New York: Wiley, 1979).
K. Tocher, 'Control', *Operational Research Quarterly* (June 1970) pp. 159–80.
J. Woodward, *Management and Technology* (London: HMSO, 1958).

4 Accounting as Social Science: Abstract Versus Concrete Sources of Accounting Change

Tony Lowe and Tony Tinker

1. INTRODUCTION

The purpose of this paper is to argue and illustrate that in its present stage of development Accounting is at one and the same time an unhappy mixture of abstracted and pragmatic scientism. A prevalent view of 'modern' Accounting in Western society may be said to be reflected in the idea that Accounting is an instrumental discipline (of management control) and moreover that its scope as such is primarily and largely confined to micro-organisations. Some would probably argue that it is really no more than a technique of (micro) organisation analysis and moreover that it hardly deserves the respect accorded to a subject when it is called a discipline. It is merely a pragmatic technique of business book-keeping and as such a 'service activity' (Peasnell, 1978) or technical activity (Burchell *et al.*, 1980) for business organisations.

In the light of its professionally dominated traditions this 'service or technical activity' view is a plausible one but it rests, in part at least, upon a neglect of an essential aspect of the subject of Accounting: its societal nature, as conspicuously evidenced by many public financial and accounting incidents and scandals. Accounting as a discipline and accountancy practice should, for this reason be regarded as integral parts of social science and social behaviour. In contrast the prevailing more recent professional and academic orthodoxies in both the UK and USA have been loath to contemplate the idea of Accounting as a social science. Rather this modern orthodoxy has been concerned to adopt a 'scientific' (inductive) approach based mainly upon (economic) abstraction. Whilst helpful in some respects to the development of scientific thought in Accounting it has been dysfunctional in so far as it has ignored (seemingly deliberately) much of what has been so evidently happening in the Western financial and accounting social and business environment, as well as the essentially dualistic nature of social science knowledge (to include *Geisteswissenschaften*). For instance, whilst 'decision usefulness' criteria have been a highly useful development in accounting theory (see, for instance, Sterling, 1970), the seeming insistence on developing it almost single-mindedly in terms of aggregate economic market behaviour with a general, sweeping assumption of efficient markets (see, for instance: Beaver, 1981) may be disastrous for the practical usefulness of financial accounting statements. A closely related (economic-theory based) development to which similar strictures can be applied has been that of accounting information as an economic commodity to which supply and demand analysis can both be applied (see for instance: Demski, 1972; Demski and Feltham, 1976) and also agency theory (Jensen and Meckling, 1976; Watts and Zimmerman, 1978).

However slowly and grudgingly it seems the profession has been compelled more recently to recognise this possibility as the implications of various modern, financial scandals and in their wake the seemingly never-ending contortions of the professional accountancy bodies policies on Accounting Standards, have unwound (Tinker, 1985). The argument of this paper will support the contention that these contortions are primarily due to a reluctant recognition of the true societal nature and corresponding responsibilities of the Accountancy profession. In this sense a charge of professional myopia may be justified because of many expressed concerns about the nature of professional practices and their foundations in the light of the needs of UK society, such as:

- the lack of independence as between auditors and their clients;
- the increasing weakness in competition amongst professional auditing firms, as the fashion for mergers amongst them increases;
- the domination of the professional accountancy institutions by the *business interests* of large professional auditing firms and the exclusion of the needs for developing the whole subject as it applies to all aspects of both industry and society;
- the partial dominance of the accountancy profession business interests over academic accountancy interests and the latter's need for emancipation;

- the relative neglect of the needs of 'management accounting' in the development of accounting theory despite its intrinsic importance;
- a neglect of the accounting aspects of 'value-added theory' which thereby masks some of the fundamental conflicts and antagonisms in Western society concerning profit definition, efficiency and wealth accumulation and appropriation;
- the failure, above all, to develop the discipline as a social science, recognising its wider implications, especially as testified by the *ad hoc* nature of the approach to 'Accounting Standards' and increasing impatience about the profession's inability to satisfactorily regulate itself.

A number of academic scholars have expressed concerns bearing on such matters. One may cite, for instance: Mautz and Sharaf (1961), Stamp and Marley (1970), Briloff (1972), Lowe and Tinker (1977), Burchell *et al.* (1980), Laughlin (1981), Tomkins and Groves (1983), Cooper (1984), as well as many others. A critical question to ask is why, despite the cogency of much of their argument, they have largely had little influence on the main thrust of accountancy research and teaching?

For instance, it has been suggested that:

> Few issues appear to cause accountants to jump into their ideological trenches quite as fast as that of the function of the accountancy profession in society.... It would seem that other subjects within social science such as economics and politics should have community, national and even global criteria of human welfare but accounting only operates at the detail of the individual enterprise level. Is this the nature of our subject? Or is it simply a rather large oversight on our part?
> (Lowe and Tinker, 1977)

Also:

> Until recently scholars interested in accounting seemingly have been content to accept the ends which it is seen as serving, focusing their efforts on further refinement of the craft.
> (Burchell *et al.*, 1980)

And:

> a case also can be made for the study of accounting as a social and organisation phenomena to complement the more prevalent analyses which operate *within* the accounting context. . . . Like other modes of inquiry, it to has the potential to change our conceptions of the accounting craft.
>
> (Burchell *et al.*, 1980)

To summarise the assertions of this introductory section: it is contended that there is a crisis in Accounting, both as regards its development as a discipline of Social Science and in the state of its practice, and that the latter is in some significant sense conditioned and 'caused' by the former. It is suggested that fundamentally this state of affairs is mainly exhibited by the inability of the practising profession of accountants (broadly defined) to perceive the significance of 'accounting behaviour' in its social context. The argument is developed in the two following main sections of this paper: 'Defining Accounting', and 'Displacing the instrumental definition of Accounting'. The paper ends with some suggestions and speculations.

2. DEFINING ACCOUNTING

This section does not attempt to provide a general definition of Accounting but rather one suited for the purpose in hand: to consider its instrumentality (or lack of it).

There are at least three kinds of general justifications for the use of accounting as a pragmatic, instrumental discipline of control, as follows:

1. Accounting as a business technology, emphasising the importance of a double-entry book-keeping system as a mode of accounting for resources and as a description of the fiduciary relationships between the principal participants within enterprise: shareholders, managers, workers, lenders, suppliers, customers, government, etc.
2. Accounting as a regulator of business particularly as exemplified by the advocates of Postulates, Principles and Standard Setting. Such schools of thought have emerged during the 1950s and

1960s. They emphasise the need for a de facto agreement amongst accounting practitioners about the appropriate rules for accounting statements, sponsored by the professional bodies of accountants (such as the Institute of Certified Public Accountants in the USA and the Institute of Chartered Accountants in England and Wales in the UK). Their whole emphasis appears to be to serve finance capital interests.

3. Accounting as an integral part of a regulator of society and as a means of planning for and co-ordinating the allocation of resources within society as a whole. This can be achieved through its use within and between financial and business institutions which facilitate the flows of financial and productive capital. But it can also be achieved through indicative or mandatory social planning, using Accounting as one of its 'tools'.

In terms of the above three kinds of justifications, the accountancy profession as a whole (in industry, commerce, public enterprises, local and state government, as well as in public (audit, taxation and consultancy practice) has necessarily been concerned to emphasise its pragmatism and capabilities for assisting in the allocation and management of both financial and productive capital as a useful professional service to a capitalist society. For these reasons it is tempting to define Accounting as is often done in a somewhat offhand manner as for instance:

Accounting is the language of business.

It is possibly for such (pragmatic) reasons that a researcher such as Peasnell (1978) asserts that:

Accounting is not a science, it is a service activity.

Similarly Burchell et al. (1980) refer to it as being traditionally regarded by the accountancy profession as:

a mere assembly of calculative routines.

The statement by Peasnell is a useful one to examine since although it has several interpretations it may represent (possibly without that intention) something of the pragmatic tendencies found present in professional accountancy practice. The statement may be interpreted to be one about the present (temporary) state of development or alternatively it may be one about the essential (time-invariant) nature of Accounting as a subject. The form of the statement tends to suggest the latter interpretation. If so it is surely rather a cultural statement about the inherent tendencies of the Accountancy profession since it would surely be most difficult to assert that Accounting as a subject is not even potentially a possible candidate scientific discipline?

The tendency towards an over-emphasis on pragmatism seems to be a dilemma faced by academic researchers in Accounting more generally. Yet at the same time it seems clear that they also espouse the most abstracted forms of (economic) theory construction as referred to in the previous (introductory) section of this paper. Such a dilemma seems to face any would-be academic contributor to a discipline's theoretical status where it has a brief intellectual history, such as Accounting does, where those academic practitioners have the unenviable task of achieving intellectual recognition amongst peers.

What is in fact both integral and indispensable to the identity sought (pragmatic usefulness) may be said to be what is being disowned by exclusion from such definitions: perhaps primarily the 'dualism' essential to all 'good' social science: that is, sympathetic understanding of human states of mind. To follow this line of thought and thereby undermine the boundary which is unhelpfully imposed by pragmatic, inductivist definitions would require much further analysis of modern orthodox accounting theorists and for which space is not available here.

However such analysis can be helpfully illustrated by reference to a recent contribution by R. R. Sterling (1970). In his (introductory) Chapter 1 Sterling raises the important question as to whether, and in what circumstances, we can say that one particular (accounting) theory (of income measurement in his particular instance) is better than another, or other, competing theories; or whether we can say, in relation to a particular phenomena, one theory is 'correct' and another is 'incorrect'.

Sterling apparently sees the problem of the superiority of one theory over another as the essentially pragmatic one of whether a theory is 'self-evident'. To be self-evident a theory must:

> make all the assumptions explicitly insofar as we are aware of them and we have tried to set down the reasoning in meticulous

detail. It is hoped that this will allow the reader who disagrees to know precisely where the analysis errs. The reader can then challenge the argument at the point of disagreement instead of challenging the conclusion.

Whilst Sterling's pleas for more scientific and explicit statements of Accounting theories may be necessary for the improvement of Accounting as a discipline it is surely not sufficient; and given what appears to be his notion of 'Science' discussed there it may not be at all helpful.

Sterling for instance provides no attempts to answer the following important questions:

1. How do we distinguish between two impeccably enunciated (in Sterling's terms) alternative competing, yet contradictory theories? Which is better and which is worse?
2. Indeed how do we tell whether one theory is 'better' than another in terms of the degree to which it is 'self-evident' (or explicit) in terms of assumptions, etc., as Sterling advocates?
3. More fundamentally, however impeccably explicit a theory is, in Sterling's terms, it can still be just plain 'wrong' from other equally vital viewpoints. For instance in terms of the logic of social science, or as scientific explanation (understanding). Which is to say that a 'good' theory necessarily requires other, equally important qualities apart from explicitness. In Sterling's discussion these seem to be recognised but only referred to somewhat vaguely as 'reasoning' and 'level of analysis'?

The two quotations at the beginning of Sterling's text provide strong indicators of the guiding 'principles of science' which he favours:

> We have to isolate for study a few simple aspects of science just as science has to isolate a few simple aspects of the world; ... This admittedly is over-simplification. But conscious and cautious over-simplification far from being an intellectual sin, is a prerequisite for investigation. We can hardly study at once all the ways in which everything is related to everything else.
> (Nelson Goodman, 1947)

The second quotation is from Charles S. S. Pierce (1957) and reinforces the general tenor of the first, from Goodman.

The first problems to suggest themselves to the inquirer into nature are far too complex and difficult for any early solution, even if any satisfactorily secure conclusion can even be drawn concerning them. What ought to be done, therefore, and what in fact is done, is at first to substitute for those problems others much simpler, much more abstract, of which there is a good prospect of finding probable solutions. Then, the reasonably certain solutions of these last problems will throw a light more or less clear upon more concrete problems which are in certain respects of more interest.

(Charles S. S. Pierce, 1957)

It would seem evident that both Goodman and Pierce in accepting pragmatism were unable to distinguish between the needs of natural science and social science. It is also unfortunate for Accounting that a prominent, modern researcher appears to espouse their scientistic methodologies.

Both Goodman's and Pierce's statements, quoted above, seem flawed in several respects. Whilst clearly scientists do simplify and isolate it is the manner in which this is done *in close coupling* with integrated and systemic thinking at the same time. This appears to be absolutely essential for disciplines, such as Accounting, if they are to form an integrated part of Social Science so as to adequately reflect the social and behavioural consequences of Accounting. The same is surely the case for all sciences (whether social or natural)? For instance, to take two grand-scale theories: Newton's Law of Gravity and Einstein's Theory of Relativity. Both are good examples of specific, detailed experimentation and analysis but within a context of a conception of the Universe as a whole, *as an integral part* of that more particular theory. Thus it is suggested that scientists will generally seek in their detailed experimentation, to relate to and justify that experimentation by and with reference to a large (meta) system of knowledge related to each more specific theory. That larger system of knowledge, what may be termed the meta-theory of the particular discipline, contains the justification for the more detailed, more specific research which a scientist (natural, social, etc.) would tend to devote most of his endeavours to. That is to say all good scientists must *first* find a good theory about what is the *hallmark* of a good, specific, particular theory within his discipline. Thus it seems important for an accounting researcher to first justify why (s)he believes it essential to have a theory of income. It is surely not sufficient to wade into the subject (or part-subject) of income theory without attempting firstly: to justify why Accounting must have such a theory; and secondly, what are the general hallmarks of a 'good' rather than a 'bad' theory about income, capital or any other accounting concept in terms of the theory of Accounting as a whole.

A further important point to make about the statement by Sterling is that it is more or less impossible for the theorist 'to set down the reasoning in meticulous detail . . . (to) allow the reader who disagrees to know precisely where the analysis errs'. Each theory, which is part of a discipline, cannot be complete in itself in the manner that Sterling seems to wish. Also it is not desirable that it should attempt to do so. For it is precisely the function of the meta-theory of a discipline to state the context for each and every more special theory which forms the subject-matter of that discipline. In other words its function it may be said, is to examine critically what more specific, limited theories within the subject take for granted.

The objective of this section has been to consider, by means of illustrations, the definition of Accounting as a (social science) discipline from the particular. The inadequacies of these instrumental viewpoints are highlighted when we try to use them to apprehend contemporary problems that afflict accountancy practice: the phenomenon of 'green mailing' (and the accountant's culpability in that respect); disputes over 'proper' accounting for large state-run and corporate enterprise (such as the National Coal Board and the National Health Service in the UK; General Dynamics and the Banking Industry in USA; the terms and conditions of the flotation of British Telecom; etc.). These problems are frequently seen as pragmatic, or 'practical' (and not academic). Attempts to disown such problems by pejorative labelling underscore the incompleteness of the orthodox, present theoretical system of Accounting. The essence of such problems lies not in some definitional elixir of economic income or 'efficiency' or 'effectiveness', but through an understanding of the nature of social conflict and how the Accounting function may be involved in it. Orthodox Accounting does not acquire an impartiality or neutrality through the neglect of the social consequences of the Accounting function; but rather by evading 'the social' and thereby forming the accounting agenda, it conserves the status quo and impedes emancipatory change (Hopwood, 1983).

3. DISPLACING THE INSTRUMENTAL DEFINITION OF ACCOUNTING?

A conflict-based view of Accounting is suggested by the following:

firstly that an understanding of the actual status and significance of the Accountancy profession within a capitalist society rests upon a knowledge of the complexities of the Western, capitalist societal context; especially the inter-dependent and interlocking relationships between groups, factions, interests and classes etc., which form its main constituents;
and
secondly, the extent to which Accounting purposefully and intentionally mediates those relationships.

In the context of this argument it would be simplistic to assume that the Accountancy profession itself can be regarded, for the purposes of such understanding, as an entity, having a single common, interest. Indeed it would seem much more plausible to regard the Accountancy profession as having a diversity of interests as between sub-groups within it, which can be shown to be in at least partial conflict. One such analysis of its internal division can, for example, be elaborated in terms of the distinction between finance and productive capital and how different parts of the profession serve the various principal parties involved in the organisation of and utilisation of capital resources within a society dominated by capital interests. Indeed in order to understand the function of the Accountancy profession in Western societies, it is clear that a formidable intellectual task still lies ahead in the form of a general analysis into the function of the professions in general and of the Accountancy profession in particular. What research work there is on this matter so far has been mainly confined to a narrower, functionalist kind, although a beginning has been made (see for instance: Burchell *et al.*, 1980; Watts and Zimmerman, 1979; Hope and Gray, 1982; Lowe, Puxty and Laughlin, 1983).

Formulating the constituent parts of a theory leading to an understanding of the part that the Accountancy profession plays in society is clearly a formidable task, both in terms of its scope in Social Science thinking and in the size of research effort required. A theory of 'the accountancy profession *in* society' may, for instance, need to possess the following constituent parts (within a wider

Social Science context) and moreover those parts will need to be integrated and related one to another to form a holistic theory:

1. A general theory of society and the general power structure within it.
2. A theory of the State and the function it performs within that society, making specific assumptions, for instance, about maintaining it in an equilibrial condition with a given structure.
3. A theory of the professions and how they function within society and relate to the State. A more specific theory related to the Accountancy profession and, if necessary, its constituent parts.
4. A theory of the immediate environment within which the Accountancy profession operates. For instance, in a capitalistic economy this might be the markets for both productive and finance capital.
5. A general theory of 'great people' (together with a theory of theorising about great people) and how they influence the affairs of State and society and including a particular theory of 'great accountants' and persons with accounting interests.

To propose that such a complex theory as the above is required is itself an assault on the professional integrity of the Accountancy profession. It implies that the behaviour of the profession is not determined by a professional code of morals and ethics suitable for Accountancy practice but that rather it is the product of a set of complicated societal relationships as between the Accountancy profession and the rest of society. But, as suggested previously a theory (of outright independence) at the opposite extreme, is equally damaging in a moral sense for it implies that the profession may be socially and politically neutral, or amoral; that it may be employed by whichever interests, factions, groups, etc. have the power to command it, or to pay its fees. For instance, it might be argued, in a context of 'Corporatism' (Streeck and Schmitter, 1984) that the profession is used by the State for its own function in society. Corporatism for these purposes might be defined as:

> An organisation of a needed, societal institution (such as the Accountancy profession) so that it both represents the interests of its privileged individual members and also controls and regulates them collectively in the interests of a managed, general, societal order.

Alternative theories such as the above, are mentioned briefly to indicate the problematic situation of any profession within society. It seems essential for its status, as a profession, not only to be concerned about the status of its technical content – the theories that make up its stock-in-trade of outputs, such as (in the case to accounting): capital, income, financial valuation, costs, control, budget, etc., but that it requires also a theory of its status within society, *as part of a theory of society* and incorporating the purposes served by its 'technical stock-in-trade'.

To appreciate the status and role of the Accountancy profession, particularly with regards to its revolutionary potential we need to understand what kind of accommodation Accounting experts have reached with the capitalist social order. The dominant form of organisation which pervades Western capitalist society, in both government and business, the bureaucratic – is characteristic of these broad social dilemmas. We note that it is often argued that the advance of bureaucratic organisation has been and remains its 'technical' superiority over any other form of organisation. But it would be quite misleading and erroneous to assume that bureaucracy remains the paramount organisational form and ideal because of its relative efficiency over other forms. Rather it is a form especially suited to a particular kind of domination in our society – Western capitalism – with its particular forms of domination of some humans over others and of social class over class. Joan Woodward's observation that 'Principles of Administration' so-called are little more than expedients in certain circumstances is most apt here. The instrumental effectiveness and efficiency of the bureaucratic form of organisation which is so widely adopted in Western capitalism is in no small way due to the later and more recent development of the necessary professional and technical expertise forming the cadre of bureaucratic forms of organisation. Like its other members the modern Accountancy profession is part of a much larger system of certificated expertise: in the natural sciences, applied sciences, and social sciences professions, valued by virtue of the authority bestowed on them in their role performance within bureaucracies as the possessors of rationalistic, scientific and technical knowledge necessary for maintaining society in equilibrium. Such certification is valued because it is conferred by independent training and credentialing institutions, comprising not only universities and polytechnics but also professional institutions, such as the professional accountancy bodies. In the case of accountancy the expert knowledge rests in part upon a development of 'accounting principles' over many decades, tested and approved (at least in some sense) by the experience of both the profession's individual members and its recognised corporate institutions. But that expert knowledge is grounded it may be argued in the prior development of the bureaucratic form on which it depends and for which it has been created.

A critical question to ask is clearly the question of the goals for this social system and the motivations of the role-players within it, and particularly those of the professionals which maintain the well-oiled bureaucratic machines of Western capitalism. It is beyond the scope of this paper to consider, in any detail, the goals for this capitalist system requiring as it does an analysis of the whole system itemised earlier in this section (page 57). These goals are survival-based in so far as they are tied to reproducing the conditions that sustain wage labour and individual property accumulation – the defining traits of capitalism as a social system. These 'conditions of existence' penetrate the social practices of large bureaucracies (state governmental and private) which form the main edifices of Western capitalism. Clearly the leaders of such bureaucracies form a vital link in this respect. For not only do they require the appropriate rationalistic, technical, scientific and professional credentials of competence but they also must possess the appropriate 'non-rationalistic' credentials: those pertaining to the external interests served by those bureaucracies. In that sense the overriding goals are legitimated by ideology, value system and interests which are non-negotiable within those bureaucracies. In that sense they may be defined as non-rational.

What about the motivations of those within the management of those bureaucracies? It may be argued that to some extent this is coped with by a partial defocalising of the real goals of those enterprises (Gouldner, 1976). Essentially this defocalising rests upon a substitution of the means for the end so far as those outside the hegemonic class are concerned. So long as there is a reasonably stable rate of economic growth and thereby a general maintenance of existing vested interests generally in society, a protective shield is maintained, through the obscuring and mystification of this substitution. Essentially the goals of the social system are set from outside its bureaucracies and are in this sense non-rational, ideological and essentially non-negotiable in character, as distinct from the rationality of the systems *modus operandi* which is subject always to scientific criteria and the best, most up-to-date, technical knowledge and expertise.

A partial solution to the problem of human motivation within this social system (except at 'the top') is provided by its own dynamic growth in the process of maintaining and improving its own rationalistic efficiency as a bureaucracy. Clearly it has what appears to be a solution of ideology through the politics of personal gratification. Gouldner argues that it is 'the sheer experience of gratification' rather than a new belief that partially solves the problem of motivation within the capitalist system of domination and ideological suppression.

CONCLUSION

The argument of this paper is for an augmented discipline of Accounting which not only embraces the technical aspects of an Accounting 'craft' or 'service' to the management of bureaucracies in Western capitalism but adopts also a reflexive understanding of the part that those techniques play within its social and political context. In this respect it has been argued that Accounting cannot be an instrumental, objective, independent discipline. Rather it is essential that its practitioners perceive themselves as non-instrumental in their behaviour and attitudes to the practice of the profession and should recognise that they themselves do and must necessarily bring their ideological prejudices to their work and that moreover Accounting itself, as part of Social Science, is also ideological in its content.

The purpose of this paper has been a polemical one: to help extend the scope of what is 'proper' Accounting by argument which is intended to open up discussions amongst accountants, both academic and practising.

References

W. H. Beaver, *Financial Reporting: An Accounting Revolution* (Prentice-Hall, 1981).
A. Briloff, *Unaccountable Accounting* (Harper & Row, 1972).
S. Burchell, S. Clubb, A. Hopwood, J. Hughes and J. Nahapiet, 'The Roles of Accounting in Organisations and Society', *Accounting, Organisations and Society* (1980) pp. 5–27.
D. J. Cooper, 'A Political Economy of the U.K. Accounting Profession', UMIST, Dept. of Management Sciences, Working Paper, 1984).
J. S. Demski, *Information Analysis* (Addison-Wesley, 1972).

Demski and G. A. Feltham, *Cost Determination: A Conceptual Approach* (Iowa State University Press, 1976).

Goodman, 'The Problems of Counterfactual Conditions', *Journal of Philosophy*, XLIV (1947) pp. 113–28.

W. Gouldner, *The Dialectic of Ideology and Technology* (Macmillan, 1976).

Hope and R. Gray, 'Power and Policy Making: The Development of an R. & D. Standard', *Journal of Business Finance and Accounting*, vol. 9, no. 4 (1982) pp. 531–58.

G. Hopwood, 'On Trying to Study Accounting in the Contexts in which it Operates', *Accounting, Organizations and Society* (1983).

C. Jensen and W. H. Meckling, 'Theory of the Firm: Managerial Behaviour, Agency Costs and Ownership Structure', *Journal of Financial Economics* (Oct. 1976) pp. 305–60.

C. Laughlin, 'On the Nature of Accounting Methodology', *Journal of Business Finance and Accounting*, vol. 8, no. 3 (1981) pp. 329–51.

A. Lowe A. G. Puxty and R. C. Laughlin, 'Simple Theories for Complex Processes: Accounting Policy and the Market for Myopia', *Journal of Accounting and Public Policy*, vol. 2, no. 1 (1983) pp. 19–42.

A. Lowe and A. M. Tinker, 'Sighting the Accounting Problematic: Towards an intellectual emancipation of accounting', *Journal of Business Finance and Accounting*, vol. 4, no. 3 (1977) pp. 263–76.

K. Mautz and H. A. Sharaf, *The Philosophy of Auditing* (American Accounting Association, 1961).

V. Peasnell, 'Statement of Accounting Theory & Theory Acceptance: A Review Article', *Accounting & Business Research* (1978) pp. 217–25.

S. S. Pierce, *Essays in the Philosophy of Science* (The Liberal Arts Press, 1957).

Stamp and C. Marley, *Accounting Principles and the City Code* (Butterworth, 1970).

H. Sterling, *Theory of the Measurement of Enterprise Income* (University Press of Kansas, 1970).

Streeck and P. C. Schmitter, 'Community, Market, State and Associations?' European University Institute Working Paper, no. 94, 1984.

Tinker, *Paper Prophets: A Social Critique of Accounting* (Praeger, 1985).

R. Tomkins and R. E. V. Groves, 'The Everyday Accountant and Researching this Reality', *Accounting, Organisations and Society*, vol. 8, no. 4 (1983) pp. 361–74.

L. Watts and J. L. Zimmerman, 'Towards a Positive Theory of the Determination of Accounting Standards', *The Accounting Review* (1978) pp. 112–34.

Watts and G. Zimmerman, 'The Demand for and the Supply of Accounting Theories: The Market for Excuses', *The Accounting Review*, vol. LIV (1979) pp. 273–305.

5 Authority, Accountability and Accounting

Tony Berry

Unless we have some clear notions about authority we have little or no basis for accountability to others and hence no basis for accounting. Here accountability is viewed as the process through which delegated or granted authority is exercised and hence is a process of control.

In the first section of this chapter, Weber's ideal types of authority are used as a basis for understanding the prevalence of hierarchy as a structure of authority. The second section moves on to a consideration of alternatives to hierarchy in organisations. The conclusion is an argument for a radical rethinking of authority, accountability and control in organisations along the notions of the regulation of the boundaries of self-managing groups.

1. AUTHORITY AND HIERARCHY

A central role of accounting has been and is to support the processes of accountability, whether of individuals, groups or organisations. This idea of accountability is normally embedded in relationships where the person of lower status is accountable to the person of higher status. Mutual or reciprocal accountability does not get much attention, in the literature of management control or, indeed, in the literature of organisations. Such Accountability, from one level to another, is a characteristic of hierarchies.

Hierarchy, suggest Tannenbaum *et al.* (1974), is a universal and basic dimension of organisation and carries with it an unequal distribution of valued goods. Taken to its extreme point it is observable that as there are no organisations which do not have such an unequal distribution there are no organisations which do not have hierarchies. Originally the Christian idea of hierarchy meant holy leadership; now its common meaning is a vertical authority differentiation; its emphasis being more on the observable structural and role differences rather than the relationships between persons.

Weber (1947) proposed three ideal types of authority: the rational-legal, the traditional and the charismatic. The basis of accountability in each is quite different. In the charismatic form it is the duty of individuals to conform to the moral authority of the leader, the act of joining and belonging carries with it the obligation to accept the leader's authority. In the traditional form accountability is based upon loyalty to the individual who has the highest status – that is, subjects must obey and be accountable to the king. In the rational-legal form authority is derived from an office and accountability is based upon the conduct or stewardship of that office.

In the rational-legal form authority is legitimated by task and office and hierarchy takes the form of a series of delegated levels dealing mainly with elements of the task. In the charismatic form authority is legitimated by the moral imperative and hierarchy exists to serve or to be obedient to that, hence Bishop, Priest and Deacon. In the traditional form the hierarchies (e.g. King, Nobles, Commoners) and the exercise and acceptance of authority embody the legitimacy.

Weber acknowleges that these three 'ideal' types are not necessarily stable: he put forward the idea that while the charismatic produces change, there is a tendency for the structure of authority to drift toward the traditional – and hence tradition might be seen to be the most stable form of authority structure.

It is not necessary to rehearse all of the criticisms of Weber – which have been made with considerable force – except to have some sympathy with Burrell and Morgan's (1979) desire to be theorists of change rather than theorists of a stability of any of these ideal types. For implied in all of these ideal types is the demand of accountability to some institution or person or state of power independent of oneself. They all appear to speak of constraint rather than of freedom, of dependence rather than an individual choice.

The rational-legal form of authority, with its attendant structures, roles, rules and procedures, is the form within which most accounting and control notions of accountability have been developed, that is accounting control is strongly related to the bureaucratic form of organisation.

The chain of command and the constructs of accountability in bureaucracies appear to encourage the qualities of dependence in their participants. Dixon (1976) has demonstrated, from military history, that this inculcated dependence generates an incapacity to cope with independent command, with massive denial of reality being used to sustain an unreal conception of external events. (In Dixon's case histories these behaviours led to real deaths of real persons. In the reality of organisational life, 'murder' takes place as well – that is, persons are effectively separated from the 'life' of the organisation.)

Uni-directional structure of accountability either satisfies persons with highish dependency needs (in which case bureaucracy is socially useful, as Jaques (1976) appears to argue) or such structures only reward dependent behaviour in which case bureaucracy can be parodied as creating and nurturing dependence and hence destructive to human life and, perhaps in our new consumerism, so advertised. Smith (1978) supports Jaques and argues that many persons are happy to accept the narrowest of bureaucratic control because work and the workplace is not where they expect much and are hence oriented to cope with the attendant limitations. This is powerful witness to the destructive nature of dependence.

In contrast to the bureaucratic notions of control the quasi-cybernetic models of control, which are in part aligned with the co-ordination and control constructs of bureaucracy (Hofstede, 1975), admit the problems of uncertainty. Berry and Otley (1975) demonstrated that the response of hierarchy in the process of budgeting was to suppress uncertainty and distribute the risks of failure to the lower levels. The linking of budgets down the hierarchy was manipulated to reinforce authority and distribute punishments. Perhaps hierarchies are useful because they do produce, through such processes, tenable notions of quasi-certainty and serve to contain anxiety about potential disorder.

From the evidence of Tannenbaum *et al.* (1974) and of Hofstede (1977) it is observable that the forms of authority may well be products of a given culture. For example, Hofstede relates the degree of uncertainty avoidance of his national samples with their desired power distance. Further, his evidence shows that in some country samples a high power distance index (many levels, rather bureaucratic) was accompanied by small desired uncertainty avoidance and vice versa, which would indicate that notions of control developed in an Anglo-Saxon culture may not be applicable to other cultures. Further evidence for these differences was provided by Tannenbaum (1974) who reported from his study of hierarchy in industrial organisations in five countries, Italy, Austria, USA, Yugoslavia and Israel, that Italian, USA and Austrian plants were more hierarchical (as measured by the slope of perceived influence down the hierarchy) than Israeli or Yugoslav plants. In the USA he noted that there were moves to mitigate the worst effects of hierarchy by participation and involvement. Significantly, however, Tannenbaum concluded that 'Psychologically, at least, superiors in socialist plants, as in capitalist ones, are rewarded more than subordinates...', They were 'more motivated, involved and interested', that is, in very different cultures the hierarchies were delivering unequal amounts of valued goods to their participants.

If, for the purposes of this argument, we can accept the notion that if we do not wish to perpetuate any of the Weberian ideal types of authority we must at least seek an alternative source. That is, if God and the King have been replaced by rational-legal forms which have undesirable consequences – where do we turn.

To ask the question – from where does authority derive? – is to take an almost revolutionary stance. The injunction of the human growth and development movement – which is 'to take one's own authority' is one approach to the question. It focuses the individual on to his own responsibility as a citizen – to make a role in life – as Lawrence (1979) put it. This idea is echoed in anarchist and revolutionary thought. De Monthoux (1983) reviewing this tradition argues that the notion of alliances between people not only assumes that mutual behaviours will be generous but that the alliances will oppose external authority so that human beings can discover their personality. The response of these authors to the question of authority is to take an existential position as a point of departure for the structuring of institutions and societies wherever legitimate authority and hence control as mutual accountability can be conceived through a process of granting authority to others.

And yet as Parsons (1947) put it

> A certain 'Utopianism' which tends to minimise the significance of authority, coercive power and physical force in human affairs has been a conspicuous feature of a large part of modern society and perhaps particularly economic thought.

This quotation taken from Parsons' essay on Max Weber, rings more sharply in my mind now than it did some fifteen years ago when I first read it, and indeed catches a different cadence than it would have done had I read it when this piece was mooted some five years ago. Over those years the 'Utopian' spirit, if it properly existed, has given way to an increasingly authoritarian mood in the United Kingdom. The Government takes the style of a directive school-mistress, (convinced of the rightness of its own views) rather than that of the tutor (in consultative dialogue). The style seems to be permeating organisations. Most Trades Unions are said to be muted and defensive as managers exert the right to manage. If nothing else, these trends bring back into focus the questions of power and authority, and of the conflict between persons which the existential position assumes can be dealt with by generosity.

While Jaques (1976) hopes that bureaucracies can be transformed to become agents of human feeling, pluralism and community, his book, it seems to me, rests upon a recognition that people have a powerful desire for order and, by implication, control. For some men order is desirable to 'diminish men's suspicions of one another' (Mill, 1861), and for others 'Hierarchy is part of the system of authority that is essential to the maintenance of order' (Tannenbaum et al., 1974). The fear of charisma and tradition as bases for order is that they may be arbitrary and unreasoning, the fear in respect of rational legal forms of order is that it may be limiting and death-dealing. The fear of no order is the fear of chaos, of demoniac forces unleashed, of random human violence and no place of safety. Proposals for changes in existing structures almost always trigger such fear.

Taking a trusting view of generous behaviour in alliances is difficult when the number of persons becomes large (in my view greater than 12 or so). The very complexity of larger groups seems to exhaust the possibilities of a unique negotiation of generous mutuality. It is as though the very confusion leads us back to constructs of order as a means of simplification, and in order to ensure some conformity with minimal expectations and needs, some procedures of control and accountability may have to be constructed as defences against anxieties from the inner world and defences against the actions of others. Parsons, noting that the exercise of all modes of authority generate resistance and resentment, pointed to the fact that because the structures of authority are functionally limited, that is much of life is left untouched, they may themselves generate widespread feelings of insecurity and hence anxiety. Means of dealing with such anxiety, he suggested, are dependence upon archetypes such as parent figures. For example, the Conservative

Party in the UK offers a Father archetype, the Labour Party offers a Mother archetype. In my view the archetype of Management is also a Father archetype, while Trades Unions, in concert with Personnel, provide a Mothering. Hence, while structures exist to aid tasks to meet the dependency needs and to act as defences, their very incompleteness in this regard leaves individuals with considerable ambivalence about authority, and potentially locked up in the dependent position.

The tendency towards hierarchic form may flow from the logic of tasks and accountability for tasks, but it is compounded by social experience with its overlays of social status, power, titles and rewards.

Accounting as an element of accountability has been developed in relation to notions of authority which derive from the rational-legal form, that is bureaucracy.

Unlike the charismatic and traditional modes of authority, the rational-legal has the advantage of checking upon the conduct of an office. It acts as protection. In the bureaucratic form we find lots of puzzles – about certainty and inflexibility and rule-bound behaviour. It induces and nurtures dependent behaviour. It limits creation.

Are there any alternatives? The problem is to discover or create processes of control or regulation which give us the logic of tasks without the drift into social hierarchies.

2. ALTERNATIVES AND MODIFICATIONS

Alternatives to Hierarchy (Herbst, 1976) are presented as complex hierarchic alternatives to a simple hierarchic model. Matrix structures and networks may be applicable to differing cultures and tasks (Handy, 1974) but they are also examples of a complex ordering of complex reality. Here the problems of uncertainty and ambiguity are not ignored but neither are they as explicitly embraced as causal elements in the approach to self-designing organisation of Hedberg et al. (1976),[1] a self-designing organisation which has considerable scope for hierarchy. Interestingly, both success and failure appear to these authors to lead to stability, a state which they view with acute suspicion. There is more than a hint that these authors, having abandoned the desirability of a stable state, are caught up in making tolerable the impermanent transitory state of both their personal constructs and perhaps their own organisation to produce the paper. A key feature of these authors' approach (sufficient to forgive the delightful tautologies of the last two paragraphs) lies in their concentration upon processes rather than upon structures. Processes are defined by these authors rather gnomically as 'the media by which an organisation creates future acts out of its past experiences'.

The alternatives to hierarchies on offer vary from bureaucracies modified by consultation and participation; matrix structures which reflect differing needs but seem to institutionalise multiple hierarchies and autonomous groups such as joint professional practice.

An extreme point of what might at first sight appear to be a non-hierarchical organisation is the autonomous work group. This autonomy is usually centred upon the sequencing of tasks – but not the nature of the output (e.g. the Durham miners of Herbst (1976) still produced coal: the Volvo workers of Brown and Blackler (1978) still produced trucks). However, such groups, like a professional legal partnership, may well have a normative or democratic approach to tasks but will almost certainly have differentiated roles within them. These roles may take the form of a relatively stable status hierarchy, (oldest-serving partner, longest-serving employee) or a mobile set of leadership roles depending upon the nature of the task, internal evolution of the group and the immediate or relevant environment of the group (Bion, 1961; Miller and Rice, 1967).

The self-managing enterprise in Yugoslavia certainly has a structure of hierarchy (Jerovsek (1976), Tannenbaum (1974)), but Jerovsek reports that 'We found that work organisations operating on the basis of the participative model were highly efficient: those employing autocratic principles were less efficient, and thus did not maximise profitability'. This author suggested that the degree of participativeness was dependent upon the values of the senior management group.

Self-management, co-ownership and co-operation have a long history in the UK, with the reality of management a little different from the vision of the Quakers, Socialists and Christian Socialists which inspired its foundation. See for example, Hoe (1978). Not too surprisingly, the values which inspired the founders of these enterprises are not shared by all of those who work in them. My own experience in the London Co-operative Society in the 1960s, was that apart from a small handful of people only the employee members voted in elections. The nominal shareholder members were largely passive and in the event went off to shop at Marks and Spencer, Tesco, etc. Perhaps self-management or democratic control of producer and consumer co-operatives is simply too difficult to establish; the producer interests being concentrated and the consumer interest being diffuse.

It is posited (Hedberg et al., 1976) that some organisations are inherently flexible and adaptive. Certainly the move away from technically-determined production processes into group technology and self-managing groups does offer a chance that the production process would be partially determined by human needs and that the socio-technical system might be responsive to product, service and production technologies as well as human requirements. But this flexibility might be a transitional mirage. For as Miller and Rice (1967) argue, the detailed alignment of what they call the sentient and task boundaries of the group would lead to stability, then closedness and hence a lack of capacity to adapt.

The experience of the workers' co-operative formed after a company collapse in Kirkby, the KME Co-operative, lends some support to the notion that some self-managing groups are protective vehicles rather than vehicles through which the groups achieve an economic independence. (Eccles, 1981; Cowe, 1977). It was observed that as the workers' leaders had managed to obtain large tranches of money from the government of the day (thus excluding the opportunity cost issue from their perceptions) and had formed a closed group which not only found difficulty in getting members to take up representative roles but also were resistant to any financial information on the work of their own sub groups.[2] Lupton has commented that some of the groups he has studied have become stable with equitable but externally-managed payment systems.

Hofstede (1975) reports on a case of assembly workers being organised into semi-autonomous groups with the result that 'the number of constraints for planning had increased, the process had become less flexible'. For this and other reasons the tasks and control responsibilities of the groups were modified to 'more classical management control procedures'. Similarly, in a brief study of the history of a highly participative organisation established to manage the development and commissioning of a new plant in an old chemical factory, it was found that the new organisation was reverting to the style and relationships in the rest of the factory (cf. Hedberg et al., 'transplanted designs arouse rejection mechanisms').

In contrast to these rather negative experiences there is recent evidence that less hierarchical structures do produce benefits. The introduction of self-managing groups, autonomous groups (not necessarily the same thing), job enrichment, participation and changes in formal structure were examined by Srivasta (1974) who found that costs, productivity, quality of output, withdrawal behaviour and attitudes all tended to improve. Mumford also reports (1983) gains in both technical efficiency and human satisfactions. That is, these classes of changes, usually advocated from a Christian or humanist perspective, were found to be economically beneficial. It could be argued that there has been an insufficient attention to the economic costs and benefits of such changes (as compared to their social and political benefits) and suggests that an investment decision model would help to provide a structure for an evaluation of changes in work style. A problem is the assessment of the opportunity costs which would provide the bench mark for evaluation. This requires some notional relationship between goods and services and the human conditions of dignity, self-esteem, independence, etc. This promises to be a difficult calculus.

But what is clear is that the standing of the groups in the new forms of work is still one of systemic dependence with local group interdependence. This standing is based upon the fact that the decision to create the new work style is not wholly within the working group and, when created, the group boundary which seems to generate most interest is the outputs of physical goods or services, which are delivered to the next user. From what I can find out, and I would welcome information, it seems that wage payment systems are held outside such groups[3] as is most accounting information on costs of resources used. It is as though the individual's discontent and difficulty with authority is dealt with by making the group the unit of accountability – but not taking hold of the task of accounting.

These examples, admittedly limited, of self-managing groups and co-operatives, do illustrate the problem of the decay of ideals in the transformation of one form of authority into another. Orwell's *Animal Farm* describes a rational legal form and decays into a traditional form. As de Monthoux (1983) put it, 'Why are the joyful springtimes of political liberation so short?' Ignorance and innocence seem to be the answers. The aspirations outreach the capacity to meet them and too much is promised. The shift from bureaucratic forms of production and work to self-managing groups with different authority relationships is clearly a difficult step.

It is sometimes argued that the main thrust for new styles of working should not lie in the realms of economic and technical efficiency, rather the thrust should be simply (perhaps over-simply) seen in terms of the needs of men and women to achieve their own potentials (to self-actualise, as Maslow might put it) and to explore for themselves new dimensions of human potential which might redefine the meanings of their experience, thus echoing the Utopianism to which Parsons referred. Cooper (1976) points to the same issues when he notes that 'the proper object of work is ourselves', echoing Pope's assertion that the proper study of mankind is man.

Before moving to a consideration of the relationship of people to work it is useful to pause to examine whether the self-managing group has an economic rationale. In the classical liberal economic theory it is postulated that resources are allocated efficiently when markets operate as fully as possible at every stage in the production of goods and services. Thus breaking production into smaller autonomous groups appears to fit with these notions provided market conditions obtain. These ideas appear to underpin notions of entrepreneurial organisations. Of course, the obvious criticisms of self-interest in relation to community interest arise but such notions do have the merit of confronting dependence and offering possibilities of independence as an economic form of mature dependence. Clearly any such move would require economic decision-discretion to be available: it is intrinsically different from the self-managements groups which still make bits of a Volvo truck. There is, though, a danger that innocence in regard to the virtuous effects of 'free markets' might lead us to ignore the context in which they might exist and the damaging consequences which flow (Woodham Smith, 1962) from the surrender to the 'Authority' of the Hidden hand.

Etzioni's (1961) typology of organisations, (coercive, instrumental, normative) indicates something of the patterns of relationship of people to organisations and to work, especially to the basis of authority which might be exercised. Of course, all these can co-exist which suggests both complexity and caution.

The thesis that persons and work are related in extensive ways finds support in the work of Lischeron and Wall (1975) who concluded that job satisfaction, as measured, did not increase following upon participation and then argued that the style of participation or the nature of the work relationship was an important variable to examine. The survey of Attachment to Work by Dubin *et al.* (1976) concluded with the statement,

> We think the working man is a whole man – he is simultaneously an economic, psychological and sociological person. It is only

when the whole man idea is taken seriously that we can perceive that there are multiple attachments to work.

These multiple attachments were grouped rather mechanically into three areas: Systems of the Work Environment, Work-place Objects and Human Conditions and Pay-offs. The structure of work attachments would carry implications for any changes in work arrangements and the introduction of any accounting information into a work group would need to be analysed against its impact on the variables affecting attachment. This approach appears to be helpful because it relates to human growth as a process of change from dependence to interdependence and avoids the atomisation of independence. It also offers a way of thinking of self-authorisation about the process of attachment, the fact of a continuing belonging to an organisation, a persistence in the patterns of organisation life.

3. MOVING ON

The establishment of new work styles has been predicated on Christian and humanist concepts of the potential and actual value of human life. The constraints of human action are the consequent effects on other persons. What seems to me to be the next significant step is to bring the emerging new work groups into a more self-directing posture – by making the economic dimension of their activities a part of their self-management task. Hence we can begin to see a role for accounting *within* the self-managing group. The diagram below illustrates the shift from an external management control over the new style working group (demanding accountability for resources supplied) to the internal regulation and boundary control of the new style working group.

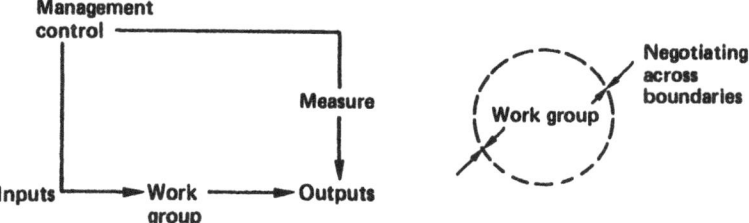

Figure 4.1

It might be thought that providing the technology of accounting and accounting information to workers, even those with the 'ability' to be in self-managing groups, would be subversive of the control which management wish to exercise on the behaviour of the group. One can readily see that a shift to a conception of the group as an independent economic entity transfers this problem to the current debate of the role of accounting in a complex organisation. But the new style working groups would necessarily operate in a state of interdependence with a variety of other such groups and the managing group. I would expect a group to want accounting information in relation to the inputs they use and the manner in which these are converted into the desired outputs. With such information the group could examine alternative arrangements of its work in relation to resource costs and its members could consider criteria for continuing membership. A statement of value added (if possible) would point to some of the mix of resources used by the group.

Of course, such working groups are not independent entities. They would need a process of mutual planning and accountability at their boundaries in order to make sense of that interdependence. The planning process would lead to the establishment by negotiation of the external conditions, output objectives and resource requirements together with a means of distributing the available incomes among the participants in the enterprise. Here the role of the 'control professional' would be to consult to the group and inter-group processes in order to help groups arrive at an acceptable plan and to help groups keep track of their activities in order to handle the processes of accountability. Broadly this conception of management control is that of building the capacity for self-regulation into the very notion of belonging to an organisation and in this manner distributing authority rather than institutionalising it.

To push the notion of free markets into organisations in too naïve a manner will almost certainly generate a fake optimism about the likely gains. If a useable notion of opportunity costs is engendered then much will have been achieved. Certainly the temptation to construct a regulatory structure based on continuously negotiated transfer prices would be to pretend that there are no other human dimensions to working; it would be a naïve and destructive simplification. The significant gains could come from a greater awareness of the boundary constraints to the whole organisation.

What is proposed here is a notion of managerial control which attempts to hold together that which is usually fragmented. The two diagrams below illustrate the change in conception. This fragmentation reflects not only a division of labour but given the Western social structure, it reflects class and socialisation. An alternative conception is to remove the fragmentation by changing the nature of the relationships, in order to hold together that which was fragmented. This socio-tech-nomic [sorry!] would bring with it some implications.

An hierarchic model of economic, social and technical fragmentation

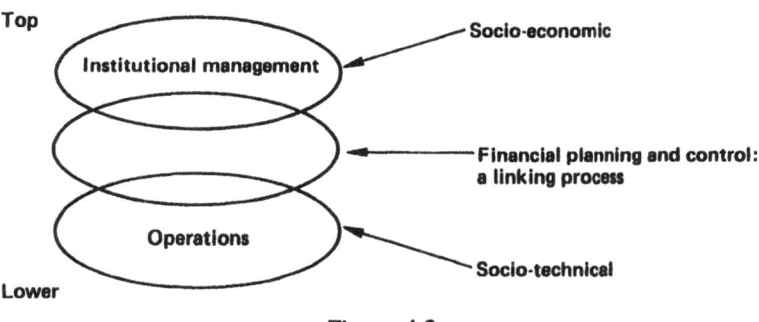

Figure 4.2

Figure 4.3

1. Management is no longer a superordinate function. It becomes a necessary task to be accomplished. It lies in the process of boundary regulation. Authority might be given to a person or group to handle some of this task.
2. The regulation of the enterprise becomes a matter of managing the internal and external boundaries, membership criteria and activities, to ensure that adequate resources are available for the tasks.
3. The task of accountability is one of mutual accountability within the enterprise and one of exchange accountability with others, i.e. suppliers and purchasers.

4. The task of accountants is to equip groups with the technology of economic measurement and evaluation and to assist in providing some of that data: i.e. Accounting is not something done to people: it is done with and on behalf of them.

Authority here is a matter of mutual giving and taking in the sense that a member's legitimacy in action is the consequence of such mutuality. This should not mean that there is no scope for initiative or development. Some examples of these kinds of organisations exist – collegial communities, professional practices, academic faculties. In using these as examples it should be clear that my argument is not for an ideal type filled with ideal people – but it is, I admit, tinged with the Utopian dream to which Parsons alluded.

It seems to me that there are some questions still unresolved. To move away from the traditional and the rational-legal a point of view was taken that Authority comes from the author and that it thus comes from the individual self; only that authority is legitimate (i.e. everyone has charisma). Now clearly that cannot be enough – an instant's reflection on the problem of moral good will make clear. There is no a priori certainty that good consequences for others will follow from a free market in individual authority. [Otherwise what is theft, murder, etc.] Hence it is imperative for the conception of legitimate self-authority and indeed the authorising of others, that the consequences to others be at least not harmful. You may recognise a turning circle here; 'order is desirable to diminish men's suspicions of one another' (Mill). Does it mean that even a self-authorising group must then have an internal order which has elements of the rational-legal and exist in a social context of order? And how can that rational-legal basis be established? It seems idle to re-create at this stage all of the problems of moral philosophy and social order. It might be better to be empirical.

Secondly, while the control notion here is of mutual accountability with generous behaviour what will be made of the problem of uncertainty? Will the uncertainty be transduced willy nilly throughout such a process or will the separate groups be able to handle uncertainty for and on behalf of each other and hold on to these notions and handle mutual accountability with integrity?

Thirdly, how would such organisations deal with the relations with the wider society? Particularly, what would be the effect of such a control structure as authority structure upon recruitment, training, etc? Would the facsimile of markets lead to the view that the survival of the entity would be the dominant criterion of behaviour?

Fourthly, should such a control structure be established, what would prevent it from decaying to either a technocracy and, further, to a bureaucracy? In what way does this new organisation of authority stand a chance of survival; in what conditions could it survive? Perhaps it is merely innocence and ignorance that lead to these conjectures.

I can imagine no obvious answers to these questions, nor do I know how to predict the 'success' of such an organisation. Further, it seems to me relatively unhelpful at this stage to continue the conjectures. What is needed is some systematic empirical investigation, which means that a programme of change should be instituted in an organisation or that some study would have to piggy-back upon an existing change event.

The research problem is to examine the role of control and accountability in the working of self-managing groups within an organisation.

The focus of the research would be the processes through which external control and internal regulation are effected by the provision and demand for accounting and accountability, whether that be marketing, production, personnel procurement or finance.

The style of such research raises immediate problems such as the intervention of the researcher in the functioning of work groups. At this stage, I would favour an action research style which would mean participating in a group; perhaps partly in a teaching role and partly in a consultative role.

Notes

1. The implicit assumption in this paper is that most persons will want to live in tents and camp on seesaws and those that don't are somehow lessened by their search for a warmer and calmer locale. There seems to be a confusion of existential ambiguities and the need for enduring relationships.
2. See Eccles, *Under New Management*; Cowe, R. unpublished MBA dissertation at Manchester Business School.
3. In contrast to the old sub-contract system in coal-mining where groups of miners could be paid as a collective and sort the distribution out themselves.

References

A. J. Berry and D. T. Otley, 'The Aggregation of Estimates in Hierarchical Organisations', *Journal of Management Studies* (May 1975).
W. R. Bion, *Experiences in Groups* (Tavistock, 1961).
C. A. Brown and F. H. Blackler, *Job Redesign and Management Control* (University of Lancaster, 1978).
G. Burrell and G. Morgan, *Sociological Paradigms and Organisational Analysis* (Heinemann, 1979).
R. Cooper, 'Work and Meta Work', *Personnel Review* 5 (1976).
R. Cowe, Financial Control in a Co-operative. Unpublished Dissertation: Manchester Business School, 1977.
Pierre De Monthoux, *Action and Existence: Anarchism for Business Administration* (Wiley, 1983).
N. F. Dixon, *On the Psychology of Military Incompetence* (Jonathan Cape, 1976).
R. Dubin, R. A. Hedley and T. C. Taveggia, 'Attachment to Work', in *Handbook of Work, Organisation and Society* (ed.) R. Dubin (Rand McNally, 1976).
Tony Eccles, *Under New Management* (Pan Books, 1981).
A. Etzioni, *A Comparative Analysis of Complex Organisation* (Free Press, 1961).
C. Handy, *Understanding Organizations* (Penguin, 1974).
B. Hedberg, P. Nystrom and W. Starbuck, 'Camping on Seesaws: Prescriptions for a Self-Designing Organisation', *A.S.Q.* (March 1976).
P. G. Herbst, *Alternatives to Hierarchies* (Martinus Nijhoff, 1976).
S. Hoe, *The Man Who Gave His Company Away* (Heinemann, 1978).
G. Hofstede, The Poverty of Management Control Philosophy, EIASM Working Paper, 75–44 (Dec. 1975).
G. Hofstede, *Culture's Consequences* (Sage, 1977).
E. Jaques, *A General Theory of Bureaucracy* (Heinemann, 1976).
J. Jerosvek, *Exploring Individual and Organisational Boundaries* (Wiley, 1979).
J. Lischeron and T. Wall, 'Employee Participation: An experimental field study', *Human Relations*, vol. 28 (1975).
J. S. Mill, *Representative Government* (1861).
E. J. Miller and A. K. Rice, *Systems of Organisation* (Tavistock, 1967).
E. Mumford, N. Bancroft and B. Sontag, 'Participative Design – Successes and Problems', *Systems, Objectives, Solutions*, vol. 3, no. 3 (Aug. 1983).
T. Parsons, M. Weber, *Theory of Organisations* (1947).
D. Smith, 'Control and Orientations to Work in a Business Organisation', *Journal of Management Studies* (May 1978).
S. Srivasta *et al.*, 'Productivity, Industrial Organisation and Job Satisfaction: Policy Development and Implementation', Report to National Science Foundation (Case Western Reserve University, 1974).
A. S. Tannenbaum, B. Kavcic, M. Rosner, M. Vianello and G. Wieser, *Hierarchy in Organisations* (Jossey Bass, 1974).
M. Weber, *The Theory of Social and Economic Organisations*, trans A. Henderson and T. Parsons (Free Press, New York, 1947).
C. Woodham Smith, *The Great Hunger* (Hamish Hamilton, 1962).

6 Power and Management Control

Keith Robson and David J. Cooper

Management control is conventionally regarded as a set of practices designed to ensure that individuals, organisations and societies satisfy their goals (Anthony, 1965). This statement, bland in itself, has been elaborated, explored and criticised in the management control literature (see, for example, the chapters in this book). Yet the above argument is also one about power or at least there is a theory of power (as authority) present, even in its absence. Individuals have goals which they act to satisfy. The statement also suggests that organisations have goals which individuals act to satisfy. But what is the relationship between the two? Are these goals themselves interdependent with the social world in which they are located? How is it we can account for the construction of these 'goals'? This is itself a question of power. Further, if conflict and resistance inhabit organisational life, then management control practices can be evaluated as power systems, reproducing or undermining the economic social and political patterns in organisations and society.

Yet the notion of power is problematic, there being several ways of approaching the concept, with each approach emphasising particular themes. The aim of this chapter is to explore various approaches to the incorporation of power and to elaborate what are the implications, more generally, of treating management control as a power relation. We argue that power and knowledge are intertwined and that an appreciation of this interrelationship offers a fuller and more critical understanding of the roles of management control practices in organisations and society.

Elaborating the four approaches outlined here involves the outlining of a number of thematic commonalities and differences between them. Power is presented variously as a positive (i.e. enabling) or negative (repressive) phenomenon. The issues as to what is the appropriate field of study (the organisation or the social totality) how this 'field' is characterised (static, suggesting constant order, or dynamic, providing accounts of change and the potential of change) and how to depict the structure of social relations (as antagonistic or harmonious) are given a variable response. Not independent of these themes is the account of human action presented: alternatively voluntistic or deterministic (the individual and society as subject and object). Finally there is a question of the necessity, or not, of providing an historical content to the present.

Thus we focus on themes such as opportunity/repression, part/whole, static/dynamic, consensus/conflict, subject/object, present/past. From these themes (and others) included, excluded, and differentially intertwined, concepts of power have emerged. In presenting our argument[1] we outline four paradigms on power, where each embodies a different world-view through their analysis of these themes. We show how research in management control has tended to adopt one or other of these views. Three of the four positions outlined are based on the framework of Therborn (1978). The first is the subjectivist approach (looking for the subject of power and asking, 'Who has power?'). The second we refer to as the integration approach (looking for 'the power to command things' and focusing on social integration by asking the question 'Power to do what?') and the third is the historical materialist approach (looking at the production of systems of power and asking 'What are the sources and effects of power?'). Our fourth approach, referred to as the 'analytic of relations of power' (Foucault, 1980, p. 199) focuses on the specific technologies by which power is exercised through its intersection with knowledges.

For each approach we briefly review the general literature on power to identify the applied implications for management control. We suggest that views of management control which do not recognise the movement of power throughout organisations and society are deficient from a theoretical point of view. Further, a failure to recognise power and the possibility of resistance has major practical consequences. It is likely to lead to incomplete prescriptions for the design or modification of management control systems which will, in turn, render problematic the designer's expectations of the effects of any proposed change.

SUBJECTIVIST APPROACHES

In this view the concern is not with the individual's subjectivity but rather 'on the power holding and exercising subject' (Therborn,

1978, p. 3). The approach is characterised by a behavioural and empirical concern with 'who has power'. This is to be identified in the outcomes of particular issues and thereby related to the actions of the powerful. Power is treated as a negative phenomenon: the denial of others in the pursuit of the subject's interests. Simplifying, the paradigm identifies power as the causal link between interests and outcome(s), in empirically verifiable situations.

Within the subjectivist approach, there are three ways of answering the question 'Who has power?' Each reflects a different view of the pattern of social relations:

(a) *Pluralism*: regarding society (and organisations) as a collection of individuals, each with their own interests and potential for influencing the world;
(b) *Elitist*: regarding society as composed of a coherent leadership or elite and an undifferentiated mass of people, the latter with limited influence;
(c) *Radical*: viewing society as composed of distinct groups or classes with one group essentially dominant and in conflict with the other(s).

The bulk of the literature concerned to study power and its relationship to management control practices utilises this paradigm. In this section we explore its theoretical location and identify its strengths and weaknesses.

Pluralism

The concern with the empirical identification of individuals exercising power leads Dahl (1957, 1963) to focus upon the process and outcome of decision-making. Individual interests are empirically located through an analysis of debates embodying 'significant issues'. Power is measureable through the notion of 'scope of power': the differences in the ways individuals respond to the exercises of power to which they are subject.

The empirical focus is upon instances of observable conflict in the process of decision making over significant issues. Conflict is assumed to arise out of differing interests, which represent the policy preferences expressed by actors in relation to the key issues. Whilst the approach allows straightforward empirical studies of who has power (and has been widely used in such exercises) there are a number of problems with it which render the interpretation of such studies rather problematic.

What is to be regarded as a key issue is not explained and the method does not recognise the possibility of gaming or strategic behaviour (for example, an individual failing to act in one situation in the expectation of acting at another time or over a related issue). Further, the focus on power over others leads to an excessive concentration on linking interests and outcomes (i.e. who gets their way?). This ignores the possibility that there is not a simple and casual link between interests and outcomes, due for example to accidents, unanticipated consequences and mistaken calculations. Nor does it attempt to take the *context* of action seriously as not merely reflecting actors' interests but also assisting in the construction of their interests. Dahl provides no historical dimension to his work on power, as the conditions of action of the power-exercising individuals bear no relevance to their interests or their present context, the latter being essentially static.

Elitism

Bachrach and Baratz (1962, 1963, 1970) present the weakness of the pluralist approach to power as one of undue concentration on the strictly observable conflict in the decision-making process. This, they claim, leads to viewing only 'the first face of power' i.e. 'when A participates in the making of decisions that affect B'. To this they would add 'the less apparent face of power', namely: 'Power is also exercised when A devotes his energies to creating or reinforcing social and political values and institutional practices that limit the scope of the political process to public consideration of only those issues which are comparatively innocuous to A' (1970, p. 7).

The above exercise of power, the 'non-decision', can result in the thwarting of any latent challenge to the interests of the decision makers. As Lukes (1974) comments 'Bachrach and Baratz are in effect redefining the boundaries of what is to count as a political issue' by adding potential issues to Dahl's concern with 'key issues'.[2] The study of power is extended to empirically locate those 'covert grievances' that lie outside the decision-making agenda. Who determines what is to be decided in an organisation and the range of policies to be considered, are important in identifying power. The elite approach, however, only identifies these issues by focusing on observable conflict. In the absence of grievances either inside or outside the decision-making arena, there is assumed to be consensus.

Radicalism

Lukes (1974) characterised the pluralist and elitist conceptions of power as one and two dimensional views. He presented a third dimension which is intended as a 'thoroughgoing critique of the behavioural focus' of the aforementioned. Firstly, attacking the individualism of Dahl and Bachrach and Baratz, Lukes argues that this ignores: (a) collective action – where this may not 'be attributable to particular decisions or behaviour' – contesting intentionality; (b) the nature of any organisation as a potential 'mobilisation of bias'.

Secondly by concentrating on instances of *observable conflict* the pluralist and elite approaches ignore the possibility that power may shape or determine the wants of those over whom it is exercised, even in the absence of overt conflict, for example, 'through the processes of socialization' (1974, p. 23).

Maintaining the link between power and interests, Lukes proposes that the empirical identification of power must rest upon notions of the interests of those over whom power is exercised (B). Having already identified the manipulation of B's wants as a power-effect, Lukes locates power in *latent conflict*: 'a contradiction between the interests of those exercising power (A) and the *real interests* of those excluded (B)' (1974, p. 24–5). The empirical concern involves Lukes in attempting to identify 'real interests'. He suggests that this is possible by the counterfactual argument that interests are objectively identifiable were B 'exercising choice under conditions of relative autonomy', (as opposed to, and distinguishable from, B's espoused wants).

One difficulty in sustaining this approach is the empirical basis for the identification of 'real interests'. The argument rests on a highly speculative ascription of 'interests' in a position of relative autonomy. Assuming society were to reach such a condition, such that any speculation could be empirically verified, would we be aware of this (Knights and Willmott, 1985)? This is a rather peculiar method of examining the power implication of 'socially structured and culturally patterned behaviour of groups, and practices of institutions' by appealing to the mythical free individual in a position of relative autonomy. Quite apart from the paternalism the 'objective' ascription of real interests implies (Benton, 1981) it leaves the present pattern of social relations untheorised (e.g. what are the power implications of our social practices?) in preference to a distinctly hazy world of 'relative autonomy'. What constitutes 'relative autonomy' is not understood and is a construction of the researcher.[3]

In positing his radical view of power Lukes was quite rightly concerned with the error of voluntarism (people produce society) which is implicit in the pluralist and elitist positions. The identification of patterns of 'socially structured' (Lukes, 1974, p. 22) practices is an attempt to deal with the society that pre-exists the individual. Yet Lukes's failure to incorporate such socially structured practices can be seen as part of the continuing subjectivist preoccupation with 'interests'. Just as Lukes suggests that conflict is not logically tied with power, so it is sensible to de-couple the notion of interests from power (Giddens, 1979). To see power as the medium of causation between interests and outcomes is to ignore both the arena of struggle with other groups and the historically contingent conditions of action of the parties involved. Furthermore, outcomes are then presented as a functional consequence, and not as possibly unintended. (Yet this is not to deny that interests and power have much to do with one another.)

In summary, the subjectivist paradigm treats power as an exercise and a simple relation between individuals – 'A's power over B'. Both the pluralist and elitist approach are premised on the ontological position that people produce society. Consequently the analysis of power presented is ahistorical, and unconcerned with the society that can be said to pre-exist the individual. The radical approach is somewhat set apart from the other two in that Lukes recognises that the structure of social relations of any society will have consequences for the exercise of power between people. Lukes backs away from any attempt to analyse power and its relation to social and economic practices that pre-exist and are reproduced by the individual. The counterfactual appeal to 'real interests' ultimately leaves the radical approach as located within the subjectivist framework of tying individual interests to power to produce, and thus account for, outcomes.

Management Control Applications of the Subjectivist Approach

The traditional literature on management control ignores the issue of power and conflict and treats organisations as unitary entities with well defined and essentially agreed purposes. For example, influential management control texts such as Anthony *et al.* (1983), Dermer (1977) and Maciarello (1984) rarely even mention terms such as power or conflict. Those studies that identify power as a significant element in management control practices are to be appreciated for recognising organisations as contested terrains both between managers (e.g. struggles between departmental managers) and between managers and the workforce (e.g. industrial relations conflicts). The subjectivist approach to power has been influential in those studies that focus on power in management decision-making.

The study of power in management control from a subjectivist set of assumptions, emphasises specific themes which were referred to in this chapter's introduction. Power is seen as a repressive phenomenon, emphasising the ability of a manager to fulfil his or her interest against the wishes of others. Conflict, normally overt, is regarded as a normal concommitant to power; without conflict, power is rarely recognised. The appropriate field of study is the organisation itself, rather than the wider social totality. The analysis of management control is regarded as an organisational analysis, independent of general social features or changes. The organisation is characterised as basically static, with only minor shifts of emphasis in organisational activity resulting from the exercise of power. There is no consideration of the source and origins of power in organisations because the subjectivist position has neglected history and tended to regard the past as somewhat irrelevant for understanding the present. Fundamentally, power in management control is treated as if it can be understood as the result of autonomous actions of individuals, pursuing their own interests. The emphasis on these themes can be illustrated through examples of the literature on power in management control from the pluralist, elite and radical views.

Within the subjectivist approach the identification of who has and who exercises power is normally conducted from a pluralist perspective. Thus Pfeffer and Salancick describe the 'power model' as where 'there is conflict among participants and the answer to what decisions will be made is to be found in examining *who has power to apply* in a particular decision contest. Thus power, rather than what is optimal for achieving some organisational objective, becomes an important decision variable' (1974, p. 136, emphasis added). This model is also implicit in studies such as Wildavsky (1965), Pettigrew (1973), Hills and Mahoney (1978), Jonsson (1982), Rosenberg *et al.* (1982), Boland and Pondy (1983) and Markus and Pfeffer (1983) which focus on the politics of identifying who influences budget and the strategies they adopt. Studies of interdepartmental relationships and the effects of the introduction of computerised information systems have also focused on the exercise of power (Bjorn-Andersen and Pedersen, 1980; Bariff and Galbraith, 1978). All these studies proceed by identifying key decisions and then defining the powerful as those whose interests are satisfied in situations of conflict.

The pluralist analysis of power has also dominated the literature on accounting standard setting. To the extent that accounting standard setting can be interpreted as an aspect of developing organisational rules for the accounting profession (see Cooper et al., this volume), this application may also be interpreted as concerned with management control of the accounting profession. Studies of the accounting standards setting process have recognised that it is a 'political process' and have concentrated on studies of 'key decisions', namely specific standards. Because no single individual or group seems to explicitly dominate across a range of standards (Haring, 1976), even though it may be possible to identify powerful individuals and groups for a specific standard (Hussein and Ketz, 1979; Hope and Briggs, 1980; Hope and Gray, 1981), it is implied that the standard setting process is pluralist. Yet, as has been observed in relation to similar studies on community power, this assumption of pluralism is built into the analysis itself. The focus on explicit decisions and an individualistic approach (there is no coherent approach to what constitutes a group) means that many possibilities for power (e.g. the control of the agenda and shared perceptions) cannot be identified.

There are very few studies of power and management control which adopt an elite or radical analysis. Pahl and Winkler (1974) in their study of 'power and decision making at board level' (p. 102) address the issue of control of agendas and found that many company boards in their study were non-functional, with other senior managers 'in control', often manipulating the board.

Whilst Pahl and Winkler are concerned to contribute to the elite approach, Clegg's early work (1975) would seem to offer a radical perspective, focusing on the use of language to structure organisational decision making. There have been a considerable number of studies which indicate the way management information can structure the content and form of industrial relations (e.g. Bougen and Ogden, 1982). There has, however, been little empirical research on the ways and the extent to which management control systems, through their role in producing, reproducing and modifying organisational patterns of responsibility and authority and their role in developing organisational cultures and patterns of visibility, can affect the decision premises, taken-for-granted views of the organisation and subjective interests of organisational members (Burchell *et al.*, 1980; Cooper, 1981, 1983).

Yet for all the considerable insights offered by these subjectivist studies of power and management control, they are all firmly rooted in the decisions and action of individuals and do not offer comprehensive explanations for the source of this power and their relationship to social and economic practices.

INTEGRATION APPROACH

Whereas the subjectivist approach focuses on the exercise of power, the integration approach to power is concerned with the 'power to do'. Therborn (1978) described it as an 'economic' view because power, like money, is treated as a circulating medium. Power is treated as if it can be exercised to the benefit of all. There is an emphasis in the integrative or systemic nature of power. With this approach the legitimate, functional and socially cohesive possibilities for power are emphasised, at the expense of other themes. This can be illustrated by the way in which Parsons has responded to the question of 'power to do what' (which follows from the general concern with power to do). For Parson's power is 'a generalized capacity to secure the performance of binding obligations by units in a system of collective organisation when the obligations are legitimized with reference to their bearing on collective goals' (1963, p. 237).

The 'system of collective organisation' includes the social sphere as a whole, though it is also applicable to sub-systems of this, such as organisations. The social world is conceived as a system bound by a normative consensus or ('collective goals') which *legitimise* the pursuit of 'binding obligations'. Power, as the *generalised* capacity to ensure these obligations are fulfilled, then becomes authority. This has a number of consequences:

(a) Power is divorced from any logical connection with 'conflict'.
(b) The absence of conflict, however, rests upon the assumption that society is entirely harmonious – the existence of genuine, normative consensus.

(c) The assumption of the existence of collective goals repeats a major difficulty in the subjectivist approach, namely of conceiving power and interests as *logically* tied.
(d) The equivalence of power with authority serves to ignore the sense of power as coercion (which need not correspond with conflict). For example, the existence of 'common goals' may derive from a relationship of unseen manipulation.

The view of society as a system belies the organismic origins of Parsons' theory. 'Units', like cells, function 'to the profit of the social system (i.e. organism) as a whole'. If they do not, one assumes, then the social body 'dies'; indeed Parsons is most concerned with the functional imperatives that must be performed for society to survive. In society, 'units' receive their genetic-like blueprints, so to speak, not at birth but at school, the 'agency through which individual personalities are trained to be motivationally and technically adequate to the performance of adult roles' (Parsons, 1969).

In contrast to the highly voluntarist notion of society portrayed by the subjectivist approach, the integrationist position tends to treat behaviour as determined by functionalist imperatives; the individual is portrayed as an 'unthinking dupe' (Giddens, 1968).

Parsons' account of power, contains some valuable insights. Power is presented as a *generalised* capacity which is an important advance on the notion of power purely as an individual capacity. Power is a property of societies and is theorised in relational terms; it is not a resource to draw upon but a *medium* of action rather than just a constraint upon it. Parsons perceives the flows of power in a society at its most effective ('efficient') in its *unseen* guises in the reproduction of everyday life (see also Foucault, 1977).

More dubious, however, is the assumption that persons in relations of dependence live their lives in the pursuit of collective goals because of their 'internalised need dispositions'. This is a reification of the social system (with its functional imperatives). It proves incapable of theorising changes in the form of society. Organisations and society are, therefore, conceived as static systems of harmonious relations.

Management Control Applications of the Integration Approach

The management control literature which has adopted the integration paradigm has tended to emphasise legitimate authority and the deterministic nature of managerial activity. This approach emphasises specific themes which were referred to in the introduction to this chapter. The tendency is to regard power as enabling; the exercise of managerial power results in the right things being done. Management control is seen in systems terms, the environment being an important source (perhaps even a determinant) of managerial actions. However the environment, and the organisation, is seen as essentially harmonious and unchanging. The lack of concern with understanding the historical dimension of management control and the contexts of managerial behaviour leads to a naturalisation of the status quo. The existing patterns of authority and power are seen as both legitimate and desirable because they represent the inevitable and most efficient way of satisfying social and environmental imperatives. The ways in which these themes are emphasised in integrationist approaches to management control is illustrated by taking two applications of the approach, namely studies of legitimate power (i.e. authority) and studies of the sources of power.

An emphasis on the legitimacy and functionalism of power can be illustrated by studies of managerial authority. Such studies tend to follow Parsons' lead to conflating power with authority. For example much of the economics orientated literature on management control has been concerned with hierarchy and the information which should be provided to the appropriate level in an hierarchy to ensure management control. Issues of power tend to get reduced to ones of hierarchy. Thus, Williamson's analysis of markets and hierarchies (1975) has been criticised for distorting issues of power into issues of hierarchical form. Further it treats the existence and nature of specific hierarchical forms as evidence of the superiority of that organisation form over market modes of coordinating economic activities (Francis *et al.*, 1983). Indeed, hierarchy is seen merely as functional coordination. Further, the approach naturalises the status quo in that the organisational form in existence is assumed to be the best form for all participants, independent of any particular historical process (du Boff and Herman, 1980).

Another strand of the economics orientated literature goes even further than merely assuming that existing patterns of power, authority and hierarchy are functionally necessary. It focuses on the design of information systems and incentive schemes to support the hierarchy (Baiman, 1982; Spicer and Ballew, 1983). The emphasis is on an analysis of superior and subordinate (alternatively referred to as principal and agent) relationships. The themes of the integrationist approach relating to the enabling characteristics of power and the harmonious nature of social relationships is illustrated by the unselfconscious concern with the 'principals' problem (Ross, 1974) of designing appropriate incentive and reporting schemes. The significant issue is not that the analysis merely focuses on the principal's problem. Rather it is that it assumes that resolving the principal's problem is synonymous with satisfying the agent, in that designing suitable information and incentive systems will result in both the principal and the agent (the superior and subordinate) being better off.

The second application of the integration economic approach to power in management control, has been to focus on the sources of power. The strategic contingency approach to organisational power (Hickson *et al.*, 1971; Hinings *et al.*, 1974) is concerned to identify the resources which departments within organisations possess, in order to assess their capacity to influence decisions. This approach conceives of power in terms of the formal managerial structures of an organisation (as depicted, for example, on an organisational chart) and is thereby able to identify differing capacities of departments in specific organisations. Following Crozier (1964) it locates the source of this power in the control of critical uncertainties, although it does not explain either the origin of the uncertainties or what departments do with their power.

An influential attempt to identify the sources of power has been that of French and Raven (1959) who identify five such bases: reward, expert, coercive, legitimate and referent. These are heavily influenced by Parsons' analysis and this influence is reflected in the non-problematic way these bases are discussed. All such bases arise, for French and Raven, out of the functional imperatives of the social system and these are assumed to be legitimate. For example, the concept of expertise is not seen as a social and political construction but rather as a reflection of those skills that are functionally required by the system.

The apparent poverty of the integration approach to management control is lessened if it is recognised that so called 'external' factors may be important in an analysis of power and management control. This recognition is associated with the population ecology model of organisation (Aldrich, 1979) and the resource dependence model (Pfeffer and Salancik, 1978; Mintzberg, 1983). However both these models implicitly adopt an integration approach to power, focusing on legitimate authority and accepting the current structure as natural and the external environment of the organisation as relatively fixed. Indeed all the research within this approach has a decidedly ahistoric quality. For example, Aldrich focuses on inter-organisational relationships and the ability of organisations to create 'niches' for themselves in their environments. The environment is seen as powerful: selecting and retaining those organisations which fit its needs.

Alternatively (although still consistent with the integration approach) the power of environments is seen as 'a source of scarce resources which are sought after by a population of organisations which competes as well as shares them' (Aldrich and Mindlin, 1978, p. 156). In this analysis we see an ahistorical and reified analysis similar to that of Parsons, but one which emphasises the importance of moving beyond common sense notions of the boundaries of an organisation. The insight of this approach is that to study power in management control or to design management control systems may mean that the 'environment' should be conceived as a central part of the approach.

HISTORICAL MATERIALISM

'Men make their own history but they do not make it just as they please; they do not make it under circumstances chosen by themselves, but under circumstances directly encountered, given and transmitted by the past' (Marx, 1852).

The above quote elegantly summarises the materialist view of history: human activity is paramount, the primary force in history. It is from this perspective that power is theorised; not through its subjects or quantity, as in the two previous schematas.

Marx suggested that as human beings need to work to survive (the labour premise), the development of society is generated primarily by economic practices. The concept of the mode of production was abstracted to account for the distinctive economic practices of specific social formations (e.g. capitalism, feudalism). The mode of production represents the dominant relationship between the forces of production (materials, tools, technologies) and the relations of production (crudely, the capacity to control the product). In capitalist society the mode of production embodies a fundamental contradiction that, in conjunction with contradictions in non-economic structures, will provide episodes of societal transformation. The capitalist mode of production contains a contradiction between the manifest experience of it and that which is revealed by analysis. The latter indicates an antagonism between the forces and relations of production, capital and labour, exchange value and surplus value, socialised production and private ownership. These are all aspects of the same phenomenon and all of them can provoke crises and the possibility of social change.

The variety of social formations and their associated systems of power are the object of focus in historical materialism. However this variety is considered primarily from the perspective of the mode of production which provides the primary source of social transformation. The analysis of the history of social transformations provides distinct episodes but a feature of Marxian analysis has been the concern to account for the relatively enduring structures of social relations and the mechanisms by which they are continually reproduced, through the exercise of *power*.

As we maintain throughout this chapter power is inextricably involved in the practical activities carried out in the enactment of everyday life. Yet 'power' as a separate and particular analytical concept has been poorly developed within the materialist framework and particularly in the writings of Marx himself. Within a Marxian conceptualisation Althusser (1969, 1970) has sought to incorporate power and to develop a sustained and systematic attempt to refute the economism and mono-functionalism of much Marxian work (for example, the suggestion that the economic 'base' determines the pattern of state and religion in a society).[4] Further, Poulantzas (1973, 1975) and Therborn (1978) taking Althusser's work as an essential backcloth, have been specifically concerned with the theorisation of power from a historical materialist position.

For Poulantzas power represents 'the capacity of a class to realize its specific objective interests'. 'Objective' is inserted 'to rule out any question of behavioural motivations' (Poulantzas, 1973) and indeed power in a historical materialist framework is not concerned with the 'power holding' (Therborn, 1978) subject. The subject is analysed with respect to his or her 'position' in the pattern of structural relationships, i.e. 'the ongoing social process of reproduction and transformation' (Therborn, 1978, p. 131).

Though specifically tying his view of power to class interests Poulantzas denies that class is the 'foundation' of power. Rather, power 'points to the effects of the structure on the relations of conflict between the practices of the various classes in "struggle"'

(1973). Further, power is neither located nor resides in the levels of structures but rather 'is an effect of the ensemble of these levels' (1973). This 'ensemble' of the various levels does not *determine* the ability to realise objective interests, rather this 'ensemble' provides its *limits* or horizon. The power of class is also dependent upon the 'economic, political and ideological organization of each class itself'. Thus Poulantzas provides a 'double delimitation', of structure and class, in his assessment of power.

Power is both limited by 'the ensemble of the levels of structure' and the particular organisation of a class. However these 'limits' do not appear to meet and thus structure (external) and the active organisation of classes (internal) are set in a dualistic opposition. Instead of recognising that 'action' and 'structure' presume and preserve the other (the 'duality of structure', in Giddens' (1982) phrase) the subject is presented in a position that, while not totally determined by the dominant social structures, is nevertheless left with little apparent autonomy.

Poulantzas ties his concept of power to both 'conflict' and 'interests'. The power–conflict link repeats the subjectivist problem of the failure to recognise the possibility of coercion without 'struggle' and, indeed, the process by which subjects may invest in their own regulation.

We would wish to place more emphasis in a materialist view of history which theorises the subject as a conscious being. The problem with much of the analysis that derives from Althusser is that the subject becomes the 'bearer of definite relations of production' (Therborn, 1978) – Garfinkel's 'cultural dope' (1967). Althusser's analysis treats actors as if their own consciousness was not important. Yet it is human beings who make history by what they 'know' and what they do, and power is directly implicated in this process, and not limited within 'the ensemble of the levels of structure'.

Power is quite explicitly tied to class in both Poulantzas' and Therborn's writings. This link leads to the risk that the approach is treated economistically, that is, the economy is the only important force for social development.[5] We recognise the importance of the economy as a force for change in the social field. But power as implicated in the development of societies can take many forms, each of which can provide the conditions of possibility for societal transformation.[6] For example, exploitation by the nation-state, gender conflict and racial domination may each provide particular forms of domination encountered in any society. They provide the conditions for the circulation of power that reproduces these conditions and can transform them. Though the materialist framework has advanced us little in understanding the operation of power in everyday life, it has served to emphasise the importance of the historical context in its production. The opening quotation of this section preserves the notion of the duality of structure which is central to our analysis. It is unfortunate that the emphasis upon economic domination may serve to obscure as much as it highlights. Historical materialism provides an understanding of the dispersion of sites of domination that can be said to generate power but not the media through which power is exercised. This will be the subject of the final section of this paper.

Management Control Implications of the Historical Materialist Approach

Only recently has the historical materialist approach had any explicit influence on management control research. The value of the historical materialist approach is that it opens up the question of organisational goals and the role of management in achieving such goals. This question recognises that the very concepts 'goals' and 'management' are socially and politically created. These concepts are understood by locating them at a particular historical time, as part of a social dynamic, and in the context in which the organisation operates. The historical materialist approach to the question of 'what do the rulers do?' (Therborn, 1978) is not answered through an atheoretical and ahistorical study of management practices (Mintzberg, 1983; Stewart, 1967). Rather it is addressed through analysis of the role of management in capitalism, theorising management in processes of appropriating surplus value for capital and the reproduction of capitalist relations of production (Clegg and Dunkerley, 1980; Willmott, 1984).

The management control literature that has built upon historical materialism has illustrated both the strengths and weaknesses of this approach to power. It locates managerial strategies within a wider organisational and social context at a particular point of time. Management control practices are seen as dynamic and contingent on the specific economic, ideological and political structures that constitute the social totality. Organisations are regarded as a middle range concept; their management control systems, beliefs and actions reflect and help produce the social world in which they operate.

However, primacy is given to economic interests, to surplus value appropriation, which by assumption is regarded as the source of change. Management is seen as having little autonomy; they have little option but to carry out the wishes of capital and to operate in conflict with labour. For example, much of the literature on industrial relations has focused on class relations and conflict over the economic surplus (e.g. Beynon, 1972; Nichols and Armstrong, 1976). Whilst this focus may be a reaction to a prevailing orthodoxy of integrationist analyses which have dominated much industrial relations, issues such as the gender, racial and nationalistic bases of conflict have not been widely addressed within this approach.

Power is implicated, as class power, in studies that adopt the historical materialist approach. 'A given kind of relations of production may be reproduced without the exploiting (dominant) class defined by them being in 'control' of the government in any usual and reasonable sense of the word, even though the interventions of the state further and/or allow these relations of production to be reproduced. And yet the fact that a specific form of exploitation and domination is being reproduced, *is* an example of class rule and is an important aspect of power in society' (Therborn, 1978, pp. 232–3).

Many of the analyses which have taken a historical approach to power in management control have focused on the labour process, which has frequently been interpreted as the organisation and control of work. Braverman (1974) and Gorz (1976) injected a new vigour into the analysis of the labour process. The emphasis in labour process theories has been on the nature and control of work and on particular historical analyses of the management strategies for control. It traces a transformation from the formal subordination of labour (where workers are brought into the factory to be under the control of the capitalist) to the real subordination of labour (where the use of science and machinery such as management science and new technology results in the domination of labour). Braverman, for example, places considerable emphasis on management control techniques such as standard costing which results in the practical knowledge of those who carry out work being transferred to managers who then control the work. This separation of the execution from the conception of work strengthens the real subordination of labour. He also emphasises the significance of measures such as return on investment as a means of developing the capitalist enterprise into a divisionalised form and thereby facilitating greater specialisation and extraction of surplus value from labour power. Power is inherent in management control techniques and for Braverman these techniques are consistently applied for the benefit of the capitalist.

Braverman's analysis has been criticised for its historical inaccuracies, his neglect of resistance, management's assumed rationality and the emphasis on class in itself (Clawson, 1980; Stark, 1980; Wood, 1982; Knights and Willmott, 1985). In an elaboration of Braverman, Friedman (1977) introduces two alternative management strategies of control, direct control (which Braverman discusses) and responsible autonomy where management provide concessions to labour to enhance their commitment to the organisation and capitalist values. Edwards' (1979) historical and comparative analysis of US firms suggested three forms of control: simple, (e.g. direct observation and unsystematic rewards and punishments) technical (embodied in the technology through, for example, the pace of work) and bureaucratic (administered systems of management control). Friedman and Edwards locate these forms of control in the specifics of the organisation's historical and competitive position (e.g. workplace conflict and economic contradictions) and the social totality (e.g. of current ideologies). They stress that management control strategies are located in the particular historical relations of production and their relationship to the productive forces.

The detailed historical studies of Clawson (1980) Burawoy (1979) and Littler (1982) provide detail about how managerial and worker power operates in a relational manner, and how it reflects wider social developments. These studies concentrate attention on conflict at the workplace and make little attempt to systematically account for the differences in control strategies, the success of resistance and the degrees of managerial autonomy which they identify. However such accounts assume a direct link between changes in managerial and workplace practices, the surplus value appropriating process and the interests of capitalists. This may be illustrated by work informed by Gordon et al., (1982) and Johnson (1980).

Gordon et al. (1982) directly link control of the labour process with the surplus value appropriating process. They introduce the concept of the 'social structures of accumulation' which are institutions involved in the reproduction of labour, systems of class struggle and exchange and credit arrangements. The nature of these social structures is related to long waves of economic development so that Gordon et al. develop a periodisation analysis which indicates how control systems in the enterprise are related to the changing nature of the social structures. Building on their analysis, Hopper *et al.* (1986) undertook a detailed study of financial control in the National Coal Board and they illustrate how the State has been involved in capital accumulation through its investment, pricing and financial management (and information) policies. More specifically, Hopper *et al.* suggest that changes in management control practices (e.g. the use of profit centres, the investment in elaborate systems of financial management and the elevation of market prices as a signal for strategic action) are linked to changes in the British economy and the British State (which is seen as having a degree of limited autonomy from the economy). However the economy in these formulations is posited as fundamental, rather than demonstrated to be so. Managerial autonomy whilst not neglected by Hopper *et al.*, is almost ignored in the more economistic analysis of Gordon *et al.* The strength of the latter work is its elaborate historical analysis which locates changes in internal management practices within the dynamic of waves of economic growth and decline. Power as a distinct analytical category is not very obvious in these applications of historical materialism. However it is central in Johnson's analysis of work.

Using an Althusserian framework, Johnson seeks to explain that work is a relationship of power. This statement 'refers to the view that when people enter into relationships of production they are, at the same time, engaged in a political process out of which emerge structures of domination and subordination, mechanisms of social control and forms of exploitation' (1980, p. 335). The primary relationship of production is between the producer and non-producer, which in capitalism is between the producers and appropriators of surplus value. For Johnson, the processes of production and appropriation of surplus value involves three aspects, the appropriation process, the realisation of capital and the reproduction of the relations of production.

Much of the literature concerned with the organisation and control of work as a labour process focuses upon the appropriation process. This involves direct surveillance and coercion of productive labour and strategies such as formal organisation, hierarchical planning and reward and training systems which may be used in an attempt to increase productivity and profits. For Johnson, the realisation process may take place either internal or external to the particular enterprise. It is concerned with 'the means by which surplus value is transferred, struggled over and allocated' (Braverman, 1974, p. 304). These struggles within capital may take place within a holding or multi-divisional company where head office allocates and receives capital from its branches (Williamson, 1970) or it may involve the institutions of finance capital such as the stock market, banks and the fiscal policies of the State. Francis (1980) shows how changes in ownership structures have tended to be related to a shift from industrial to finance capital. Management control in the realisation process involves financial management, of 'watching over capital, of checking and controlling the process of its enlargement' (Braverman, 1974, p. 362).

Where Johnson goes further than Braverman is to emphasise the significance of the reproduction of the relations of production. Burawoy's (1979) emphasis on the manufacture of consent focuses on the importance of subjective factors and ideology, but at the level of the industrial plant. However, Johnson's analysis is more general, dealing with the structures of the society. In this he follows Althusser (1969) and Therborn (1978), by indicating the centrality of a further 'set of control mechanisms which are not directly related to the appropriation of surplus value or its realisation but operate to reproduce the social conditions for the maintenance of such relationships' (Johnson, 1980, p. 362). The reproduction of social relations involves not only those institutions which maintain labour power (e.g. health and education) but also those which maintain and develop knowledge and science (e.g. education). The state has a dominant role in these processes, particularly that associated with reproduction. The emphasis of Johnson on the state illustrates a distinguishing feature of this historical materialist approach to power in management control. The organisation is not regarded as an adequate focus for the analysis of power in management control; much of management control may rely upon the State (e.g. in developing attitudes to work and in the use of repressive mechanisms in industrial disputes) or upon economic, social and ideological features of society.

Several recent articles in management control have begun to explore aspects of this historical materialist approach in a manner informed by the Althusserian approach. Armstrong (1985) has discussed inter-professional rivalries within the labour process of management control and the ascendancy of accountants in UK manufacturing enterprises. He emphasises the latter's centrality in the realisation process in the UK (notably the merger boom and bankruptcies). Armstrong suggests that accountants have both taken advantage and reinforced the specifics of historical developments in the UK, and their role in the appropriation process (including the management of work) has thereby been strengthened.

Neimark (1983) and Neimark and Tinker (1986) have used an analysis of annual reports to illuminate the 'social functions of corporations' in reproducing ideological structures: 'The conditions necessary for continuing capital accumulation at the firm level are created by the mechanism of reproduction at the societal level – the political, cultural, ideological and juridicial superstructures of institutions and patterns of belief' (Neimark and Tinker, 1986). They demonstrate that analyses of management control which are located within the firm are incomplete and that the management control process is a dialectic one of resolutions and impediments between the corporate control system and the specific conjunctures of the socio-historical environment. Their emphasis on ideology is also characteristic of the historical materialist approach, particularly as they lay emphasis on the economic and class basis of ideology. An economically based periodisation analysis serves as the mechanism through which they trace the way in which the corporation reflects and reproduces the social ideology of the period.

Finally, some of Clegg's more recent work (Clegg, 1979 and 1981; Clegg and Dunkerley, 1980) has sought to articulate a historical materialist approach to power and control in organisations. However, he draws on theoretical developments since Braverman to emphasise not only the contested nature of control but also the contradictory and discontinuous nature of the historical processes of control. Although his use of theories of long waves of surplus value accumulation is less specific than Gordon *et al.* (1982), he draws attention to the autonomy of management and the enduring patterns of organisational practices, through the metaphor of 'sedimentated rules'. Together with his emphasis on the significance of the state, the extraorganisational rules (principles of organisations) and the view that 'organisations are the sites of the social relations of production that define class structure' (Clegg, 1981, p. 551), he offers an analysis of organisations that provides historical and case specificity, considerable managerial autonomy and a structuralist approach firmly rooted in the surplus value appropriation process.

THE ANALYTICS OF RELATIONS OF POWER

'Human social life is formed and reformed in praxis' (Giddens, 1984). This is a central tenet of our account of power and summarises the general position of historical materialism conveyed by the earlier quote from Marx (1852). Indeed it is the crucial role of power in social change that we wish to emphasise in this chapter and the ways power can account for management control in the present. Yet historical materialism need not rest on the primacy of the 'economic' (even 'in the last instance'). The Marxian analysis of domination recognises the importance of economic practices in the movement of capitalist society. Nevertheless, other forms of domination (ethnic, gender, religious, nation-state) are also present in various mixes in particular societies. Power presumes and sustains these forms of domination but the analytics of relations of power seek to understand the means through which power is exercised to accomplish these outcomes.

Foucault has attempted to analyse the circulation of power effected in the discourses and practices of our social world and his work complements the absence of the everyday exercise of power in historical materialist analysis. Much of the historical materialist concern with domination forms a background to Foucault's work and whilst recognising that there are 'silences' between the two frameworks this does not negate their complementary positions.[7] Foucault regards the concept of 'truth' as 'our longest lie'. He focuses on the general politics of truth; the historical conditions that allow some forms of discourse to be taken seriously, while setting aside the question of their essential truth. Our discussion will focus on Foucault's analysis of disciplinary power (1977). Foucault is concerned to undermine notions of progress by 'delegitimising' the present. To this end he employs the geneological method, probably best understood through example.

In *Discipline and Punish* (1977) Foucault takes as his starting point the spectacle of torture and executions present in the seventeenth century and the contrast with the regulation of everyday life within the new carceral institutions less than one hundred years later. The regime of 'punishment' underwent a quite remarkable transformation. Rather than suggesting these changes present the accomplishments of humanist reforms, Foucault discusses how these alterations effected a new 'efficiency of power' in the processes of social control. By the growth of human sciences (criminology, psychology, medicine, sociology and even psychoanalysis) the 'knowledge' these practices effect has constituted the individual and brought him/her into a complex web of surveillance and regulation of the 'self' encompassing the social field. The consequences were to be important in providing conditions for, amongst other things, the growth of state activities and the possibility of what we now know as the factory.

Foucault is intent to undermine the 'common sense' antagonism perceived between power and knowledge: 'we should rather admit power produces knowledge ... that power and knowledge directly imply one another' (1977, p. 27). Through the strategy of decentring the subject, he suggests that it is ultimately pointless to speculate about the 'nature' or 'intention' of actors; attention is more fruitfully focused upon cultural discourses and practices 'themselves neither true nor false' (1980, p. 118) for their 'power-effects':

> People know what they do: they frequently know why they do what they do; but what they don't know is what what they do does.
> (1982, p. 187)

Power presents itself at its most powerful when unseen. Violence and force are not its ideal form: 'leniency' can be more efficient. In the minute details of everyday discourses and practices power is exercised between people by what they understand as truth. Thus the human sciences appear suspect in their truth content. Foucault suggests that the proliferation of the human sciences is significant for their negotiation of 'problems' of social order: problems that are themselves a social construction. They offer a 'grid of technologies' which have the individual as their object of knowledge. Disciplinary power emphasises the part knowledge has played at its intersection with power to produce the human being as an object, or 'docile body'.

Disciplinary power

The crossing of power and knowledge presents power with its greatest strategy for attaining invisibility. This tactic finds an expression in *discipline*, a term that is itself ambiguous in use.

Discipline has been concerned to organise bodies, time and space. By distributing bodies at functional sites into a network of relations that can be surveyed, discipline provides not only an increased domination (subjection) but an increase in productive force (utility).

The architectural, functional and hierarchical meet in the distribution of cells, places and ranks; the complex space of the subject (1977, p. 148). Time was also to be given more consideration. Occupations became more closely defined with regard to the placing of the body in time and space. For example the use of timetables and meticulous attention to gestures and movement affected a control of time, which became continuous.

The effects of discipline were not simply to *totalise* the domination of the subject by organisation and observation of bodies, space and time. This is to overlook the importance of *rank* as the measure of discipline (1977, p. 145). Knowledge of the body becomes the process by which discipline 'makes' individuals; the body as a machine becomes superseded by the 'problem' of the individual and behaviour. The body is 'offered up' to new forms of knowledge; surveillance offers the capacity to *differentiate* as well as coerce by the act of observing. Disciplinary power can constantly refer the individual to the whole (i.e. the population) for comparison. The Norm becomes the standard which is then enforcible by ever more finely tuned 'micro-penalties' (1977, p. 178).

For example, surveillance, knowledge and normalised judgement find their integrated form in the examination, the crucial tool of differentiation and normalisation in our society. The examination presents the 'superimposition of power relations and knowledge relations at its intersection with writing' (1977, p. 185); it represents the start of the individual as a 'case' to be known in all its details. The growth of the file containing details of the individual has also been co-existensive with the development of the state. 'Knowledge' of the individual is made visible while its power-effects remain invisible to the subject. Power and knowledge have thus combined to produce the individual as object of knowledge under increasing forms of subjection.

Power in Foucault's work is revealed in its positive, enabling forms. Force and violence seem ineffectual media of power by comparison. Disciplinary power has helped 'create' individuals; how to position them, how to judge them and how to induce self-regulation. The individual has been constructed as an object.[8]

Power circulates in the exercise and involves everyone to varying extents. Discipline alerts us to the exercise of power at the everyday level as an effect of discourse and practices. Although power presumes domination (Giddens, 1984) the concrete technologies of power are not reducible to it. So in following the rise of disciplinary technologies, Foucault stresses that their point of origin is dispersed: 'It is rather a multiplicity of often minor processes of different origin and scattered location, which overlap, repeat or imitate one another, support one another, distinguish themselves from one another'. The social totality becomes an horizon of thought not its object (Poster, 1984).

Discipline was not the product of capitalism but one of the conditions of its possibility. Since that time it has served to strengthen the 'coercive link to the apparatus of production' at the intersections of power and knowledge. With regard to shop-floor practices, Foucault argues that Taylorism was a restatement of already existing disciplinary technologies, with longer and more complex histories. The role of the state in the use of technologies of power is a clear implication of Foucault's work, even though the micro-powers he identifies often operate at the fringes of state activity. Nevertheless the notion of the state as a particular 'generator' of power in itself (Foucault, 1982) re-emphasises the multiple modes of domination in our society. Foucault does not neglect class domination, as Dews (1984) suggests, he just refuses to reduce all power to it.

It has been suggested that Foucault underplays any possibility of resistance to power. However within any relation of power there may be a 'space', or area of darkness, from the all-embracing gaze for the individual to counteract. For example, neither factories nor prisons have ever worked in the way the discourse suggests they would. Yet that still leaves us to uncover what it is they do achieve, i.e. 'actual effects are often very different from their intended effects' (Cousins and Hussain, 1984, p. 230). With regard to the role ascribed to prisons as one of 'reform', criticism of their inadequacy in achieving this is not as modern a debate as is widely believed. Indeed it seems to have followed from the birth of the prisons. When technologies of power and the knowledge do fail, the limits of the discourse often only justify the need for more of the same (Dreyfus and Rabinow, 1982, p. 196).

Implications for Management Control

The historical materialist analysis emphasises the role of power as providing the medium for the reproduction of modes of domination in society be they economic, nation-state, ethnic, or whatever. Power presumes domination but this does not provide much assistance in understanding how it is exercised. The strength of Foucault's 'analytics of power relations' is its concern to address the specific mechanisms and technologies by which power circulates in the social world.

This may be related to the techniques of management control. A starting point is to recognise that practices are often accounted for in discourses (e.g theorised) in ways which seem remote from actual consequences. Rather than presenting the rise of 'management sciences' and their applications as a simple reflection of the growth of rationalisation, this paper suggests it is their 'power-effects' in specific historical situations that provide an important explanation for the significance of techniques of management control.

The growth of cost accounting in organisations is an illustration. The vision of accounting as functioning within organisations 'for decision-making' has a problematical relationship to how accounting operates in practice (Burchell et al., 1980). This could suggest there are other consequences to accounting. One such consequence is suggested by Foucault's discussion of the Panopticon (1977). Bentham's Panopticon was an architectural model for a prison. A central tower stands in a courtyard surrounded by a continuous building or buildings. The buildings are divided into levels and cells. Cells are arranged so that the occupant is totally visible to the guardian in the tower through the spatial arrangement of windows. Yet screens within the tower itself are arranged so that the prisoner never knows whether (s)he is under surveillance or not. This uncertainty affects the prisoner, who becomes his òr her own guardian. The Panopticon represents a technology of power that is continuous and anonymous. The principle of the Panopticon is effective in the practices of cost accounting. As Cyert and March (1963) noted, standard operating procedures, budgets, performance reports and other formal mechanics of management induce a continuous regulation and supervision of the person while effecting a particular internal visibility to the organisation. Furthermore as the 'eye' operates, as it were, in an entirely impersonal manner, the individual consciousness of the possibility of surveillance induces his or her own self-regulation. The growth of communicative technologies has greatly assisted this process by their reduction of 'time-space distanciation' (Giddens, 1979) allowing the absence of face-to-face contact without absence of control. That management control techniques such as cost accounting present only a partial visibility further provides one quite crucial aspect of its power. (Their techniques indicate what aspects of organisational life are regarded as important and worthy of attention.)

A great many of the human sciences that form the decisive bases for management practices in organisations have longer and more involved histories. Many have continually reproduced the name of 'efficiency' as their rationale. Miller and O'Leary (1986) offer a genealogy of the discourse of efficiency, taking as their main period of analysis the first three decades of this century. The apparent concern of management thinking in terms of scientific management, industrial psychology and standard costing, for example, and their linking with efficiency, share a common ancestry in various discourses surrounding politics, wealth and eugenics at the turn of the century.

All strands of these human sciences have continued to construct the individual as an object of knowledge through their concern with 'behaviour'. In focusing on the 'problem' of human motivation, defining norms of behaviour and designating attributes to be measured, management sciences have been implicated in the construction of the lived body of the individual, as well as reinforcing the 'body of knowledge' of each science through the institution and collection of data records.

The power of such *individualising* human sciences has two aspects. One can be subject to control from without and management practices are often seen in this regard. But one can also be subject to oneself, by identity or what it is one 'knows' about oneself – the conscience or self-knowledge of the person. The discourses of management here discussed act to inform that self-knowledge and self-discipline, with their specific rationalities oriented particularly towards production and utility. This aspect of the person tied to oneself represents a crucial instance of the intersection between power and knowledge contributing to the achievement of a social order in organisations.

The problem of tying power to questions of intentionality and interests is demonstrated by the Foucauldian analysis of specific 'power effects'. We have already reiterated the suggestion that discourses surrounding 'efficient resource allocation' are a most tenuous reflection of accounting in action. Indeed the historical context in which cost accounting arose within organisations was one concerned to address the problems of fraud and the lack of adequate records (Pollard, 1965). There was nothing 'essential' to accounting theory that could 'create' a market for accounting services (as Hoskins and Macve demonstrate (1986), much of the necessary technology of accounting was already in existence before the 1800s).

Rather the actions of a war-time state played a crucial and unintended part.

The response of the state reflected public concern over 'profiteering' of private suppliers to the Ministry of Munitions and others during the First World War (Loft, 1985). Through the secondment of eminent accountants to investigate the pricing of contracts, the state quite unintentionally expanded the possibilities of accounting becoming centrally involved in the presentation of organisational activities. A changing role for accounting began to define the terrain by which organisations could be interrogated or made accountable.

In similar fashion state regulation of the workplace during the First World War was responsible for the introduction of welfare officers in munitions factories. The prospect of personnel management as a preemptive management control was realised. Between the wars larger organisations in the UK, such as ICI, Courtaulds, Pilkingtons and Marks & Spencer, set up the first specialist personnel departments (Watson, 1977). A file for each employee was thus created. The person began now to be 'referenced' for 'good character' and particular aptitudes. 'Intelligence' and how to measure it was introduced as a problem, and personnel became intertwined with many of the selfsame discourses as eugenics: the degradation of the race, the need for selective breeding and a functional hierarchy based on IQ, (Gould, 1981). The use of 'aptitude' tests increases today and is derived from many of the same premises.

The focus upon specific management discourses and practices present within organisations today and their genealogies highlight how the field of their development is social and not simply organisational. Yet vague descriptions of environmental ('static' or 'uncertain') determination of management practices ignores the duality of their change, (as well as the often significant consequences of state action).

As an illustration, we are not suggesting that accounting's representation of the economic is at all unambiguous (Berry *et al.*, 1985) *nor* that the purposes of accounting in organisations are simply contingent on its environment. For example, Burchell *et al.* (1986), have shown that the issues were present in the discourses surrounding the Value Added Statement in the UK during the 1970s. As a technology, the value added statement was sufficiently ambiguous to appeal as a mediator in the conduct of industrial relations. Management control could be facilitated by the construction of employee incentive payment schemes based upon value added. Yet the disciplinary role the value added statement could play in the operation of incomes policy was to some extent in conflict with its discursive roles as presenting the economic activities of the organisation as a cooperative venture. The extent to which the 'three arenas' of accounting standards, industrial relations and national incomes policy overlapped, demonstrate the manner in which accounting both reflects its social context and also has the power to constitute the terms of, and interests in, the value added event. This reflective and constitutive role for the value added statement, however, had particular power-effects at a specific historical episode, the conditions of which were soon to alter.

In 'The Subject and Power' (1982) Foucault generalised the kinds of social struggle that have characterised history. He characterised the present as a struggle against the forms of subjection or individuation. But this is not to present the individual as somewhat *totally* in the grip of power. Whatever form of control is present the individual often has sufficient space to resist. Indeed the process of individualising tends to obscure the relations of interdependence between people and promotes instrumental relations between organisational actors (Knights and Roberts, 1982). The 'dialectic of control' (Giddens, 1979) allows always the possibility of resistance. Society is not a prison. The prison, however, was a response to the growing popular revolt against the spectacle of torture as a social control and it is often in these instances of resistance to management practices that power is revealed and, perhaps, new technologies of power also arise.

CONCLUSION

Management control practices have not 'evolved' to the condition they now occupy within organisations as a result of any technological need in the past or present for rational resource allocation. As we have sought to demonstrate the consequences of many management activities have little to do with such narrative ideals. So what do they do?

We suggest more research be devoted to the history of knowledge that, once outside organisations, now reside within them and to thereby understand the power of management control. Suspending judgement on the truth of many management techniques it is hoped to come to terms with their histories from the awareness of 'power-effects'. In constructing such histories, the organisation is not the obvious boundary of analyses. Rather, management techniques active in today's organisations have longer histories in the social field as a whole. With respect to those studies which work in the new directions we have outlined, the consequence of state actions serves to have played a by no means insignificant role.

In conceptualising the notion of power there has been an attempt to stress the ontological pitfalls of tying power to interests. By linking power and interests the subjectivist approach explains outcomes without a serious consideration for the historical conditions of action, the context of 'struggle', or the possibility of unintended outcomes. This limits the value of the approach as our society seems to display a mix of intended and unintended outcomes. This view may be contrasted with the integrationist account of social systems with functional imperatives. As well as supporting the general historical materialist position that human beings make history, this literature on power has served to demonstrate the link with modes of domination which both generate and are the outcome of the exercise of power. This, still leaves the question of 'how is power exercised?' unanswered.

Finally our argument develops into an appreciation and advocacy of the work of Michel Foucault in understanding the strategy by which power attains its greatest form of efficiency – through what we regard as knowledge.

There is also important conceptual and empirical work to be done on the role of power in managerial discourse (particularly the politics of classifying people and normalising actions) and on its embodiment in concrete practices (Foucault, 1977). Like the historical materialist approach, the analytics of relations of power conceives power as being everywhere and reproducing social relations, but unlike that approach, Foucault urges the analysis of the events and conjunctures of specific historical episodes.

Finally, important conceptual work remains to be done on designing management control systems for differing social formations (e.g. social enterprises). Whilst historical materialism offers a powerful critique of existing systems and indicates why non-exploitative (in the technical sense of surplus value appropriation) management control in the organisation is impossible without change to the social relations of production, it has not yet yielded positive designs for non-exploitative management control systems. The insights from analysing power relations suggest that the effects of such interventions may be quite different from the intentions of the designer. This insight has profound implications about the efficacy of design and the power of the designer!

Notes

1. The expression of power demonstrated in the classification and general arguments of this chapter is acknowledged by the authors.
2. Key issues are defined as those that 'involve a genuine challenge to the resources of power or authority of those who currently dominate the process by which policy outputs in the system are determined' (Bachrach and Baratz, 1970, pp. 47–8).
3. We agree with Clegg (1979) that the source of the difficulty with the radical approach is its attempt to *build upon* the one and two *dimensional* views of the subjectivist approach.
4. Althusser identifies three structures that constitute the social totality: the economic, political and ideological. Although each structure operates with relative autonomy, at any moment in history there will be a 'structure in dominance' which is, in the last instance, determined by the economy.
5. Again the charge of economism may result from an over reliance on Althusser's analysis. For Althusser does not clearly explain why the economy will determine the structure in dominance; his crucial concept of structural causality remains ambiguous and indeed arbitrary.
6. Mouzelis (1978, 1984) argues that the tendency towards economism rests upon a failure to recognise that in historical materialist analysis of ideological and political structures those are no conceptual equivalents to the economic mode of production and its contradiction. Althusser is to be praised for discussing the possibility of contradictions in the non-economic levels of the social formation, but must be criticised for suggesting these contain within them a 'reflection' of the fundamental economic contradiction. For example, there has been little attempt to discuss modes of political domination (Mouzelis, 1984).
7. Foucault has himself acknowledged his debt to Marx, in a typically elliptical manner (Foucault, 1980).
8. The power of 'pseudo-science', in particular the social sciences, in producing 'truth-effects' that reinforce the tendency towards surveillance and classification of the human being as subject, is the concern of *The History of Sexuality* (1981).

References

H. E. Aldrich and S. Mindlin, 'Uncertainty and Dependence: The Perspectives on Environment' in L. Karpic (ed.) *Organization and Environment* (London: Sage, 1978).

H. E. Aldrich, *Organisations and Environments* (Englewood Cliffs, N.J.: Prentice-Hall, 1979).

L. Althusser, *For Marx* (London: Allen Lane, 1969).

L. Althusser and E. Balibar, *Reading Capital* (London: NLB, 1970).

R. N. Anthony and J. Dearden, *Management Control Systems*, 5th edn (Irwin, 1984).

R. N. Anthony, *Planning and Control Systems* (Harvard, 1965).

P. Armstrong, 'Changing Management Control Strategies: The Role of Competition Between Accountancy and other Organisational Professions', *Accounting, Organisations and Society* (1985) pp. 129–48.

P. Bachrach and M. S. Baratz, 'Decisions and Non-decisions: An Analytical Framework', *American Political Science Review* (1963) pp. 641–51.

P. Bachrach and M. S. Baratz, *Power and Poverty: Theory & Practice* (New York: O.U.P., 1970).

S. Baiman, 'Agency Research in Managerial Accounting: A Survey', *Journal of Accounting Literature* (Spring 1982) pp. 154–213.

M. Bariff and J. R. Galbraith, 'Intraorganizational Power' Considerations for Designing Information Systems', *Accounting Organizations and Society* (1978) pp. 15–27.

Ted Benton, 'Objective' Interests and the Sociology of Power', *Sociology* (May 1981) pp. 161–84.

A. A. Berle and G. C. Means, *The Modern Corporation and Private Property* (New York: Macmillan, 1932).

A. Berry, T. Capps, D. J. Cooper, T. Hopper and E. A. Lowe, 'NCB Accounts – A Mine of Misinformation?', *Accountancy* (Jan. 1985).

H. Beynon, *Working for Ford* (Harmondsworth: Penguin, 1972).

Roy Bhaskar, *The Possibility of Naturalism* (Brighton: Harvester, 1979).

N. Bjorn-Andersen and P. Petersen, 'Computer Facilitated Changes in the Management Power Structure, *Accounting Organizations and Society* (1980) pp. 203–16.

R. B. Du Boff and E. F. Herman, 'Alfred Chandler's New Business History: A Review', *Politics and Society*, vol. 10, no. 1 (1980).

R. J. Boland and L. R. Pondy, 'Accounting in Organizations: A Union of Natural and Rational Perspectives', *Accounting Organizations and Society* (1983) pp. 223–34.

H. Braverman, *Labour and Monopoly Capital* (New York: Monthly Review Press, 1974).

M. Burawoy, *Manufacturing Consent: Changes in the Labour Process under Monopoly Capitalism* (Chicago U.P., 1979).

S. Burchell, C. Clubb, A. Hopwood, J. Hughes and J. Nahapiet, 'The Roles of Accounting in Organizations and Society', *Accounting Organizations and Society* (1980) pp. 5–27.

S. Burchell, C. Clubb and A. G. Hopwood, 'Accounting in its Social Context: Towards a history of Value Added in the UK', *Accounting Organizations and Society* (1985).
P. Bougen and S. Ogden, 'Power in Organizations: Some Implications for the Use of Accounting in Industrial Relations', *Managerial Finance* (1982).
D. Clawson, *Bureaucracy and the Labour Process: The Transformation of U.S. Industry 1860–1920* (New York: Monthly Review Press, 1980).
S. Clegg, *Power, Rule and Domination* (London: RKP, 1975).
S. Clegg, *The Theory of Power and Organisation* (London: RKP, 1979).
S. Clegg and David Dunkerley, *Organisation, Class and Control* (London: RKP, 1980).
S. Clegg, 'Organization and Control', *Administrative Science Quarterly*, vol. 26, no. 4 (1981) pp. 545–62.
D. J. Cooper et al., 'Accounting in Organized Anarchies', *Accounting Organizations and Society* (1981) pp. 175–91.
D. J. Cooper, 'A Social and Organizational View of Management Accounting', in M. Bromwich and A. Hopwood (eds) *Essays in British Accounting Research* (London: Pitmans, 1981).
D. J. Cooper, 'Tidiness, Muddle and Things: Commonalities and Divergencies in two approaches to Management Accounting research', *Accounting Organizations and Society* (1983) pp. 269–83.
D. J. Cooper, E. A. Lowe, A. G. Puxty and H. Willmott, 'The Accountancy Profession Corporatism and the State' (this volume).
M. Cousins and A. Hussain, *Michel Foucault* (London: Macmillan, 1984).
M. Crozier, *The Bureaucratic Phenomenon* (London: Tavistock, 1964).
R. M. Cyert and J. G. March, *A Behavioural Theory of the Firm* (Englewood Cliffs, N.J.: Prentice-Hall, 1963).
R. A. Dahl, 'The Concept of Power', *Behavioural Science*, 2 (1957) pp. 201–5.
R. A. Dahl, *Who Governs?* (New Haven: Yale, 1963).
J. Dermer, *Management Planning and Control Systems* (Homewood Illinois: Richard D. Irwin, 1977).
P. Dews, 'Power and Subjectivity in Foucault', *New Left Review* (1984).
H. Dreyfus and P. Rabinow, *Michel Foucault: Beyond Structuralism and Hermeneutics* (Brighton: Harvester, 1982).
R. Edwards, *Contested Terrain: The Transformation of the Workplace in the Twentieth Century* (London: Heinemann, 1979).
Michel Foucault, *Discipline and Punish* (London: Allen Lane, 1977).
Michel Foucault, *Power/Knowledge* (ed.) C. Gordon (Brighton: Harvester, 1980).
Michel Foucault, *The History of Sexuality*, vol. 1 (Harmondsworth: Penguin, 1981).
Michel Foucault, 'The Subject and Power' in H. Dreyfus and P. Rabinow *Michel Foucault* (1982).
A. Francis, 'Families, Firms and Finance Capital: The Development of UK Industrial Firms with particular reference to their ownership and control', *Sociology* (1980).

A. Francis, J. Turk and P. Willman (eds), *Power, Efficiency and Institutions* (London: Heinemann, 1983).

J. R. P. French and B. H. Raven, 'The Bases of Social Power' in D. Cartwright (ed.) *Studies in Social Power* (Ann Arbor: University of Michigan Press, 1959) pp. 150–67.

A. Friedmann, 'Responsibility versus Direct Control over the Labour Process', *Capital and Class* (1977) pp. 43–57.

H. Garfinkel, *Studies in Ethnomethodology* (Englewood Cliffs, N.J.: Prentice-Hall, 1967).

Anthony Giddens, *Central Problems in Social Theory* (London: Macmillan, 1979).

Anthony Giddens, *A Contemporary Critique of Historical Materialism* (London: Macmillan, 1982).

Anthony Giddens, *The Constitution of Society* (Cambridge: Polity Press, 1984).

D. M. Gordon, R. Edwards and M. Reich, *Segmented Work, Divided Workers* (CUP, 1982).

S. J. Gould, *The Mismeasure of Man* (Harmondsworth: Penguin, 1981).

A. Gorz, (ed.) *The Division of Labour: The Labour Process and Class Struggle in Modern Capitalism* (Sussex: Harvester Press, 1976).

J. R. Haring, 'Accounting Rules & "The Accounting Establishment"', *Journal of Business* (1979) pp. 507–20.

D. J. Hickson, C. R. Hinings, C. A. Lee, R. E. Schneck and J. H. Pennings, 'A Strategic Contingencies Theory of Intra-organisational Power', *Administrative Science Quarterly* (1971) pp. 216–29.

F. S. Hills and T. Mahoney, 'University Budget and Organizational Decision-Making', *Administrative Science Quarterly* (Sep. 1978) pp. 454–65.

B. Hindess, 'Power, Interests and the Outcome of Struggles', *Sociology* (1982) pp. 498–511.

C. R. Hinings, D. J. Hickson, J. M. Pennings and R. E. Schneck, 'Structural Conditions of Intraorganizational Power', *Administrative Science Quarterly* (1974) pp. 22–44.

Anthony Hope and John Briggs, 'Accounting Policy-Making Some Lessons from the Deferred Taxation Debate', *Accounting & Business Research* (1982) pp. 83–96.

Anthony Hope and Rob. Gray, 'Power and Policy Making: The Development of an "R & D" Standard', *Journal of Business Finance and Accounting* (1982).

T. Hopper, D. J. Cooper E. A. Lowe and T. Capps, 'Financial Control and the Labour Process in a Nationalised Industry' in D. Knights and H. Willmott (eds) *Managing the Labour Process* (London: Gower, 1986).

A. Hopwood, 'The Archaeology of Accounting Systems', *Accounting Organizations and Society*, 1987.

K. Hoskin and R. Macve, 'The Power of Accounting', *Accounting Organizations and Society* (1986).

M. E. Hussein and J. C. Ketz, 'Ruling Elites of the FASB: A Study of the Big Eight', *Accounting Review* (1980) pp. 354–67.

M. Jensen and W. H. Meckling, 'Theory of the Firm: Managerial Behaviour, Agency Costs and Ownership Structure', *Journal of Financial Economics*,

vol. 3 (Oct. 1976) pp. 395-60.
T. Johnson, 'Work and Power' in G. Esland and G. Salaman, *The Politics of Work and Occupations* (Milton Keynes: Open University Press, 1980) pp. 335-71.
Sten Jonsson, 'Budgetary Behaviour in Local Government – A Case Study over 3 years', *Accounting Organizations and Society* (1982) pp. 267-304.
David Knights and John Roberts, 'The Power of Organisation or the Organisation of Power?', *Organizational Studies* (1982) pp. 47-63.
David Knights and H. C. Willmott, 'Power and Identity in Theory and Practice', *Sociological Review* (Feb. 1985).
G. Littler, *The Development of the Labour Process in Capitalist Societies* (London: Heinemann, 1982).
A. Loft, 'Towards a Critical Understanding of Accounting: the Case of Cost Accounting in the UK 1914-25', Paper presented at the Interdisciplinary Perspectives on Accounting Conference, Manchester, July 1985.
Steven Lukes, *Power: A Radical View* (London: Macmillan, 1974).
J. Maciarello, *Management Control System* (Englewood Cliffs, N.J.: Prentice-Hall, 1984).
L. Markus and J. Pfeffer, 'Power and the Design and Implementation of Accounting and Control Systems', *Accounting Organisations and Society* (1983) pp. 205-18.
S. A. Marglin, 'What do Bosses do – The Origin and Functions of Hierarchy in Capitalist Production', *Review of Radical Political Economies* (1974) pp. 60-112.
K. Marx, *The Eighteenth Brumaire of Louis Napoleon* in K. Marx and F. Engels, *Selected Works in One Volume* (London: Lawrence & Wishart, 1968).
P. Miller and T. O'Leary, 'Accounting and the Construction of the Governable Person', *Accounting Organizations and Society* (1987).
H. Mintzberg, *Power in and Around Organisations* (Englewood Cliffs, N.J.: Prentice-Hall, 1983).
N. Mouzelis, 'Ideology and Class Politics', *New Left Review* (Nov. 1978).
N. Mouzelis, 'On the Crisis of Marxist Theory', *British Journal of Sociology*, vol. 35, no. 1 (1984) pp. 112-21.
M. Neimark, *The Social Construction of Annual Reports: A Radical Approach to Corporate Control* (Unpublished PhD dissertation, New York University, 1983).
M. Neimark and A. Tinker, 'The Social Construction of Management Control Systems', *Accounting, Organisations and Society* (1986).
T. Nichols and P. Armstrong, *Workers Divided* (London: Fontana, 1976).
T. Nichols and H. Beynon, *Living with Capitalism* (London: RKP, 1977).
R. E. Pahl and J. T. Winkler, 'The Economic Elite: Theory and Practice' in P. Stanworth and A. Giddens (eds) *Elites and Power in British Society* (Cambridge: 1974).
Talcott Parsons, 'On the Concept of Political Power', *Proceedings of the American Philosophical Society* (1963) pp. 236-62.
Talcott Parsons, 'The School Class as a Social System: Some of its Functions in American Society' in Halsey, Flaud and Anderson *Education, Economy, Society* (1969).

A. Pettigrew, *The Politics of Organizational Decision Making* (London: Tavistock, 1973).

J. Pfeffer and G. R. Salancik, 'Organisational Decision-Making as a Political Process', *Administrative Science Quarterly* (1974) pp. 135–51.

J. Pfeffer and G. R. Salancik, *The External Control of Organizations: A Resource Dependence Perspective* (New York: Harper and Row, 1978).

Sidney Pollard, *The Genesis of Modern Management* (Harmondsworth: Penguin, 1965).

Mark Poster, *Foucault, Marxism and History* (Cambridge: Polity Press, 1984).

Nicos Poulantzas, *Political Power and Social Classes* (London: NLB, 1973).

Nicos Poulantzas, *Classes in Contemporary Capitalism* (London: NLB, 1975).

John Roberts and R. W. Scapens, 'Accounting Systems and Systems of Accountability – Understanding Accounting Practices in their Organizational Contexts', *Accounting Organizations and Society* (1985).

D. Rosenberg, C. Tomkins and P. Day, 'A Work Role Perspective of Accountants in Local Government Service Departments', *Accounting Organizations and Society* (1982) pp. 123–38.

S. A. Ross, 'On the Economic Theory of Agency and the Principle of Similarity' in M. S. Balch *et al.* (eds), *Essays on Economic Behaviour under Uncertainty* (Amsterdam: North Holland, 1974).

B. Spicer and V. Ballew, 'Management Accounting Systems and the Economics of Internal Organization', *Accounting Organizations and Society*, vol. 8, pp. 73–98.

D. Stark, 'Class Struggle and the Transformation of the Labour Process: A relational approach', *Theory and Society* (1980) pp. 89–130.

R. Stewart, *Managers and their Jobs* (Macmillan, 1967).

Goran Therborn, 'What does the Ruling Class do when it rules?', *The Insurgent Socialist* (1978).

J. B. Thompson, 'Ideology and the Analysis of Discourse', *Sociological Review* (May 1983) pp. 212–30.

C. Tomkins, D. Rosenberg and M. Day, 'A Work Role Perspective of Accountants in Local Government Service Departments', *Accounting Organizations and Society* (1982) pp. 123–37.

T. J. Watson, *The Personnel Managers* (London: RKP, 1977).

O. E. Williamson, *Corporate Control and Business Behavior* (Englewood Cliffs, N.J.: Prentice-Hall, 1970).

O. E. Williamson, *Markets and Hierarchies: Analysis and Antitrust Implication* (New York: Free Press, 1975).

A. Wildavsky, *The Politics of the Budgetary Process* (New York: Little, Brown, 1965).

H. Willmott, 'Images and Ideals of Managerial Work: A Critical Examination of Conceptual and Empirical Accounts', *Journal of Management Studies* (July 1984) pp. 349–68.

S. Wood, *The Degradation of Work: Skill, De-skilling and the Braverman Debate* (London: Hutchinson, 1982).

7 Ideology, Rationality and the Management Control Process

Tony Puxty and Wai Fong Chua*

A theory of administration or of organization cannot exist without a theory of rational choice. Human behaviour in organizations is best described as 'intendedly rational'; and it merits that description more than does any other sector of human behaviour.

(Herbert Simon, *Models of Man*)

There seems to be a distinction, not always recognised, between organisation theory and management theory. Organisation theorists base their concern in sociology or social psychology and ask questions concerning the way organisations operate. Management theorists take as a much closer focus the question of what a manager should do to make his organisation operate better. Management theorists frequently take note, in their research and in their textbooks, of what some organisation theorists are saying: the latter is not always so true.

The field which we can call 'management control' is no doubt part of management theory, and as such is generally seen by those concerned in it as an essentially pragmatic, normative subject. Its subject-matter is the question of efficient and effective organisational operation, frequently linked to those information and control systems such as accounting which are supposed to lead to efficiency and effectiveness. In this instrumental approach, however, something is lost which is central to the best organisation theory: the context of the organisation in society, its rationale for existence, and hence the broader criteria for its operation.

Two of the aspects of organisations which tend to be filtered out by the exclusive nature of most management control inquiry are rationality and ideology. As Simon suggests above, at least some kind of limited rationality is an essential presupposition for organisational analysis to take place: management theory supposes a particular kind of rationality. However, the more problematic questions concerning rationality (such as its nature, its presuppositions and its consequences) are assumed away in most inquiry. Similarly with ideology: this is relegated to a minor role, and its meaning constrained in the way Shils (1968) constrains it (see below, p. 127) so that its only importance is as an 'explanation' of why some organisational members are antagonistic to others. But rationality and ideology, which at first sight are only distantly related as phenomena, have one particular common characteristic: they both appear to have a governing relationship to action. It is the link between these two concepts which is the concern of this paper.

To say that rationality and ideology govern action is over simple. The relation is not monocausal. It would not be possible to understand organisational action through these two concepts nomologically because there is an interactive relationship of the kind described in Figure 7.1.

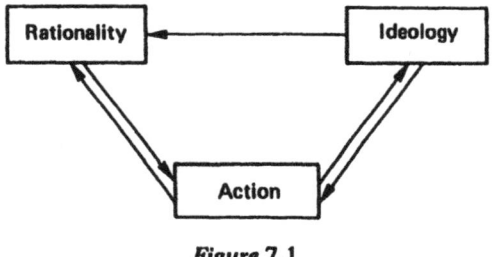

Figure 7.1

First, there are various relationships between rationality and ideology themselves (for example, the application of formally rational action is itself the result of ideological processes). Second, because the expression 'action' refers to a self-regenerative social process, the action will itself affect what is perceived as rational, and will also have an effect on the construction of the *Weltanshauung* which is the outworking of ideology. This paper concerns itself with the complex relation between all three variables.

Beliefs about rationality and ideology underpin the theory and practice of management control. They underlie the ways in which theoreticians express beliefs both about normative control strategies and positive control procedures. They underlie the ways in which managers take action – since action must be founded on beliefs, which in turn, being value-laden, are expressions of the value-sets which those managers accept.

Chiefly, however, this distinction between theory and practice is a misleading one. The manager is, in acting, implying beliefs about the outcomes of his actions: that is, he is relying upon theories concerning the cause-and-effect of his subject matter. Many of these theories, moreover, are based on the theory of management control: the ways in which, according to the textbooks, things should be done and consequences arise. But the interaction is two-way: the theoreticians themselves are grounded in the reality of management, and are obliged to expose their ideas to the empirical test of managerial reality, so that theory grows from practice just as truly as practice is enriched by theory. However, there is a fundamental law of the market place which states that *only those theories of action which are acceptable within the existing ideology* will be sufficiently acceptable to the majority of management teachers and managers to be considered seriously to be taught, to be considered as bases for case analysis and to be applied by the student when he has left the classroom and faces the organisational world. This means that there is a circle of mutual support, in which a certain kind of approach and solution (theory) will continue to be believed in however inferior it may be, simply because alternative approaches are unacceptable in practice. For example, the explanation of strike action as the result of class-based repression will not in general be found in personnel management texts. It is filtered out as an unthinkable hypothesis.

The structure of this paper will be as follows. We shall consider first the definition of rationality in organisations; we shall examine the extent to which it is supposed to underlie organisational behaviour. We shall then examine recent research which suggests that the 'rationality' implied by certain theories is not the way actual organisations operate. Next we shall examine theories of ideology and argue that concepts of rational action are rooted in ideologies. Next, we explicate Habermas's (1978) hypothesis that our knowledge to date has an interest only in technical rationality and ideology. Hence, management control researchers must strive to develop other forms of rationality and interest in order to understand organisational action and 'make sense' of 'practical' action within its full societal context.

RATIONALITY IN ORGANISATIONS

As Simon notes in the quotation which opens this paper, rationality is seen as fundamental to the study of organisations – that is, some kind of assumption about rationality must be made in any organisational theory; and in addition to this, rationality underlies the assumptions made by organisation members themselves in their day-to-day dealings with each other. The way in which this takes place is described by Salaman (1979):

> Organizational structures, decisions, technologies, procedures and systems are frequently defined – by senior members and others – as rational, or the result of 'rationalisation'. By this they imply that the decision or event or technology is (a) related to, or deriving from, scientific, modern, efficient principles and criteria; (b) an inevitable and unavoidable aspect of modern life, of progress; (c) beyond choice or politics.

It is the validity of such an approach which is open to question: in particular, the extent to which this is a 'true' rationality. If we turn first to Simon (1976) we find that he defines rationality in the following way:

> Roughly speaking, rationality is concerned with the selection of preferred behaviour alternatives in terms of some system of values whereby the consequences of behaviour can be evaluated.
> (p. 75)

He goes on to contrast different actions which might be considered rational and finally decides that 'rationality' in the context of his own work must always be accompanied by an adjective. Thus there is 'objective' rationality, 'subjective' rationality, 'conscious' rationality and so on. We shall follow Simon in making such distinctions, but we suggest a fusion of his approach with that of Weber (1964) and introduce two axes on which rationality can be considered.

There is, first, the distinction made by Weber between 'formal' rationality and 'substantive' rationality. 'Formal rationality involves certain processes or operations which are seen as rational. . . . These processes are, essentially, the conversion of situations, problems, and decisions into numerical, calculative, terms or the application of technical rules. . . . They are not necessarily rational in the 'real' sense (i.e. efficient in achieving goals, or reasonable in terms of the various parties' needs and expectations)' (Salaman, 1979). Substantive rationality, on the other hand, involves

> a relation to the absolute values or to the content of the particular given ends to which it is orientated. In principle there is an indefinite number of possible standards of value which are 'rational' in this sense.
> (Weber, 1964, p. 158)

Second, there is Simon's distinction between 'organizational' rationality and 'personal' rationality:

> A decision is 'organizationally' rational if it is oriented to the organization's goals; it is 'personally' rational if it is oriented to the individual's goals.
> (Simon, 1976, pp. 76–7)

The former distinction is particularly important, since formal rationality is so frequently confused with substantive rationality. It might be suggested that there is an element almost of ritual or religious belief in the application of methods which are merely formally rational: the unsubstantiated belief that the actions taken will lead to the ends sought. It might be suggested that the application of the principles of Scientific Management, for example, is formally rational. Indeed, there is an implication of rationality within a great deal of management writing.

The approach which underlies such thinking might perhaps be described as follows: that there is, to a greater or a lesser extent, rational behaviour of individuals within organisations, and that rational, deliberate action should be taken to ensure that 'control' is effected over their actions for the purpose of the organisation itself. It is in this sense that management control is more purposive and more consciously rational than the general run of studies of 'organizational behaviour'.

Now since the general tenets of management control theory imbue both management practice and management theory, it would seem that the majority of research would be conducted within a rationalist framework, and would frame its findings within such a construct. Rationality would be sought and 'found': and prescriptions for management action would be based on the same set of ideas. In particular, what would be sought would be a set of principles whereby substantive personal rationality on the part of organisational members could be made consistent with a substantive organisational rationality, such that both members and organisation achieved their goals by 'rational' means. Similarly, prescriptions for management action would be based on a framework of formal rationality in the belief that this would lead to substantively rational results. It is such approaches that we have referred to above.

There is an increasing body of recent research, however, which appears to suggest that there is a break in the chain between pedagogy and practice: in particular, which refutes a proposition that the formally rational practices which we might expect to find in organisations do in fact occur in the way in which both members of the organisations say they occur, and prescriptions suggest that they should occur. It is to evidence of this that we now turn.

A FRESH LOOK AT OLD CONCEPTS

Management control has often been described as 'the process by which managers assure that resources are obtained and used effectively in the accomplishment of the organization's objectives' (Anthony and Dearden, 1976). Anthony's approach to the concept and process of management process has equally often been chastised for being narrow, lacking in theoretical rigour and for ignoring the effects of an organisation's environment. (See Lowe and Puxty.) Yet, as pointed out earlier, the concept of an organisational goal or of a pre-set strategic plan which an organisation seeks to realise is prevalent and implicit in this and other approaches to management control. For example, 'Control is essentially concerned with regulating the activities within an organization so that they are in accord with the expectations established in policies, plans and targets' (Child, 1977). Or, the purpose of the organisation is postulated to be long-run survival at a desired level of welfare which is consistent with maintaining boundary conditions (Lowe, 1979).

The issue of organisational goals has been much discussed in the literature (Georgiou, 1973; Perrow, 1961; Lowe, 1973; Mohr, 1973; Silverman, 1970). Some of the points of debate will be briefly mentioned here as it is not intended to embark on an in-depth analysis of this particular issue. To begin with, questions have been raised as to whether it is possible for collectivities of individuals to have goals when a total consensus does not exist amongst them. The concept is also accused of reifying an organisation, or attributing concrete reality, particularly the power of thought and action, to social constructs. Then there is the debate as to what exactly organisational goals are. Official goals were discarded in favour of operative goals. Simon (1964) suggested that they be viewed as sets of constraints on human behaviour. Currently, there seems to be an acceptance amongst some American theorists that they be identified as the objectives of the dominant coalition within the organisation (Pennings and Goodman, 1977; see also Cyert and March, 1963).

What most interests us here is a criticism that the 'goal paradigm' has over-rationalised human behaviour within organisations. For the concepts of objectives, plans, strategic choice and a variety of other control terms are based on the fundamental assumption that the model of man is a rational one. However, he may possess only a bounded rationality (Simon, 1957). The essence of this notion is that individuals have perceptual as well as information-processing limits, and even though they may intend to act rationally, they can do so only in a limited fashion. When transplanted to the organisational level, purposive action may now be seen to have intended or manifest consequences as well as unanticipated latent ones.

Not everyone, however, agrees with this model of man and it is hoped that, by highlighting opposing models of rationality, more insight will be gained into the ideological assumptions behind different concepts of control. One of the foremost attacks on goal-directed, planned forms of rational behaviour comes from Weick (1979). Arguing from Mead, and from Schutz (1967) and other phenomenologists, Weick maintains that the creation of meaning in an enacted environment is always a retrospective process. This is termed reflective meaning. He asserts that meaningful experience is lived, it is not living or to be lived. 'Hence, we can know what we've done only after we've done it. Only by doing is it possible for us to discover what we have done.' And 'It is only possible to direct attention to what has already passed; it is impossible to direct attention to what is yet to come.' Garfinkel (1967) makes a similar point when he argues that any person undertaking an inquiry about social structure can 'assign witnessed actual appearances to the status of an event of conduct only by imputing biography and prospects to the appearances'. This he does by submerging the appearances in his presupposed knowledge of social structures. Thus it frequently happens that in order for an investigator to decide what he is now looking at he must wait for future developments, only to find that these features are in turn influenced by their history and future. Garfinkel concludes that the investigator, in the calculable sense of the term 'know', does not and even cannot know what he is doing prior to or while he is doing it.

If everything is retrospective, what are we to do with the fact that people seem to plan and to guide their actions according to their plans? Schutz's (1967) answer is that when one thinks about the future, this thinking is not done in the future tense, but rather in the future perfect tense. When one says 'I will write a memo to the president requesting a budget increase', Schutz argues that one really says 'I shall have written a memo to the president requesting a budget increase.' Hence, although a plan appears to be something oriented solely to the future, in fact it also has about it the quality of an act that has already been accomplished. The meaning of the actions that are instrumental to the completion of the act can be discovered because they are viewed as if they had already occurred.

For Weick, rationality seems better understood as a postdecision rather than a predecision occurrence. Rationality makes sense of what has been, not what will be. According to him, it is a process of justification in which past deeds are made to appear sensible to the actor himself and to those other persons to whom he feels accountable. This is because it is difficult for a person to be rational if he does not know precisely what it is that he must be rational about. He can create rationality only when he has available some set of actions which can be interpreted in several ways. Similarly, Weick feels that goal statements are better understood as summaries of previous actions. He writes '[m]uch of the organization's work does not seem to be directed toward goal attainment. Instead, it can be understood more readily as actions with a primitive orderliness, this orderliness being enhanced retrospectively when members review what has come to pass as a result of the actions.'

What are the implications of such a view on rationality and organisational goals? As Perrow (1979) pointed out, Weick seems to be suggesting that organisations run backwards. The thought is not necessarily the father to the deed; in fact, the deed may be the father to the thought. This means that (a) the idea that organisations may run backwards much of the time is not simply a matter of 'covering one's tracks, making excuses, lying or fabrication supporting data to justify what we want to do'. Such activities exist to be sure, but they are much more a part of a planned world that we (often mistakenly?) believe we can consciously direct or influence to some extent. What Weick seems to refer to is the creation of new meanings, the construction and reconstruction of a world that we sincerely believe was there all along. 'We do not cover our tracks, we unwittingly reconstruct the deed because we think that thought must have been behind it.' (b) Our world might be less subject to rational human planning than we thought, and more stimulated by accidents, random events, luck, chance, memory failures. (c) Statements of goals may only serve to give a symbolic rational meaning to this more random, loosely coupled, accidental and stumbling process. (d) And though actors within organisations may make elaborate, detailed statements of their plans, instructions, rules, these may not control their behaviour. If we watch closely, it may seem that the behaviour is under the control of other determinants which may be 'nonrational' and that rationality only emerges during the actors' interaction.

Garfinkel (1967) and others make the same point about the myth of rationality and they demonstrate how social actors again employ rationality retrospectively as a rhetoric to account for actions that, from a rationalistic point of view, were chaotic and stumbling when performed. For example, he describes how jurors initially do not know what they are doing and are not guided by the rules. But as their arguments take shape, they begin to invoke rules of evidence and rationality to justify positions they have taken or are in the process of forming. The rational justification of their decision crystallises at about the time the decisions do and indeed even afterwards, when a summary is being prepared for presentation to the court.

Yet another thought-provoking application of the idea that organisations may run backwards comes from March and his associates. Back in 1963, Cyert and March argued that people have a rather disorganised file drawer of goals at hand, which they are ready to pull out when the circumstances warrant. Hence, organisational goals may emerge in a somewhat fortuitous fashion. These ideas were further extended by Cohen, March and Olsen (1972), who formulated a 'garbage can' model of organisational choice and control. They postulated that solutions look for problems, rather than the other way round. Problems are convenient receptacles for people to toss in solutions that happen to interest them, or for interests that are not being met at the time. The can, with its problems, becomes an opportunity or resource. Depending upon the number of cans, the mixes of problems in them and the amount of time people have, they stay with the particular can or leave it for another. The problem then gets detached from those that originally posed it, may develop a life of its own, get transformed into another problem or simply waste away. Again, solutions no one originally intended or even expected may be generated, or no solutions may arise. March and Olsen (1976) give an example in which the problem of rewarding a particularly valuable secretary gets mixed up with a stream of quite unrelated and quite unpredictable other problems and interests and accidents. Some years later, the consequences are the restructuring of several university departments. The process is then rationalised as the inevitable modernisation of the university due to forces in the environment! No pre-set, coherent goal guided the total process, but after the event a coherent goal was presumed to have been present.

A more extreme emphasis upon the arguable symbolic character of goals and management rules is found in the work of Meyer and Rowan (1977). They define formal organisational structure as a blueprint for activities within organisations; it includes a listing of the departments, offices, policies, programmes, rules and goals that make up a rational theory of how, and to what end, activities are to be fitted together. They then argue that many of these formal organisational structures arise as reflections of rationalised institutional rules, where institutionalised rules are defined as classifications built into society as 'reciprocated typifications or interpretations' (Berger and Luckmann, 1966). Because elements of rationalised formal structure arise in highly institutionalised environments, which typically characterise post industrial society in the West, they reflect widespread understandings of social reality and these two sets of meanings mutually enforce one another. Many of the policies, positions, procedures rules are enforced by public opinion, by the views of important constituents, by knowledge (of how to manage and control organisations such that they will be successful, prosperous and survive in the long-run) legitimated though the educational and academic system, by social prestige and by the legal system. They then argue that these institutionalised rules and formal structures function as powerful myths, and many organisations adopt them ceremonially so that they can increase their social legitimacy and their survival prospects, independent of the immediate efficacy of the acquired practices and procedures.

For example, they argue that ideologies define the functions appropriate to a business – such as production, advertising, or accounting; to a university – such as instruction and research in history, sociology, engineering. Such classifications of organisational functions, and the specifications for conducting each function, according to them, are prefabricated formulae available for use by any given organisation. Similarly, as new domains of activity are codified in institutionalised programmes, professions, or management techniques, firms incorporate the packaged codes. For example, the discipline of psychology creates a rationalised theory of personnel selection and certifies personnel professionals. Personnel departments and functionaries appear in all sorts of extant organisations, and new specialised personnel agencies also appear. As the issues of industrial democracy, safety and environmental pollution arise, and as relevant professions become institutionalised in laws and public opinions, organisations incorporate these programmes and professions.

Meyer and Rowan further argue that conformity to these myths and rules often conflicts sharply with efficiency criteria (however, they are never clear as to who does the evaluation of organisational efficiency). They argue that organisations therefore tend to buffer their formal structures from the uncertainties of day-to-day technical work activities by becoming loosely coupled, building gaps between these two structures. Rituals of confidence and good faith between both internal participants and external constituencies are also used to make certain organisational aspects appear useful. Such rituals include delegation, professionalisation, goal ambiguity, the elimination of output data, the maintenance of face, avoidance, discretion and the overlooking of anomalies (see Goffman, 1967). Such practices may help to preserve the formal structure of the organisation by absorbing uncertainty (March and Simon, 1958).

Meyer and Rowan's propositions make us question and rethink our past management techniques such as variance analysis, various means of budgetary control, gap analysis, etc. Do formal structures actually co-ordinate and control work? How do we account for loosely coupled forms of control (March and Olsen, 1976; Weick, 1976; Glassman, 1973)?

A further extension of this discussion on goals, rationality, and plans is to look at the prospective use of rationality in organisations. For the organisational plan, so beloved of management control theorists, may be reinterpreted not as a set of instructions for what actually will take place, but rather as an ideological device that functions to build constituency, to define the limits of 'responsible opinion'. Instead of attempting to co-ordinate and control work activities, the plan may be a tool to impose the planners' or managers' definition of reality upon discourse and conduct within and around the organisation. Such unobtrusive forms of premise controls, or control of the parameters of decision-making and non-decision-making (Baratz and Bachrach, 1962) are seldom researched in detail at the organisational level. But they must surely be one of the most powerful forms of *management* control. The question that Bendix (1956) posed: why are some given the right to command and others the duty to obey in organisations, can only be asked once the premises of the economic order are held in abeyance. For most people, even management researchers, the question is not meaningful; it is just the way things are and perhaps have always been. So thoroughly have social researchers adopted the premises of management, their concepts, meanings, language and thought; that they tend to see the world and carve it up in similar ways.

A similar critique of the conventional view of rationality comes from neo-Marxists such as Horkheimer (1974) and Adorno (1973). They have argued that means-end rationality has provided an instrument as well as a rationale for technocratic domination. Not only can the redoubtable plan, e.g. the annual budget, be used to close off unwanted alternatives and to advance one's own agenda, it may obscure class-based issues. By focusing attention on alternative means, 'instrumental reason' may displace discussion on the appropriateness of pregiven ends and the class interests that they serve. Thus, they argue that 'bourgeois rationality' constitutes, in effect, a class ideology. There may be some truth in their contentions for many of our management techniques could be better termed managerial techniques, in that they are geared towards higher levels of productivity, profits and dividends within a given social, economic and political framework. One seldom questions the underlying structure and order of production, exchange and control.

Enough has been said to cast doubt on our prevailing theories of human behaviour and control, which may be over-determined. For the truth might be that there may be less than we think we can explain. Perhaps this over-determinance is part of the reason why our current theories seem to lack predictive power and our statistical models contain such large unexplained correlation coefficients. But one must balance these opinions with other empirical facts. As Perrow (1979) points out, there are significant regularities in our world, such as stable distribution of wealth, increasing concentration within industry, urbanisation, the persistence of class and racial discrimination. Though goals and plans may be used as ideological devices, and they interfere with technical activities, yet organisations do exhibit an orderliness and tasks are accomplished. We may 'muddle through' (Lindblom, 1959) and planning may be nothing (Wildavsky, 1973) but organisations are not often chaotic anarchies. Goals do not fluctuate all the time, they are stabilised through the budget process and past commitments. And though man is less rational than we thought, yet dominant organisations and their rulers do get their way. They do influence their environments, 'win battles and share the nature of the contest that goes on around them'.

THE INSEPARABILITY OF RATIONALITY AND IDEOLOGY

The feeling with which the reader is left after this discussion might well be that there is a 'rationality' which might be expected of the managerial world, a rationality which appears to be demanded of managers by the very task with which they are charged, and which they are prevented from attaining by what might best be called an ideology. Ideology is, in this sense, a false consciousness, a perceptual and analytical blockage which prevents desirable rationality. Such a view of managerial ideology would imply two things: first, that it is possible to eliminate this problem and uncover the underlying rationality: the second, that it is adequate to do this. As we discuss these matters it will be clear that these are not, as they at first seem, separable matters, and they will accordingly be treated here together.

We may start our enquiry with the nature of ideology. The meaning of such a term cannot be separated from the implications of it, and we find, therefore, that the various social theorists who have looked at the problem of ideology have tended to use it in different ways which are consonant with the theses they are proposing.

We may reject the curiously narrow view of the term proposed by Shils (1968) who gave various characteristics of ideology in evidently political terms, remarking that 'Ideologies . . . are not usually espoused by the incumbents and custodians of the central institutional and value systems' (p. 66) and 'All ideologies – whether progressive or traditionalistic, revolutionary or reactionary – entail an aggressive alienation from the existing society' (p. 68). This would prevent our using the expression 'ideology' to describe the orientation and beliefs of groups in society such as managers, because such orientation and beliefs do tend on the whole to be in harmony with society's central value systems. Yet many have used the expression 'managerial ideology': it appears to be a useful way of describing a phenomenon. Shil's approach is, therefore, we feel, too restrictive to be helpful.

Marx's use of the term is enlightening, implying as it does that the ideology is by definition a false consciousness which serves to buttress a given exploitative system, since it would be generally agreed that in any social system the managers do have a set of beliefs which is similar to the ruling values of the society as a whole; and since there is also at the least a great deal of truth in Marx's maxim that in any epoch the ruling ideas are the ideas of the ruling class (Marx, 1963), we should have an explanation of the interdependence between the position in society of the managerial class and the ideology which they hold. It can hardly be coincidental that managerial value-sets support the view of hierarchy as a natural part of society which confirms and legitimates their own power position.

Nevertheless, it might be more useful from our viewpoint here to consider a broader approach to ideology, an approach which throws light upon the problems we appear to be faced with. We may begin this by considering the problem of the individual in understanding the world which surrounds him.

Our knowledge of the world is based upon the information we receive through our senses. 'As no one can see or hear anything except through his powers of perception, social reality consists in every case ... of "objective facts" which have been interpreted, given meanings and, thereby, transformed into "social facts"' (Allen, 1975). That is, actual social reality is the result of perceptual processes. We may, however, follow Kant in rejecting the view that our knowledge of the world is the sole result of a continuous flow of sensory information: this sensory information is organised into meaningful (classified) information by our sensory processes, and is thus potentially different for different people. Whether this classificatory process is inherent or itself the result of social circumstances is not germane to the present discussion. In either case, it would differ as between individuals, although the basis within which classifications of 'sorting processes' might be made would differ depending on the view taken.

Now if we suppose that the 'premiss' we are considering is one which sees ideology as a distortion of reality, and thus dysfunctional (since it is a barrier to 'true rationality') then it would appear that nothing which has so far been discussed would contradict this. Yet this 'premiss' would be denied, from different points of view, by both Althusser and Mannheim. 'Strictly speaking it is incorrect to say that the single individual thinks. Rather it is more correct to say that he participates in thinking further what other men have thought before him' (Mannheim, 1936). Ideology is, then, 'the necessary condition of human society, and the medium of individual consciousness . . . Mannheim also emphasised that it is mistaken to treat total ideologies as merely "systems of ideas" or "thought-systems": they are incorporated within, and make possible, the everyday practical conduct of actors' (Giddens, 1979, p. 181). Similarly, for Althusser, ideology is a '"social cement", the indispensible source of social cohesion: through ideology, human beings live as "conscious subjects" within the totality of social relations. Ideology is not the conscious creation of human subjects; it is only through and in ideology that conscious subjects exist' (Giddens, 1979).

We may relate these ideas to the phenomenological insights into the construction of reality. Persons interacting in social situations build their interpretations of those situations on the meanings they ascribe to the actions of others. It is not the actions themselves which matter, but the meanings which appear to inhere in them. Through interactions continually building upon themselves in this way the social world is created. Because life consists of a whole complex series of interactions between people the world is being constantly redefined through interactions, and thus is constantly being changed by them. Moreover there is a further definition which is affected: one's self-definition, and this is also continually being redefined by interaction.

The implications of the above ideas regarding ideology would appear to be that there is an interchange between the ideological framework within which actors evaluate their world and the continual redefinition of situation, self and other which takes place in the consciousness of one's social situation. To take the specific case of the manager: he is continually being confronted with situations which question or confirm his conception of himself in terms of the dimensions which make up his self-evaluation – for example, the esteem in which he is held by others, the extent to which he is in control of a situation or comprehends the ramifications of a situation

– and the reality of these dimensions will impinge upon his perceptions of the dimensions. At the same time, the way in which his senses process the stream of impressions available to him will be affected by the ideological presuppositions which create his *Weltanschauung*. The interaction is clear: because the results of the re-evaluation of his situation will feed back to confirm or deny not only the specific reality of the circumstances, but also the *Weltanschauung* which he will carry over into future situations.

The implications of the discussion so far, then, are the following. The ideological apparatus which governs the way each of us sees the world will mean, for the acting manager, a shifting but essentially constricted view of reality, the restriction being caused by his ideology. Now there is generally supposed to be a type of course of action which is 'rational': it is this which the manager is expected to strive for, *and he knows this*. But this concept of rationality has no roots in objective reality: it is just the result of the ideologies of both the manager and those who set the criteria by which he is judged. These criteria, in turn, are based upon the power structure of society, and the power structure of the manager's own organisation (these two structures being of course closely interwoven). Hence if we wish to understand the full relationship between ideology and rationality we must investigate the nature of this power relationship and the precise way in which it emerges in a formal, conventional view of the meaning of rationality. To understand the way in which this works we turn to the views of the eminent social theorist Jürgen Habermas.

Before we do so, it is necessary to issue a warning which would be true for almost any theorist, but is particularly true of Habermas: the ideas we shall be explicating are part of a total and internally-consistent framework which it has taken him many years to develop and expound (and which, he says, is by no means yet complete): any short and selective summary is bound to distort by the very brevity and selectivity necessary, and the ideas we shall be extracting are by no means situated in the framework within which Habermas would situate them.

HABERMAS'S KNOWLEDGE-CONSTITUTIVE FRAMEWORK

The creation of the social world by the actors within it is founded, as we have said, on their interpretation of the sense-data which reaches them. This is in turn founded on the ideological bases we carry with us. 'Every (competent) member of society is a practical social theorist; in sustaining any sort of encounter he draws upon his knowledge and theories' (Giddens, 1976, p. 15). By knowledge here it is evident that Giddens intends us to understand a store of knowledge: however, this store is itself the result of cognition, and it is this cognition with which Habermas is concerned. What determines what shall be cognitively recognised by an actor? That is, how do we explain those objects which are accepted in the perception-assimilation process of social actors? The answer, according to Habermas, is their *cognitive interests*, or *knowledge-constitutive interests*. 'I term *interests* the basic orientations rooted in specific fundamental conditions of the possible reproduction and self-constitution of the human species, namely *work and interaction*' (Habermas, 1978, p. 196). These interests are hence fundamental to the constitution of the social world. It is they which 'determine what shall count as knowledge, not intrinsic autonomous elements of cognition. In fact, cognition is inseparable from practical concern' (Hamilton, 1974, p. 60). Bernstein expands on this:

> Such interests or orientations are *knowledge-constitutive* because they shape and determine what counts as the objects and types of knowledge: they determine the categories relevant to what we take to be knowledge, as well as the procedures for discovering and warranting knowledge claims.
> (Bernstein, 1976, p. 192)

Habermas defines three kinds of interest, each of which corresponds to a 'dimension of human social existence' and a kind of knowledge. This is summarised in Table 7.1 (adapted from Giddens, 1977).

Table 7.1

Dimension of human social existence	Knowledge-constitutive interest	Type of study
Labour (instrumental action)	Prediction and control (technical)	Empirical-analytic sciences
Interaction	Understanding (practical)	Historical-hermeneutic disciplines
Power/authority	Emancipation	Critical social sciences

It is now necessary to elaborate on the meaning of these categories. We begin with the technical interest.

Habermas is concerned that it is the technical interest which has, since the time of Kant, received most attention both by analysts (that is, philosophers of science) and by actors in regulating their activity. As to science, he attacks scientism, which he defines as 'science's beliefs in itself: that is, the conviction that we can no longer understand science as one form of possible knowledge, but rather must identify knowledge with science' (Habermas, 1978, p. 4). The ramifications of this go beyond any questions of scientific methodology in a narrow sense: because such an approach to life has affected the orientation by which we approach our knowledge of reality and hence our approach to reality itself. This is because our approach to cognition of the world, within this frame of reference, is directed to *technical control*.

> The empirical-analytic sciences, which include both the natural sciences, and economics, sociology and political science, are aimed at the discovery of nomological knowledge about natural and social relations. Their particular status as knowledge is constituted by their interest in technical control, in increasing the possible extent of human domination over natural and social reality.
> (Keat and Urry, 1975, p. 223)

This orientation is in itself beneficial: because the reason for it, as given in the quotation by Habermas earlier (p. 19), is that such technical control is necessary for the continued biological and cultural development of the human species. Nor would Habermas object to the way in which the knowledge itself develops: through continued experiment, through hypothesis and scientific testing (which forms a negative feedback process). But the technical interest is not confined to 'science': the following quotation shows that Habermas recognises the way in which this leads to the 'administration of society' and the implications of this:

> The real difficulty in the relation of theory to praxis does not arise from this new function of science as technological force, but rather from the fact that we are no longer able to distinguish between practical and technical power. Yet even a civilization that has been rendered scientific is not granted dispensation from practical questions: therefore, a peculiar danger arises when the

process of scientification transgresses the limit of technical questions without, however, departing from the level of reflection of a rationality confined to the technological horizon. For then no attempt at all is made to attain a rational consensus on the part of citizens concerned with the practical control of their destiny. Its place is taken by the attempt to attain technical control over history by perfecting the administration of society, an attempt that is just as impractical as it is unhistorical.

(Habermas, 1978, p. 255)

This quotation seems to us crucial in our understanding of the problem we have set ourselves. However, before tackling its implications for managerial control we need to consider another aspect of the quotation: its clarification of the distinction between technical and practical interests (see Table 7.1). As Bernstein has remarked, these tend to be confused: we tend to associate the practical with the application of technology. But when the practical is recognised in its full meaning, as concerned with the total existence of man and his relation to his natural environment (and of the individual to his social environment) it is clear that the application of technical knowledge is merely instrumental, and cannot in itself form a criterion for action. Yet the very pervasiveness of technical interest in society tends to replace concern with the practical by concern with the technical. Habermas is concerned to expose and criticise 'this ideological consciousness which seeks to suppress the distinction between the practical and the technical, and to treat all problems of action as technical' (Bernstein, 1976, p. 188). A full understanding of the practical, in particular, involves reflection: it requires a hermeneutic *Verstehen* in understanding the true social circumstance of human interaction, of the fulfilment of the citizen through his social and political (in the original Greek sense) existence.

Yet for Habermas, this more reflective level of knowledge is still insufficient, and he accuses the historical-hermeneutic sciences too of scientistic consciousness because 'much as the cultural sciences may comprehend their facts through understanding and little though they may be concerned with discovering general laws, they nevertheless share with the empirical-analytic sciences the methodological consciousness of describing a structured reality within the horizon of the theoretical attitude. Historicism has become the positivism of the cultural and social sciences' (Habermas, 1978, p. 303).

Thus, concerned as he is with the emancipation of man, Habermas suggests the third 'level' of knowledge and interest: the critical theory of society. It is difficult to describe the nature of critical theory as conceived by Habermas, involving as it does a further analysis of problems within non-emancipated society (in particular, his theory of communicative competence, which concerns the discovery of truth through interchange and his application of the methodology of psychoanalysis to the understanding of society). Enough has, however, been said to enable us to consider the way in which Habermas's clarification can help us in a critique of management control theory and practice in present social formations.

A RECONSTRUCTION OF RATIONALITY AS A CONCEPT IN MANAGEMENT CONTROL

Management control processes, as at present conceived, are essentially tied to the technical interest. They are concerned with the cognition and application of, ideally, substantively rational choice models for enterprise control. Within such a framework they find space for sociological research into the nature of 'irrationality', in particular into such matters as motivation and group processes. They do this for technical reasons: to improve the functioning of enterprises within a given societal framework. They do not question the very framework within which they function: their sole concern is with, in Habermas's phrase, the administration of society.

This applies at all resolution levels. It would appear that the very existence of given institutions in society which cry out to be managed creates an ideology that the institutions should be managed in the way in which their stability both for the enterprise/institution and for the society as a whole is not questioned, because within the confines of the technical interest, there are no grounds for questioning it. The means has become the end. The confusion of the technical with the practical has diverted attention from man's needs as a *zoon politikon* towards a bland search for administrative perfection.

The question of rationality may now be re-examined: and in particular the view that man is less rational than 'we' might have thought in his organisational actions. It may be suggested that in fact the question of rationality–irrationality is itself invalid. It is the wrong question – that is, such a dichotomy is the wrong metric. This is because, essentially, rationality is in the eye of the beholder, and the rationality of any act is not structurally intrinsic to that act but inheres only in the perception of the observer which may to a greater or lesser extent be grounded in the norms of society. Thus, if we claim that actions within organisations are in some way 'irrational' we are merely stating that they do not conform to the norms of society as we perceive them. This means that the correct question to ask becomes a question which includes societal norms: and this returns us to Habermas's concept of technical interest. The displacement which has taken place, which replaces practical interest in the eye of the societal beholder with technical interest, make actions which are not in accordance with technical effectiveness seemingly irrational. In fact they are not irrational: they are simply leading towards the practical interest of man and they happen to consist of that subset of such actions which are not consonant with the technical interest. 'Rational planning' may at times be justifiable in both the technical and practical interests: the human actions detailed earlier in this paper are not.

We may take as an example of this the point we made on page 122. There it was suggested that organisations in some way 'run backwards' (point (a)). Weick's explanation was in terms of 'unwittingly reconstructing the deed because we think that thought must have been behind it'. This can be looked at in an entirely different light: that Weick's explanation is part of the broader practical interest, relating as it does to the world-of-interaction in which we consciously live. When we then take the course Weick suggests this is simply because we believe that, in a scientific culture, a planned approach to constructing the future is in some sense 'proper' and that since we are self-legitimating, we would obviously have been acting within the norms of such a scientistic value-action system.

We can now see our way clear to approaching the question posed earlier in this paper: what is the relation between ideology and rationality, and if as so much recent organisation theory has suggested, man's behaviour within the organisation is in so many ways 'irrational', how do we explain the stability of the organisation and the continued attempts to (in at least some cases) use rational means of analysis for managerial problems? The answer, it is clear, lies in this distinction between the practical and the technical. For, within his historical-hermeneutic interest, which governs his interactive behaviour in society and creates a kind of criterion function for his social being, man perceives a need for empirical-analytic science – which may well include such 'rational' activities as planning and control. In many cases perhaps such instrumental methods will be found to be used: but this will be within the constraints of the practical interest which may loosely be equated with the Mannheimian concept of total ideology, which governs the actor's *Weltanschauung* and governs his construction of reality. If research is to go forward in management control, by implication, it should eschew its present technical concern and enquire more fundamentally into a broader question of human need in society than that implied by positivist frameworks: and in particular it might perhaps reflect on Habermas's characterisation of critical theory:

> The systematic sciences of social action . . . have the goal, as do the empirical-analytic sciences, of producing nomological knowledge. A critical social science, however, will not remain satisfied with this. It is concerned with going beyond this goal to determine when theoretical statements grasp invariant regularities of social action as such and when they express ideologically frozen relations of dependence that can in principle be transformed.
> (Habermas, 1978, p. 310)

If we are concerned, as we should be, with the true emancipation of man in a way which is not restricted to any extant social formation, then in *any* theorising we should be concerned with such issues. It is not enough to accept a social formation and understand man's role within it; nor is it enough within that social formation to go beyond this and consider man's control of his environment (whether social or natural) in such a way as to optimise his relation to it: but rather the nature of man within his social environment should itself be the subject of enquiry, the criterion for consideration, and the basis of theorising about the world.

This suggests, then, that we must go forward from our present preoccupation with technical issues such as further elaborations on the perfectibility of the planning process. We should even go further than to consider these within the context of human interaction, of the practical interest which sustains relations between men in society. In the research we do – and even 'descriptive' research is so value-laden in its framework that its implications for policy cannot be ignored – we must have as a goal, in our concepts for management control, a far broader set of issues than we at present do have.

A criterion for such research is needed which is not immanently wedded to particular present social constructions. If we have moved away from the concept of management control as being the way in which management controls others into a concern with the way the enterprise's relations with its environment are maintained, then perhaps we should not stop there. To take such an approach would mean accepting a host of societal conditions without enquiry. Management control is a branch of social research and the investigator must take societal problems as lying within his purview just as much as problems upon technical or practical rationality. Control of the enterprise within society is not a separate issue from control of society itself: the better organisation theorists have recognised this. Hence notice must be taken of the criterion for such investigation.

Note

*The authors acknowledge the helpful comment of Simon Archer on an earlier draft of this paper.

References

T. W. Adorno, *Negative Dialectics* (The Seaberry Press, 1973).
V. L. Allen, *Social Analysis* (Longman, 1975).
R. N. Anthony and J. Dearden, *Management Control Systems* (Irwin, 1976).
M. S. Baratz and P. Bachrach, 'Two Faces of Power', *American Political Science Review*, 56 (1962) pp. 947–52.
R. Bendix, *Work and Authority in Industry* (Wiley, 1956).
P. L. Berger and T. Luckman, *The Social Construction of Reality: A Treatise in the Sociology of Knowledge* (Doubleday, 1966).
R. J. Bernstein, *The Restructuring of Social and Political Theory* (Methuen, 1976).
J. Child, *Organization* (Harper and Row, 1977).
M. D. Cohen, J. G. March and J. P. Olsen, 'A Garbage Can Model of Organizational Choice', *Administrative Science Quarterly*, 17 (1972) pp. 1–25.
R. M. Cyert and J. G. March, *A Behavioral Theory of the Firm* (Prentice-Hall, 1963).
H. Garfinkel, *Studies in Ethnomethodology* (Prentice-Hall, 1967).
P. Georgiou, 'The Goal Paradigm and Notes Towards a Counter Paradigm', *Administrative Science Quarterly*, 18 (1973) pp. 291–310.
A. Giddens, *New Rules of Sociological Method* (Hutchinson, 1976).
A. Giddens, *Studies in Social and Political Theory* (Hutchinson, 1977).
A. Giddens, *Central Problems in Social Theory* (Macmillan, 1979).
R. B. Glassman, 'Persistence and Loose Coupling in Living Systems', *Behavioral Science*, 18 (1973) pp. 83–98.

E. Goffman, *Interaction Ritual* (Doubleday, 1967).
P. S. Goodman, J. M. Pennings and Associates, *New Perspectives on Organizational Effectiveness* (Jossey-Bass, 1977).
J. Habermas, *Knowledge and Human Interests* (Heinemann, 1978).
P. Hamilton, *Knowledge and Social Structure* (Routledge and Kegan Paul, 1974).
M. Horkheimer, *Eclipse of Reason* (The Seabury Press, 1974).
R. Keat and J. Urry, *Social Theory as Science* (Routledge and Kegan Paul, 1975).
C. E. Lindblom, 'The Science of Muddling Through', *Public Administration Review*, 19 (1959) pp. 79–88.
E. A. Lowe, 'Comments on Georgiou's "The Goal Paradigm and Notes Towards a Counter Paradigm"', *Administrative Science Quarterly* (1973) pp. 253–4.
E. A. Lowe, 'Towards a Definition of Management Control', Paper presented to the Management Control Workshop.
E. A. Lowe and A. G. Puxty, 'The Problems of a Paradigm', this volume.
K. Mannheim, *Ideology and Utopia* (Harcourt, Brace and World, 1936).
J. G. March and J. P. Olsen, *Ambiguity and Choice in Organizations* (Universitetsforlaget, 1976).
J. G. March and H. A. Simon, *Organizations* (Wiley, 1958).
K. Marx, 'The German Ideology', abstracted in *Karl Marx: Selected Writings in Social Philosophy* (ed.) T. B. Bottomore and M. Rubel (Penguin, 1963).
J. W. Meyer and B. Rowan, 'Institutionalized Organizations: Formal Structure as Myth and Ceremony', *American Journal of Sociology*, 83 (1977) pp. 340–63.
L. B. Mohr, 'The Concept of Organizational Goal', *American Political Science Review*, 67 (1973) pp. 470–81.
C. Perrow, 'The Analysis of Goals in Complex Organizations', *American Sociological Review*, 26 (1961) pp. 854–66.
C. Perrow, *Complex Organizations: A Critical Essay* (2nd edn: Scott Foresman and Co, 1979).
G. Salaman, *Work Organizations: Resistance and Control* (Longman, 1979).
A. Schutz, *The Phenomenology of the Social World* (Northwestern University Press, 1967).
A. Shils, 'Ideologies' in *International Encyclopaedia of the Social Sciences* (1968).
D. Silverman, *The Theory of Organizations* (Heinemann, 1970).
H. A. Simon, *Models of Man: Social and Rational* (Wiley, 1957).
H. A. Simon, 'On the Concept of Organizational Goal', *Administrative Science Quarterly*, 9 (1964) pp. 1–22.
H. A. Simon, *Administrative Behavior* (3rd edn: Free Press, 1976).
M. Weber, *The Theory of Social and Economic Organization* (Free Press, 1964).
K. E. Weick, 'Educational Organizations as Loosely Coupled Systems', *Administrative Science Quarterly*, 21 (1976) pp. 1–19.

K. E. Weick, *The Social Psychology of Organizing* (2nd edn: Addison Wesley, 1979).
A. Wildavsky, 'If Planning is Everything, Maybe it's Nothing', *Policy Sciences*, 4 (1973) pp. 127–53.

8 Accounting and the Pursuit of Social Interests
Anthony Hopwood

Accounting is coming to be regarded as an interested endeavour. Rather than being seen as merely residing in the technical domain, serving the role of a neutral facilitator of effective decision-making, accounting is slowly starting to be related to the pursuit of quite particular economic, social and political interests. The active and influential ways in which accounting is implicated in the construction and propagation of notions of organisational and social control are now starting to be addressed.

At both the tactical and the strategic level, accounting is coming to be seen as being able to have a positive rather than merely enabling influence on the specification of the problematic, the delineation of the desirable and the possible, and the conduct of action in organizational and social settings. Indeed, accounting, so conceived, is coming to be recognised as not being independent of the very organisational and social contexts in which it operates. It is implicated in the specification of organisational boundaries, in the internal segmentation of organisational space, in the delineation of social practices which can cut through that organisational space, and in the creation of a means of visibility which can penetrate into the internal functioning of the contexts in which it operates. Perceived in such terms, accounting is a creative rather than merely reflective endeavour. It can positively shape rather than merely enable the settings of which it provides an account. What is more, those accounts are themselves starting to be acknowledged as being selective and partial. Only certain phenomena, concerns and activities enter into the accounting domain. In helping to mobilise the actions which it does, accounting also excludes and relegates a whole array of equally meaningful potential actions and concerns. It plays a role in constructing an organisational or social domain not only by its positive acts of creation and enablement but also by its equally significant acts of demarcation and exclusion.

Increasingly both the partiality of accounting and its positive roles in the creation of organisations and society as they now are have come not only to be recognised but also to be seen as problematic. Together such conceptions contrast sharply with conventional notions of an impartial, neutral and merely facilitative account. Spurned on by such a recognition, questions now are being asked about the organisational and social origins of the accounting craft, the nature of its functioning when seen in organisational and social rather than purely technical terms, and the wider consequences of the accounting endeavour. A new vocabulary is in the process of entering accounting discourse. In addition to interrogating accounting in the name of its facilitative roles in organisational decision-making, the social and political aspects of the craft also are being examined and questioned. The language of the social is being intertwined with that of the technical in order to come to a different appreciation of the accounting phenomenon.

It is in such a context that the interested nature of accounting has arisen as a problem. Questions now are being asked of the origins of accounting as we know it. Just what has mobilised the development of so particular an accounting art? What other practices and concerns are implicated in accounting as it is? What set of mobilising interests might explain the form that accounting takes? For if accounting is such an influential but partial endeavour, what organisational and social factors have been at stake in its emergence and continued elaboration? Just what interests can accounting be seen to serve?

As of yet, however, the interested nature of accounting practice remains a vague and only partially articulated notion. Rather than representing any well developed theory of accounting's development and functioning, it is best seen as representing a context for a different way of questioning and understanding the accounting craft. Specific accounts can be related to the organisational and social settings from which they emerge. The ways in which accountings can be infused with a language of organisational and political mobilisation can be subjected to explicit investigation. The actual consequences of the craft can be examined and critically appraised. In such ways the interested language of the social and the political can be used as a platform on which to interrogate accounting in terms very different from those conventionally applied. Despite its embryonic ambiguities and its poorly delineated form, the conception of an interested account can be used to mobilise very different inquiries into the development, practice and consequences of the craft. Indeed, although preliminary in its form, the new conception nevertheless is already starting to become influential.

Aware of this, the present discussion seeks to examine a few quite specific aspects of the newly emergent view of the accounting domain. Appreciating the contexts which have given rise to current concerns, the analysis aims to further the understanding of what is at stake in the presumption of an interested accounting. However, although the analysis is not a critical one, it does attempt to tease out a few of the problems that need to be confronted if the social understanding of accounting is to progress.

Initially the conventional disinterested view of accounting is examined in order to explicate some of its presumptions and modes of analysis. Thereafter a strong form of the interested view of accounting is subjected to a similar review. On the basis of the latter examination, a number of significant questions requiring further examination are identified. Consideration is given both to some of the ways in which accounting itself can help to shape the very interests in the name of which it is advanced and reformed, and to the multitude of different interests that can become implicated with the organisational and social practice of the accounting craft. Some attention also is given to the possibilities for accounting change which can emanate from within its own sphere of action and to the uncertain relationship between the functions and interests in the name of which accounting is advanced and the precise organisational and social consequences which it can be seen to have. Although the discussion of these questions is of necessity a tentative one, it is suggested that the further analysis of these and related issues is necessary if a social appreciation of accounting is to advance.

ACCOUNTING AND THE TECHNICAL FACILIATION OF ORGANISATIONAL FUNCTIONING[1]

The majority of conventional discussions of accounting see it in terms of organisational reform and improvement. Accounting is implemented in and changed within organisations in order to make them more efficient and effective. Albeit slowly, the accounting craft and the organisations to which it has been applied are seen as having progressed. Analysis, inquiry and sustained experiential learning together are seen as resulting in the increasing joint realisation of an accounting and an organisational potential. In becoming what they were not, accounting and the organisations in which it operates have been in the process of becoming what they should be.

Such characterisations of accounting appeal to the ways in which it enhances organisational performance. Moreover organisational economy, efficiency and effectiveness are seen not only to be capable of being improved by accounting means but also to have an existence independent of the accounting or other calculative representations of them. Not only is profit for real but also the accounting representation of it is getting better, almost all the time.

The contributions which accounting makes to organisational performance are seen as being achieved by the roles it plays in organisational functioning. Once again, these roles are defined prior to and independently of the specific organisational practices, including accounting, by which they are effected. Accounting is seen as being implicated in processes of direction, planning, coordination, control and the management of motivation. In all of these areas specific practices of accounting can be, and indeed are, compared with an abstract conceptualisation of what they essentially should be about. The actual practices thereby can be seen as manifestations of the realisation or frustration of these abstract imperatives. They can be seen as being more or less adequate in ways which are not solely dependent on their specific functioning in specific organisations. And because of this, attempts can be made to improve accounting in the name of what it should be rather than what it is. The accounting potential seemingly is always a future one.

As a discipline, accounting has invested a great deal in the elucidation of abstract bodies of knowledge concerned with what it essentially should be about. Ideas exist as to good costing practice, good planning, good modes of management reporting and good approaches to the appraisal of new investment opportunities. Attempts have been made to tease out the abstract characteristics of good coordination, control and direction, and their implications for the reform of accounting practice. Regimes of thought thereby have been developed which have an existence and dynamic of change partially independent of the practice of the craft. Accounting can be evaluated in terms of what it is not. Specific practices can be appraised on the basis of their conformity to more general notions of management and the manageable. An abstract, external body of knowledge can be imposed on them in order both to assess their adequacy and to reform them so that they can become what they really should be.

So presuming that the functions of accounting exist independently of its practice and that the problem of practice is to reform, albeit slowly, organisational procedures so that the intrinsic goals to which they are orientated are achieved, accounting is known, described and evaluated by reference to a body of knowledge that is presumed to be external to accounting itself. Therefore, although the realisation of the accounting potential may be problematic, the potential itself is only rarely, if ever, seen in problematic or emergent terms. It is endowed not only with a privileged organisational status but also with a privileged epistemological one as well, such that although accounting is seen as being laboriously constructed, its essence is not.

Many questionable assumptions are implicit within such a view of accounting. The presumption that the ends towards which accounting is orientated exist independently of the accounting practices which embody them is, for instance, a highly problematic one. For in historical terms, the emergence of the concepts of organisational goals and functions cannot be dissociated from the development of the specific means of action and calculation which enabled them to function. The apparatus of organising has profoundly influenced our conception of the organisation. Equally, the organisational participants to which and on which accounting information is reported cannot be defined externally to the practices in which they are engaged, including those of an accounting nature. The concepts of management and the manager were actively constructed in a particular way at a particular socio-historical juncture and are inseparable from the practical means of administration and calculation which were, and still are, implicated in their emergence and functioning. There was no a priori, pre-given (primitive savage) manager to whom one can appeal as having interests and needs which mobilise the development of accounting practices. Equally, there was no primeval concept of accounting which shaped the development of accounting as it now is. Accounting has emerged in a more positive way than the mere realisation of an essence. Indeed, in part, at least, the present imperatives of accounting – its potential, which can and do guide its development, have emerged from the practice of the craft. And, in similar terms, accounting practice needs to be seen as playing a more active role in creating rather than merely enabling organised endeavour as we now know it. Accounting development is as much a history of organisational construction as organisational realisation and enablement.

That is not to deny that external discourses of the accounting potential can and do mobilise accounting change. They provide an incentive for action. An understanding of specific organisational targets for intervention can be constructed on their bases. And they can provide criteria for both gauging the presumed need for change and reading its effects. But such appreciations of the discourses that can mobilise accounting still do not provide insights into the forces underlying the deployment of different accountings and the use of an abstract rhetoric of the accounting potential, the precise practices involved, the resistances which they engender and the precise organisational consequences which they give rise to. For it would be inappropriate to assume that there is any invariant relationship between a rhetoric and discourse of accounting and a programme of intervention in the organisation conducted in the name of it. That relationship should be a problem for investigation rather than presumption.

It is precisely such problems that social analyses of accounting are starting to explore. From a social perspective, the accounting potential is seen as having not only a privileged but problematic status in terms of its knowledge bases but also a claim to a technical rationale that is divorced from its organisational and social functioning. Despite the fact that accounting is quite centrally implicated in many significant organisational and social processes, including those through which the results of organised endeavour are allocated, the ends of accounting traditionally have been seen as residing outside the sphere of legitimate social debate. In conventional discussions accounting is treated as an asocial, technically rational phenomenon. Even though it is explicitly stated as being involved in processes of organisational control and the mobilisation of a vocabulary of organisational motive, accounting discourse still is abstracted from the social processes which give rise not only to its emergence, functioning and continued elaboration but also to the very achievement or frustration of the ends which it seeks to serve. Organisational conflict, power and disagreement know no place in the official rhetoric of an abstract and seemingly technical accounting. The organisational ends which it seeks to further are seen as unproblematic, having a rationality that is and should be detached from the specific organisational and social functioning of the craft. Conflict seemingly is not endemic to the organisational terrain, despite the fact that action cannot be taken for granted but needs to be mobilised, constrained and controlled by organisational norms and practices, including those of accounting itself.

Nor are the partialities of accounting seen as problematic in the conventional discourses of the craft. Repeated emphasis is placed on what accounting is rather than on what it is not. The processes of calculative exclusion do not enter into accounting rhetoric. Its role in creating a very particular and privileged organisational visibility is ignored. What is not accounted for seemingly has little relevance for those who want to further accounting as it is. Such problems are emphasised by those who wish to analyse accounting in its social terms. For them, accounting cannot be divorced from the social relations which accompany its emergence and functioning. Organisational and social conflict and debate are endemic to the accounting craft. The domain of the unaccounted for is, from such a perspective, as significant as that which is. Looking, thereby, at the partial and contested trajectories of accounting's social development and functioning, they have appealed to the concept of interest to explain accounting as it is rather than as it might have become. They have tried to account for accounting in terms of the ends which they see it as serving rather than those in which it has sought to account for itself.[2]

Although somewhat extended, the discussion of the conventional rhetoric of a disinterested facilitative accounting has tried to demonstrate how it is problematic on its own terms as well as from a wider social perspective. Such a view of accounting's contribution to organisational improvement provides neither an adequate insight into accounting as it is nor an understanding of how it has become or might otherwise have been. By appealing to an abstract, organisationally detached, technical essence of accounting, conventional discourses endow their subject with a metaphysical existence that is difficult to ground in or relate to the specifics of the organisational and social functioning of the craft.

ACCOUNTING AND THE ARTICULATION OF THE SOCIAL

Aware of such problems, accounting increasingly is coming to be seen as having its origins in the social conflicts which are enacted in the organisational arena. Rather than being seen as a technical reflection of pregiven economic imperatives facing organisational administration, accounting is now starting to be seen as being more actively constructed in order to create a particular economic visibility within the organisation and a powerful means for positively enabling the governance and control of the organisation along economic lines. Accounting, so seen, is not a passive instrument of technical administration, a neutral means for revealing the pregiven aspects of organisational functioning. Instead its origins are seen to reside in the exercising of social power both within and without the organisation. It is seen as being implicated in the forging of a particular regime of economic calculation within the organisation in order to make real and powerful quite particular conceptions of economic and social interests.

From such a perspective, accounting is seen as having played a very positive role in the creation of a manageable organisational domain, actively furthering both a particular segmentation of work and a particular distribution of its outcomes to quite specific economic ends. Economic interests are seen as having been reflected in now legitimate and accepted economic facts. Seen in such terms, a regime of economic visibility and calculation has positively enabled the creation and operation of an organisation which facilitates the exercising of particular concepts of power. Economic motives have been made real and influential. The work process in the organisation has been exposed, ordered and physically and socially distributed in quite particular ways. The resultant organisational facts, calculations, schedules and plans have positively enabled the construction of a management regime which is abstracted and distanced from the operation of the work process itself.

So, although functioning in the organisation, accounting is best seen from such a perspective as an artifact residing in the domain of the social rather than the narrowly organisational. It has been implicated in the radical change of the organisation in the name of the social. Indeed, so conceived, accounting is seen as being one of the important means by which the organisation has been incorporated into the realm of the social.

Strong forms of such an analysis, whilst making problematic the social origins and consequences of accounting, also tend to endow a relatively unproblematic status to accounting itself. Accounting, and indeed other organisational practices, are seen as being merely reflections of wider and underlying social interests. The interests themselves, however, are defined prior to and outside of the context of the specific organisational and social arenas in which they intervene. They are abstract phenomena with a privileged epistomological status. Apparently having a logic, dynamic and power of their own, they infuse particular organisational and social arenas, radically shaping, if not determining, the outcomes of conflict and debate. From such a perspective accounting as we now know it is a reflection of an abstract conceptualisation of directed social relations and interests. It can, thereby, be reduced to its social core. Indeed the potential inherent in the social is seen as being made concrete and real through its embodiment in specific organisational and social practices, of which accounting is not an insignificant one.

It is somewhat paradoxical that so significant a conception of an accounting potential should feature so dominantly in a perspective which seeks to undermine the pretensions of the accounting potential of old. However, be that as it may, some emerging social analyses of the accounting craft do find it tempting to attribute to accounting a mobilising essence which is abstracted from the practice of accounting itself. Although this is seen to reside in the realm of the social rather than the technical, it too is regarded as giving a particular functionality to the accounting craft. Albeit they are cast in very different terms than those that are conventionally articulated, the new social analyses nevertheless also attribute abstract roles of accounting, the practice of which is seen as being a reflection of (or only rarely a frustration of) its underlying potential.[3]

Whilst not seeking to deny that actions can be mobilised on the basis of interests that are formulated prior to their engagement in particular organisational and social arenas or that accounting can be influenced by forces residing outside of the practice itself, some of the difficulties encountered by the stronger forms of social analysis nevertheless need to be recognised. If future social analyses of accounting are to be more robust, the inadequacies implicit in their formulation must be recognised. Only in this way can a more adequate basis be constructed for the social understanding and guidance of the accounting craft.

Some of the significant difficulties already have been discussed. Whilst making no presumption of a comprehensive critique, some further problems are now introduced.

SOME PRECAUTIONS NECESSARY WHEN TRYING TO INTERTWINE ACCOUNTING WITH THE SOCIAL

Accounting is a purposive endeavour. Through it individuals, groups, and whole societies seek to articulate their concerns, worries and preferences. Accounting is called upon in the pursuit of certain goals and objectives. It is implicated in making calculations, evaluating trade-offs, taking and then justifying decisions, and the furtherance of certain desired courses of action. So to this extent, it is appropriate to endow accounting with a purposive, interested nature.

Accounting and the Construction of the Interests in the Name of Which it is Advanced

However, the interests which accounting seeks to further are not necessarily independent of the accounting of them. Cost may be a powerful rhetorical category but the pursuit of cost reduction requires a practical means for its enablement. Nor is there any easy relationship between the idea of costing and specific programmes of organisational intervention conducted in the name of that idea. Costs have to be laboriously constructed rather than merely revealed. There is no singular, obvious and automatic relationship between the notion of cost and its practical representation, as many volumes of scholarly accounting research testify. An organisational economy grounded in a domain of the facts of cost has to be painstakingly forged rather than merely exposed (see Hopwood, 1987). Similarly for profit, capital, value added and so on. All these can function as powerful rhetoric categories, and have consequences because of that, but to serve as a means for specific organisational or social interventions they depend on particular discursive means for their articulation and elaboration, and particular organisational practices for their practical furtherance. And here too there is never an easy and unproblematic relationship between the particular and the specific, and the more general categories in the name of which they are introduced. One is not simply a reflection of the other. The relationship between the two always is mediated by a mass of quite particular, partial and often inadequate discursive and organisational practices. So whilst accounting may be centrally implicated in the celebration of the economic, the economy, be it of the enterprise or the nation, as a specific governable, manageable entity is not independent of the accountings of it. Social analysis must always seek to investigate both the precise relationships between the general and the specific and the actual consequences of the latter rather than the presumed consequences of the former.

Accounting and the Diversity of Interests Acting on It

Because of its powerful potential, accounting frequently is utilised in the name of a multitude of different interests. Inflation accounting, for example, was acted upon in the name of national economic management, government taxation policies and a heterogeneous politics surrounding the declaration of corporate surplus, as well as in the furtherance of particular, but conflicting, conceptions of accounting regulation (see Hopwood, 1988). Value added, perhaps now best seen as a relatively temporary accounting phenomenon of the late 1970s, arose in the context of strategies for the management of national incomes policies, reinvestment in British manufacturing industry, the regulation of the accounting profession and the contested extension of conceptions of industrial participation and democracy (see Burchell, Clubb and Hopwood, 1985). Similarly, within the enterprise, accounting developments can be implicated in responses to competitive pressures, changes in information processing technologies, attempts to further regulate the work process and so on (see Hopwood, 1987, for further more detailed examples). Whilst on occasions it might be possible to point to a dominant interest or strategic intervention in accounting, or some complementarity between an array of such interests, in general there can be no prior assumption that this will be the case. The different pressures impinging on accounting can be articulated through different institutional and policy arenas, use different discursive means for their representation, intersect with an array of very different organisational and social practices,[4] and seek to utilise accounting in very different ways. Any assumption as to the functional orchestration of such diverse influences must always be a tentative, even if subsequently correct, one and subjected to a detailed examination of the very particular factors and practices associated with it.
associated with it.

Accounting's Influences Upon Itself

Accounting may also serve as a significant influence upon itself. Both in terms of the technical properties of the accounting discourse and the labour process associated with the accounting craft, there are possibilities for accounting to develop some internal logics of elaboration and change. Not least as it seeks to adjust to an ever expanding array of quite particular accounts, but also because of its partial and incompletely specified nature, the accounting discourse can itself provide a momentum for accounting to become what it was not. Attempts can be made to reconcile internal inconsistencies, of which there still are many. Accounting can be elaborated as it is made to confront the novel and the new. And significant developments can occur, and indeed have occurred, as attempts are made to intertwine the discourse of accounting with those of commensurate and often initially incommensurate disciplines and bodies of knowledge.

The accounting labour process, broadly conceived of in terms of its institutional embodiment, its internal segmentation and the conduct of accounting as an occupational task, also can influence the paths of accounting development. Professional rivalries and ambitions can result in a more or less intensive regime of accounting control in organisations (Armstrong, 1985). Professional interests in examination, certification and internal regulation and administration have all served as influential bases for the enlargement and elaboration of a discursive practice of accounting (Hopwood, 1988). The will to talk accounting as well as merely to do it has been a significant and influential factor. Although not unrelated to the concerns of the state, the conduct of the judicial process, the management of the wider educational system and the maintenance and enhancement of professional powers and privileges, it still would be difficult to embrace many, let alone all, such internal dynamics of development under the name of wider and all too ill-defined social interests.

When seen in such terms perhaps some of the internal logics of accounting development can be compared with the biological mutations which pepper the natural world with added variety if no additional functionality. As Jacob (1982) has commented:

> adaptation is not a necessary component of genetic evolution. A population is evolving whenever its gene pool changes in the course of generations whether it be gradually or suddenly. Such statistical alteration in the relative survival of genetic elements does not obligatorily imply adaptation. It can merely reflect some change effect at any level of the reproductive process. Obviously random evolution cannot explain why land animals have legs, birds have wings, and fish have fins. Yet a number of mechanisms are now known to be operative in evolution besides natural selection, for instance genetic drift, random gene fixation, indirect

selection due to genetic linkage, and differential growth of organs. Many of these factors help to randomise the effects of natural selection and to produce structures that may well be of no use. The problem is to determine the relative weight of all these processes in evolution.

The same problem most certainly applies in an accounting context.

Accounting and the Inadequacies of the Accounting Craft

One final significant reason for exercising some caution in seeing accountancy as simply a reflection of wider ends relates to the very real inadequacies of the accounting craft. Both the conventional rhetoric of accounting and stronger forms of social analysis presume that accounting is an efficient functional endeavour. In the vast majority of circumstances both see it as being adequate to the ends in the name of which it seemingly is advanced. Such a presumption is far from being an obvious one, however, not least if it is to serve as a general rule.

In many respects the accounting craft is not only a very tentative one but also one that has only a partial understanding of the bases for its own effectiveness and the processes through which to fulfil its own aspirations. Accounting may be seen as being orientated towards the enhancement of organisational economy and efficiency, but the paths by which that can be achieved in the context of specific organisations, meeting particular resistances and intersecting with other influential organisational practices remain little understood, and certainly do not enter into the texts and manuals of the craft. Moreover this problem is only intensified amidst the crisis situations, pressures and short deadlines in which accounting is so frequently called upon.

The unanticipated consequences of the craft are both real and increasingly recognised (Kaplan, 1983). The impact which accounting has on the organisational construction of time, the rigidity of organisational processes and the monopolisation of the visibility of the economic do not enter into the accounting rhetoric but they are entering into the vocabulary of corporate worrying about accounting (Hopwood, 1985). The constitutive role of accounting (see Burchell, Clubb and Hopwood, 1985) provides a further basis for accounting's own inadequacy (Hopwood, 1987). For to the extent that accounting positively changes the organisational conditions of its own functioning, it provides a basis for a dynamic by which it can sometimes create the possibility for its own malfunctioning. Paradoxes such as those which occur when accounting attempts to integrate a segmented organisation result in increased difficulties of coordination and when newly decentralised accounts facilitate the exercising of centralised control seem to bedevil the accounting art.

Functional accounts of accounting's organisational potential also tend to attach little significance to the very real resistances which accounting engenders. Although the incorporation of slack into budgets is a well documented phenomenon, other strategies for both managerial and work place resistance and inertia towards accounting are little understood and assigned relatively little importance.

For a while now I have been fascinated by the thought that the resistances to accounting may provide at least a little insight into the very heavy British investment in professionalised accounting expertise. Having one of the highest ratios of accountants per capita in the western world and utilising this resource very selectively, predominantly in the manufacturing sector, to some extent in the area of local government and, very recently, in the previously unaccounted for sphere of central government (Hopwood, 1984), questions can quite legitimately be raised about the functionality of the accounting craft and the adequacy of the accounting rhetoric. Recently I have been impressed by the extent to which accounting appears to be called upon in circumstances where the difficulties facing the meeting of its own objectives seem to be greatest. Faced by the growing power of the labour movement generally, and the shop steward movement in particular, cost accounting was advocated as a means of gaining effective economic control of the work place. During the turbulent years following the First World War accounting was suggested as a means to provide a more adequate account of the 'labour problem'. In the depressed and conflictual conditions of the late 1920s and 1930s, legitimate professional accountants entered the higher ranks of British manufacturing industry. With the relative re-emergence of the power of labour during the 1970s, accounting once again was called upon to provide a different account. Interest emerged in value added, financial data was provided to employees and trade unions and an active politics emerged concerning the procedures implicated in the declaration of corporate surplus. On each of these occasions accountants maintained their occupational presence after the crisis was past. Also on each of these occasions the technical rhetoric of accounting was appealed to amidst social turbulence and conflict. And yet on each of these occasions the social resistances which seemingly mobilised the accounting response resulted in an unknown but perhaps equivocal relationship between the rhetoric and the achievement of any particular accounting potential. In the process, however, a professionalised calculus of the economic could well have become unintendedly ever more entrenched in the fabric of British institutional life, having its own very particular set of economic, social and political consequences.

At this stage such thoughts must remain only a tentative hypothesis for further social investigation. They suggest the need, however, for exploring beyond the conventional assumptions of accounting's adequacy to the functions in the name of which it is elaborated and reformed. At the very least, the functionality of accounting must be investigated, not assumed. More generally, there might be bases for presuming that accounting can sometimes change because of its failure to satisfy the aspirations which are held of it.

CONCLUSION

Social understandings represent an important means for exploring the origins, functioning and consequences of the accounting craft. In this chapter I have sought to argue sympathetically for the advance of such a perspective. At the same time, however, I also have tried to point to some of the dangers that can all too readily be implicit in the task of social analysis. For an understanding of accounting in the name of the social is neither an unproblematic nor homogeneous endeavour. Without conceptual care and consideration there is a possibility that an overly socialised conception of accounting might result in insufficient attention being given not only to the powers of human agency on the path of accounting's development but also to the rich and varied texture of the social terrain which accounting both traverses and creates. If this happens not only will the resultant social analyses fail to realise their potential of enriching our understanding of accounting as it is but also, somewhat paradoxically, they might curtail the recognition of the very arenas in which an active politics of accounting might take place.

Notes

1. Some of the following discussion and that of the next section is based on Hopwood 1987).
2. Interestingly many of the same criticisms apply to recent organisational analyses of the accounting craft. The pretensions of the accounting potential still mobilise inquiries into the organisational functioning of the craft. Accounting still tends to be viewed on its own terms. Resistances, although recorded, are seen as something to be corrected by behavioural or organisational means. The analyses that have been made of accounting diversity are not dissimilar. Although the differences in the contemporaneous practice of the craft have provided an incentive for an analysis of some of the factors that impinge on the forms that accounting practice takes, the resultant contingent analyses retain many of the unquestioned presumptions of the accounting potential. The organisational calculus implicit in accounting adaptation is still one that is posited on the functional roles that accounting plays in the enhancement of an abstract concept of organisational performance. The path of accounting movement is seemingly an unproblematic one. Accounting becomes what it next should be, apparently guided by a rational, even if still poorly understood, calculus of organisational improvement which is not dissimilar from that which is implicit in more traditional conceptions of the craft. Little role is acknowledged for managerial discretion and choice, let alone the active exercise of politics and power.
3. In many senses such strong forms of social analysis share the same problems as agency theoretic formulations of accounting development and change. There too an abstract conception of an economic interest mobilises the form that accounting takes. Perhaps even more so than in even the stronger forms of social analysis, a concept of a prior nature is conceived of as an origin or cause of phenomena such that specific histories and particular organisational forms assume a secondary role in the analysis: history tends to be used rather than confronted. And there too the underlying conceptions of interest are seen as being independent of the specific organisational and social practices which they give rise to. The latter presumption is a particularly paradoxical one in the case of agency theory since organisational alternatives are assumed to be evaluated on the basis of an economic calculus that results in the furtherance of the principal's interest. Apparently a pre-given, if not a God given, and wholly unproblematic meta-accounting guides the choice of particular organisational accounts. Not too surprisingly, such metaphysical presumptions are not discussed by agency theorists.
4. Despite the attention given to accounting as a relatively independent discipline, the dependency of accounting practice on other organisational practices and bodies of knowledge needs much closer attention. In the context of management accounting, its development can be shown as being intertwined with those of industrial engineering, time and motion study, personal management and the emergence of a psychological concept of the person, and factory design and layout. Many of these different functions and disciplines provide important conditions of possibility for the present pursuit of the accounting craft.

References

P. Armstrong, 'Changing Management Control Strategies: The Role of Competition Between Accountancy And Other Organisational Professions', *Accounting Organizations and Society* (1985).

S. Burchell, C. Clubb and A. G. Hopwood, 'Accounting in its Social Context: Towards a History of Value Added in the United Kingdom', *Accounting, Organizations and Society* (1985).

A. G. Hopwood, 'On Trying to Study Accounting in the Contexts in Which it Operates', *Accounting Organizations and Society* (1983).

A. G. Hopwood, 'Accounting and the Pursuit of Efficiency' in A. G. Hopwood and C. Tomkins (eds) *Issues in Public Sector Accounting* (Philip Allen, 1984).

A. G. Hopwood, 'The Development of "Worrying" About Management Accounting', in K. B. Clark, R. H. Hayes and C. Lorenz (eds.), *The Uneasy Alliance: Managing the Productivity–Technology Dilemma* (Harvard Business School Press, 1985).

A. G. Hopwood, 'The Archaeology of Accounting Systems', *Accounting, Organizations and Society* (1987).

A. G. Hopwood, 'Accounting Research and Accounting Practice: The Ambiguous Relationship Between the Two', the Deloitte, Haskins & Sells Accounting Lecture, The University College of Wales, Aberystwyth (1988).

F. Jacob, *The Possible and the Actual* (Pantheon Books, 1982).

R. S. Kaplan, 'Measuring Manufacturing Performance: A New Challenge for Managerial Accounting Research', *The Accounting Review* (1983).

Part II
Critique in Action

9 Labour and Deskilling: A Critique of Managerial Control in the Glass Industry

John Black and Fiona Neathey

INTRODUCTION AND SYNOPSIS

The approach taken to the issue of control in this paper is one which is in marked contrast to other contributions to this monograph. Otley, as an example, accepts 'a broad view of control as involving both the selection of ends to be attained and means to attain them'. His approach ignores the economic context of organisations whose dynamics he attempts to explain, thus he neglects the possibility that fundamental conflicts of interest may exist within organisations, which would make the selection of ends and means a far more problematic process than he suggests. The fact of this conflict is a key assumption in our analysis. Thus we see control in capitalist organisations as inherently conflictual since its aim, we suggest, is the effective utilisation of factors of production to the end that outputs are optimised whilst costs are minimised. Hence control is focused on labour utilisation and unit costs. This is the source of conflict in the control process: control of labour as a resource is in direct conflict with workers' interests to maximise income and maintain some control over their activity at work. The definition of the nature of control implied in this approach could be criticised as overly simplistic. However a key purpose of this paper will be to examine the details of control relationships in capitalist organisations, and thus to demonstrate that the processes underlying such a definition are, in fact, highly complex. We are concerned, for example, with the implications which changes in technology have for managerial control and how the feasibility, and potential impact of these changes is mediated by other factors. Thus in this paper we will explore the issue of managerial control, its relationship to the logic of capitalist realisation of profit, and how this relates to a general dynamic of the deskilling and control of work.

The purposes are, by reference to both relevant literature and our own empirical research, to:

1. examine certain weaknesses, not only in the central deskilling thesis as presented by Braverman (1974) – which has been done extensively elsewhere – but also in widely quoted responses to his work, and through the example of one particular industry;
2. demonstrate, contrary to universalistic analyses, that
    (a) management behaviour needs to be understood in the context of its particular operational setting, and
    (b) the assumption that the realisation of maximum profit is the central motive force of capitalism is a crude generalisation which requires significant qualification. Firstly in the light of how oligopoly characterises many markets in the capitalist economy. Secondly because, implicit in the taken-for-granted acceptance of profit maximisation, is a unitary model of the organisation which, by assuming consensus over goals, distracts attention away from the plurality[1] of interests which typify the business organisation. Thus the assumption, which is implicit in a wide variety of literature, from 'Managerial' to 'Marxist', that managerial behaviour can be directly related to the search for lower unit cost and hence greater profit, must be questioned. So must the assumption that where the reduction of unit cost is a motivator of management behaviour, this is achieved by increasing the technical division of labour and its concomitant, the creation of a deskilled labour force.

In section 1 we argue the centrality to management control of knowledge and thus of measurement and recording at the point of production. The development of managerial control, both personnel and financial, can be seen as deriving from these requirements. As Babbage (1971) puts it, the need 'to know the precise expense of every process'. Hence the impetus to cheapen, and by implication deskill labour, finding expression in Industrial Engineering and Cost Accountancy, might lead one to accept a deterministic deskilling analysis as found in Braverman (1974). We outline in section 2, the core of Braverman's analysis apropos deskilling. Against this we present the salient features of the literature which has arisen as a response to Braverman, looking at the work of Friedman (1977),

Edwards (1979), and Burawoy (1979) as representative for our purposes of both the major advances and the major deficiencies of this literature. We then indicate the ways in which the critique should be developed, both in terms of the further definition of terms and of the implied need for empirical research. We look particularly at the status of the term 'control'. Having expressed the need for a study of specific industrial situations, we next introduce our own empirical research. We describe the labour process in crystal glass manufacture in the context of the industry and examine the nature, and some implications, of the 'skills' employed. In the following section we point to the survival of skill and consider the conditions under which it will survive in terms of technology, the nature of the product and the product and labour markets. Evidence is presented as to the way in which skill has been defended historically in this industry.

The issue of control raises questions of the nature and mobilisation of managerial power. Next we draw attention to how a failure to consider the origins of a power differential focuses attention away from important sources of managerial power, based for example in trade union 'incorporation'. Workers' perceptions of their subordinate role may be ambivalent. Hence we argue that management may not only attempt to limit entry to the organisation to applicants with suitable attitudes, but may also be wary of exercising their objective power for fear that this might shatter their precarious legitimacy in the eyes of the workforce. Craft consciousness is thus seen not so much as an impediment to management purposes, but rather, in this context, as beneficial. Management then, we suggest, will not necessarily press home its domination of the workforce, either through discipline or deskilling.

MANAGEMENT AND CONTROL

Control, as Baldamus (1961) argued, is central to the management function.

> The organization of industry ... ultimately revolves on a single process ... through which the employees' effort is controlled by the employer ... [through] a system of administrative controls which regulate quantity, quality and distribution of human effort.'
> It is the variation in form and rationale of management controls which requires explanation.

The exercise of control requires knowledge. Thus the development of cost accounting was motivated by the desire of manufacturers for more precise knowledge of the component cost of the finished product, such that control over each element could be exercised. Solomons quotes Babbage (1971), who, drawing upon Adam Smith's famous example of pin manufacture, states that,

> The great competition introduced by machinery, and the application of the principle of the subdivision of labour, render it necessary for each producer to be continually on the watch, to discover improved methods by which the cost of the article he manufactures may be reduced; and, with this in view, it is of great importance to know the precise expense of every process, as well as of the wear and tear of machinery which is due to it.

This knowledge, Babbage goes on to argue, should be used to reduce labour costs:

> One of the first advantages which suggests itself as likely to arise from a correct analysis of the expense of the several processes of any manufacture, is the indication which it would furnish of the course in which improvement should be directed. If a method could be contrived of diminishing by one-fourth the time required for fixing the heads of pins, the expense of making them would be reduced about 13 per cent; whilst a reduction of one-half of the time employed in spinning the coil of wire out of which the pins are cut, would scarcely make any sensible difference in the cost of manufacturing the whole article. It is therefore obvious that the attention would be much more advantageously directed to shortening the former than the latter process.
> (Solomons, 1968, p. 9)

Indeed, as Solomon states,

> It is impossible to take any discussion of the origins of standard costing far without acknowledging its close connection with the scientific management' movement in America generally, for standard cost means little without standard process and standard operating times such as F. W. Taylor's famous paper on 'Shop Management' of 1903, without seeing that many of the elements of standard costing are there.
> (Solomons, 1968, p. 37)

In Taylorism, then, the questions of costing and manpower control, converge. Taylor employed the principles of the division of labour enshrined in the work of Charles Babbage,

> the master manufacturer, by dividing the work to be executed into different processes, each requiring different degrees of skill or of force, can purchase exactly that precise quantity of both which is necessary for each process: whereas, if the whole work were executed by one workman, that person must possess sufficient strength to execute the most laborious of operations into which the work is divided.
> (Babbage, 1971, pp. 175–6)

> The purpose of work study was never, in [Taylor's] mind, to enhance the ability of the worker, to concentrate in the worker a greater share of scientific knowledge, to ensure that as a technique rose, the worker would rise with it. Rather, the purpose was to cheapen the worker by decreasing his training and enlarging his output. In his early book, *Shop Management*, he said frankly that the full possibilities of his system 'will not have been realised until all of the machines in the shop are run by men who are of smaller character and attainments and who are therefore cheaper than those required under the old system'.
> (Braverman, 1974, pp. 117–18)

It is notable that Taylorism, like earlier cost accounting, focused attention on control at the level of the labour process to the neglect of factors pertaining to investment or market considerations, or indeed to any consideration of wider social and economic factors.

BRAVERMAN AND HIS CRITICS

We move now specifically to the issue of labour control and deskilling as expressed in Braverman's influential work and some important critiques thereof. The focus is upon those features of Braverman's work, and of the labour process debate, which are salient to our purpose.

In his seminal book *Labour and Monopoly Capitalism*, Braverman (1974) addresses important and neglected questions concerning the nature of work and employment in advanced capitalist society. His central thesis revolves around the imperative of capitalism which, through the application of the principles of Taylorism, increases management control over work. This being a process by which labour is inevitably and systematically deskilled. Taylorism then, as the epitome of capitalist control, comes to dominate man-management. Its major principles are the appropriation by management of all the skills and knowledge previously in the hands of individual workers; the separation of the 'conception' of all tasks from their 'execution'; and the use of the monopoly of knowledge thus acquired to control each step of the labour process and its mode of execution. Braverman sees the development of all machinery as having the aim of maximising managerial control in this manner. And further that managerial techniques and technology of this nature are not only evident on the shop floor but also in the office and the service sector.

Many critiques of *Labour and Monopoly Capital* have developed Braverman's approach of giving a central position to the labour process in examining control in organisations. Significant modification to Braverman's ideas has come from Andrew Friedman (1977). Friedman's key concern is the relationship between the twin notions of control and resistance. He has developed a typology which locates two 'ideal type' managerial control strategies at opposite ends of a continuum. Workers controlled through a 'responsible autonomy' type strategy will be those whose work is of central strategic importance to the organisation, and/or who have considerable industrial muscle. They are allowed significant autonomy on the job, and are employed on favourable terms and conditions relative to other workers. This strategy 'attempts to harness the adaptability of labour power by giving workers leeway and encouraging them to adapt to changing situations in a manner beneficial to the firm' (Friedman, 1977, p. 78).

'Direct control', on the other hand, limits workers' freedom through close supervision, by minimising the worker's sphere of responsibility and in the last resort, through threats. Workers managed in this way tend to be employed in jobs which are bounded, routinised and limited to one small part of the production process. The greater predictability provided by direct control makes this the preferred strategy for managers, even though it produces workers who are less cooperative and adaptable than the more privileged group. Thus it will be used with any group whose willing compliance is not crucial to the success of the organisation.

Richard Edwards (1979), in 'Contested Terrain', shares Friedman's concern with resistance and control. He examines the way in which prevalent forms of control over labour, will change over time as a response to the industrial conflict which they generate. He describes an evolution from 'simple control', through 'technical control' and finally to 'bureaucratic control', which he sees as necessarily the dominant form of control employed in post-war capitalism.

In *Manufacturing Consent*, Michael Burawoy (1979) has developed Braverman's ideas in an area given only scant consideration by either Edwards or Friedman. His central concern is the process by which management gains the accommodation and compliance of the workforce. He compares the structures and ideologies of control in operation in an engineering factory in 1975 with those employed in the same workplace, in 1945. He demonstrates how the combination of a more relaxed style of management, which turns a blind eye to the various 'fiddles' employed by pieceworkers to earn their maximum bonus, plus the growth of internal labour markets, produced a much higher level of accommodation amongst the workforce in 1975 than was apparent in 1945.

Braverman's work and that of his major critics, has provided the basis for significant debate within the social sciences in recent years. The extent of this debate must be seen to reflect the importance of the issues addressed, but also as partly due to the limitations inherent in the work outlined above. The value of Braverman's work in demonstrating that technology is not an objective, independent force, to which industry must adapt, but rather an instrument of managerial control, is undoubted. However, his approach tends to reify the relations of production and therefore ignore the dynamics of relations between management and worker. As Friedman notes, Braverman, by concentrating on Taylorism, isolated *Capital's* solution to the control problem from the struggle which necessitates such solutions (Friedman, 1977, pp. 80–2). At one level, the existing structure of control and work practices are the result of the interaction between management behaviour and the degree and type of worker response. This dialectic is acted out on a stage upon which material factors (product and labour markets), interact with subjective social forces (beliefs, values and ideologies). Braverman fails to consider subjective forms of control. He attempts to justify his neglect of the subjective elements of workers experience by arguing that he is concerned with the objective effects of capitalist control, on the working class. However in ignoring workers' perceptions he neglects important elements of this control, specifically the ideological resources which may be available to management. This omission also means that he does not consider worker reactions to the control to which they are subject; that which may determine their acceptance of a large measure of managerial authority, and therefore allow it to go unquestioned. Neither, therefore, are the manifestations of management authority, which are the subject of conflict considered.

The weaknesses in Braverman's work, stemming from a preoccupation with technical forms of control, the most damaging of which is the neglect of subjective/ideological aspects of control, are only partially overcome in the critiques cited. Friedman (1977) and Edwards (1979) also neglect questions of ideology – of the acceptance or otherwise of managerial definitions of work relationships. Their failure to consider these issues of ideology and legitimacy means that they do not properly analyse the ambiguous position of the trade union organisation in the workplace. Where, for example in the glass industry, there is a sharing of certain values and of an interest in order, the trade union can be seen to assist management in the control of the workforce. Their neglect of the question of managerial legitimacy means that they fail to discuss reasons why workers may accommodate with managerial decision-making despite the objective conflict of interests. The origins of this compliance arguably lying outside the organisation (Hyman and Brough, 1975). Burawoy (1979) also has a very limited conception of the external factors which may influence orientations to work and work relationships. He fails to consider the potential of prior-socialisation and the dialectical relationship between the values held externally to work and those evident within a work organisation. Thus he concludes that the major determinants of these perceptions are necessarily internal to an organisation.

A common criticism of Braverman is that as well as portraying workers as totally passive, his model of management is of a totally unified, all-knowing, all-powerful body. The major critics also tend to have images of management which suggest a view of managerial activity as necessarily strategically planned. Friedman's use of the term 'strategy' to describe different patterns of managerial behaviour, demonstrates such an assumption. Also Burawoy, in his description of the process by which consent is 'manufactured', portrays management action as consciously planned towards this end. As

Wood and Kelly have asked in their critique of Friedman, do we really want to attribute the characteristics of comprehensiveness, coherence, long-term perspectives and consciousness, which the term 'strategy' implies, to capitalist management? It might be more appropriate to use concepts such as tactics or practices (Wood and Kelly, 1982, p. 84).

A problem which arises in those critiques of Braverman which seek to establish models of control to be used in understanding the operation of a wide variety of organisations, is that they tend to over-generalise from the case-studies which have formed the basis of their theories. This criticism is particularly applicable to Edwards' work, whose case-studies are undertaken entirely in American industry, and have proved very difficult to replicate in Britain. As well as showing over-generalisation at a macro level, at a micro level Edwards' models are too crude to explain the effects of different control strategies, since they omit details of the realities of managerial action at the level of the firm.[2] Friedman in aiming for simplicity, also produces models of managerial strategy which are too general to usefully analyse the dimensions of managerial practice in different organisations. Finally Edwards fails to consider the possibility that different systems of control, apart from bureaucracy, may exist in industry today for positive reasons in terms of profit accumulation.

DEVELOPMENT OF CRITIQUE

What then is now required? It is, we suggest, necessary to qualify an overly deterministic analysis of (a) the degradation of labour; that the 'labour process is rendered independent of craft tradition and workers knowledge' (Braverman, 1974, p. 113), and (b) of workers' resistance – that they will necessarily resist managerial initiatives. There is a need to examine how control structures, and the tendency to deskill, are constrained or facilitated by social, economic and legal factors. As Storey argues, where deskilling is treated as a universalistic imperative of capitalism 'analysis of managerial control strategies is insufficiently located within a wider theoretical scheme, which would permit investigation of why control was required and under what circumstances it would be pressed home. The unevenness across sectors and within sectors is accordingly under-emphasised and under-explored' (Storey, 1983, p. 6). There is then, we argue, a need to examine specific industrial situations with an awareness and sensitivity to the complexity of contending factors, thereby to transcend overly deterministic generalisation.

The focus on control found in the literature discussed tends to be associated with certain ontological problems, whereby control becomes dissociated from the ends for which it exists, and to which ends it may be put. Friedman, as an example, portrays 'control' as an end in itself, neglecting discussion of its purposes. Wood and Kelly make the point that,

> There is a strong tendency in Friedman, as in Braverman, to treat management under capitalism principally as a control function, in which the recalcitrance of labour – class struggle – is elevated to paramount status. Yet for Marx the two principal defining features of the capitalist mode of production were that labour existed as a commodity and that the major objective of social production was the production and realization of surplus value. Although formally acknowledging these features, Friedman draws the conventional (but crude) distinction between the coordinating (or technical) and the authoritative functions of management: the latter is specific to capitalism while the former is 'part of any complicated economic process' (1977a, p. 77). What is missing from either of these functions is the production of profit in its various modes, an activity that has been reduced to the a-historical category of 'coordination'. Capitalism therefore ends up being characterised in effect specifically by control over labour and its various modes.
>
> (Wood and Kelley, 1982, p. 84)

In this work then, the weakness is in the reification of 'control' to the neglect of its purposes for particular groups. Our earlier criticisms (pp. 161–3), dealt with those authors who provide an overly-simplistic analysis of the relationship between managerial behaviour and the pursuit of profit. Further, in Edwards' work as shown above, there is an assumption that bureaucracy is the inevitable and most efficient form of control in modern organisations. This determinism in part stems from a failure to consider ends as paramount rather than means, such that he neglects the possibility that other forms of control within the social relations of production may prove more convenient for management. Increased control over the labour process may[3] be pursued to the end that expropriation is greater, yet it is misleading to conflate control with appropriation. The objective is an increase in the surplus rather than an increase in control.

Turning our attention more closely to the central deskilling thesis, Solomons (1968) has been quoted stressing the role of Taylorism in the origins of standard costing. 'It is impossible,' argues Braverman, 'to overestimate the importance of scientific management in the shaping of the modern corporation' (Braverman, 1974, p. 86). The two great contributions of Taylor, insists Braverman, were in that he 'gave, to a disconnected series of initiatives and experiments, a philosophy and a title' (Braverman, 1974, p. 89).

> The second distinctive feature of Taylor's thought ... was his concept of control. Control has been the essential feature of management throughout its history, but with Taylor it assumed unprecedented dimensions. The stages of Management control over labour before Taylor had included, progressively: the gathering together of workers in a workshop and the dictation of the length of the working day; the supervision of workers to ensure diligent, intense and uninterrupted application; the enforcement of rules against distractions, (talking, smoking, leaving the workplace etc.), that were thought to interfere with application; the setting of production minimums; etc. A worker is under management control when subject to these rules, or any of their extensions and variations. But Taylor raised the concept of control to an entirely new plane when he asserted as an absolute necessity for adequate management the dictation to the worker of the precise manner in which work is to be performed.
>
> (Braverman, 1974, p. 90)

Braverman further argues that,

> Workers who are controlled only by general orders and discipline are not adequately controlled, because they retain their grip on the actual process of labor. So long as they control the labor process itself, they will thwart the efforts to realise the full potential inherent in their labor power. To change this situation control over the labor process must pass to the hands of management, not only in a formal sense but by the control and dictation of each step of the process, including its mode of performance. In pursuit of this end, no pains are too great, no efforts excessive,

because the results will repay all efforts and expenses lavished on this demanding and costly endeavor.

(Braverman, 1974, pp. 100–101)

The concept of deskilling as found in Braverman has four elements. Firstly, there is the separation of planning from working, of 'conception' from 'execution', involving a total divorce of mental from manual labour (Braverman, 1974, p. 114). Secondly, work is thus fragmented through the technical division of labour into meaningless segments. Thirdly, deskilled tasks are distributed amongst the labour force. Thus, finally, work organisation is transformed from 'traditional' craft forms to 'modern' Taylorist forms. As Littler (1982, p. 122) has pointed out, elements one to three represent the deskilling of labour – the process is made independent of the autonomy, creativity and ability of the individual worker and following Babbage (1971, p. 2) labour is cheapened. The fourth element, however, represents the transformation of the structure of control, which, as noted above, is perhaps Taylor's most significant contribution. Capital comes to control every step of the labour process in the 'modern' form of work organisation. Subordination is now 'real' rather than 'formal' as in pre-capitalist forms of production. With formal subordination the manager has the right to manage, but only with the advent of 'real' subordination does he gain the capability.

We now turn to the specific industrial context where we carried out research for two years. How far does this analysis bear scrutiny in the context of the cut-lead crystal industry?

THE LEAD CRYSTAL INDUSTRY

Our subject firm operates in Stourbridge in the West Midlands, which is the centre[4] of the industry which started there in the seventeenth century. Five lead crystal firms are presently operating in Stourbridge. They have a variety of forms of ownership, some retaining links with their founding families and having associated structures and styles of management, while the other two, including the subject of this case-study, are owned by multi-national conglomerates. The industry produces luxury tableware, which ranges from liqueur glasses, through wine glasses to large decanters and bowls, all of which are decorated by cut patterns. All of the firms market their products in a way which gives emphasis to the hand-crafted nature of the process and to the quality and exclusivity of its products.

The five firms have a total workforce of approximately 1500, the vast majority of whom live within a five-mile radius of their work. More significantly 85 per cent of the employees in the firm studied live in four clusters of half a mile or less in radius. The glass industry is a major employer in the area, although it has faced competition, at various times, from employers in other parts of the West Midlands. Due to the long historical association between the industry and the locality it is common for several generations of the same family to have had a life-time of employment in glass production.

Workers in the industry are all organised into the National Union of Flint Glassworkers, which is the product of a merger in 1948 between the unions representing the two crafts in the industry; glass 'making' and glass 'cutting'. The union represents glass-workers in other parts of the country – but its main branch, and the centre of its organisation, is in Stourbridge. The union has no full-time officers, although both its President and General Secretary are retired glass-workers. Negotiations on the basic pay and conditions of glass-workers are carried out between the National Officers of the NUFGW and the Stourbridge Crystal Glass Manufacturers Association, representing the employers. However details of payment are negotiated within the individual firms, which has lead to considerable disparity in the form and level of earnings received by workers in each firm.

The process by which cut lead crystals ware is produced can be divided into two parts, glass 'making' and glass 'cutting'. Glass-making is the production of 'blank' (uncut), pieces of glass. Glass-cutting is the process by which 'blanks are decorated'. As far as records go back – to the mid-seventeeth century – glass-making has been carried out within what is known as a 'chair'. A chair is the archetype of work group production. Dependent on the type of item being produced, the chair consists of a hierarchy of four or five men who work together in close harmony. The nature and pace of the interaction between the members of the chair is heavily influenced by the nature of the material being handled, that is molten glass or 'metal'. The 'blower' (second in the chair hierarchy), gathers the appropriate quantity of metal from the 'pot'[5] on a blowing iron. He uses a hand-held open mould to shape the lump of metal. The blower then begins the blowing process. Firstly he gives quick puffs down the blowing iron so that the metal becomes a small balloon.

The most skilled part of the blowing process is then undertaken. He distributes the glass at different thicknesses around the balloon. While doing this he keeps the metal swinging to aid the distribution. Finally he places the metal in a mould, and blows it to its full size. The shaped bowl of the glass is then passed to the 'servitor', who is the senior member of those chairs which make wine glasses. The servitor determines the pace of work of his team. He adds the stem and foot to a wine glass. The tools he uses for this are extremely simple: a large pair of calipers is employed to shape the leg of the glass, and the foot is finished off by being rolled against a truing board ('marver'), made of burnt pearwood. The metal for making the leg and foot of the glass is gathered from the pot by the third member of the team – the 'bit-gatherer', using a solid iron known as a 'bit-iron'. The bit-gatherer assists the servitor by holding the main bowl of the glass at the end of the blowing-iron while the servitor adds the foot. Finally the junior glass-maker, the 'taker-in', 'cracks' the finished blank off the iron and takes it to the 'Lehr' which is a slow-moving belt passing through an 'annealing kiln'. This kiln, which slows down the speed at which the glass cools, so as to ensure the release of internal stresses induced in articles by the making process, is the last phase of making.

The skill content of the work of members of the chair is high, not only in terms of the technical and manipulative requirements of the job, but also in terms of the knowledge of the nature and variability of the metal. Both a new pot and one which is low on metal make it more difficult to 'gather' without collecting impurities. Additionally the metal is prone to discolouration which may not be apparent in the pot but which will flaw the finished blank. (A vocabulary has developed to describe inadequacies in the pot mix, referring to the metal as 'stony' or 'cordy'.) It is therefore necessary to produce those items of glass which will make best use of the metal available. Knowing how to evaluate this is one of the foundations of the glass-maker's craft, and hence a mechanism of craft control.

None of the four elements which it is argued (per Braverman, 1974, p. 12), are the specifically capitalist forms of management control, characterise crystal glass manufacture. Intensification through deskilling may be a means of increasing expropriation, however, as Hobsbawm argues, there exists a variety of initiatives which have been accepted to this end, of which deskilling is just one. Each may be applied at different times according to the exigencies of the particular context. Intensification may only be applied when 'pressure of profit margins, increased competition, the demands of labour, or other inescapable facts forced a change'. Otherwise 'it was safer, if less efficient to stick to the old ways'[6] (Hobsbawm, 1964, p. 356). In other words, management may prefer to conserve existing stable profits rather than gamble them against the *possibility* that changed practices might increase the level of surplus.

THE 'OLD WAYS' - STABILITY AND CHALLENGE

The research of Bryn Jones (1982) throws light upon the conditions in which the 'old ways' may survive. From his work in the field of technology and deskilling, Bryn Jones argues that there is no inherent tendency to deskilling. Three features of the enterprise, he suggests, are pertinent to the conditions in which deskilling will occur. Firstly there are 'the traditions, strengths and strategies of the trade unions concerned and their relationship with the relevant labour markets'. The second feature is the nature of the product and product market. Jones refers to Bright's (1958) study which compared mechanisation between the electric light bulb industry and the footwear industry. The latter's lower level of mechanisation was related to the variability of the product and the changing product market. The third feature is the structure of the organisation, its technology and managerial control systems.

Technology and managerial control systems are, as both Palmer (1975) and Zeitlin (1979) demonstrate, interrelated. Palmer argues that craft was destroyed in the US steel industry because of the nature and appropriateness of the available technology (Palmer, 1975, p. 31). With the arrival of the stop watch, paternalism was eroded and resistance to the new methods engendered worker solidarity. As a result, where technology was not available or was not appropriate, it was possible for workers to resist skill dilutions and the new Taylorist methods. Palmer charts working class resistance to the 'thrust for efficiency' in the US 1903-22 (Palmer, 1975, pp. 41-7). Zeitlin shows how the fates of engineers and compositors (1890-1930) flowed from their ability to control new technology in the context of the relative power of the employer. The latter emanated from their solidarity, the nature of the product (machine tools and newspapers), and product market and the potential utility of the new technology to the employer (Zeitlin, 1979, pp. 267-8).

Resistance to deskilling in the crystal glass industry has been rooted in a solidarity based upon control of entry to the craft. Strikes in the industry have been rare. From 1851, when the National Flint Glass Makers Friendly Society of Great Britain and Ireland was formed, until the First World War, there appear to have been only five strikes. In each dispute the issue of craft control looms large[7] (Hopkins, 1974). Two disputes, of 1858–9 and 1902–4, were over the issue of the trade union right to fill vacancies and the ratio of apprentices to journeymen (skilled men). In 1886 a dispute over the recruitment of additional men led to a lock-out[8]. The dispute of 1896 illustrates the importance of craft control. The strike in 1896 writes one authority, was 'over the offer of wages of less than the standard rate to a glass-maker' (Hopkins, 1974, p. 26). However according to contemporary sources[9] the dispute revolved around (a) the right of the society to appoint workers when vacancies occurred, and (b) the maintenance of an agreed rate of pay for a given class of worker, rather than the class of work currently engaged upon. Further evidence that factors challenging craft control lay behind the dispute is found in the biography of John Northwood who worked as a manager in the industry from 1850 to 1902. 'In 1896,' writes John Northwood, 'a regrettable dispute arose . . . the firm[10] had by this time greatly increased the manufacture of . . . mould blown tableware[11] "servitors" had to make the legs and feet after the bowls had been blown into the mould. The skill to cast the small quantity of glass onto the centre of the bottom of the bowl for the making of the leg, was only acquired after long practice. The making of the foot [however] . . . was comparatively easy and could soon be learnt' (Northwood, 1958, p. 129).

In order that the skilled labour of the 'servitor' could be dispensed with Northwood,

> devised a plan to use short canes of glass for the stems. After having a long length of cane of suitable thickness drawn out he had this cut up into the length of the desired stems and given to the boys they were teaching in the glasshouse. One end of these short canes was held in a special 'grip' or 'gadget' so that it could be heated at the other end of the furnace. When this was sufficiently hot the boy holding it sat in the glassmakers chair and another boy gathered the required quantity of hot glass on another iron and brought it to the boy in the chair. He cast sufficient glass onto the heated end of his cane stem and then

proceeded in the usual way to roll the lot along the arm of the chair while using the glassmakers' foot boards to squeeze the lump of glass into a thin circular plate and so form the foot. He now had a stem and foot in one piece and after annealing it was then taken to another department where the wine glasses were to be completed. The boys soon became skilful in this operation. Meanwhile the bowls of the wine glasses had been blown in the paste moulds by other boys, who also soon became practised hands at this.

(Northwood, 1958, p. 129)

Thus we see the grounds of the 1896 dispute[12] as for the other major disputes in the industry, in craft control. Control of entry was the basis upon which the union attempted to sustain its negotiating power with management. This power was then deployed, when and insofar as market conditions allowed, to maintain wages and the skill content of work.[13]

Extracts from the *Pottery Gazette* of the period give the flavour of both the extent of the control and the employers' attitude towards it:

So senseless is the attitude of the workmen's leaders, and so much do they seem to arrange beforehand for embarrassing the masters, that the only conclusion left to a glass-master is that some of the leaders could do no worse if they were secretly subsidised by the German glasshouses to ruin the English trade ... there is no industry in the Kingdom where better wages are paid and less hours worked, and yet every obstacle is put in the way of prosperity by the most tyrannical society ever organised in the United Kingdom.[14]

It was in their power to have helped themselves as well as their employers by lightening the conditions which fettered production, but they would not budge from the narrowness and restrictions of their 'laws',[15], written and unwritten.... One position the men take up is that workmen must be paid alike, and the drone under their rules have been paid the same as the best hand. The tail was the head, and the interests of the best man are made subordinate to the interest of one of inferior ability. A certain number of articles have to be made per 'turn'[16] and the number is fixed to suit the drone. The good workman could make more and could earn more money by doing so, and benefit his employer, but he is made to feel that it would be apostasy to his society to do so.[17]

The importance of technology in the deskilling thesis is linked to Jones' second feature; the product and product market, by the way in which the concept of 'skill' is employed. There is implicit in the Braverman argument concerning the necessary separation of 'conception' from 'execution' the assumption that 'conception' is nil-sum. The implication is that one person, or group's enhancement of understanding over a particular process or series of processes is accompanied by the equivalent loss in understanding by others. However the acquisition by a supervisor or manager of overall knowledge of a process does not mean that each individual worker's knowledge is thereby reduced over part or whole of the process[18] (Elmbaum and Wilkinson, 1979; Littler, 1978). Managerial recruitment from below has been the norm in the crystal glass industry. It is seen as a means of maintaining a management which has the ability – based upon knowledge – to manage. Owing to the nature of the process – as described above – it is not possible, nor indeed desirable to reduce the skill levels of the glass-makers. This is, as we have noted, not unconnected to the nature of the product and the product market, the latter being based on the products craft content. Crystal glassware is aimed at the luxury market, great play being made of the 'hand-made' and 'hand-cut', nature of the articles. The aim is thereby to differentiate the product from the mass-produced, machine-made commodity. The product market is, then, small, specialised and with the emphasis on quality selling at a high markup. Looking, then, at the demand side of the labour market, we see an absence of economic pressure to intensify work, plus an awareness that attempts to intensify the labour process may mean a trade-off in cooperation and quality.

Present-day crystal glass manufacture is a form of production where the possibilities for the intensification of labour are limited by the nature of, and the workers detailed control over and knowledge of, the process.[19] In glass-making incorporating work methods, where opportunities for intensification are absent (or limited), surplus value may be created or increased by the lengthening of the working day. By the 1840s a pattern of working hours in crystal glass had been established which survived in Stourbridge until the late 1930s. Work began at 6.00 a.m. on Monday[20] with a six hour 'turn'. It then recommenced after a six hour rest period with a further six hour turn finishing at midnight. This pattern of six hours on and six hours off continued until midnight Thursday, making an eight turn, four day week. The glassmaker had Friday to Sunday free.[21] This pattern appears to have suited both employers and union. Both parties claimed that such highly skilled work could not be maintained for more than a six hour period (Hopkins, 1973; Enquiry into the workings of the Factories and Workshops Act 1875–6).

This structure of work and leisure thus incorporated a long weekend which could be used for setting up production for the following week. This would include the servicing and rebuilding where necessary of the pots. 'Pot-setting', which involves charging the pot with a batch of the required raw materials and starting the 'melt', was done on Friday morning. A minimum of 36 hours of firing the pot is then needed before a metal of the required properties is ready for making to commence. For employers then, the system of turns had the advantage of high capital utilisation within a process, the technology of which would otherwise have severely limited it. Neither union nor employers attempted to alter this system, until the economic upturn prior to the Second World War. The employers did however attempt to intensify work. The makers of Stourbridge limited output to two moves per turn. A move being a unilaterally imposed level of output – particular to each type of article – for a three hour period. In 1882, during the Great Depression, the employers' organisation[22] approached the Stourbridge makers with a view to abolishing the two move per turn level of output restriction. Although other areas, including Birmingham, had already conceded this and were producing up to two and a half moves per turn, the Stourbridge makers were intransigent.[23] This position was maintained until the interwar period.

Intensification of labour is not synonymous with deskilling. Where appropriate, as above, management may attempt to increase the rate of execution rather than, as Babbage (1971) argues, break down tasks into their component operations. Glass-making is such a situation. Management has made few attempts to alter the process of production and those which it has made have tended to be firmly resisted by the glassmakers themselves. However management has had some success recently in increasing output without the substitution of technology for skill. A major factor in this success has been the weekly production meetings instigated by a new production manager[24]. These are attended by all the supervisors from the different departments in the factory. These meetings can be understood to have a dual function. Firstly they have a coordinating[25] function, they provide a venue for the discussion of any production problems and make it possible to 'iron-out' any which are the result, for example, of failures of communication between different departments. However, more significantly the production meetings also have an important role in control. The production manager is able to confront each supervisor with the performance of his department, in the presence of management from the rest of the factory, and demand evidence of improvement for the next meeting. In this forum he has publicly challenged the arguments, based in the mythology of glass-making, put forward by the glasshouse supervisor, to justify 'low' production levels in his department. This mythology is tied to the special vocabulary[26] of glassmaking discussed above. It stresses that the peculiar qualities of metal make it extremely difficult to work with and take a life-time of learning to understand. As a respone to the pressure from higher management, supervision in the glasshouse has made some direct attempts to encourage the glassmakers to raise production levels. However it has also taken advantage of more indirect methods to the same end. The union representative was requested to tell his members that their jobs would be under threat unless they modified their behaviour in terms of punctuality, and attendance on the job. Thus not only was the management in the factory able to increase production without introducing deskilling, the role of the trade union in the plant minimised the need for increased supervision.

CONTROL AND POWER

It has been argued above that it is misleading to conceive of management as all-seeing and all-powerful. There is inherent in such an approach a misconception concerning the nature and mobilisation of managerial power. Control by management over the workforce implies an imbalance of power between the two groups. The overt deployment of objective power over the workforce by management is a strategy of last resort. The most significant power which management has is the willing compliance of the workforce. The mobilisation of coercive power jeopardises the precarious legitimacy which management may possess in the eyes of the subordinates. But compliance with managerial wishes may not have its origins in shared values, as suggested by a systems model, but rather in an engineered commitment. Behaviour is not understood then in terms of the internalisation of organisational norms, but rather in terms of positive oppositional and survival strategies by the workforce.

There exists an extensive literature on the 'institutionalisation' of industrial conflict, demonstrating that managerial interests are best served by (a) the recognition that employees perceive a conflict of interests within the employment relationship, (b) by conceding limited (and often superficial) control and autonomy over work task execution and (c) by developing structures and procedures, which, rather than suppressing conflict, encourage its overt expression. There is evidence that such practices enhance managerial legitimacy and that paradoxically, the overt expression of conflict, rather than being detrimental, is functional for managerial interests.[27]

In the case study firm there are two union representatives, one for the glasshouse and one for the cutting shop. They are known as Factory Secretaries. These secretaries are widely consulted by management on a range of issues. Indeed they often receive information on proposed changes in the factory before the relevant supervisors. One supervisor said of the secretary in his department 'He's always been in the know, far more than we have, us supervisors and managers ... because [the Technical Director] always had him up there discussing it before he told us.' This consultation is not to be seen as entirely or even largely in terms of the sanctions available to the Factory Secretaries if they were not consulted. Rather it can be seen as a reflection of the union's importance to management in containing conflict in the plant.

The senior secretary has served for 20 years. He demonstrates a clear acceptance of managerial norms in the factory, indeed, in some instances he has been more concerned with efficiency in the plant than some members of management. He has, for example, urged redundancies in the factory for the 'survival' of the company. His position is clear, that 'bad' workers – those who are late, absentee or dishonest – are therefore bad craftsmen and do not deserve the protection of a union embodying many craft values. This principle was employed when management requested his help in selecting a group of workers to be made redundant. Thus in this example it is shown how the application of craft norms by a union representative can be clearly functional in terms of management's interests. At times the union representatives are used to put over what are essentially managerial ultimatums. An example of this was given above: in a meeting of glassmakers, their union representative assured them that there would be no further redundancies in the near future. But he stressed that this was contingent upon the 'discipline' of the glassmakers. They must endeavour to increase their output, they must improve their time-keeping and attendance, and there must be no informal breaks from the glasshouse without clocking out.[28]

The institutionalisation of conflict is one aspect of the exercise of managerial power, another, equally important, relates to the external context of the organisation and concerns the control of entry. Management in the glass industry puts considerable stress on a recruitment policy which by employing people from particular parts of the local community provides workers who already share many of the values of the industry and who accept its particular conditions of employment as the norm. For this reason, traditionally, recruitment was almost entirely based upon the recommendations and contacts of existing trusted employees. As a result the workforce was composed of a tight network of friends, neighbours and relations. It is still the case that a new employee is more likely than not to have a member of his family already employed, at least in the industry and probably in the firm. A further important aspect of recruitment policy in the industry is the preference for school-leavers. It is felt that people employed straight from school will be free of the conflictual norms which experience in another workplace may have given them. The use of the extended family not only has a function for management in controlling entry into the organisation, it can also provide a secondary internal control mechanism: senior members of a family who have achieved considerable status and respect as craftsmen, may use their authority over junior relations to prevent their behaviour from damaging this position.

The crude exercise of power only becomes necessary when and where the legitimacy of one party to exercise authority over another is questioned. As Fox (1974) has written, whereas authority implies an obligation on the subordinate to accept the position and legitimacy of management and hence will result in cooperative behaviour, the exercise of power (implying a lack of legitimacy) generates resistance, expressions of conflict and hence produces diminishing returns to management (Fox, 1974, pp. 33–4). Thus as Cressey and MacInnes point out, 'contrary to the implications of the real subordination of labour argument, capital has an active interest in suppressing its own domination in the workplace'. In other words the great or careless use of material power threatens management's ideological power. In practice in the employment relationship, albeit there is unequal access to ideological and material resources, management needs the cooperation of the workforce. It is, drawing again on Cressey and MacInnes, 'precisely because capital must surrender the use of its means of production to labour that capital must to some degree seek a cooperative relationship with it' (Cressey and MacInnes, 1980, p. 17; quoted in Storey, 1983, p. 47).

It is hence evident that whereas Braverman (1974) presents craft control as an obstacle to the realisation of surplus (p. 57), this is not necessarily the case. Craft workers may resist deskilling, or as above, the conditions which compel or facilitate it may be absent. Further, high levels of surplus value may accrue to the owners of capital without high levels of overt control being exercised over the workforce. Where worker resistance is anticipated management may, as we have seen, attempt to 'organise production in such a way as to minimise opportunities for resistance and even to alter workers' perception of the desirability of opposition' (Wood, 1982, p. 116).

Now the very existence of certain types of craft consciousness, may, particularly in the context of the institutionalisation of conflict referred to above, facilitate or even render superfluous the latter strategy. Further if craft control creates and sustains a sense of control, this is functional for management. It becomes part of a process of insitutionalisation, complementing a paternalistic style of management and encouraging any tendency for trade union incorporation. Craft control must be seen within the context of particular social and economic values. Control over the immediate work process may be itself embodied within a structure of subordination.[29] This tendency is evident, where, as in the crystal glass industry, craft consciousness is associated with a trade unionism which displays labouristic orientations (Nichols and Armstrong, 1976).

CONCLUDING COMMENTS

Control is thus a complex issue. Industry is not, as it is often portrayed, monolithic nor is it homogenous. The extent of deskilling and the form of managerial control are the result of an interaction between; rational choice;[30] historical development and continuing intra and extra organisational negotiation. In practice managerial action is limited by formidable constraints, thus choice is never free and often marginal. Management's control strategies, then, must be seen in terms of both competing demands and the variety of constraints upon their actions. Additionally the extent and nature of worker resistance is played out in a dialectic between what is feasible in terms of market, product and technology, and the degree to which labour can marshal the power to resist managerial initiatives. The role of trade union organisation in this relationship can be either an enabling or a constraining one. Where the terrain is contested (Edwards, 1979), the frontier of control is negotiated and renegotiated continually.

Action is to be understood in terms of structure and consciousness. Explanation of action is adequate, in Weberian analysis, only when it operates at both the level of 'cause' and of 'meaning' (Weber, 1948). An explanation of managerial initiative or of worker response is inadequate then, if it fails to analyse both the objective ability (power) and the subjective inclination (desire) to pursue a certain course of action. Each may be pursued at various times according to the exigencies of the particular context.

Notes

1. This is not to adopt a 'pluralist' model of organisations. It is a recognition that a simple dichotomous model of 'labour' and 'capital' is crude. The more or less permanent coalitions of interest groups that arise, will however, form along hierarchical lines. That is along the dimension of the 'capital' – 'labour' struggle, rather than randomly as in a pluralist model.
2. Some of the deficiencies referred to here are met in Gordon, Edwards and Reich (1982).
3. Control 'may' be exercised so as to increase the power of a group or profession. See Burns and Karlson (1979).
4. Lead crystal forms operate in other parts of the country including London and Edinburgh, but Stourbridge is very much the centre of the industry, both in terms of the level of production and of organisation.
5. A 'pot' is a crucible holding up to three-quarters of a ton of metal, set in and fired by a furnace. The pot is enclosed, save for a small access hole for the collection of the metal.
6. It should be noted that Bobsbawm's use of the term 'efficient' here, is vague and therefore somewhat problematic.

7. The glasscutters, whose organisation the United Glass Cutters Mutual Assistance and Protective Society had been formed in 1844, also had an arduous battle over the apprenticeship issue in 1865–6.
8. The *Flint Glassmakers Magazine* 27 Nov. 1866 and 26 Nov. 1887.
9. The *Pottery Gazette* Oct. 1986, pp. 814–15.
10. The firm is Stevens and Williams of Stourbridge, one of the prominent long-established enterprises, where John Northwood worked.
11. Mould blowing was generally introduced in the industry in the 1880s.
12. Interesting corroboration of the nature of this dispute is found in the *Pottery Gazette* Dec. 1896, pp. 1083–4. A paper is in preparation.
13. We are here simply attempting to demonstrate how in crystal glass, craft was defended when conditions allowed. It is necessary to look at wider market conditions in order to explain why, for example, in the 1880s, when mould blown techniques were introduced in 'wine' production, making workmen redundant, that this appears not to have been fought by withdrawal of labour.
14. *Pottery Gazette* 1 Sep. 1896, p. 716.
15. 'Laws' refers to the societies' rules concerning promotion and recruitment, including rules on the ratio of apprentices.
16. 'Turn' refers to a period of time, which during this period was six hours.
17. *Pottery Gazette* 1 Dec. 1896, p. 1083.
18. Further it should be noted that the widespread use of sub-contracting in many craft-based industries demonstrates that employers did not need to subsume to themselves knowledge of the process, but rather, gained considerably from not being directly involved in supervision.
19. The glass 'chair' having been operational in a period of the small owner-producer, possibly having antecedents in the guild system of production.
20. By the 1870s, with the existence of 'St. Monday', the working week had become Tuesday to Friday (J. Northwood, 1911, p. 131).
21. A selected few would take a 'turn' on Friday to 'pot-set'.
22. The Midland Association of Glassmakers.
23. Stourbridge, by mid-century, seems to have established itself as the major centre of the craft. The Birmingham Branch appears to have included workers employed upon less skilled work such as lamp chimneys. See *Pottery Gazette*.
24. This manager was appointed approximately seven years ago and represents the new regime who came from outside the glass industry and are critical of its myths.
25. cf. Carchedi (1975). Although it should be noted that Carchedi's typology over-simplifies a complex problem.
26. For an interesting discussion of the role of vocabulary in power relationships see Mills (1956). For a more recent treatment see Batstone (1979).
27. See Coser (1956) for the classic argument on the functions of the expression of overt conflict; Purcell (1979) is an explicit encouragement to management to employ such strategies; See Hyman (1972, ch. 4) for a review of the literature in this area.

28. There is no intended implication here that the trade unionists discussed are acting irrationally. Clearly elements of a realistic perception of survival inform their behaviour.
29. This may be compared with the obfuscating notion that alienation is eliminated by conceding control over immediate work tasks yet leaving workers within a wider and more pervasive structure of control.
30. That is, related to identifiable goals.

References

C. Babbage, *On the Economy of Machinery and Manufactures* (London: Charles Knight, 1971).
W. Baldamus, *Efficiency and Effort* (London: Tavistock, 1961).
E. Batstone, 'Systems of Domination, Accommodation and Industrial Democracy' in T. R. Burns and E. Karlson, ibid.
H. Braverman, *Labour and Monopoly Capital* (Monthly Review Press, 1974).
J. R. Bright, 'Does Automation Raise Skill Requirements?' in *Harvard Business Review*, vol. 36, no. 4 (1958).
M. Burawoy, *Manufacturing consent* (University of Chicago Press, 1979).
T. R. Burns and E. Karlson, *Work and Power* (London: Sage, 1979).
O. Carchedi, 'Reproduction of social classes at the level of production', *Economy and Society*, vol. 4, no. 4 (1975).
L. A. Coser, *The Functions of Social Conflict* (Routledge and Kegan Paul, 1956).
P. Cressey and J. McInnes, 'Voting for Ford', *Capital and Class*, no. 11 (1980).
R. C. Edwards, *Contested Terrain: The Transformation of the Workplace in the Twentieth Century* (Heinemann, 1979).
B. Elmbaum and F. Wilkinson, 'Industrial Relations and Uneven Development', *Cambridge Journal of Economics*, vol. 3 (1979).
Enquiry into the Workings of the Factories and Workshops Act (1875–6).
A. Fox, *Man Mismanagement* (Heinemann, 1974).
A. L. Friedman, *Industry and Labour: Class Struggle at Work and Monopoly Capitalism* (Macmillan, 1977).
D. Gordon, R. C. Edwards and M. Reich, *Segmented Work, Divided Workers* (Cambridge University Press, 1982).
E. J. Hobsbawm, *Labouring Men* (Weidenfeld and Nicolson, 1964).
E. J. Hopkins, 'An Anatomy of Strikes in the Glass Industry 1850–1914', *Midland History*, vol. 11, no. 1 (1973).
R. Hyman and I. Brough, *Social Values and Industrial Relations* (Basil Blackwell, 1975).
R. Hyman, *Strikes* (Fontana, 1972).
B. Jones, 'Destruction or Redistribution of Engineering skills? The case for numerical control' in S. Wood (ed.) (1982).
C. R. Littler, *The development of the Labour Process in Capitalist Societies* (Heinemann, 1982).

C. R. Littler, 'Understanding Taylorism', *British Journal of Sociology*, vol. 29 (1978).
C. W. Mills, *The Power Elite* (Oxford University Press, 1956).
T. Nichols and P. Armstrong, *Workers Divided* (Fontana, 1976).
J. Northwood, *John Northwood I: His Contribution to the Stourbridge Glass Industry* (Mark and Moody, 1958).
B. Palmer, 'Class Conception and Conflict', *Review of Radical Political Economy*, vol. 7, no. 2 (1975).
J. Purcell, 'A Strategy for Management Control in Industrial relations' in J. Purcell and R. Smith (eds) *The Control of Work* (Macmillan, 1979).
E. Solomons, *Studies in Cost Analysis* (Sweet and Maxwell, 1968).
J. Storey, *Managerial Prerogative and the Questions of Control* (Routledge and Kegan Paul, 1983).
M. Weber, *From Max Weber: Essays in Sociology*, ed. H. H. Gerth and C. Wright Mills (Routledge and Kegan Paul, 1948).
S. Wood, (ed.) *The Degradation of Work* (Hutchinson, 1982).
S. Wood and J. Kelly, 'Taylorism, responsible autonomy and management strategy' in S. Wood (ed.) 82, op cit.
J. Zeitlin, 'Craft Control and the Division of Labour: Engineers and Compositors in Britain 1890–1930', *Cambridge Journal of Economics*, vol. 3, no. 3 (1979).

10 The Management and Control of Experts and Expertise: The Case of the Nurse

Wai Fong Chua

I INTRODUCTION

Authors in this volume have analysed management control from a variety of perspectives. It has been equated with control by a dominant managerial/capitalist class (Black and Neathey) and with holistic control of the organisation (Otley). In the first paper, control is seen as being exercised oppressively by one class over another. In the latter, control is conceptualised as a system of structures and processes which are 'managed' by both superiors and subordinates in order to ensure organisational viability and prosperity.

The concept of management control illustrated in this paper has both these facets. Control is seen as a fluid set of strategies and structures which are instituted by actors to ensure the 'success' of their organisation. But the organisation in this case is not a manufacturing or commercial concern like British Petroleum or Woolworths. It is an organisation of experts – professionals who claim a common identity through training and certification. The concern here is with the management and control of these experts and their expertise by fellow experts. Such control may be the result of overt elite power or it may simply emerge in a non-intentional, complex way.

Three aspects of the control of and by experts justify its position as a distinct subject for analysis. First, the growth in the number of 'experts' has been substantial. At the beginning of the nineteenth century there were only three recognised professions in the Anglo-Saxon world: divinity, law and medicine (Larson, 1977). Today, Foucault (1977) writes that the 'judges of normality' are everywhere. We have the professional accountant, lawyer, information scientist, etc. Second, professions whether deserving or not are special occupational groups which are ascribed high status and unique privileges such as peer control, a relative lack of state regulation and greater economic rewards.

Third, there remain important gaps in our knowledge of the processes through which experts are created and controlled. Although much energy has been devoted to a study of the 'man of knowledge' and the 'intelligentsia' this has tended to analyse their cultural impact and role (Mannheim, 1935; Znaniecki, 1940) and the tension which exists between an expert's professed technical and social image (Benveniste, 1977; Ravetz, 1973). It was not until recently that the claims to privilege of the professional were critically examined and located within the class and labour divisions of Anglo-Saxon society. In the last 15 years, the work of Freidson (1970, 1972), Larson (1977), Navarro (1976) and Gramsci (1971) have led to certain insights into the structure of professions and the process of professionalisation.

The professional's claims to privilege and universal service are no longer seen as stable and a priori characteristics. Instead they are identified as being both a product of and an input to a territorial quest: the carving-out of a niche in the social division of labour. As Larson (1977) points out, a profession, whatever else it may be is first and foremost a class-based, self-interested monopoly of people who seek to transform:

> one order of scarce resources – a special knowledge and skills – into another – social and economic rewards. To maintain scarcity implies a tendency to monopoly: monopoly of expertise in the market, monopoly of status in a system of stratification.
> (Larson, 1977, p. xvii)

A profession thus has to *make* itself into a special and valued type of occupation. In addition, a profession does not always act as a harmonious, homogeneous whole. Its apparent internal cohesion, like its strategic and social importance needs to be managed and controlled via a myriad of relations.

This macro-structural critique of the profession has contributed much to the debates about professionalism. However, it still leaves unanalysed the cognitive basis of professional control. The claim of the professional to scarce expertise remains uncontested. But are those skills intrinsically scarce or is that scarcity created and managed? What are the processes which aid a profession in the monopolistic appropriation of a skill? What role does 'training' play in imparting 'scarce' expertise? How do the needs of the community and the State become intertwined with the organisational problem of achieving professional prosperity?

This paper seeks to complement the recent structural critique of professional power by analysing the management and control of the cognitive base of one of the largest corporation of 'new' professionals – the nurses. Its purpose is to examine how 'nursing skill' and 'training' have been socially constructed such that monopoly power was engendered and maintained.[1] Nursing is a skill. But its claims to scarcity have, in part, emerged and in part been managed by nursing elites. Like the directors of BP or BSC, nursing leaders have sought to ensure organisational viability by creating a strategic advantage within its environment. At times, such overt control was clearly observable. At others, events did not appear to be the intention of any one group/person; their emergence appearing to flow from a complex balance of forces both social and individual. The final outcome, however, is one of scarcity, whether through intent or otherwise.

The emergence-creation of scarcity has, in turn, generated contradictions within nursing which threaten to undermine its claims to 'professionalism'. These tensions include (a) a rise of unionisation among younger nurses; (b) an imposition of an industrial management structure (the Salmon Plan, 1966) within a 'caring' occupation; and (c) the elevation of 'mental' labour in a traditionally pragmatic occupation.

We begin an analysis of these present contradictions with a brief, historical discussion of nineteenth-century nursing.

II THE ORIGINS OF MONOPOLY

(i) Untrained but not Unskilled: The Nurse before 1840

The history of the nursing profession in England has been ably documented by numerous historians.[2] It is not the intention here to recount these descriptions of the origins of nursing. Instead, these histories will be relied upon to highlight the processes and means by which nurses came to gain monopoly over an area of competence.

British nursing has its historical antecedents in a lowly Victorian social class – domestic servants.[3] As Abel-Smith (1960) points out, although there had been religious orders which dedicated themselves to the service of the sick, British nursing at the start of the nineteenth century was no more than a specialised form of charring. Nursing in the workhouses was carried out by people of an even lower social class – able-bodied paupers.

A nurse then was not formally trained and did not carry out the wide range of duties now performed by the hospital nurse, but this did not mean that she was unskilled. Braverman (1974) defines skill as that combination of knowledge of materials and processes with the practical manual dexterities required to carry on a specific service or branch of production. And the untrained nurse did require and in some cases possess skill. Illness creates dependency and the sick not only require medical diagnosis and treatment but personal service. It is in the provision of this service, the administration of the treatment prescribed by the doctor and the careful monitoring of a patient's state of health which, even in those early days, constituted nursing skill. It was the nurse who was the 'doctor's eyes' when he was not present.

In addition, the doctor whether consciously or not 'trained' the nurse. This was because the nurse and 'sister' tended to stay on one ward for a long time and thus learnt what was required of her from a particular doctor. Historians agree that this did produce some very skilled nurses.[4] However, the level of skill was very variable. If nurses were carefully selected, adequately supervised and sufficiently taught by the medical staff, the standard was high. But where the hospital or workhouse did not take proper steps to ensure the level of skill, the standard of nursing was extremely low.

In summary, nursing before the institution of formal training was essentially a low-status job. It was performed by woman servants or paupers. Neither the pay nor the conditions of work were such as to attract educated women from the truly 'genteel' families. However, skill was not absent and was usually acquired in an informal fashion through practice, supervision and teaching by the medical staff.

(ii) **The Institution of Nurse Training: The Germ of Monopoly**

The second half of the nineteenth century saw the introduction of training within nursing, a process often regarded as highly important in any occupation's march to professionalism (Larson, 1977). Larson argues that training, or more specifically the monopoly of instruction and credentialing helps secure monopoly power because it aids product/service differentiation, standardisation, quality control and marketing. It is training which gives the professional a commodity to sell, demarcates him/her as a privileged knower and imparts exchange value to the practitioner. It is also a means of professional socialisation and of inculcating a sense of solidarity.

Such a depiction of the role of training though characteristic of the later struggles within nursing does not adequately analyse the early development of training. For there was no one single group seeking to control the market for their services purely to reap economic benefits. Also, training was not apparently intended to restrict supply or to advance the profession for its own sake. Instead diverse interests, relations and localised desires merged to form the early structure of nurse training.

It was Nightingale, more than any other nursing leader, who focused on the benefits of training. It would standardise skill but in a way which would be beneficial to patient care. It is important to highlight that Nightingale's concept of a nurse was not the modern one of a woman equipped with large amounts of examinable knowledge and technological interests. Indeed, she believed that neither the doctor nor the nurse cured, it was Nature who did so. The duty of the nurse (invariably female) was then to place her patients in the most appropriate situation for Nature to act upon them. This notion of training gave rise to a pragmatic training course which was based on several principles.

First, Nightingale insisted on a maximum of moral stature and a minimum of educational attainment. No longer were nurses to work unsupervised on the wards or to sleep on male wards. Uniforms had to be worn at all times and the wearing of jewellery was frowned upon. Indeed, any lapse in sobriety or truthfulness meant instant dismissal. This stress on sexual morality, was understandable. Like other Victorians, Nightingale believed that morality preceded all other virtues. She had particularly admired the 'high tone' and 'pure devotion' of the nurses at a German religious order. But personal preference aside, Nightingale knew that in order for the occupation to be reformed, it had to obtain recruits who could read and write. And mothers of literate daughters were not in favour of their girls entering nursing unless their morality could be 'protected'. It was in fact *politically expedient* for the emphasis to be placed on sexual morality.

Second, nursing was not seen as being the prerogative of any class. Women from even the lowest social strata were accepted into nursing. If Nightingale discriminated it was to the disadvantage of the upper classes. For she thought that highly educated ladies, who by definition came from the upper classes, were 'given to spiritual flirtations with the patients'. She therefore insisted that applicants for the 'lady class of probationer' had to display a 'desire to qualify themselves for the superior situations'. They had to come into nursing with a 'settled purpose, free from all romance and affectation, but yet not wanting in some genuine enthusiasm' (Abel-Smith, 1960, p. 22).

Third, Nightingale saw nursing as a means of emancipating women. For her, a 'life without love' and 'an activity without aim' was horrible in idea and even more wearisome in reality. It was due to Nightingale's liberal tendencies that she sought to make nursing an occupation that would free the large pool of idle Victorian spinsters from a dependence on either fathers or brothers. She emphasised that nursing had to be a paid job thus preventing it from becoming yet another form of female Victorian charity. A training certificate justified that a woman now be paid for her services.

Training did empower the trained nurse to appropriate an area of competence and call it her own. Now, it was the trained matron, rather than the doctor who would be responsible for the selection, training and discipline of nurses. No longer were sisters the loyal assistants of particular doctors. Instead, it was the matron who in the name of 'better training' rotated nurses among various wards. Also, the trained matron reported directly to the hospital committee rather than to lay administrators. And the status and financial position of the trained matron became much enhanced after the institution of training. Nightingale herself was in no doubt as to the role of the trained matron. She wrote:

> The whole reform in nursing ... has consisted in this; to take all power over the Nursing out of the hands of the men, and to put it into the hands of one female head and make her responsible for everything.... Don't let the Doctor make himself Head Nurse.... It is so odd that practical Englishmen cannot see this without being told.
>
> (Nightingale, 1867)

However, almost unintentionally this new cadre of trained matrons was drawn largely from lady-nurses of the upper classes. Once the notions of respectability and morality had been successfully launched as the cornerstone of nursing, lady-pupils came forward in significant numbers to train. From the beginning their class distinction introduced inequalities within nursing (see Abel-Smith, 1960). The most important of these was that the training of lady-nurses lasted only one year because they were better educated. Other nurse-probationers had a two-year period of training. Due to this shorter training, lady-nurses gained promotion quicker. It was the ladies who rapidly became sisters, then assistant superintendents and ultimately heads of nursing departments in hospitals. In this manner, inequalities in access to class, wealth and education ensured that the production of producers became focused on women from the upper classes. And although Nightingale did not expressly set up class barriers in nursing, the profession came to be led by ladies from the richer class.

The management of training at the end of the nineteenth century did not appear to have a single 'aim' – the restriction of supply. Researchers seeking to establish such a clear motive could argue that the training initiated by Nightingale did provide nurses with a means of negotiation with other occupational groups. It did allow them to take over certain responsibilities in both voluntary hospitals and workhouses. The inequalities of class and education were beginning to create a nursing elite which would eventually dominate the profession. Yet it is clear that Nightingale's concept of training was not intended to create an elitist cognitive exclusiveness. Training to her was essentially a practical course within the capacity of even a country girl. Indeed, she distrusted the highly educated nurse trainee. And her stress on morality appears to have introduced class divisions accidentally. There is, therefore, little evidence that training was expressly intended to reduce supply, to reserve nursing for the educated/rich or to create a body of esoteric knowledge divorced from the perceived needs of patients. Also, training appeared to have liberal roots in Nightingale's desire to emancipate women.

In addition, wider social factors influenced the shape of training. There was a war in the Crimea, a demographic imbalance between the numbers of men and women and the first stirrings of a suffragette movement. The first projected nursing to the forefront of public debate, enabled Nightingale to finance the first training course and gave nursing its militaristic culture. The second resulted in a large number of unmarried women who were well-educated but unemployable. This and the third factor enabled a reformed system of nurse training to attract recruits.

Thus, training when it was first initiated took the form it did due to a complex of relations within a certain historical and social milieu. There were localised events and objectives, which though clear at their inception resulted in outcomes which could not be said to be the intention of anyone. There was no overriding controller. Neither was there a natural evolution of knowledge or a simple causal chain. This ambiguity, however, did not characterise the later development of monopoly power.

III THE CONSOLIDATION OF MONOPOLY

The profession came to power on a different historical stage with different protagonists. It was the twentieth century. There was the First World War, a full-grown suffragette movement and a Mrs Bedford Fenwick. In addition, nursing itself exhibited certain characteristics which made the creation of 'scarcity' feasible and opportune.

First, nurses remained an extremely varied group of people despite the introduction of a small degree of standardisation. There were ladies with excellent education and servant girls with a minimum. Quality control of the product marketed, i.e. nursing service, was in fact extremely poor. Second, despite destandardisation, the market for nursing had expanded considerably (Abel-Smith, 1960, pp. 50-60). 'Disciplined' nursing had been seen to work, especially in the prevention of cross-infection. In addition, the system of medical care was developing. Medicine's own institutionalisation and greater effectiveness increased the demand for medical care. Both these processes increased the demand for trained nurses in the voluntary hospital and the workhouse.

Third, and most important of all, nursing skill had become a distinguishable, marketable commodity. Due to Nightingale's reforms, the nurse was now seen to have an important, distinct role in the management of health; a role which required training and one which was as necessary as the doctor's. A nurse's prerogative was 'care' whilst the doctor's was diagnosis and treatment. The nurse-patient relation had in effect undergone a successful process of product differentiation. It now formed a part of a triadic set: nurse-doctor-patient, the hospital equivalent of the Victorian familial father-mother-child structure.

These characteristics of nursing at the end of the nineteenth century – unstandardised supply, expanding demand, the 'universal' nature of the product – made it ripe for the creation of scarcity. Not surprisingly the move to restrict entry came from those nurses of upper class origin – the lady nurses. A group of them became afraid that they had lost social caste by becoming nurses. The ladies now found they had as colleagues and peers women from the lower strata of society with perhaps a minimum of education. Also, their nursing duties did comprise of many routine, housekeeping tasks, some of which were clearly unpleasant and embarrassing. It thus seemed as though, by choice, they had descended the social ladder such that their servants were now their equals. Abel-Smith (1960) suggests that the lady-nurses were also spurred by a form of militant feminism and snobbery. It was the age of the suffragettes and it seemed appropriate to demonstrate to male doctors, many of whom did not originate from the highest social classes, just how high women could climb.

Apart from these motives, there were also highly skilled nurses who knew better than anyone the damage that could be done by an incompetent nurse. There was a genuine danger to the community when the public had no means of knowing the level of skill deemed 'adequate' and 'safe'. It was precisely because there was a real need for the institution of some form of quality control that the lady-nurses were successful in advancing their 'public interest' arguments.

But it is clear that the lady-nurses sought more than quality control, they desired monopoly (see Abel-Smith, 1960, pp. 61–98). For the former purpose, a register of practising nurses accompanied by testimonials of ability and good character could have sufficed. Such a register was proposed by Burdett, the spokesman of the Hospitals' Association. But the lady-nurses dismissed this as 'a registry office similar to that in vogue for domestic servants'. They wanted more and their demands included:

(a) a register of practising nurses which would prevent other 'unqualified' people from working as nurses;
(b) a central body which judged which schools provided adequate training;
  (c) a national examination which ascertained whether each individual trainee had benefited from the course; and
(d) three years' training.

In addition, firm educational and financial barriers were to be erected in nursing schools to keep out 'undesirable' recruits. Also, nurses undergoing training would receive no salary and would be charged five guineas for examination and registration. The net effect of these proposals would have been not only to reduce the number of women permitted to train (and hence the future supply of nurses), it would effectively have debarred many practising nurses from being registered.

Training was now being redefined. No longer was it only a means of imparting knowledge and skill. It became an entry barrier, an initiation rite. As Abel-Smith writes:

> The militant lady-pupils on the other hand saw training in a different light. It was an apprenticeship, a period of trial, almost an initiation ritual, to test who was fit to bear the title 'nurse'. The greater the severity, the higher its intellectual demands, the longer its duration, the greater the status of the profession. The very fact that every woman thought she could nurse made it the more necessary to emphasize and exaggerate training requirements.
>
> (Abel-Smith, 1960, p. 62)

This ideological stress on a large amount of technical and examinable knowledge contradicted sharply with the view of Nightingale. She opposed registration vigorously precisely because she felt the professional competence of a nurse could not be judged by an examination. All an examination could test was knowledge, and a nurse could acquire all the knowledge she needed in six months. What she deemed more important was not knowledge but personal qualities of sensitivity, devotion and practical intelligence. Nightingale submitted that:

> The idea of the new-fangled people seems to be to put nurses on the level of dictionaries – a dictionary can answer questions.
> (The Select Committee on Registration, 1905, p. 52)

But influential though Nightingale was, the lady-nurses who pressed for state registration had powerful allies. These included Princess Christian, the daughter of Queen Victoria, and the matrons and consultants of the large London teaching hospitals. These allies helped the nursing elite to set up the British Nurses' Association which persuaded a Select Committee of the House of Lords enquiring into the management of London's hospitals to adopt three years as a requisite period of training. By 1897, a three-year training had become standard practice in nursing schools and was expressly required for superintendent nurses in workhouses. Today nearly a century later, nurses training for the Register still undergo a three-year training.

The State finally granted nurses an official licence for monopoly in 1919. A number of factors are responsible for this victory for pro-registrationists. First, the nurse's cause was helped by the setting up of 'registers' for other occupational groups such as doctors, midwives and teachers. Second, the First World War had served to reaffirm the nurse's strategic 'public' role and to unite the rank and file of the nursing profession in a pro-registration lobby. The increased solidarity arose because during the war many 'untrained' women had been recruited to work in Britain's civil and military hospitals. After the war, these members of the Volunteer Aid Detachment (VAD) were seen by many nurses as a threat to their power and status. This perception of a common 'enemy' led many nurses to press for state certification of their expertise. Third, public sympathy for the nurses' demands was particularly high after the war. Fourth, women had earned the vote. Fifth, Florence Nightingale had died. And, finally, above all else, the experience of war had produced a willingness to accept change. There was a national sense of unity and a desire for conciliation.

The Nurses' Registration Act incorporated many of the demands which the nursing elite had pressed for some 30 years earlier. For instance, persons without formal training were only eligible for registration provided they had been 'for at least three years before the first day of November 1919 bona fide engaged in practice as nurses in attendance on the sick . . .'. Also, a Nursing Council would be established to approve training schools.

However, not content with these advances in monopoly control, the new Nursing Council sought to further narrow the eye of the needle. Abel-Smith (1960) documents how on two occasions the State intervened in the profession's restriction of supply via training requirements. The first intervention centred round the Council's definition of a 'bona fide' nurse. This was to be a nurse who had one year's formal training in a hospital approved by the Council. This rule effectively kept out all the VADs but allowed in the lady-nurses. It also excluded practical nurses employed in domiciliary nursing and in nursing homes, district nurses and old-style nurses. Its blatantly restrictive nature caused Parliament to overturn this requirement. In the second instance, the Council had drawn up a highly detailed training programme which it sought to make compulsory for all nursing schools. This would have presented difficulties to the small hospitals which could not 'train' and hence recruit as well as the larger hospitals. Eventually, the Government, aware of the shortage of manpower decided to make the training syllabus advisory but not mandatory.

Despite these initial State interventions (which have not been repeated since) the shortage of nurses had begun. When the Registration Act was first debated, it was expected that 70 000–80 000 nurses would be registered. In the event, only 40 451 applications were received and a shortage of nurses continued through the 1920s and 1930s. There were several factors for this. First, the demand for nursing services continued to expand. Substantial developments in medicine, particularly in surgery meant that hospitals were no longer the last resort for the sick poor (Abel-Smith, 1960, p. 119). And doctors began to send their patients to hospital for specific courses of treatment. The development of more complicated treatment, the expansion of medical research, the need to teach these procedures to nurse trainees and the growth of specialised out-patient departments all helped increase the demand for hospital nurses. The State, too, demanded more trained nurses for its poor law hospitals, particularly after the Local Government Act of 1929. This transferred control of the poor law hospitals from the Boards of Guardians to the Counties and County Boroughs. In most areas these local authorities sought to improve the quality of treatment to a standard comparable to that of the voluntary hospitals.

More trained nurses were also needed for work in the district clinics, an expanding number of nursing homes and in the home. As Abel-Smith (p. 129) points out, this service was particularly demanded by middle income earners who could not afford to enter the voluntary hospitals as paying patients and who did not qualify as needy members of the public. They, however, could afford and thereby fuelled the expansion of nursing and convalescent homes.

This increased demand partly explains why despite a higher proportion of working women entering nursing after registration, the scarcity continued. There is, however, an important second factor, the long period of training and the stiff examinations now required by the General Nursing Council. There are several implications of this requirement.

First, it made it extremely hard for widows to enter the profession.

They could not subsist on the low pay received during training if they had family responsibilities. Second, the living-in system (a cheap way for the hospital to maintain a 24-hour nursing service) kept out women whose husbands were still alive. Third, women with lower educational standards were either put off by the state examinations or failed to pass them.

Other actions by the Nursing Council and lady-nurses further contributed to this scarcity. For instance, there was positive discrimination against married women and males. Also, the conditions of work and the pay of trainee nurses were unattractive. They were subjected to Victorian notions of respectability and discipline and had to work long hours. This led to a high rate of trainee nurse turnover. Training had truly become a rite of passage, a period during which the trainee had to 'prove' her suitability for this 'high office'.

But how much of this training was 'really' necessary? If a three-year training is sufficient now, given a century of expansion in medical knowledge and techniques, it was clearly too long in 1887. Goode (1969) argues that most professionals are typically overtrained and trainees must learn far more than they will typically apply in the course of their practice. Larson (1977) suggests that overtraining serves ideological functions. This is because there is no guarantee that the professional will be able to mobilise this generalised knowledge after qualification. Overtraining also helps to create an atmosphere of complete skills and knowledge. This elicits the layman's trust and reaffirms the superiority of the expert. Finally, a generalised training allows specialisation to be seen as an added skill and for specialists to command higher economic and social rewards. The nursing elite's imposition of a three-year training period certainly appeared to serve all these purposes.

IV THE PERPETUATION OF MONOPOLY

Today, training continues to perpetuate scarcity and monopoly power. But as the times have changed, so have the alliances which the nursing elites have had to form. With the rise of 'liberal democracy', of a belief in scientific, technical thought and with meritocracy replacing patronage as a central norm in Anglo-Saxon society, the question: 'what is nursing skill?' has been re-answered. The question and the answer have always had socio-political dimensions which permeate the technical. This has been particularly perceptible in the last fifty years with the admittance of the enrolled nurse, the nurse auxiliary and increasing specialisation and territorial tensions within the health care field.

The processes by which the definition of skill and expertise has been managed since registration will now be analysed in detail. Evidence will be drawn not only from historical data but from empirical observations obtained during a four-year (1979–82) research project conducted in a school of nursing. Both the school and hospitals concerned were situated in the north of England.

(i) The Examination

This is and always has been one of the central processes by which a profession controls its members. The examination is implicated in the process of product differentiation, standardisation, quality control, exchange-value creation and restriction of supply. It is that one final event which certifies recruits as 'knowers of mysteries', as specialists and which grants them their credentials. Larson (1977, p. 31) writes that even the existence of a body of esoteric knowledge, in the absence of a certifying process, does not ensure capture of a competitive market. Foucault (1977, pp. 184–5) further emphasises the technology of power which the examination generates. It is seen as a form of discipline which provides a means of punishment, subjection and objectification of human beings.

The institution of a national examination was one of the first acts of the lady-nurses and the General Nursing Council. Its subsequent effects on scarcity and monopoly power have already been discussed. But has the analysis been too one-sided? For it could be argued that the examination does not solely serve an ideological purpose, that it serves a real need by discriminating between 'safe' and 'unsafe' methods, by removing 'incompetent practitioners' and thus safeguards the health of a community. In nursing, however, there is some indication that the examination does not always have this control or policing function. Bendall (1975), for example found that trainee nurses performed certain techniques in a particular way only during the examination and had forgotten some of the steps undertaken soon after. Our own ward observations showed that trainee nurses constructed some of the taught routines as 'finicky', 'unnecessarily tedious', 'idealistic', 'impossible to follow because of lack of time'.

The equivocal nature of the examination was especially highlighted during a three-month period of participant observation in a large English hospital. In a heated and agitated discussion, first-year learners were amazed to learn that neither the staff nurse, nor the qualified enrolled nurse nor the sister could agree as to whether a pair of 'dirty' forceps did or did not exist in an aspesis procedure. Each of these three qualified experts performed the procedure in slightly different ways and had apparently equally logical reasons for doing so. But a correct procedure had to be learnt for examination and the lack of a correct method caused some anxiety among the learners. Eventually, the sister telephoned the School of Nursing and requested a clinical teacher (who would be an examiner) to pronounce on *the* correct procedure. He too explained that variations could exist but that he himself preferred to assume the traditional existence of a pair of 'dirty' forceps. The reasons for this assumption were not clear. But the pronouncement of *one correct method* had been made. The learners visibly settled down. They now knew what was required in the examination.

In our observations, it was clear that although learners were taught one standard practice, these methods were practised in a destandardised way. Due to the vagaries of staffing, of resource scarcity, of a lack of knowledge about outcomes and differences in individual preferences, variations in method did occur. However, such destandardisation was often glossed over as 'minor', 'to be expected', 'as not involving a change of fundamental principle'. Variety in practice was thus not perceived as a threat to the legitimacy of examinable knowledge. Instead it was neutralised and individualised.

(ii) The Elevation of Mental Labour

The rise of examinable knowledge and the focus on 'intelligence' has led to a contradiction within nursing: the domination of 'mental' labour over 'physical' effort. Nursing, a hundred years before, was no more than a set of physical tasks supposedly executed with the 'proper' feminine attributes of kindness and obedience. It was a pragmatic occupation performed by working-class women. After the introduction of training, the bulk of bedside care became the responsibility of young single women of a higher social origin and even higher social aspiration than the typical patient in their care. From the 1880s until the 1950s, it was the young,[5] single woman who dominated the nursing profession, who was thought 'skilled' to deal with the physical and psychological needs of men and women.

Between 1919 and 1950, the State was unable to persuade the then Nursing Council to relax the restrictions for admission to the Register and two compromises were struck. First, the Council agreed to a second grade of nurse who would undertake the more routine, repetitive 'basic' nursing tasks. The enrolled nurse was thus designated as the 'less promising' student who could be a 'good practical' nurse. The Council was amenable to this idea for it further enhanced the 'skill' of the registered nurse and stopped the migration of trainees, who for higher pay, withdrew from registered training to become assistant (enrolled) nurses. Now, the assistant nurse was clearly a 'less able' nurse. Second, the Council agreed to recognise the role of nursing auxiliaries. These would be persons with a minimum of nurse training who would undertake the more menial domestic tasks such as dusting and cleaning.

These two compromises have helped redefine the concept of nursing skill. It now appears to have completed a full circle and reverted to a pre-Nightingale construction. Then nursing, was seen only in terms of its physical tasks. Because these tasks were performed in an ill-informed way by 'socially undesirable' persons, the occupation was not respected. The introduction of training by Nightingale gave some scientific basis to nursing and helped standardise certain procedures. Nightingale, however, retained an emphasis on qualitative care. Nursing, in her eyes, remained a labour-oriented, 'caring' service.

Today, 'basic', physical care has been relegated to the lower-paid 'less well-educated' members of the occupation. Despite professional rhetoric that the enrolled nurse is not an inferior type of nurse, her second-grade status is real. From the beginning (1943), enrolled nurses were pupils (not students) who wore different uniforms and badges and who are now lower-paid and have no structured career in management. The auxiliary is not even seen as a nurse. Her role is restricted to the performance of 'basic', quasi-domestic duties such as the bathing, feeding and lifting of patients.

It is these subordinate members who perform the bulk of direct patient-contact tasks. Ward observations during the study (Chua, 1982) showed that learners, enrolled nurses and nurse auxiliaries comprised between 70 and 75 per cent of the ward labour force. Of a shift complement of 10–13, there were usually only two qualified registered nurses, these being the ward sister and the staff nurse.

These proportions of unqualified staff were even higher during periods of night duty and at weekends. These findings are consistent with that of the Merrison Report (1979, p. 195) which reports that about 50 per cent of the nursing workforce is unqualifed and of Moores (1979a) who found that the ratios of learner to qualified staff (including qualified enrolled nurses) could reach a maximum of 2 on weekdays and 2.8 on weekends. By contrast, whilst the majority of direct-contact tasks is performed by unqualified staff, the bulk of the 'skilled' ward sister's time is spent on administration. When a sample of ward sisters (21 in total) were questionnaired on the amount of time spent on administration, their answers ranged from 25–90 per cent, with a mean of 60 per cent.

The concept of skill in modern nursing emphasises notions such as 'decision-making', 'care-planning', 'co-ordination', 'over-seeing'. In short, on control of the physical delivery of care. This surveillance is performed by the supposedly more experienced, more able nurse whilst the actual performance of nursing tasks is often delegated to the subordinate 'practical nurse'. This social division of labour and the reward system associated with it has been further reinforced by the introduction of the Salmon Plan (1966).

In the 1950s and 1960s, hospital matrons found that their authority was being eroded through the growth of professional administrators and the power of the medical profession. The General Nursing Council agitated for reform. This arrived in 1966, in a mode consistent with the rise of managerialism (Carpenter, 1977) in organisational life. The Salmon Plan was modelled on the hierarchical 'pyramid' model of commercial organisations and introduced a clear administrative career structure for registered nurses. No such plan was available however, to nurses who wished to remain within the clinical/care delivery function. Neither was there any form of career structure for the enrolled nurse. In effect, the Salmon Plan awarded to administrative controllers high pay, status and prestige.

Collectively, these structural changes in the profession have elevated the skill of administration at the expense of 'basic nursing'. But why has this relegation of the core activity of production not brought about public unease about the concept of nursing skill? Why are the following questions not asked: if nursing as a skill consists of tasks which are routine and mechnanical, if the greater expertise of a sister or a Senior Nursing Officer is in administration what difference is there between a nurse and an administrator? What need has a community of the label 'nursing officer' when it is equivalent to that of 'an administrator'? More importantly, why has society at large not reacted to the contradiction which makes the claim to nursing expertise inconsistent?

The answer appears to have several facets. First, the Salmon Plan had the support of the important Nursing Council and other nursing organisations as it improved the power and status of the nurse. Second, a government committee has decided that there is little evidence that there are too many nurse administrators (Merrison Report, 1979, pp. 31–2). The Committee, perhaps only too knowledgeable about the territorial conflicts between doctors and nurses, discounted such a complaint from the British Medical Association. Statistics produced in the Report showed that the proportion of administrative nursing staff fell from 4.7 per cent in 1966 to 3.6 per cent in 1977. These statistics seem to suggest a residual resistance among ward-based staff to the greater economic rewards of administration. However, the report fails to highlight that between 1973 and 1977, the number of administrative nursing staff increased by 23 per cent. Also, ward sisters are not classified as administrators, yet their role in patient-contact care has been much reduced. Such realities are, however, unlikely to be widely publicised by nursing leaders to the State or to the public.

Third, the educational branch of nursing has helped to contain the contradictory division of labour by coupling itself to dominant social values – meritocracy and systems of inequality – the school and university. However, as will be shown, because these linkages were not made in order to veil the elevation of mental labour, further contradictions have been generated. These undermine internal cohesion and solidarity, thus frustrating the control efforts of nursing leaders to 'professionalise'. The first strand in this complex, equivocal web of relations is the rise of a technical rationality within nursing.

(iii) The Visibility of Techne

In any occupational group, the institution of formal training and the delineation of educators as a specialist group means that, in time, their role is enhanced through consolidating the *raison d'être* for their existence (Larson, 1977). Through our hospital observations and reading of the main nursing journals, it was clear that nurse educators, in general, identified themselves with the development of a 'scientific' basis for nursing. They turned often to the biological and social sciences in their attempts to establish a 'theory of nursing'. In so doing, they were influenced by and contributed to the continued rise of a technical rationality in Western society (Habermas, 1971; Ravetz, 1973).

One only has to compare the following definitions of nursing to note the emergence of a technical rationality. Henderson writes:

> Nursing is primarily *helping* people (sick and well) in the performance of these activities contributing to health, or its recovery (or to a peaceful death) that they would perform unaided if they had the strength, will or knowledge.... The nurse is temporarily the consciousness of the unconscious, the love of life of the suicidal, the leg of the amputee, the eyes of the newly blind, a means of locomotion of the newborn, knowledge and confidence for the young mother, a voice for those too weak to speak.
> (Harmer and Henderson, 1955)

This romantic depiction of the nurse's skill is quite different from the following picture of brisk, intelligent efficiency:

> The first-level nurse [professional nurse] is responsible for planning, providing and evaluating nursing care in all settings for the promotion of health, prevention of illness, care of the sick and rehabilitation; and functions as a member of the health team.
> (International Labour Office, 1976)

The second definition uses the language of rational management science and focuses on the activities of 'planning' and 'coordination'. Such a change in emphasis is also reflected in the profession's current efforts to establish the 'nursing process' as the model of nursing skill. This is usually described as comprising four sequential functions: (a) assessment of patient needs and nursing resources; (b) planning for nursing intervention; (c) implementation of the plan; and (d) evaluation and feedback. This model is but a simple, mechanistic model of decision-making found in any elementary textbook on management science. And in the words of an experienced sister: 'we've been doing this since 1860, so what's new?' What is novel is that the model provides an apparently logical, scientific coherence to a set of diverse everyday tasks which the nurse has appropriated in an *ad hoc* manner over the last hundred years.

The emphasis on a scientific basis is not surprising. Science has been observed to have 'satisfactory' explanations for the prediction and control of events. It was through properly controlled research that Roth (1978) was able to argue that a nursing technique like regular mouth washing did not help to control infection at all. Science and scientific research has yielded material benefits to society and its status is not totally ideologically rooted. The technological developments within nursing, medicine and society more generally have helped to prolong life and ease the pain of death. But it is argued that an emphasis on science and technology also has ideological underpinnings.

First, science and scientific theory is important to the interests of nurse educators. Second, it has helped to mystify the nursing division of labour. By borrowing from the technical social sciences with their emphasis on planning, control and efficient decision-making, the educators have made sensible the 'extension' of the nurse's role to administration. The 'mental intelligence' required for planning and management is often seen by nurse educators as the cornerstone of a nursing profession which is not subservient to the doctors. Finally, technological developments have added prestige to the rise of specialist nursing experts who are skilled in the monitoring of people and machines as for example in the nursing of renal patients, theatre nursing and cardio-thoracic nursing. These specialisms are heavily dependent on the use of technology in patient care. Together, these recent changes have transformed a qualitative, physical service into a dual technology. Skill now lies mainly in the ability to relate machines to people and in the hierarchical observation of the subordinate and the sick.

What then of the qualitative aspects of nursing skill? Are activities such as bathing and feeding purely mechanical tasks or are they parts of a total service? An emphasis on the technology of skill may ignore important aspects of psychological care. For man is a whole with a mind-body which exists within a particular socio-political context. And a concentration on short-term physical intervention within an institution may fail to apprehend the totality of health and sickness.

But does an emphasis on the 'secret' personal qualities of nursing skill not help to consolidate the nurse's claim to monopoly? Such expertise is not easily quantifiable and could be used to manage the nurse-patient relation such that the nurse is less accountable for his/her actions. The mystique of the expert could once again be invoked and in a potentially more important area – an understanding and hence control of the psychological needs of a patient. But equally a process of demystification may be initiated once the limitations of technical skill are clear. For instance, patients with 'incurable' or long-term problems such as renal failure or skin disease (see Jobling, 1978) have been encouraged by nurses to develop a greater degree of dependence and self-determination in the management of their illnesses. This result could conceivably be attained in the nursing and management of acute short-term illness.

(iv) **The Role of the University**

A third relation which is important in consolidating nursing's monopoly power is its link with the modern university and polytechnic. In the UK, this liaison has only recently been forged and as yet it is not happily accepted by all nurses. Nurse educators whose interests could be furthered by this linkage are enthusiastic about the establishment of graduate nursing. Service personnel, for example, ward sisters who do not possess university credentials are less doubtful about its worth. This tension at the level of the rank and file could seriously affect nursing's attempt to gain more status by locating its training within tertiary educational institutions.

This, however, is unlikely. First, it was the General Nursing Council which actively sought to develop links with the university and polytechnic. These links have been welcomed by the polytechnics which, after the boom period of the 1960s were faced in the 1970s with falling student numbers and a shortage of State funds. In addition, the polytechnic had sought to develop a comparative advantage *vis-à-vis* the university in the teaching of vocational as opposed to 'academic' subjects. Second, there has been no active opposition from the State to the introduction of graduate nursing. This may be because at present, the number of students on these courses is relatively small and it does not affect substantially the manpower available. Finally, some younger nurses have already accepted the increased emphasis on university credentials and undertaken part-time degrees in order to gain promotion. Should such acceptance grow, the linkage with the university will be strengthened.

As always, such a linkage has both material and ideological aspects. For instance, research and development within a university could be more cost-efficient than scattered efforts by various hospitals. But a university confers other advantages. First, it fosters the profession's attempt to provide a standardised, 'scientific' and theoretical basis to the subject by allowing teachers and students access to the technical sciences. in addition, when professional training is provided by apprenticeship in a diverse group of institutions, there is always some degree of differentiation. Its concentration in a university increases uniformity for a university tends to become a major centre for the production of both producers and consumers of knowledge. Also, this knowledge will be more coherently communicated to the larger society as it is done by the same institutional mediators.

Second, the university defends the professional's claim to expertise and autonomy by granting an appearance of disinterestedness and universalism. A university is perceived as free from 'commercial pursuits', as desirous of knowledge for its sake, as independent of lay demands and private interests. This notion of universalism is clearly consonant with a profession's claim of universal service to all, removed from the inequalities of class and access to wealth. In addition, a university, through promoting meritocracy allows professionals to obscure the social determinants of their expertise and to privately appropriate this for themselves. Entry to a university is said to be based on merit. And if centres of learning appear to be open to all who desire education, then the inequalities which people subsequently experience are not arbitrary. They are the 'logical' consequences of different levels of 'natural' intelligence and personal drive. The structural determinants of many of these differences will become obscured.

Through this process of desocialisation, an expertise which is socially produced and financed becomes private property, to be dispensed at the discretion of the expert. The nurse trainee does help provide a nursing service but the cost of her training clearly exceeds the benefit of her service (see Moores, 1979b). In addition, upon qualification, a nurse's skill is his/her own. Whilst the majority of nurses do work within the National Health Service, opportunities exist for private and commercial work. Such private appropriation of a social good would have been more difficult had the ideology of equal access to education not been secured by linkages to the school and the university. Finally, a university grants status to a profession. This is partly historical and probably dates from medieval times when the university was highly prestigious. Such status is clearly useful to nurses who wish to negotiate a greater share of decision-making power with other groups of educated labour such as doctors.

At present, the number of graduate nurses is still small but if developments continue, the prestige of the university-trained nurse will be difficult to question. And the nurse-expert will be harder to unseat.

(v) The Role of Credentials

Finally, the profession has managed to maintain its strategic advantage by strengthening its links with the general educational system. At present, its entry requirements are almost exclusively based on 'O' and 'A' level results. This is especially true for registered nurse trainees. Consistent with the policy adopted by the nineteenth-century lady-nurses, modern nurse selectors have taken educational credentials as evidence of the ability to care. In part, the higher educational requirement has resulted from an increase in the general educational level of the female population. It is also due to the necessity of finding an easy selection tool. With large training schools facing several thousand applicants at times of record youth employment, it is much quicker to select on the basis of 'O' and 'A' level results.

The increased use of credentials meshes in well with the development of 'scientific' and graduate nursing and helps consolidate the administrative career structure. However, though veiling the contradictory division of labour, these processes collectively introduce new tensions: they have caused the nurse experts to compare wage levels with those of other experts. And, more importantly, to ally themselves with the trade union movement when the Royal College of Nursing appears not to champion their rights. The College is in an ambiguous position. It claims not to be a trade union but a 'professional association' which represents some 190 000 nurses. It has never repealed its founding rule not to take strike action believing that such action would undermine the nurse's claim to professionalism and public support and put patients' lives at risk. But whilst supportive of the professional aims of nurses, the College is also well-aware that the State requires a health service which is run on state-defined and not nurse-defined cost limits. These two inconsistent demands have often hampered the College in its wage negotiations.

Consequently, a significant number of younger nurses are joining labour organisations, like NUPE (National Union of Public Employees), COHSE (Confederation of Health Service Employees) and NALGO (National Association of Local and Government

Officers). These nurses complain of 'unprofessional' wages and they view aggressive trade unions as offering nurses solidarity among a broad trawl of NHS employees. In addition, the Salmon Plan has helped transplant nursing into an industrial work setting with less of its vocational mystique and altruism. Together, the increased trade union activity and the industrial metaphor have led to a decline of the myth of self-denial and universal service. This has two important effects. First, it leads to the weakening of an hitherto important means of the managerial control of professionals. Second, it defeats the profession's claims to differentiate itself from other 'unskilled' hospital workers. Trade union membership in effect allies 'skilled' nurses with other 'non-professional' occupational groups within the NHS.

Thus, on the one hand, the State seeks to maintain low employment costs and the nursing leaders agitate for a bureaucratic administrative structure, cognitive exclusiveness, status and restricted supply. On the other, the professional learns to demand higher economic and social rewards. When these are not available a rise in unionisation and industrial unrest result in a demystification of the service ethic and the professional. The result: a system shot through with contradictions.

V CONCLUSION

This paper has sought to demonstrate that professional expertise and the definitions of 'skill' and 'training' are not *a priori* characteristics of an expert. They are social constructs whose meaning depends on a complex set of forces which may be managed intentionally or otherwise by a range of constituencies. Like other workers within an industrial organisation, professional experts as a corporate body are subject to control which seeks to ensure their survival and prosperity. And using historical and case-study research it has been argued that the execution of such management control is a constantly changing, equivocal task.

Notes

1. The paper is informed by what is now termed the 'closure' perspective on professions (Murphy, 1983, 1984). This theoretical approach stems from Weber's notion of social closure and has been developed in the writings of Parkin, Collins and Bourdieu. It explores the manner in which occupational monopolies maintain a delicate balance between maintaining occupational exclusivity and market competitiveness.
2. See Abel-Smith, 1960; Seymer, 1949; Haldane, 1923; Cope, 1955; White, 1978.
3. Nursing historians are apt to disagree with this perspective. They regard the medieval religious orders as the 'true' ancestors of the nursing profession; the Victorian era was but an atypical, temporal phase in the 'progress' of the profession. The 'evils' of the nurses of this period are in fact more roundly condemned by nurses themselves than by other historians. Such a construction of history, however, is questionable for it assumes that there are patterns of cause and effect in the amorphous unity of some great evolutionary process. But it may be the historian who imposes these patterns and sees evolution within a web of events. Indeed, Foucault (1972) contends that such a construction of history is an ideological use of history that tries to restore to human beings a position of power which has always eluded them.
4. Abel-Smith (1960) writes that even in 1830, the sisters at St Bartholomew's had an admirable sagacity and a sort of rough practical knowledge which was nearly as good as any acquired skill. Also, Mrs Roberts, the best nurse to accompany Nightingale to the Crimea had been 'untrained' whilst at St Thomas's.
5. The youth of the trained nurse was due partly to a deliberate policy of lowering the age of entry into nursing in an attempt to alleviate the scarcity of manpower. After 1919, the entry age was reduced to 18, at times it was as low as 15 or 16 years.

References

B. Abel-Smith, *A History of the Nursing Profession* (London: Heinemann, 1960).

E. Bendall, *So. You Passed, Nurse. An exploration of some of the assumptions on which written examinations are based* (Cavendish Square, London: Royal College of Nursing and National Council of Nurses of the United Kingdom, 1975).

G. Benveniste, *The Politics of Expertise* (2nd edn, San Francisco: Boyd & Fraser Publishing Co., 1977).

H. Braverman, *Labor and Monopoly Capital* (New York and London: Monthly Review Press, 1974).

M. Carpenter, 'The New Managerialism and Professionalism in Nursing' in M. Stacey et al., *Health and the Division of Labour* (London: Croom Helm, 1977).

W. F. Chua, Organizational Effectiveness: A Study of the Concept with Empirical Reference to a Nurse Training System, unpublished PhD

Z. Cope, *A Hundred Years of Nursing at St Mary's Paddington* (London, 1955).
M. Foucault, *The Archaeology of knowledge*, trans A. M. Sheridan (London: Tavistock, 1972).
M. Foucault, *Discipline and Punish: the birth of the prison*, trans A. M. Sheriden (London: Allen Lane, 1977).
E. Freidson, *Profession of Medicine* (New York: Dodd and Mead, 1970).
E. Freidson and J. Lorber, *Medical Men and their Work* (Chicago: Aldine–Atherton, 1972).
W. J. Goode, 'The Theoretical Limits of Professionalization' in A. Etzioni (ed.) *The Semi-Professions* (New York: Free Press, 1969) pp. 266–313.
A. Gramsci, *Selections from the Prison Notebooks* (London: Lawrence and Wishart, 1971).
J. Habermas, *Towards a Rational Society*, trans J. Shapiro (London: Heinemann, 1971).
E. S. Haldane, *The British Nurse in Peace and War*, (London, 1923).
B. Harmer and V. Henderson, *Textbook of the Principles and Practice of Nursing* (New York: Macmillan, 1955).
International Labour Office, Employment and Conditions of Work and Life of Nursing Personnel. Report 7(2), International Labour Conference, 61st Session. The Office, Geneva, 1976.
R. Jobling, 'Nursing with and without professional nurses: the case of dermatology' in R. Dingwall and J. McIntosh (eds) *Readings in the Sociology of Nursing* (Edinburgh, London and New York: Churchill Livingstone, 1978) pp. 181–96.
M. S. Larson, *The Rise of Professionalism. A Sociological Analysis* (University of California Press, 1977).
K. Mannheim, *Man and Society in an Age of Reconstruction*, trans E. Shils (London: Routledge and Kegan Paul, 1935).
B. Moores, 'The cost and effectiveness of nurse education – 2', *The Nursing Times*. Occasional Papers, vol. 75 (28 June, 1979a) pp. 71–2.
B. Moores, 'The cost and effectiveness of nurse education – 1', *The Nursing Times*. Occasional Papers, vol. 75 (21 June, 1979b) pp. 65–8.
R. Murphy, 'The Struggle for Scholarly Recognition: The Development of the Closure Problematic in Sociology', *Theory and Society*, vol. 12, no. 5 (September 1983) pp. 631–58.
R. Murphy, 'The Structure of Closure: A Critique and Development of the Theories of Weber, Collins and Parkin,' *British Journal of Sociology*, vol. 35, no. 4 (December 1984) pp. 547–67.
V. Navarro, *Medicine Under Capitalism* (London: Croom Helm, 1976).
F. Nightingale, Letter from Miss Nightingale to Mary Jones. St Thomas's Hospital Archives, 67/1 (1867).
J. R. Ravetz, *Scientific Knowledge and its Social Problems* (London: Penguin University Books, 1973). First published by Oxford University Press in 1971.

Report of the Committee on Senior Nursing Staff Structure. Ministry of Health Scottish Home and Health Department (London: HMSO, 1966). (The Salmon Plan).

J. Roth, 'Ritual and magic in the control of contagism' in R. Dingwall and J. McIntosh (eds), *Readings in the Sociology of Nursing* (Edinburgh, London and New York: Churchill Livingstone, 1978) pp. 153–63.

Royal Commission on the National Health Service (Merrison Report) Cmnd 7615 (London: HMSO, 1979).

Select Committee on Registration (London: HMSO, 1905).

L. R. Seymer, *A General History of Nursing* (2nd edn, London: Faber and Faber, 1949).

R. White, *Social change and the development of the nursing profession: a study of the poor law nursing service, 1848–1948* (London: Kimpton, 1978).

F. Znaniecki, *The Social Role of the Man of Knowledge* (New York: Octagon Books, 1940).

11 Accounting in the Production and Reproduction of Culture

Teresa Capps, Trevor Hopper,
Jan Mouritsen, David Cooper and
Tony Lowe

This paper explores through case study research of an Area of the National Coal Board (NCB) the role of an accounting system in producing and reproducing organisational culture. It seeks to illustrate how accounting systems are both influenced by, and influence, behaviour in organisations (Burchell *et al.*, 1980; Hopwood, 1983; Roberts and Scapens, 1985; Cooper *et al.*, 1981; Boland and Pondy, 1983).

Accounting reports are necessarily ambiguous because of the nature of the uncertainty surrounding their subject-matter: the values of rights in enterprises. This allows for different interpretations of their meaning and significance which enables them to be an important vehicle for conflict resolution within uncertain organisational contexts. The particular significance of an accounting system is closely connected to the interests of people and to the culture of their organisational context. Following this theme, this paper is part of the 'culture-debate' in accounting (Ansari & Bell, 1985).

The particular interpretation of the concept of culture utilised is Giddens's Theory of Structuration, because of its ability to relate structure to action and in particular its strength in analysing continuity and discontinuities in an empirical situation with a distinctive culture and tradition, and which appeared to be under threat. The following quotation illustrates our view of tradition and culture:

> Tradition is the purest and most innocent mode of social reproduction: tradition, in its most elemental guise, may be thought of, as

one writer puts it 'as an indefinite series of repetitions of an action, which on each occasion is performed on the assumption that it has been performed before; its performance is authorised – though the nature of the authorisation may vary widely – by the knowledge or the assumption of previous performance'. The sloughing-off of tradition in a certain sense begins with its understanding simply as how things were, are (and should be) done.

(Giddens, 1979, p. 200)

This paper focuses on the interpretation of the accounting system by managers in an Area of the NCB and on how they use it to negotiate meaning. The structure of the paper is as follows. First, we present its theoretical basis. Then the research methods are briefly outlined. The next section seeks to explicate the culture of the dominant management group, namely mining engineers. The fourth and main section explores how the dominant culture relates to accounting systems and systems of accountability. The paper concludes with a postscript which discusses the dynamic aspect of this relationship witnessed during and after the field work.

CULTURE AND THE THEORY OF STRUCTURATION

Problems in the Study of Cultures

A series of alternative approaches to accounting research have been developed in the last decade. One of these approaches is inspired by the theory and methods of interpretive sociology (Glaser and Strauss, 1968; Schutz, 1967) which has been applied to an accounting context by Colville (1981) and Rosenberg *et al.* (1982). It is based on a concern to understand the significance of accounting through the subjective and negotiated interpretations of involved people. Such research has provided an important, if partial, insight into the functioning of accounting and management by acting as a sharp corrective to the unthinking determinism inherent in conventional functionalist approaches. In particular, it argues for the importance of individual agency in the production and reproduction of meaning. However we are critical of the dualist split in the interpretive approach between the subject and social context, and its consequent neglect of institutional analysis, power, and widespread social change.

The concerns of interpretive sociology are prevalent in recent work on cultures and organisation. Felinek *et al.* note that 'the linking of culture and organisation legitimates attention to the subjective, interpretive aspects of organisational life' (1983, p. 335). Similarly Smircich states that

> the emergence of social organisation depends on the emergence of shared interpretive schemes, expressed in a language and other symbolic constructions that develop through social interaction. Human actors do not know and perceive *the* world, but know and perceive *their* world, through the medium of culturally specific frames of references.
>
> (1983, pp. 160–1; emphases in original)

Such statements suggest that research into culture may be treated, at least in part, as interpretive in nature and that an important purpose of such research is to elicit shared realities as they appear to exist among groups of people. As such, much of the cultural research associated with organisational behaviour attempts to describe the meaning-content of established behavioural practices within organisations. However, little attention has been devoted to explaining the mechanisms of the emergence and reproduction of cultures over time. The role of power in the transformation and the continuation of culture is often understated. Giddens (1976) argues that power – understood as the agents' capacity to transform (i.e. their ability to intervene in a series of events), is a major source of potential change inherent in social life. This forms an important part of his Theory of Structuration, which provides insights into how social systems are produced and reproduced by competent agents. Moreover, as already noted in an accounting context by Roberts and Scapens (1985), Giddens's synthesis of contemporary social theory seeks to provide a 'nonfunctionalist manifesto' whereby the societal insights and concerns of Functionalism, Systems Theory and Structuralism can be incorporated into a methodology that recognises human agency and the subjective creation of both meaning and structures. This paper seeks to build on Giddens's Theory of Structuration to illustrate how accounting and accountability are dynamically related within interaction to structures of meaning and power.

The Theory of Structuration

Giddens argues that a problem of interpretive sociology is its distinction between subject and object which creates a dualism; on the one hand voluntaristic theories emphasise agency, on the other hand antagonistic theories stress determinism. But neither are able to satisfactorily address the concerns of the other. Giddens argues that the problem lies in a false distinction between the subject and object. Action and structure cannot be separated, but rather each presupposes the other in the reproduction of social systems. This notion is captured dialectically in his theory of the *duality of structure* whereby:

> the structural properties of social systems are both the medium and outcome of the practices they recursively organise.
> (Giddens, 1984, p. 25)

The relationship between the subject and the object is a dialectic emphasising the impact of agents in creating social practice. Particular emphasis is lain on time; to understand human agency adequately it must be treated as a continuous flow of conduct or 'as Rilke says; Our life passes in transformation' (Giddens, 1979, p. 3). Thus a social system 'comprises of the situated activities of human agents reproduced across time and space' (Giddens, 1984, p. 25). The means which agents use in this process are defined as structures which are 'rules and resources ... organised as properties of social systems' (ibid., p. 25). The rules and resources are created and recreated in interaction because they only exist in being used.

A distinction is drawn between systems and structures. Systems are described as regularised interdependent relations between individuals and groups. They represent patterns of activities that exist over time. Interdependence is taken to represent integration, but not necessarily cohesion, nor consensus. Systems integration is differentiated from social integration. The latter represents reciprocity between actors at the level of face-to-face interaction, whereas the former describes systems of reciprocity between groups or collectivities, i.e. social systems. Structures are the 'rule resource set which is involved in the articulation of social systems' (ibid., p. 185). They exist as a set of means/rules and resources which agents draw upon in their knowledgeable negotiation of social life. Importantly, structure exists only in so far as it is used in interaction. It is the way that systems, through the application and generation of rules and resources, coupled to the context of unintended outcomes, are produced and reproduced in interaction, that is central to the Theory of Structuration. Structuration is defined as the 'conditions governing the continuity of transformation of structures, and therefore the reproduction of systems' (Giddens, 1979, p. 66). Thus the concept of structuration seeks to express the duality of structure referred to earlier by capturing the 'fundamentally recursive character of social life' whilst noting 'the mutual dependence of structure and agency' (ibid., p. 59). Giddens's duality of structure in social interaction can be shown as:

Interaction	Communication	Power	Morality
Modality	Interpretative Scheme	Facility	Norm
Structure	Signification (*Weltanschauung*)	Domination	Legitimation

(Giddens, 1976, p. 122)

The top line refers to the elements of interaction: communication, power and morality. Those on the bottom line refer to the characterisations of structure, signification, domination and legitimation. The communication of meaning in interaction involves the use of an interpretative scheme which draws from 'mutual knowledge' – that is, the 'taken-for-granted' part of their reality which enables actors to make sense of actions and words. This represents a cognitive order of the organisation which is re-created in its use. The use of power in interaction provides the facilities to influence outcomes by affecting the conduct of others – in this way the order of domination is utilised and reproduced. In the same manner, the moral order of interaction involves the use of norms which draw from the legitimate order and its use, and thus reproduces this legitimate order.

Giddens suggests that there are three forms of structure within the processes of structuration (1984, p. 29); signification (meaning), legitimation (morality), and domination (power). When people act, they draw from these structures. Signification refers to those rules (stocks of knowledge) which lie behind action and are linked to the communication of meaning in interaction. Legitimation is the actualisation of rights and obligations in interaction. These are forms of norms which are a resource from which moral interaction emanates in the sanctioning of action by others. Domination is the medium through which power is exercised and thereby structures of domination are reproduced. Power is rational in the sense that actors can only achieve outcomes in relation to other actors' agency. The power brought into interaction will influence how social systems are constituted as social practices. Thus social systems involve the reproduction of relations of autonomy and dependence in social interaction (Giddens, 1979, p. 93).

Giddens used the concept of 'frame of meaning' (1976) as a generic term for the relationship between structure and interaction. This is applied in the following sections on the NCB case-study to characterise the 'cultural systems' described.

RESEARCH METHODS

The research took place in an Area of the National Coal Board over three years (1982–4). A major research aim was to achieve a description of controls employed within the organisation and to understand their creation, continuance and significance from the perspective of practising managers. The primary emphasis was on financial control systems, but their connection with other organisational features such as formal organisational structures, production controls, the payment systems and industrial relations were also studied.

More detailed reports of the scope and methods of the two research phases can be found in Berry et al. (1985) and Capps et al. (1984). The gathering and interpretation of data was informed by interpretive sociology (Glaser and Strauss, 1968). The methods utilised included loosely structured interviews with managers; close observation of accountability meetings; observations of managers at work, following them on 'typical' work days; and the study of formal documentation relating to control systems. Whilst access to management was generous, the terms of our research access permitted little contact with the workforce.

THE FRAME OF MEANING OF MINING MANAGEMENT

Domination

A major feature of NCB management is the domination of mining engineers. Nearly all line management and many of the key staff functions tend to be filled by mining engineers. Staff functions (finance, industrial relations, marketing) were not central to the system (and language) of communication, particularly lower down the hierarchy. For example, finance was represented by professional accountants at Area and Headquarter levels, but poorly represented at colliery level, where cost clerks had a clerical role and rarely possessed formal qualifications. The system of accountability follows the 'line' and was not present in functional departments. This pattern of domination is sustained in two ways.

Firstly, legal requirements specify that a colliery manager must be a mining engineer. This is due to the considerable safety problems and attendant legislation covering this industry. However this legal requirement is not inevitable; colliery managers in the FDR and USA are not necessarily mining engineers. Secondly, when investment did not expand with demand for output in the early twentieth century then probably circumstances favoured an organisational structure directed to the purpose of 'turning coal' so as to extract as much as possible from a fixed level of investment. In this production oriented situation the mining engineers came to form the dominant managerial line of the industry.

An illustration of this domination was the failure of attempts to introduce standard costing and marginal cost systems in the 1950s and 1960s. Official explanations of why the systems did not work stress the uncertain and variable nature of conditions underground resulting in standards which quickly became obsolete. Yet physical standards remain intact for payment systems. The continuity dominance of the engineers is an important factor in the 'failure' of these more advanced systems of financial control (Hopper et al., 1986). As a senior accountant recalled, finance

> never had the power – it was trying to find its way. At the time all the emphasis was on the black stuff – producing. Finance called in consultants who recommended standard costing. It was a massive failure. The engineers kicked it down the shaft.

A consequence of the domination of mining engineers particularly at Area level, is that the structures of signification, legitimation and domination within management reflect the occupational culture of engineers, and the nature of the NCB which enables them to reproduce their culture, possibly mainly through appointments and promotions policies.

Signification

The symbolism of this culture permeates the structures of signification. The language observed consisted particularly of concepts and vocabulary emphasising mining-related matters. Communication is based primarily on 'manshifts', 'tonnage', 'cuts', 'seam', 'machine delays', 'supply of air', 'underground' and 'safety', all of which are important in defining the craft of coal extraction. 'Meaning' centred around the 'turning of coal'.

As is discussed later, work is viewed against a set of formal plans expressed in physical and financial terms. These plans established a set of formal priorities or objectives for a time period and to which the line are held accountable. However work in the main was viewed as technical. Formalised decisions, such as those contained in formal reporting systems, were considered untrustworthy unless managers had experience of such events, knew the people involved or, better still, were physically present at the time. Extraction related events reported in formal and informal reports bore a problematical relationship to actual events. Serious doubts were expressed whether formal (especially financial) reports could recognise (or as managers put it, 'define') the variability and controllability inherent in underground activities. Mining was thought to be so uncertain, difficult and ambiguous that it was felt that no accounting system could adequately make mining operations understandable and visible. Rather the (untested) adage adopted was that 'if you get production right, finance will fall into place' (Berry *et al.*, 1985b).

As a consequence of this informational uncertainty, a continuous concern of management has been to construct a 'mental picture' of what is 'really' happening underground. Managers seek to constantly add and recreate their picture of reality through cultivating multiple sources of information. Formal reports represent only one source and they are constantly supplemented by a series of planned interactions. For example, in the collieries, at least five important sources of information were cultivated by managers.

Firstly, financial and production reports: as will be discussed later, these were not simple 'objective' statements of the 'facts' of production. With regard to output and cost data a widely practised smoothing of figures was acknowledged to exist. The various output accounts, prepared daily, have pre-defined categories on 'Calculated Outputs', 'Weight Office Tonnage' and 'Reported Area'. Although these categories all describe the same set of events, the same figures often do not result.

Secondly, the line has a series of regular (daily) meetings with subordinates (e.g. the overman reports to the undermanager who reports to the deputy manager, who reports to the colliery manager, who reports to the production manager, who reports to the Area Director). A key person is the undermanager who not only receives reports from the overman, but also the assistant mechanical and electrical engineers, the linesman, and from people controlling ventilation, safety, etc. This kind of daily personal reporting is carried out between all levels of management in the collieries to discover and address short-run problems. In the process of reporting, information is filtered. This was expressed by one undermanager as 'they [the overman] only tell us what they want us to know'. Such managers internalise as normal, the everyday problem of knowing whether they have 'really' received the relevant information. Perhaps, partly as a response to such problems, undermanagers spend a considerable time underground, observing whether the reports received are actually 'true', since they appreciate the problematic status of underground mining reporting.

Thirdly, much information on repair work and delays is provided by craftsmen. This information is reported to the 'line' both at the level of undermanagers by assistant engineers and at the level of colliery managers by the colliery engineers. This type of information may be used to cross-check reports given through the 'line' e.g. by overmen, since both the assistant engineers and the overmen report on the same breakdowns. This often forms the basis for serious discussions about the functioning of the mine, because the highly interdependent production technology rarely permits a simple cause-effect relationship to be established. For example, the discussion of the cause of delays may frequently be inconclusive about whether it was caused by mechanical, electrical, geological or other (human) faults.

Fourthly, information provided through computer systems (e.g. MINOS) reports on delays and break-downs (as well as ventilation and other environmental data within the mine. There is considerable doubt whether these reports are reliable. Essential inputs are human, since explanations of the causes of delays and breakdowns are provided by the machine operator. Since the computer limits the number of acceptable explanations (e.g. machine failure, operator failure, etc.), the allocation of explanations is to some degree 'constrained'. often such operatives are not concerned about the accuracy of the explanations offered. Further, not all delays are recorded in this system. 'Minor' delays (which are 'paid' for by the men through the incentive scheme) tend not to be captured by the system. As a consequence delays frequently endure till the 'minor' delays are turned into 'larger' ones, for which the miners are compensated by the NCB. No attempts are made to accompany print-outs of delays with costs (Hopper *et al.*, 1986).

Lastly, the 'grapevine' is a further source of information. It is thought important by both colliery managers and undermanagers to 'keep one's ear to the ground'. In view of the problem they have in obtaining valid information about the mine, managers place great emphasis on developing extra lines of communication. For instance, one colliery manager claimed to have a 'fifth column' in the pub, which he regarded as an excellent place to get to learn about the mine. Other managers used trusted secretaries or ex underground staff. This kind of information is by nature problematic but managers believed that it provided important background, e.g. about how the men felt, which was useful for generally managing the mine, as well as occasionally providing significant detailed insights, e.g. on unsanctioned early leaving.

This detailed description of patterns of communication utilised illustrates Gidden's point that one can only examine structure through action. The formal information systems represent only a part of the communication systems utilised. Its usage, adoption and interpretation is variable and selective, and is often not consistent with the ways intended by the designer. Rather structures of languages and signs which inform meaning reside in the complex patterns of interaction. It is in such interaction that structures and patterns of meaning are created and recreated.

Legitimation

The structure of signification and the power of mining engineers must be legitimated through behaviour. The pattern of management employed in the line tended to be centralised, hierarchical, and paternalistic. Given the difficulty in establishing 'reality' underground, much of the management works on the assumption that people cannot be trusted. If they are not checked, policed and controlled then it is assumed that they will break rules and manipulate information. Hence, it can be argued, the need to constantly create different 'stories' from alternative sources arises in order to enrich and cross-check stories obtained elsewhere.

Considerable power, status and deference are accorded to the managerial roles of the Colliery Manager and Area Director. The legitimation of such key roles is ever-present. Firstly, the mining engineers filling such roles constantly display their expertise to peers and subordinates, by detailed scrutiny over, and intervention into, the work of subordinates. This requires detailed knowledge of workings which is problematic. However the legitimacy of the key roles resides in the ability to be seen to know the details of work and hence to be able to coordinate it. Consequently the key managers need to be able to publicly dispute subordinates' versions of the 'truth', with justification, to illustrate their ability to know and hence direct. This 'need to know' is coupled to a need to demonstrate the strength, status, and power of mining engineers.

However, the norms expressed in behaviour reside in a broader morality which sustains the balance of domination and signification. This emphasises the importance and continuity of coal extraction. External constraints, such as governmental policy, markets and financial demands, whilst not disregarded, tend to be seen, by lower subordinates, as less pertinent (often with justification) and hence in need of dampening. Thus mining norms need to be legitimated to the community and to the industry by supporting notions of turning coal and maintaining collieries when coal is still available, though not necessarily 'profitable' in accounting terms. Consequently, until recently, closure decisions were made on grounds of workable capacity rather than on economic criteria. If disputed by unions the debate became conducted through mining engineers on grounds of whether workable reserves existed. Similarly output allocations and cuts tended to be negotiated on the basis of 'fair shares' and 'equal agonies' between Areas and between collieries within Areas. In addition, cross-subsidisation of collieries through the accounts could also counteract the problems of closure for communities.

Such behaviour is legitimated through references to a broader morality. Collieries often exist in one-industry communities. The concerns of the industry are the concerns of the community because the enterprise is a major source of personal survival and 'meaning'. The work force, as well as management, are mainly recruited from such communities. Although moves between pits are common they are socialised in traditions that reinforce the importance of coal extraction for the survival of the community. Managers tend not only to be recruited from a community with its heritage in coal but through their training they are also socialised into mining norms. An important part of their education consists of gaining practical experience in supervisory positions underground. Because of their intensive underground training, senior managers know in detail the duties of subordinate managers. Therefore they are 'legitimately' able to specify the decisions to be carried out by subordinates and to oversee the work based on traditional mining values. Authority is legitimated because it is based on shared knowledge which is widely regarded as appropriate. A paternalistic leadership style is legitimate because the older and experienced managers know the 'correct' answers to mining-problems. In short the legitimacy of management practice is based on 'hard' mining experience and knowledge and an understanding of the heritage and the broader morality within coal-mining communities.

However, Colliery Managers and Area Directors work to attain two major objectives; 'to turn the coal', and to gain profit figures displayed in the budgets. Management strongly identifies with images of running an efficient, well-managed, flexible, profitable, private-like organisation, and resents attitudes that nationalised industries neglect such concerns. The extract from an interview with a colliery manager is typical in terms of the strong sense of commitment to, and also some confusion about, the necessary conditions for financial viability as it relates to production and profit:

> I'd like more financial accountability – the key factor I look to is the bottom line. Not OMS or bulk tonnes. It's profit, I don't need people to tell me we're over budget. I can read that . . . It's not a social service. I don't want to be part of a national embarrassment . . . You never see money – it's all a paper exercise. Yet there's satisfaction in turning in a paper profit. As a measure of efficiency; a measure of your own performance . . . We've got to work within national constraints. We try to produce as much coal at the right quality as we can.

Mining management also seeks legitimacy through efficiency and profitability, particularly with regard to important sectors external to the mining community. Financial considerations are incorporated by an emphasis on total unit costs and the associated belief, sometimes erroneous, that maximum output is the most efficient way to secure profitability. Little reference is made to cost-volume relationships, cash-flows or return on investment. The attempted reconciliation of profitability with increased output understandably helps rationalise the demands of the mining community for continuity with those emanating from other sectors of society seeking efficiency. The tensions of the countervailing moralities are explored later.

ACCOUNTING AND STRUCTURATION

Giddens's approach emphasises the need to observe actions rather than relying upon descriptions by involved parties. The dynamics of structuration are encapsulated by his notion of systems described earlier. The dialectical approach stresses how resources in the form of structures may be transformed as subjects borrow from them selectively and differently over time. Roberts and Scapens (1985) outline how Giddens's methods of analysis might be employed in accounting research. They distinguish between the abstract system and the systems in use, calling the former 'the accounting systems' and the latter as structures, i.e. 'a body of rules and resources which are drawn upon in the practice of accounting' (ibid., p. 447), whereas systems of accountability are seen as integral to structuration. They comment that, 'how and why and in what way [accounting systems] are drawn upon will vary over time, from situation to situation and from person to person. It is an understanding of the nature of this variety, its origins and consequences, which is the object of our attempts to understand accounting practices' (ibid., p. 447). This section employs the distinction between accounting systems and systems of accountability made by Roberts and Scapens in an attempt to explicate how accounting was observed to be used within the NCB.

NCB Accounting Systems

NCB accounting systems need to be seen in their context of physical colliery plans, from which they flow. Each colliery prepares an Action Programme for at least the next six quarter-years covering face layouts and physical resources required; and long-term plans (up to 20 years) covering physical factors and resources. Colliery Action Programmes set out the colliery manager's physical objectives including saleable tonnage, manpower, and development work. The financial assessments required to achieve the plans for each colliery are used to form the basis of Area and Colliery budgets (MMC Report, 1983). As would be expected such plans involve a series of iterations hierarchically up the line and with staff departments. Action plans are updated regularly and periodically translated financially as projections, although these updates and projections are not synchronised.

The financial reporting system is based on two sets of accounts. The first is the *Profit and Loss Account* (F23) which details proceeds and costs and computes a profit figure for each colliery. These are aggregated to form the Area profit or loss. However a degree of 'slack' is built into the Area budget by a system of 'relaxation allowances'. The Area budget is normally less than the aggregated colliery budgets. This permits senior management scope for discretion which, inter alia, permits them to cope with uncertainties. During the period the Area was studied the key-statistics for control purposes appeared to be: (i) output (tonnes) per manshift, (ii) earnings (wages) per manshift, (iii) costs per tonne of coal produced, (iv) percentage of overtime incurred, (v) total output and proceeds, (vi) total costs. The other set of reports is a *Wages Cost Summary* (F22) which gives details about the deployment of men in terms of face work, development-work, transport work and different kinds of surface work. These categories specify the usage of manshifts and how labour was paid (ordinary pay, overtime pay, incentive pay). These statistics focus on output, on material costs and on the use of manshifts, giving a set of ratios for labour productivity.

The management accounts can be criticised from a conventional accounting viewpoint on several important counts. This occurred prior to the subsequent national dispute (MMC, 1983) and during it (Berry et al., 1985b; Glyn, 1984; Kerevan and Saville, 1985). There is little recognition of variability in costs and profits; the financial reports do not distinguish between fixed and variable costs; the cost of capital investment is not adequately reflected in the accounts; an arbitrary practice of allocating Area and Headquarter costs to collieries is employed; proceeds are identified on the basis of coal produced rather than coal sold. Berry et al., (1985a) attempted to explicate from the managerial perspective why the accounts had developed in such a form. They noted that the 'Accounting statements have evolved into ambiguous documents with well known uncertainties about the reliability of data and the extent of controllability. However, the ambiguity, as well as assisting direct control of the collieries, has permitted management to cope with conflicting and often inconsistent demands from trades unions and government' (ibid., p. 24). However problems associated with sharp environmental discontinuities were noted, especially market and governmental shifts.

The next section seeks to elaborate and extend these observations by reference to subsequent research observing accountability meetings.

Systems of Accountability

The accounting system described above forms the basis of accountability as attempted by the NCB. To the extent that the accounts are utilised our observations suggest they are used in comparisons of budget with decisions about the future taken on the basis of physical, engineering data. Accountability is formally effected through an elaborate set of meetings: daily and weekly in the colliery; monthly and quarterly between colliery and Area; and quarterly between Area and Headquarters. The daily meetings took place during the morning and consisted of highly elaborate, and time consuming procedures of subordinates reporting to their superiors, mainly verbally. They focused on the day-to-day activities of the mine on a technical basis. Their aim seems to be the allocation of men and materials around the pit on a short-term basis. Accountability meetings at the other levels also concentrated on the interpretation of physical activities in reviewing and producing plans. These are reviewed both by reference to the Action Programme (which is a blue-print of the physical work to be done) and also the Development Programme (which is a blue-print of the planned development work). The review also embraced actual performance physically and against budget, i.e. the F22 and F23s and revisions also applied to the financial budget in terms of projections. It is difficult however, to see the financial control consequences of these projections since colliery managers appear to be held responsible to a fixed revenue-cost budget (Berry et al., 1985a). Accountability meetings were by no means inconsequential: they were serious and time-consuming. For example, the Colliery to Area meetings normally lasted half a day and involved extensive preparations on both sides and were rehearsed for on critical occasions. On the Area side they normally involved the Area Director, deputy directors, the relevant production manager and Area heads of marketing, industrial relations, and accounting. On the colliery side the team normally consisted of the colliery manager, his assistant, and chief engineers. Similarly careful preparation and much managerial time was spent on the meetings between Area Management and Headquarters.

Ostensibly, from the data supplied to meetings, it might appear that the financial aspects were of major significance. Certainly financial statements formed a significant part of the briefing papers. Such statements act as a series of codes for signification. It has been argued that accounting systems not only define a set of categories but also fashion the preoccupations of people in organisations (Jain, 1973, Burchell *et al.* 1980). For example, Burchell *et al.* (1980, p. 5) suggest that

> what is accounted for can shape organizational participants' views of what is important, the categories of dominant economic discourse and organizational functioning that are implicit within the accounting framework help to create a particular conception of organizational reality.

The language and categories of accounting systems (e.g. profit, loss, waste, labour cost) tend to provide meaning for people and what is *not* accounted for has less legitimate meaning. Both reflect the emphasis in the discourse of the organisation. However, the precise meanings interpreted from the financial reports will themselves be open to dispute since financial reports are themselves ambiguous and based on a multitude of underlying relationships in production (Cooper *et al.*,1981). Further, categories that do not exist in accounting systems (quality, safety, alienation, etc.) reflect and constitute those issues which it may not be legitimate to manage or be concerned about. The way in which financial reports are used is most apparent in accountability meetings, where the particular interpretation of the categories is created and recreated.

It is important to observe however that accounting systems by no means constitute the only source of meaning since our observations of these meetings suggest that the financial reports are in fact not even the main point of reference for discussing underground activities. Attempts are not made to evaluate different potential courses of action in financial terms. Rather, detailed discussion concerned the use of specific machinery and the particular organising of pit-bottom supervision. Detailed short-run commands were frequently given by the superior and invariably accepted by the subordinate. The mode of intervention was hierarchical and the superiors' decisions deferred to. These accountability meetings tended to concentrate almost entirely on technical issues relating to production, to staffing and occasionally to industrial relations. The apparent lack of financial evaluation of potential courses of action was explained by managers in terms of financial reporting not taking into consideration the uncertainties (geological, engineering and perhaps industrial relations) inherent in mining. Also finance was not thought to reflect the long-run character of mining because it emphasises a short-run and marginalist conception of performance.

The lack of use of financial reports, as revealed through the accountability meetings, tends to reinforce the primacy of production, technology and physical output considerations. Decisions are based primarily on the application of well-tested and well-known engineering and production methods. Financial reports are not considered relevant it seems. However this does not necessarily mean that financial concepts and language do not underpin discussions of what are essentially seen as mining type problems. The concerns for operating efficiency in terms of allocation of men and materials and of ensuring that work is actually carried out is clearly related to a concern for financial efficiency. This latter concern (ensuring that work is done) reflects the nature of coal mining: of apparent invisibility, high uncertainty, important interdependencies in the production processes (e.g. integration of face-technology and conveyors), and long spacial distribution of the physical lay-out. This situation creates a particular problem for managers to get to know what 'actually' goes on in the pit. This is seen in physical terms and finance and accounting is assumed to be taken care of by getting production 'right'.

Earl and Hopwood (1980) argue that frequently there are several competing sources of information in organisations. Formal financial reports are clearly not the only medium through which managers get information about what goes on in the organisation. Accountability is only possible if there is at least one medium through which 'visibility' of production may be created. Given that the nature of the information provided is so varied and ambiguous in this industry, the process of interpretation is one based on the premise that what counts as 'reality' is debatable. For example, although the Area Director tended to emphasise effective cost control in his accountability meeting to Headquarters, he found that Headquarters officials argued that improvements were due to phasing variances and were not attributable to anything that the Area management did.

The discussion of the formal reports is not only a question of 'accountability'. Because of the hierarchical and centralised way in which the accountability meetings are carried out, there is a strong element of the superior defining concrete actions to be carried out by the subordinate. As such the accountability meetings tend to provide 'correct' answers – and perhaps even the 'correct' problems, the accounting systems being drawn from selectively by superiors to create and recreate fresh issues. For example, at a previous accountability meeting with Area management a colliery manager had been extensively criticised for being over budget on materials. At the subsequent meeting the item was never discussed, much to the annoyance of the manager who had achieved budget by stopping official recording of materials requisitions once the budget limit had been reached!

As our observations of accountability proceeded, the less rational models of financial control expounded in texts appeared appropriate. Rather than witnessing a technical exercise of planning and control on formal data, we realised that we were observing, in part, a social phenomenon involving power and legitimacy. With regard to legitimacy, it appeared that the technical systems and data surrounding the accountability meetings enabled management to project an image of technical efficiency and rationality to external agencies and, to a degree, themselves. However when attention was directed at the financial reports, it tended to be cursory and ritualistic. Observations of the processes within such meetings indicated major divergencies from modes of decision-making implicit in conventional models (often for good reason). Instead the meetings involved other purposes such as their use as a vehicle for reproducing the mining culture and for testing whether rights and obligations inherent within it were being adhered to. For example, the key line managers were expected to display their competence by producing a full and rich picture of 'reality' underground by utilising and cross-checking multiple sources of information. Thus the variety of information could be pulled upon selectively to 'test' for inconsistencies. Through such accounts to colleagues the methods of mining engineers are reproduced and reaffirmed, and new entrants socialised where necessary. The latter was vividly illustrated in one colliery accountability meeting where the colliery manager was able to reduce to tears a young graduate undermanager for not cross-checking reports from deputies and hence, according to the colliery manager being unable to reconcile their inconsistencies with reports emanating from elsewhere. The belief that 'you can only control if you know everything' was central to the dominance of the mining line and their claims to co-ordinate the work of others. However this had to be ritually reproduced and witnessed by others. Mining managers unable to do so were quickly sanctioned. Similarly senior mining managers legitimated their status and hierarchical powers by displaying, through detailed interventions, and knowledge, their ability to recognise and resolve mining problems. The accountability system thus provided regularised points in time whereby such legitimation could be secured.

In so far as the mining line can legitimate itself in such a manner, the systems of accountability provide an opportunity for the domination of mining engineers over other functions to be reproduced and witnessed. Accountability in concept (and as observed) involved interpersonal interactions almost exclusively concentrated along the mining line. Marketing and Finance entered in only a very limited sense, usually concerning quality. When introduced they were only briefly and deferentially spoken about by personnel outside the line. Marketing and financial issues rarely stimulated sustained comment or action. In fact Finance personnel after discussing with us our observations on meetings decided not to be present at meetings between Area and Collieries. In such a manner the meetings served to reinforce to the whole organisation the dominance of mining engineers and their concerns, to other professionals.

However, within the mining line power is neither unlimited nor absolute. As Giddens argues, 'the dialectic of control is built into the very nature of agency, or more correctly put, the relations of autonomy and dependence which agents reproduce in the context of the enactment of definite practices. *An agent who does not participate in the dialectic of control, in a minimal fashion, ceases to be an agent*' (Giddens, 1979, p. 149, emphasis as in original). Higher levels of management are dependent upon lower levels for information. Given the ability of lower management to 'smooth' information, the information itself becomes a source of uncertainty.

A 'secondary effect' or 'unacknowledged consequence' of the interventionist managerial style, can be the realisation by subordinates that smoothing is 'useful'. This serves to increase the propensity by superiors to demand more detailed information from subordinates, and this reinforces the pressure for intervention which further strains the interpersonal relationships between superior and subordinate. The social rule 'know everything in detail' seems to apply to all managers at all levels both in the colliery and at Area. One consequence is that suspicion and lack of trust becomes part of the culture of relationships between managers.

Senior NCB managers show great concern for the organisation of pit-bottom activities and because of the ambiguity in mining, planned and actual accounting figures rarely coincide on a day-to-day basis. In order to prevent the detailed intervention that this might provoke subordinates tend to smooth information. And since everybody in a hierarchy is in some sense a subordinate, smoothing occurs frequently at all levels. But since superiors want to engage in detailed intervention they tend to demand highly detailed information. The attempts to juxtapose different 'independent' sources of information reflects the concern of managers to achieve control through information and detailed hierarchical intervention. But also the use of multiple data sources reflects the resistance by subordinates to control in this manner, particularly about issues which they know are ambiguous and unpredictable. The widely practised smoothing of output figures and materials costs may also be a response to the tension between the inherent ambiguity of mining operations (in terms of geology, technology and perhaps industrial relations) and a concern to maintain the rationalistic need for a notion of stability and continuity in mining. Whilst others have focused on the use of slack as a response to performance evaluation pressures and managerial concerns with their careers (Cyert and March, 1963; Otley, 1978) we are stressing that in this industry a cause and consequence of smoothing is that it reproduces the ongoing stable (and viable) character of mining. Attempts are made to present the figures in such a way that they 'show' that the colliery is following the plan and is therefore a steady state. In creating a picture which stresses the 'successful' fulfilment of the laid-down plan managers reinforce the notion of longer-run concerns. The smoothing is an attempt by managers to make 'visible' what they see as the 'normal' state of the mine, devoid of 'random fluctuations'.

Moreover, in this particular culture bureaucratic and technical solutions to achieving visibility and hence control, which are becoming increasingly credible, may be resisted because they essentially represent an attempt to control the colliery from the surface. Such an 'office-approach' to management is not in accordance with the traditional style of management which stresses *underground experience* as the main basis for knowledge. Computer systems and formal accounting systems hence challenge the view that mining-knowledge is necessarily 'qualitative' and judgemental. The fact that 'alternative' sources of information, stressed and cultivated in mining management, are basically non-financial reflects the concern to be 'close-to-production' and to discount more bureaucratic, economic and financial approaches to mining management.

Contradictions

Giddens's analysis is not merely an attempt to relate action to structure. Rather it is concerned, through the latter, to study contradictions in social systems and patterns of stratification therein. Such analysis has tended to be neglected in much of the organisational work on culture, certainly as it relates to accounting systems. Social contradictions are defined by Giddens as an 'opposition or disjunction of structural principles of social systems, where those principles operate in terms of each other, but at the same time contravene one another' (1979, p. 141). The position that contradiction underlies or stimulates movements of historical change is consistent with Marx's argument that capitalism is intrinsically contradictory in that the socialised nature of production is at odds with its private appropriation. The message of the analysis is not to look for the functions that social practices fulfil, but instead for the contradictions they embody and in which they are played through.

Such advice is pertinent, for contradiction runs through the culture of mining engineers and their methods of management. In turn this is a consequence of having to cope with more general contradictions. Extracts from an interview with a senior mining manager illustrate the contradiction between economic management, political pressures and traditions of continuity:

> In strategic business terms my task is to maintain profitability in an adverse market. I'm doing this as others would: maintaining a low investment profile and tight cost control, just as any other managing director would.

In response to a question on alternative accounting methods:

> it would give me a different feel. But the profit and loss account is a moveable feast, as you well know . . . I have an inherent feel of

the politics that affect us. We can't do it this way – we're too constrained and the whole thing is political.

In talking about senior management in peripheral coal areas:

> Their problem is not finance, but how to cope with closures. The social consequences are so great. Showing the NUM the balance sheets would not make any difference. They wouldn't accept them or understand them, or they would realise the figures are arbitrary and start challenging them. If the Government had the political courage to make each Area a separate company then it would be different, but it's not politically feasible ... the social consequences would be tremendous...

And,

> I'll be here much longer than the Board members ... I want to make sure that there is an industry in the future.

Much later, talking of the future problems:

> If the strike ballot is yes and the government takes them [NUM] on, then I become a virtual bystander in the proceedings.

The extracts encapsulate many of the contradictions and dilemmas in the mining management culture. The task is increasingly defined in private sector terms, using private sector models and images, and defined in the language of private appropriation. Financial language is emerging from its hitherto hidden position yet, when extended and applied to the concrete, physical task, the financial models and methods are treated with scepticism. Instead the task is defined in terms of managing the politics – not only the industry with government, but also the resistance of workforce, rather than by a purely financial approach. Legitimation is secured in terms of needing to incorporate social consequences and protect the industry in the longer-run against short-run and perceived damaging intervention by politicians or their appointees who might not have such interests at heart. However if open conflict with the trades unions ensues then management becomes relatively peripheral: government then becomes dominant.

The management task is defined in contradictory terms: on the one hand justified by the models of private appropriation, on the other hand in terms of social consequences and maintaining continuity of the industry. To a degree the contradiction is recognised. Indeed the legitimacy of the role resides in the ability to reconcile or cope with such contradictions and the avoidance of outright conflict. If conflict ensues then the management role becomes irrelevant.

The NCB case is a cameo of many managers' ambiguous and contradictory position within class systems, deriving in part from their positions within organisational controls (Braverman, 1974; Wright, 1978; Willmott, 1984). Managers are potentially both victims and agents. As the above quotation illustrates, mining managers are themselves, as well as many of their communities, threatened by controls based on private appropriation. Yet their relatively privileged positions within capitalism are secured, in competition with other professional groups, by providing a peculiar set of skills that assist the control of organisations, and hence appropriation of its wealth. The mining industry has been characterised historically by a considerable degree of labour resistance, whose effects impinge on national politics. Consequently a degree of social concern has had to be incorporated in governmental and managerial policies. In addition, since nationalisation, the industry has been subjected to political ends other than mere private profitability, e.g. regional policy, employment, etc. To a degree the dominance of mining engineers has resided not only in their technical skills but also their ability to respond to the contradictions and varying pressures placed upon their industry. As the mining engineer quoted above states, to act upon 'an inherent feel for the politics that affect us'.

SUMMARY

The case presented here shows a set of practices which underline the persistence and durability of established patterns of behaviour. Action seems to be institutionalised in the daily reproduction of the status quo. In terms of the theory of structuration the character of this stable social system (of reproduced behaviour) is that production and mining form the common denominator of meaning. A second element is the moral obligation of managers to create 'viable' collieries. The third element is the domination of the 'line' to define 'adequate problems and solutions' of day-to-day mining. Hence, we argue, the creation and recreation of structures of meaning, morality and domination in the mining frame of meaning is reinforced by the way in which managers negotiate the financial reports from four aspects.

Firstly, meaning is created in relation to both the accounting model and in relation to the actual use of these figures. The accounting model focuses on production accounts (tonnage, proceeds, manpower, productivity) all expressed in non-commensurate terms and reflecting the concerns of managers with coal extraction. The actual preparation of figures (and verbal accounts) includes a certain level of smoothing as an attempt to reinforce perceived stability and continuity. Coal extraction is perceived as essentially long-run and stable despite the inherent ambiguity of day-to-day mining. Further, the fact that alternative potential courses of action are evaluated solely in technical terms and technical feasibility emphasises the 'close-to-production' character of mining management.

Secondly, morality is sustained because of the concentration on output. Maximisation of output implies maximisation of workers' wages because of the incentive scheme and, even more important, the maintenance of employment. This means 'wealth' and survival of the community and the colliery. And since managers tend to smooth figures, attempts are made to show that 'all is well' and that there are prospects for the longer-run survival of particular collieries.

Thirdly, domination by the 'line' is recreated because the way in which the financial reports are used reinforces the notion that finance is irrelevant and that mining criteria should be employed. Finance is rejected because conventional financial models it is argued do not reveal the multifaceted, long-run and uncertain nature of mining. But also, when used, the financial reports are but a point of departure into the detailed discussion of particular problems usually at specific faces in a colliery.

Lastly, through examination of the structures produced in structuration, attention is drawn to fundamental contradictions within the mining frame of meaning and reflections made upon this in respect to the ambiguous and contradictory position within class structures that managers are simultaneously in, and exploit.

By trying to relate action, structure and contradiction the case has attempted to illustrate how the purely interpretive studies of culture might be extended to include structural and power considerations.

POSTSCRIPT

In the course of the research the growing presence of finance in the affairs of the NCB was becoming apparent, e.g. MMC report, 1983. Much of the pressure for this appeared to be coming from external sources, namely government rather than from the NCB management itself. In this respect it is important to note that the Area researched was widely acknowledged to be an efficient and well managed section of the NCB. Confronted with a position of over-supply of coal, considerable energy was directed at the identification and hence closure of collieries in what was deemed to be an 'uneconomic' tail of the industry. It was widely believed that the elimination of this 'tail' would resolve the problems of over-capacity and restore the industry to profitability. As is widely known the miners union (NUM) in the bitter and prolonged coal dispute of 1984/85 challenged this strategy. Miners' representatives stressed the social effects of pit closures, e.g. on unemployment, local communities, etc., whereas NCB management, and government in particular emphasised the financial deficits of collieries within the industry. Thus the accounting system, which had to a degree lain dormant, was drawn from to provide a fresh set of meanings and morality to justify policy. As the dispute was prolonged, the financial frame of meaning appeared to be publicly expressed more and more. The ideological aspects of accounting and its relationship to control of the labour process in the industry and, to a lesser extent, the dispute is explored elsewhere (Hopper *et al.*, 1986).

Since the cessation of the dispute it would appear that financial rather than social issues predominate in governmental control of the industry and hence its management. The effect of this upon the dominant mining culture, methods of management, and systems of accountability is not known. However, we might surmise that accountability may draw from a fresh set of structures inherent in the accounting system. No doubt some mining engineers will identify and create new processes of structuration to reflect changed circumstances. With others the old culture may prevail and a cycle of resistance through their agency may ensue. Others may simply leave the industry, feeling at odds with the new concerns. Whether the dominance of mining engineers and their culture will be maintained is problematical.

There is reason to believe that the full-cost base of the accounting system may be seriously challenged, as an industry subject to increasing pressure towards 'renewal' and change requires a completely different set of management concepts, perhaps emphasising marginality and enterprise-based rather than a social concept of performance (Berry et al., 1985b). Finance represents a different mode of rationality or frame of meaning which tends to reflect, and perhaps help constitute, some of the pressures for change, particularly in view of the attempts by the British Government to privatise large parts of public industry and to induce spending limits and cutbacks. As such the financial system may become more public and a focus of resistance for workers in the industry.

References

S. L. Ansari and J. Bell, Implications of Culture for the Study of Accounting and Control Systems, paper to E.I.A.S.M. Workshop on Accounting and Culture, Amsterdam (1985).

A. J. Berry, T. Capps, D. Cooper, P. Fergusson, T. Hopper and E. A. Lowe, 'Management Control in an Area of the NCB; Rationales of Accounting Practices in a Public Enterprise', *Accounting, Organizations and Society*, vol. 10, no 1 (1985a) pp. 3–28.

A. J. Berry, T. Capps, D. J. Cooper, T. M. Hopper and E. A. Lowe, 'NCB Accounts – a Mine of Mis-information', *Accountancy* (Jan. 1985b) pp. 8–10.

R. J. Boland and L. R. Pondy, 'Accounting in Organisations: A Union of Natural and Rational perspectives', *Accounting, Organizations and Society*, vol. 8, no. 2/3 (1983) pp. 223–34.

H. Braverman, *Labor and Monopoly Capital: The Degradation of Work in Twentieth Century* (New York: Monthly Review Press, 1974).

S. Burchell, S. Clubb, A. Hopwood, J. Hughes and J. Nahapiet, 'The Roles of Accounting in Organizations and Society', *Accounting, Organizations and Society* (1980) pp. 5–27.

T. Capps, D. J. Cooper, T. M. Hopper and E. A. Lowe, Accountability and Control within the North Derbyshire Area of the NCB. Report to the Economic and Social Research Council (1984).

I. Colville, 'Reconstructing Behavioural Accounting', *Accounting, Organizations and Society* (1981) pp. 119–32.

D. J. Cooper, D. Hayes and F. Wolf, 'Accounting in Organised Anarchies: Understanding and Designing Accounting Systems in Ambiguous Situations', *Accounting, Organizations and Society* (1981) pp. 175–92.

T. Cutler, C. Haslam, J. Williams and K. Williams, 'Aberystwyth Coal Report', in D. J. Cooper and T. M. Hopper (eds), *Debating Coal Closures* (Cambridge University Press, forthcoming).

R. M. Cyert and J. G. March, *A Behavioural Theory of the Firm* (Prentice-Hall, 1963).

M. J. Earl and A. G. Hopwood, 'From Management Information to Information Management' in H. C. Lucas Jr., F. F. Land, T. J. Lincoln and K. Supper (eds), *The Information Systems Environment* (Amsterdam and New York: North Holland, 1980).
M. Felinek, L. Smircich and P. Hirsch, 'Introduction: A Coat of Many Colors', *Administrative Science Quarterly* vol. 28, no. 3 (1983), pp. 331–8.
A. Giddens, *New Rules of Sociological Method* (Hutchinson, 1976).
A. Giddens, *Central Problems in Social Theory: Action, Structure and Contradiction in Social Analysis* (Macmillan, 1979).
A. Giddens, *The Constitution of Society* (Cambridge: Polity Press, 1984).
B. G. Glaser and A. L. Strauss, *The Discovery of Grounded Theory: Strategies for Qualitative Research* (Weidenfeld & Nicolson, 1968).
A. Glyn, *Economic Aspects of the Coal Industry Dispute*. Report prepared for the National Union of Mineworkers (October 1984).
T. M. Hopper, D. J. Cooper, T. Capps, E. A. Lowe and J. Mouritsen, 'Financial Control and the Labour Process in the National Coal Board' in H. Willmott and D. Knights (eds), *Management and the Labour Process* (Aldershot: Gower, 1986).
A. G. Hopwood, 'On Trying to Study Accounting in the Contexts in which it Operates', *Accounting, Organizations and Society* (1983) pp. 287–305.
T. N. Jain, 'Alternative Methods of Accounting and Decision-Making: A Psycho-Linguistical Analysis', *The Accounting Review* vol. 48, no. 1 (1973) pp. 95–104.
G. Kerevan and R. Saville, *The Economic Case for Deep-Mined Coal in Scotland*, Report presented to the National Union of Mineworkers in Scotland (1985).
Monopolies and Mergers Commission, (MMC), *National Coal Board: Volumes 1 & 2*, (Cmnd, 8920, HMSO 1983).
D. T. Otley, Strategies for research in Studying the use made of accounting information in organisational control. Proceedings of E.I.A.S.M. Workshop, (September 1978).
J. Roberts and R. Scapens, 'Accounting Systems and Systems of Accountability – Understanding Practices in their Organisational Contexts', *Accounting, Organizations and Society* (1985), pp. 443–56.
D. Rosenberg, C. Tomkins and P. Day, A work role perspective of accountants in local government service departments, *Accounting, Organizations and Society* (1982) pp. 123–38.
A. Schutz, *Collected Papers* (Monton, 1967).
L. Smircich, 'Studying Organisations and Cultures' in G. Morgan (ed.), *Beyond Method* (Sage, 1983).
H. C. Willmott, 'Images and Ideals of Managerial Work: A Critical Examination of Conceptual and Empirical Accounts', *Journal of Management Studies*, vol. 21 (1984).
E. O. Wright, *Class, Crisis and the State* (London: New Left Books, 1978).

12 The Accounting Profession, Corporatism and the State*

David Cooper, Tony Puxty, Tony Lowe and Hugh Willmott

This paper is concerned with accounting – particularly the occupation, but also its practices and knowledge and its relationship with the state. In so far as we refer to specific occupational groupings of accountants and to specific state institutions, we will be referring to those in the UK. Focusing on the relationship between the UK state and the UK accounting profession may seem rather peculiar in a book concerned with management control, where the latter term is usually applied to the management of organisations. Our analysis is provided, however, to illustrate a social analysis of the relationship between an organisation and its environment, a relationship which is implicit in most conventional studies of management control. In so doing we also wish to explain how accountancy is intertwined with the state and those corporatist arrangements that developed (sometimes temporarily) in several countries.

The paper proceeds in six parts. Firstly, we show how the conventional model which treats the environment as separate from, and uncontrollable by, the management of an organisation, is descriptively inadequate since it ignored the power of, and constraints on, managerial action. This first section on the environment can be regarded as explaining why this chapter is relevant to the themes of this book. The second section argues that an adequate theory of management control of and in the accounting profession

---

*This chapter arises from preliminary work conducted for the project 'Accounting Regulation as Corporatist Control', which is funded by the Economic and Social Research Council (grant E04250007). We gratefully acknowledge its support, and the comments of Stuart Burchell, Anthony Hopwood, Keith Robson and Tony Tinker on drafts of this chapter.

must focus on its environment not as something that is separate from the profession but as a set of institutions that are intricately and dialectically inter-related with it (Burchell *et al.*, 1985). To understand (and control) a profession requires an understanding of those institutions which we collectively refer to as the state.

Corporatism has been suggested as a useful way of analysing the relationship between the state and quasi-regulatory bodies (Streek and Schmitter, 1985; Panitch, 1980). In so far as the accounting profession initiates regulations on behalf of its members and the state, then the corporatist model may clarify the relationship and suggest how the state may be involved in the regulation of the accountancy profession itself. We suggest that this model usefully illustrates the historically contingent, materialist basis and dialectical relationship between the state and the profession. The model is particularly valuable in emphasising the problematic nature of control due to the fragmented nature of the profession and the state. However, despite these strengths, the model has several unresolved difficulties, notably in relation to its reductionist and equilibrial tendencies (Tomlinson, 1983). The fourth section therefore returns to a review of theories and the state, with particular emphasis on the post Marxist analyses of Offe (1975; 1984) and Habermas (1976). Combining the insights of the corporatist model with the post-Marxist, 'crisis' model of the state allows us, in section five, to partially resolve the difficulties of the corporatist model and thereby offer what we believe to be a convincing and theoretically grounded explanation of the recent history of the inflation accounting standard in the UK. We briefly conclude by relating our arguments back to the 'management control' problematic.

THE ENVIRONMENT IN CONVENTIONAL APPROACHES TO MANAGEMENT CONTROL

Conventional approaches to management control tend to adopt a mechanistic systems view which identifies organisational performance as the outcome of the combined effect of environmental or market behaviour (which is regarded as uncontrollable) and the behaviour of the organisation (which is regarded as manageable, at least to a degree). Writers as varied as Anthony (1965), Rhenman (1974) and Lawrence and Lorsch (1967), all share this basic approach. Management control is seen as the ways in which management can change the organisation (e.g. its technology, personnel, information, behaviour) to respond to exogeneous and uncontrollable environmental disturbances. Even writers such as Galbraith (1973) who recognise that managers can choose which strategy or response to adopt, view the environment as separate from, and largely uncontrollable by, the organisation.

The reasons for this assumed uncontrollability of the environment are rarely made explicit. One approach suggests that an environment may be essentially unpredictable due to its complexity and turbulence (Emery and Trist, 1965; Terreberry, 1968). This complexity may be created, for example, by the interactions of many organisations, by the alleged inherent randomness of the world, or because of limitations in information. An alternative explanation for the uncontrollability of environments relates to the alleged power of the 'environment' in comparison to that of the 'organisation' (Aldrich, 1979; Pfeffer and Salancik, 1978). The environmental dominance approach to management control rarely articulates the reasons for the power of the environment (even the strategic contingencies model fails to explain why contingencies are 'strategic' or indeed, scarce) and the processes by which this power is reflected in organisational and managerial action.

These views can be challenged on ontological grounds (about the nature of 'reality') but for our present purposes it is sufficient to identify the implicit pluralism in the complexity argument. The pluralist view implies that no one element of the complex environment is particularly significant; interactions between elements, or the multiple, independent elements of the environment, are regarded as affecting the disturbance and uncontrollability of the environment. Whilst there may indeed be pluralities, our analysis will suggest that forces of class relations dominate social activity and these should be recognised in an analysis of the environment, and of power within it. In other words, environmental uncertainty is produced by agents whose action reproduces society which in capitalist societies results in the appropriation of surplus value in a social context of contradictory and conflicting forces.

Further, we suggest that it is much more fruitful to analyse the reciprocal and mutually supportive roles of organisations and their environments (Knights and Roberts, 1982; Neimark and Tinker, 1986). This emphasis serves to highlight the dialectics of power and control in the interdependent relationship between organisations and their environments. Neither can exist independently nor in ignorance of the other but instead each is part of the social fabric in which they both exist (Therborn, 1978). This social context influences the way they are related and behave much more fundamentally than is recognised in conventional, pluralistic models of 'systems' or 'contingencies'. Thus, in their analysis of power and management control Robson and Cooper (this volume) emphasise how organisations are both constitutive and reflective of the society in which they operate. Organisations exist not so much in, but also because of, their environment (Lowe and McInnes, 1971). In capitalist societies, the motivating force may be seen to be the accumulation of capital through the systematic extraction of the surplus after labour has been provided with sufficient to 'reproduce' itself and the appropriation of this capital by the owners and controllers of capital.

The argument that organisations and environments are both constitutive and reflexive of society is clearly brought into focus if we consider the management control of the accountancy profession. The accountancy profession may be likened to an organisation and its environment may be regarded as the state. Management control can exist at different levels of analysis but we will focus on the 'control' of the profession by the State and the 'control' of the members by the Institutes of the profession and how each aspect of control interrelates with the other. Management control systems are conceptualised as part of the process by which surplus value is appropriated and realised and through which social relations between capital and labour are reproduced. We then see how 'control' of and in the accountancy profession indicates the intermingling of the 'organisation' of the profession and its environment and that the organisation cannot be adequately analysed through a study of its 'internal' processes. Instead an 'external' dynamic, identifying the importance of the state in the control of the profession, is essential to understand the actions of the accounting profession and how control is affected both 'within' and of the profession.

THE ACCOUNTANCY PROFESSION

Most studies of the accounting profession have focused on accountancy firms, their structure and management processes. For example there have been studies of bureaucratisation of firms (Montagna, 1974) and management control techniques which could be applied to audit work (Dillard and Ferris, 1979). Such studies do not relate, however, to the control of the occupational group and the activities which they perform. Of more relevance for an analysis of the occupation of accountancy and accounting practices in general are studies of the historical development of what is known today as the accountancy profession and analyses of the role of professional organisations in the regulation of the economy and society.

Most historical studies of accountancy offer a picture of an accountancy profession that responds to social and economic pressures (Stacey, 1954; Gilling, 1976; Jones, 1981; Carey, 1969). The accountancy profession is seen to respond to pressures in its environment (Jones, 1981, for example cites the growth and internationalisation of business and increasing government intervention) and to thereby provide a service to the nation. Implicit in this approach is a functionalist and unitary model of society and professional groups within it (Cooper, 1984). Conflicts over society's needs are not recognised and the approach represents little more than an elaborate justification for the status quo. From this perspective, professions such as accountancy are privileged (in that they possess a degree of self-regulation and are given the freedom to monopolise their labour market, thereby ensuring high status and rewards for their members) because they are assumed to fulfil important social functions. It is usually taken for granted that these functions are indeed important or valuable to all members of society although such views are increasingly challenged. (Briston and Perks, 1977; US Senate, 1976; Briloff, 1976; Tinker, 1985). Even those studies that identify differing 'segments' (e.g. audit, consulting, taxation, insolvency work as suggested in part by Montagna, 1974, or in terms of the differing professional Institutes of the profession) adopt a functionalist approach.

Such 'segmented' theories, do however, introduce a degree of dynamism into what is otherwise a very static analysis by suggesting that different segments may respond to different social constituencies and needs. Yet they offer little explanation for the origins or development of the posited needs of a society. The plurality of needs are all assumed to be legitimate and equally significant in explaining changes in the profession. Further, the functional approach in general displays the dualism of conventional analysis of organisations and their environment which was discussed in the previous section. It treats the accountancy profession as distinct from, and determined by, its environment. As Hopwood (1985) suggests, this dualism may be more apparent than real.

Terry Johnson's work (1972; 1977; 1980; 1982) represents the most developed and coherent attempt to develop a theory of the social role of the accounting profession. His 1972 book focused on the relationship between the producer and consumer of various occupational accounting services. The crucial issue for Johnson was how the uncertainty and tension in the producer–consumer relationship was resolved. He suggests that accountancy does not conform to the 'professional' mode of resolution which involves the producer (i.e. the accountant) defining the needs of the consumer for their services (organisations and users) and the way in which these needs are catered for. Instead Johnson argues that, for the occupation of accountancy, it may be more appropriate to think in terms of corporate patronage, by which 'the consumer defines his own needs and the manner in which they are to be met' (1972, p. 46). Johnson also identifies that state mediation is an increasingly important form by which the producer–consumer relationship is resolved. As we show in this paper, state mediation is also of increasing importance for the occupation of accountancy.

Johnson's later work addresses the issue of why the tension in the producer–consumer relationship is resolved in one way for accountancy (i.e. in terms of corporate patronage or state mediation) whereas for lawyers it has been in terms of a 'profession' (the producer in control) and for other occupations, typically those popularly regarded as semi-professional, it has been in terms of state mediation, with the state intervening in the relationship. He locates the different ways in which these roles have been resolved by theorising the roles of each occupation or activity in the mode of production (e.g. capitalism, feudalism, socialism). Johnson follows Marx in arguing that the determining feature of capitalist society is the private appropriation of surplus value and this appropriation is dialectically related to the development of antagonistic relations between capital and labour. Within capitalism, for example, Johnson concentrates on a primary process (appropriation of surplus value) and a secondary process (realisation of surplus value and reproduction of capitalist relations of production) and locates the accountancy profession within them.

The distinguishing feature of capitalism is that surplus value is appropriated by non-producers and that this appropriation creates the conditions for the emergence of antagonistic social classes. Both the primary and secondary processes of appropriation and realisation require co-ordination as both labour and capital are fragmented into specialist activities. Johnson (1977) links this Marxist analysis of society to an elaborated version of his earlier, market based, analysis of professions (1972). He argues that there is an essential dualism involved when knowledge is organised as work and he uses the analysis of Jamous and Peloille (1970) to analyse this dualism. Based on their study of French doctors, Jamous and Peloille identify two components of professional knowledge, technicality and indetermination. The former refers to the technical knowledge of the profession, which can be rationalised and codified. The greater the codification, the easier it is for another occupational group to capture or undermine the knowledge (as Armstrong, 1985, clearly illustrates in his analysis of the rise of management accountants at the expense of industrial engineers) or the easier it is for the knowledge to be routinised and de-skilled (through the advent, for example, of computerisation). Indetermination refers to the unformulateable aspects of knowledge, the qualities which are necessary but not codifiable or rationalised. Examples include mystique, charisma and ascriptive qualities, such as social status and acceptability.

Johnson uses the example of the UK accountancy profession to illustrate his analysis. He links technicality with the surplus value producing process and suggests that the codifiable and potentially de-skilled element of accountancy (book-keeping and routine processing of data) relate to the control and co-ordination of the labour process. 'Much of what is designated as accountancy work might be more validly characterised as book-keeping, that is to say, a purely technical function associated with the routine day to day implementation of systems of financial and stock control' (1977, p. 107).

Johnson links interminacy with the appropriation of surplus value. He identifies a part of the accounting profession whose knowledge is seen as essentially unformulateable and nonprogrammable and whose activities are concerned with the co-ordination of capital. Whilst the bulk of routine accounting work may be de-skilled and perhaps even de-professionalised, there exists a small, high status, professional elite whose job it is to design, install and supervise systems of control and surveillance which sustain the administrative hierarchy in firms and in government. This analysis illuminates some of the causes of the fragmentation and differentiation of the accountancy profession, and also emphasises the importance of elite accountants in the allocation of capital. Further it offers a compelling explanation of why, at least in the UK, accounts are being called into government and the public sector more generally (UK Treasury, 1983; Hopwood and Tomkins, 1984). In times of economic crisis, the state in modern capitalism will seek to improve the efficiency of the appropriation of surplus value (O'Connor, 1973) and accounting techniques offer a means of improvement. This explanation requires, however, a more thorough understanding of the nature of the state and crisis.

CORPORATISM

Before developing our view of the nature of the capitalist state, the significance of crisis and the role of accounting therein, it is sensible to address the meaning of 'corporatism' which has been seen by some political scientists as offering a useful way of analysing the relations between the state and various interests (such as the accounting profession). Corporatism takes as its starting point the idea that various interest organisations may be 'recognised' or licensed by the state and 'granted a deliberate representational monopoly within their respective categories in exchange for observing certain controls on their selection of leaders and articulation of demands and support' (Schmitter, 1977, p. 9). Further, as Panitch persuasively argues, it is 'a political structure within advanced capitalism' (1980, p. 173) and it is thus a structure which is combined with, and not a replacement of, other political structures, such as a parliament.

This characterisation would depict accountancy as an occupational group which has been recognised and granted certain privileges by the state (e.g. monopolisation of audit, self regulation) in exchange for the occupation adopting certain policies which advance the interests of the state. Central to this agreement, the leaders of the occupational group not only have to pursue specific policies but also have to ensure the support of the membership for these policies. In other words we consider the relationship between the accountancy profession and the state to be a reciprocal one.

The accountancy profession regulates the information provided by productive capital (firms) to financial capital (users), supplementing other regulatory mechanisms (e.g. the Stock Exchange Council, interlocking directorships), and thereby enhancing a form of societal order. The choice of what information is to be disclosed by productive capital is made both in the state sector (in the form of company acts and the courts, for example) and in professional arenas (in the form of accounting standards of disclosure such as those relating to inflation accounting and lease payments disclosures). To a degree, disclosure rules originally made in the arena of professional bodies (as has occurred in relation to rules relating to depreciation and accounting policies) may later be incorporated into state regulations such as company acts. Measurement rules are more likely to be produced in the professional arena. To the extent to which both disclosure and measurement rules have economic and social effects (for example on the size and distribution of wealth in society), then the British State sanctions the accounting profession to produce significant policies and regulations.

The accounting profession is concerned with rather more than the mediation between productive and financial capital. Its activities also include the provision of financial statistics which may be used as a basis for the protection of property rights and ensuring the financial regularity and stewardship of economic agents. The accounting profession also produces, through these activities and the production of annual reports and accounts (Niemark, 1983, Lehman and Tinker 1985), a form of legitimacy of corporate activities and the dominance of capital over other classes in the economy (Cooper and Sherer, 1984). That is, accounting statements, largely devised and produced by accountants, in their alleged role of facilitating decision making and allocating capital into profitable uses, also facilitate what Habermas (1971) refers to as the ideology of technology and science. They legitimate the current mode of economic activity, embodying in their classification of accounts (e.g. what is to be treated as a cost, what is seen to be valuable, what is to be treated as internal and external to the enterprise, and who has legitimate claims on the enterprise) the existing pattern of wealth and domination in society. The accounts produced by the accountancy profession emphasise the technical rationality of the statistics produced. The prior conceptualisations of value and property are treated as unproblematic and neutral.

In some nation states, notably those with a stronger tradition of central planning and an authoritarian state, many aspects of accounting are directly controlled by institutions of the state (for example in the form of Central Banks, Ministry of Justice or Planning, Tax Authorities). Even within the UK with its laissez-faire traditions the production of accounts for taxation and central planning purposes remains in the hands of the State, although the accounting profession is involved in the audit of some of these statements.

We thus see that the UK accountancy profession has obtained considerable autonomy from the state in its activities and is involved in the production and re-production of rules and modes of discourse for the regulation of economic life. International comparison suggests that there is nothing inevitable about the rise of a large accountancy profession which possesses considerable powers of self regulation. Rather the persuasiveness of accounting in UK economic life is associated with distinctive features of British capitalism particularly the role of the state in wartime and the manner by which UK capitalism has been reconstructed through financial arrangements (Armstrong, 1985; Hopwood et al., 1979; Ingham, 1984).

In return for the monopolisation of audit services and the advantages of self regulation, the accounting profession is expected to both act in the interests of the state and control the membership of the profession to act in those interests. As we shall see below, the idea that the interests of the state ('the national interests' – cf. Willmott, 1985) can be identified is itself problematic. None the less, the accounting profession, in the form of its central organisations such as the Councils of the six major accounting institutes, the Consultative Committee of Accounting Bodies (CCAB) and its various sub-committees (notably the Accounting Standards Committee), take considerable care to try to identify (and influence) the interests of the state. This takes the form of state representation on the Accounting Standards Committee, formal and informal discussions with the civil service in relevant departments and regulatory bodies, the movement of personnel into and out of the respective organisations and of course the general socialisation process prevalent in British society (Miliband, 1969; Sampson, 1983). The British State has, for example, found it useful to call on the accountancy profession in its attempt to control and limit the public sector; financial analysis involving the weighing of social benefits against financial costs has become increasingly prevalent in the health service, central and local government and the nationalised industries.

Audited corporate reports can also be regarded as being in the interests of a state concerned to mediate between financial and productive capital (Offe, 1984). Indeed it was when accounting reports began to be questioned in the merger boom of the late 1960s (for example Lord Kearton's complaint to the President of the ICAEW and press comment surrounding the accounts of AEI after its takeover by GEC) that the state became concerned about whether audited corporate accounts were meeting the need to mediate between fractions of capital. The response of the various accounting institutes to this perceived state concern was to instigate a standard setting process intended, inter alia, to reduce the variability of accounting treatments. Subsequently, the British state has been content to allow the accounting profession to produce most of the specific standards. The choice of a specific accounting measure is unlikely to be important in the mediation between the various sectors of the economy or fractions of capital. There are a number of standards, however, that the state may be concerned about both in relation to supporting capital more generally or because of its involvement as an economic actor itself. Most notably we can refer to inflation accounting where the state may be concerned with the role of indexation in an inflationary economy, the incidence of taxation, industrial policy and pricing in, and performance evaluation of, the nationalised industries (Robson, 1988). Because of its significance in the relationship between the state and the accounting profession, we discuss this standard more fully in the fifth section of this chapter.

Other standards have also been recognised by the British state as having significant economic effects. The process of producing these standards has therefore involved the British state expressing its interests to the standard setters. It should be emphasised, however, that the standard setters or other parties involved in the process, may themselves, in the development of the specific regulations, help to create and articulate the state interests. Two examples may be identified. The first is the development of the standard regarding the treatment of research and development expenditure (R & D). As Hope and Gray document (1982) this standard was the subject of intense lobbying and considerable revisions were made because of the effect of the standard on the defence industry, especially aerospace, and the impact on cost-based government contracts. Furthermore, attempts between 1984 and 1988 to revise the standard are concerned not merely with the issue of capitalisation as opposed to writing off of expenditures (which itself has been found to effect the amount and distribution of research and development activity in the United States; Horowitz and Kolodny, 1980) but are also concerned with the effect of the disclosure of R & D expenditure on the amount of such activity in the economy as a whole and the need, in terms of industrial policy, to monitor and stimulate R & D activity.

A second accounting standard which has stimulated state involvement has concerned the treatment of currency translation in the consolidated accounts of multinational enterprises. The accounting problem of how and when to recognise the effects of international currency movements in assessing the performance of groups of companies (i.e. multinationals) is created by state decisions concerning floating (rather than fixed) exchange rates and the attempt to recognise concentrations of economic power which arise when an international company has assets and income in a number of different countries. The decision by the British government to revert to a 'free market' currency regime seems to have been based on a desire to reduce administrative management of the international monetary system and to stimulate world trade and the competitiveness of the City (Strange, 1971). However, the state has an interest in maintaining its independence from international pressures and the attempt to develop an accounting role for currency translation has illustrated the problems of attempting to operate independently of other major capitalist nation-states, particularly the United States. In other words the choice of accounting treatment for currency translation not only has economic consequences on multinational enterprises but also has implications for the perceived autonomy of the British state *vis-à-vis* other nation states.

Interpreting the relationship between accountancy and the state as a corporatist arrangement, suggests not only that accountancy serves the interests of the state. It also suggests that the institutions of accountancy can control individual accountants and ensure a consistency of behaviour in keeping with the state's interests. This control has often proved to be quite problematic. The recruitment, training, examinations and codes of professional ethics and practice are normally sufficient to ensure the organisations' control over the membership. However it is quite clear, as was illustrated in the revolt over inflation accounting, that the membership does not automatically behave as the Institutes would like. Similarly, the variety of 'accounts' that can occur based on the same 'objective transactions' indicates that control – in terms of consistency between accounts – is not complete. Through increased formalisation of accounting and auditing rules these inconsistencies may have been reduced since the 1970s.

Further, the accountancy profession is itself somewhat differentiated, there being six major institutes and within each of these institutes there is tension between the membership and the administrative organisation. This differentiation may partly be explained in terms of historical accidents, nationalistic tendencies, different statuses and approaches to training. The tension between the Institutes and their membership can also be explained in terms of differential perceptions of pressures for change. However another set of explanations is possible, based on a recognition of various interests within capitalism.

We might identify finance and productive (industrial) capitalism, which may be international or nationalist. Finance capital is essentially international in character, but productive capital might be international (multinational, or monopoly capitalists) or national (petit bourgeois capital and national monopoly capital) as represented by nationalised industries. Now, the differentiation between accountancy institutes and the tension within each of these bodies may be related to these fractions within the capitalist class. For example, the 'grass roots' membership of the ICAEW and the large multinational accounting and audit firms and to a degree the ICAS, may associate with the City of London, international finance capital and monopoly capital. ICMA, CIPFA, ICAI and CACA – members and organisation – may identify with national productive capital, and the tensions within these bodies may be less than those within the ICAEW. Certainly, the tensions within the co-ordinating committee of the six major bodies became particularly noticeable in relation to the demise of the inflation accounting standard, SSAP 16 in 1985.

Nevertheless, effective control of accountants by the professional bodies has been normal at least in terms of the avoidance of overt resistance or rebellion. Corporatist forms of interest mediation seem to be illustrated by the accountancy case but as we have alluded, the corporatist model is not without its difficulties, even in relation to the meso-corporatism discussed here (Cawson, 1985). We can identify three particularly important weakness of the corporatist model in relation to an analysis of the management control of the accountancy profession.

Firstly, the approach assumes that the state has 'interests' and that these can be identified. The particular view of interests is one where policies 'reflect the play of the pre-given interests', that the state is able to perfectly calculate what these interests may be and that society comprises two inherent interests (Tomlinson, 1981). This form of analysis suffers from the tendency to assume that

mechanisms of articulation, calculation and domination must necessarily exist. This position easily can degenerate from detailed investigation of the means by which particular mechanisms are produced and result in specific effects to an assertion of the interest of one or other class. Interests and outcomes are treated as if they were entirely symmetrical and all explanations for outcomes are reduced to the interests of capital. This leads to the second problem of the corporatist argument, namely that the state is a perfectly calculating subject. It is assumed to be able to not only identify the interests of capital, but it can then calculate what is the best policy to satisfy these interests. There are no unintended effects or mistakes. This assumption of omnipotence is clearly rather dubious. Finally the corporatist analysis privileges the nation state. That is, the relevant actor is seen as the state with the consequence that the possibility of a heterogeneous state is not recognised and the significance of supranational bodies such as military and economic alliances (such as the EEC) and international regulatory agencies (such as the UN) tends to be ignored. In the case of the occupation of accountancy and its relationship to the 'state', this may be particularly unfortunate. The UK accountancy bodies interact with a number of state bodies including the Treasury and the Department of Trade and Industry, each of which may be offering signals (perhaps contradictory) about the so-called interests of the state. Further, as the discussion on the development of an accounting standard for currency translation indicated, supranational bodies may increasingly be prominent as the drive for an international division of labour and capital becomes more prevalent (Frobel et al., 1980).
elaborate a theory of the state which addresses the problems of reductionism to pre-given class interests.

THEORIES OF THE STATE

Theories of the role and nature of the state differ partly because they have developed from different traditions, and partly because they have taken different directions within those traditions. Broadly, we identify three perspectives to the state each of which emphasises different characteristics. Firstly the pluralist view of the state stems from theories which view society as an arena in which influential groups compete for power and resources, and where power can shift over time from one group to another. The pluralist theory of the state is one in which different groups can influence state policy depending on circumstances. Of this theory Held (1984, p. 66) comments laconically that:

> This version had a persuasive influence in the 1950s and 1960s. Relatively few political and social theorists would accept it in unmodified form today, though many politicians, journalists and others in the mass media still appear to do so.

From the ashes of pluralism, the phoenix of neopluralism has arisen, supported by the traditional theorists Dahl and Lindblom. It still claims to see independent groups representing interests, but is now prepared to accept that for various reasons shifts in power do not happen: certain groups tend to remain in control. The neopluralists still assume, however, that there exists a free plurality of groups and concentrates attention on policy making as an interplay of free individuals. This view is reflected in almost all the research on accounting policy making (Hope and Gray, 1982; Kelly, 1980).

The second perspective on the state focuses on its bureaucratic nature and is based on the Weberian analysis of society. This analysis starts from the increasing rationality of society as traditional forms of domination give way to the domination of private and public bureaucracy, the latter being seen as the most efficient means of solving society's problems. The state is the ultimate arbitrator, being the sole institution which can legitimately use force where necessary (the police and the military). The state, it is suggested, preceded and helped to promote capitalist development.

The third perspective stresses the class-based nature of the state. It is this perspective which we concentrate on since it parallels Johnson's analysis of professions and our concern to emphasise the intertwining of the accountancy profession and its environment, whose primary characteristic is its capitalistic nature. The class perspective on the state has been developed largely in Marxist writings (Jessop, 1982) and has been applied to accounting by Tinker (1984 and 1985). Rather than review the various strands in the class perspective we focus on the work of Offe (1975 and 1984) and Habermas (1973 and 1976) whose approach we refer to as 'post-Marxist'.

Offe and Ronge (1975), for example, reject three things immediately: that the state is an instrument of the ruling class, that it is merged with the interests of monopolies, and that its actions can only be understood in negative terms i.e. as supportive of the ruling class against the masses. Their alternative is subtley but crucially different: they propose that

> the state does not patronise certain interests, and is not allied with certain classes. Rather, what the state protects and sanctions is a set of rules and social relationships which are presupposed by the class rule of the capitalist class. The state does not defend the interest of one class, but the common interest of all members of a capitalist class society.
>
> (pp. 249–50)

This passage alone is sufficient to set the approach clear of any Marxist approach, since such approaches cannot conceive of a common interest to different classes, or of an agency such as the state being willing to defend such an interest. However examples can be found for any given society: for instance, barriers to free trade, which protect jobs as well as profits. This is not to deny the exploitative nature of capitalism.

A second point emphasises the independence of the state: it is dependent on the capital accumulation process for its own existence, being funded by taxes. It is thus in the state's interest to support that mode of production which it sees as being most likely to continue to provide those funds. This is why the capitalist mode of production is promoted: not because of an alliance between the state and capital but because it is in the interest of the state itself.

To achieve its ends the state enters into interchange with the production process and takes regulatory action. This creates contradictions at three different levels. In economic terms, taxation is necessary to support the state apparatus and to take regulatory actions (e.g. by using tax revenues to redistribute funds through investment grants) and yet this takes away the freedom of the individual capitalist to use his funds as he thinks best. To sustain the free enterprise system this freedom must to some extent be removed. A second contradiction is the political: because to support the commodity form of production it is necessary to expand the state sector which is not the commodity form. In other words, state support at the same time supports and restricts it. A third contradiction is the ideological: since for the commodity form to work there must be an ideology propogated of possessive individualism: yet the state is obliged to intervene and subvert this in the 'common interest'. All of these contradictions are sources of tension.

A second aspect of the theory is crisis. Habermas (1976, pp. 48–50) defines four types of crisis (economic, rationality, motivation and legitimation crises) but we shall consider only the last in our analysis of the profession and the state. To do this we must first define crisis and legitimation. Habermas remarks that

> In classical aesthetics, from Aristotle to Hegel, crisis signifies the turning point in a fateful process that, despite all objectivity, does not simply impose itself from outside and does not remain external to the identity of the persons caught up in it. The contradiction, expressed in the catastrophic culmination of conflict, is inherent in the structure of the action system and in the personality systems of the principal characters.
>
> (1976, p. 2)

Later on the same page he expands on this: 'Crises in social systems are not produced through accidental changes in the environment, but through structurally inherent system-imperatives that are incompatible and cannot be hierarchically integrated.' This is thus an explicit and graphic rejection of a pluralist attempt at understanding.

Second, we consider the idea of legitimation. To Habermas, this can only apply to States:

> Legitimacy means a political order's worthiness to be recognised. This definition highlights the fact that legitimacy is a contestable validity claim; the stability of the order of domination (also) depends on its (at least) de facto recognition ... it is realistic to speak today of legitimation as a permanent problem ... legitimation conflicts flare up only over questions of principle ... Such conflicts can lead to a temporary withdrawal of legitimation; and this can in certain circumstances have consequences that threaten the continued existence of a regime ... Only political orders can have and lose legitimacy; only they need legitimation. Multinational corporations or the world market are not capable of legitimation.
>
> (1979, pp. 178–9)

Thus a legitimation crisis (Habermas, 1971, 1976, 1979) results from the ideological apparatus of capitalism. Without state intervention, the workings of the market are seen as the workings of fate, which cannot be altered. However, as the state does become involved, for reasons outlined above, this changes, and such things are demystified. Not only is the state seen to take actions; the state actions are more visible than the invisible hand previously. As state intervention becomes institutionalised and expected, it also becomes expected that the state can achieve more and more. Increasingly, more areas of life are seen as political and subject to choice. This leads to more demands upon the system which then needs to fulfil these demands to avoid a crisis of legitimation. This basic mechanism is still based on class contradictions, it is claimed, because the underlying reason for the problem in the first place is the contradiction of capitalism. The system must be supported by the state while at the same time seeking to hide the fact that its actions bolster the interest of one class.

Thus Habermas's analysis of legitimation crisis appears to be one that can apply only to a modern class-based state. Is it possible to extend the concept to a profession such as accountancy? We propose that it is. Habermas rightly claims that corporations cannot be legitimated because they are just artefacts within a class political system. Specifically, they can only exist under capitalism: they constitute capitalism. Professions on the other hand, as institutions which can take quasi-state functions (such as the regulation, in the case of accountancy, of corporations through the audit certificate), do hold out contestable claims of legitimacy: and they can be adjudged legitimate or not independently of the contemporary state itself, since the state can alter its constitution to include or exclude them from such quasi-state functions. We can therefore proceed to analyse the legitimacy problems of both the accountancy profession and the state independently of each other, even though clearly the validity of their legitimation claims may (and as we shall see, do) interact.

Using the Offe-Habermas theory of the state, we now turn to a particular area of concern to the control of accountancy in the last few years, the regulatory debate over inflation accounting, and consider the illumination which can come from a clearer view of the state's role in society.

A BRIEF CHRONOLOGY OF THE INFLATION ACCOUNTING DEBATE IN THE UK

The Accounting Standards Steering Committee (ASSC), set up by the accountancy profession in 1970 as an explicitly regulatory body to supplement the state regulations of the Companies Acts, proposed in 1973 to issue a standard on inflation accounting. A standard was felt to be necessary partly because the inflation rate had grown to unusual levels in the recent past. The state reacted by setting up its own enquiry into the desirability and method of inflation accounting, and the committee, chaired by Francis (later Sir Francis) Sandilands, reported in 1975. It recommended that there should be a system of inflation accounting, but that it should not be the system proposed by the ASSC. The ASSC responded very quickly by accepting that the alternative system should be used, although at the same time pointing to its faults in the context of the system it had originally proposed, and after deliberation recommended a complex system which was similar to, but not the same as, the Sandilands recommendations. The members of the Institute of Chartered Accountants in England and Wales, at a specially convened meeting (the membership was not usually involved directly in accounting standards) rejected the proposed system, and subsequently a second standard was proposed which was to last for a three-year experimental period. That standard came into force, although not without signs of opposition from members. Amidst considerable dispute among the accountancy bodies the standard was eventually dropped, after extensive non-compliance by companies.

To understand this process we need to investigate two types of question. First, why did the actors involved do what they did? This breaks down into (a) why the ASSC proposed the standard in the first place (b) why the State felt it necessary to intervene – which it had not done for any previous standard (c) why the ASSC changed to a government system, albeit revised, so quickly (d) why the members rejected the first proposed post-Sandilands system and (e) why the second such draft was allowed to become a standard. Second, what were the implications of the substantive issues for the parties involved, particularly the state itself, the fractions of capital, the accounting profession as a totality and the individual members of the accounting profession?

We may consider these questions together. The passing of a standard might be seen as necessary for the accounting profession as a whole because it added legitimation at a time when the legitimacy of the profession was still being questioned. This was germane to the setting up of the ASSC in the first place, which appears to have taken place as a result of State pressure and the pressure of statements by, in particular, representatives of productive capital (for example, Sir Frank Kearton) finance capital (the Bank of England) academia (Professor Edward Stamp) and the media (for instance, the Economist). By 1973, given that inflation was perceived to be calling into question the validity of the figures in published accounts, it was necessary for action to be taken which would maintain the ASSC's legitimacy.

This legitimation however is, by the nature of the system, in a state of recurrent crisis. As a quasi-state regulator, the ASSC is subject to the same crisis pressures as the state more generally as a result of the contradictions within it. There is an economic contradiction in that professionalisation exists to protect the economic interests of its members (Carr-Saunders and Wilson, 1933): and yet to do this the profession limits the exploitation of the market and demands a subscription. This is compounded by other rules which the profession has felt bound to make, such as a ban on all advertising until recently, and even now only very restricted advertising. The individual member perceives this as a limit of his freedom to compete with the unqualified accountant, and this again therefore constitutes an economic constraint. There is a political contradiction because any professional association is supposed to be owned by its members and exist only for them: yet members find themselves being controlled by the very people they elect — for example, through accounting standards, audit standards, and ethical committees. In particular there is the contradiction of ideology: the institution which represents independent accountants, and is supposedly itself an independent actor, is obliged to take interventionist action which denies the legitimacy of the individual members exercise their judgement over accounting reports. The profession claims strongly that professional accountants are independent, whether in public practice (independently judging whether a clean audit certificate can be given) or within organisations (advising management from a quasi-independent professional standpoint as to what is appropriate): yet it intervenes with the accounting and audit standards just described. Any environmental problem which arises, therefore, such as inflation, will be difficult to solve within the ideology which the ASC's parent associations profess.

Continuing with the substantive issues for a moment, we come to the different natures of the two proposed bases for standards. The original basis (CPP) proposed in 1973 was, observers generally agree, a 'true' system of inflation accounting. The system proposed by Sandilands (CCA) was not: rather, it applied only to the maintenance of productive capital under certain conditions, since it was founded on commodity indices specific to the individual reporting entity. We may suppose therefore that CPP would have had the support of finance capital, CCA the support of productive capital. It appears not to have developed in that way, however.

More importantly for the control of the profession, the action which sparked off the original ASSC action, as an attempt to solve its own legitimation crisis, threatened to cause such a crisis for the state itself. Recognition of the level of inflation, and action predicated on that, was perceived by the state as threatening, since it was only necessary because the state had not solved the problem of inflation. The state wished to emphasise the transitory nature of the inflation problem: the ASSC's action would institutionalise it. The state's need for legitimation, in consequence, undermined the profession's need for legitimation: the solution of one crisis was the cause of the other.

The initial chain of events was therefore one in which the state and the profession were each facing a legitimation crisis, the solution of which appeared to cause a further problem for the other. Thus inflation caused such a crisis for both the state and the accountancy profession. The profession sought to solve its crisis by introducing CPP accounting. This would have worsened the state's crisis, so the state took an action (the setting up of the Sandilands Committee) which temporarily solved that aspect of its own problem but, in its existence and subsequently in its conclusions, undermined the profession's legitimacy. The turnaround in the profession's attitude – that is, the acceptance that CCA in some form had to become the new standard – was a further aspect of its struggle to maintain legitimacy: for to stand against the state's wishes would have risked undermining it further, since the state may well have forced an alternative by legislation if necessary which would have destroyed that legitimacy and any power base the profession might have built up.

This is particularly interesting for corporatist theory, according to which the state would be using the profession to control its members and their actions for its (the state's) purposes. Two things follow from this: first, that the centre of the profession should accept the signals coming from the state and second, that it would be able to control its members. It appears that in the case we are considering, the first happened without hesitation, since the profession immediately took up CCA after Sandilands had reported. The second did not: although the centre attempted to control the membership, the latter rebelled. Moreover, although the centre can clearly be seen to have been attempting to repair its perceived legitimation crisis, the membership either did not comprehend the nature of this crisis, or did not consider it sufficiently important to prevent them from voting against the first proposal for CCA accounts.

A further aspect of the events which took place is the way in which the political contradictions of the profession interacted with the ideological contradictions and the legitimation crisis. Supposedly in control of the situation by virtue of constituting the profession, the grassroots found themselves with little apparent influence in the processes which were going on. The normal situation of resolution (that the grassroots tacitly accept instructions from the leaders they have supposedly appointed) broke down: the resolution was turned on its head with the ICAEW's members overruling the centre. This linked with the reassertion by the grassroots of their desire to control the content of accounting reports in a way they wished, and which they perceived themselves as competent to do: in other words, a response to the ideological contradictions of the profession. Thus the reason the centre's solution to its legitimation crisis did not proceed was the result of two longstanding contradictions in the nature of the accountancy profession and its constitution. However it must be said that this revolt may, in its effects, have been more apparent than real. The standard which was eventually passed (SSAP16) was hardly simpler than the draft standard rejected by the members (an overt reason for objections to it) and it was still based upon CCA, the Sandilands system, with further modifications. A subsequent attempt at revolt in late 1983 failed narrowly, and thus confirmed the centre in its control of the membership.

The position of capital in this has not so far been considered. Given that we have conceptualised the state as separate from, though dependent on, capital, it must be seen as a separate actor. The role of capital in the whole debate appears uncertain and contradictory. For example, it would appear to be in the interest of both finance and productive capital to institute inflation accounting: the former because it gives more efficient signals of profitability, the latter because it acts to reduce paper profits and hence aids capital in its struggle with labour. Over the years of the debate, the response by capital was in fact mixed, with some representatives of each of these factions supporting, some opposing, the introduction of inflation accounting. One aspect of this was undoubtedly the non-determinist nature of the process: capital is not itself always aware of what is in its interests. Inflation accounting was complex, apparently theoretical, and unfamiliar to individual representatives of capital.

We may suggest a further reason for the minor effect capital had on the struggle: the real effects of inflation accounting on global capital were marginal at the most. Although it would have had some minor redistributive effects between individual capitals, the signals from accounting reports are in fact of little significance either in individual wage-bargaining situations, or in the more general struggle between capital and labour. Capital did not therefore affect the outcome.

CONCLUSION

When the inflation accounting debate had been analysed in the past, certain surprises have been expressed. These involve, for example, the intrinsic worth of particular proposals and the surprise has involved the non-acceptance of supposedly 'good' solutions. These analytic approaches assume a pluralistic society, with interest groups interacting on the basis of a free opportunity to influence events. When however the underlying nature of capital accumulation and the state's role in society is considered, a different picture emerges where the intrinsic case is of less relevance than the social processes involved.

References

H. E. Aldrich, *Organizations and Environments* (Englewood Cliffs: Prentice Hall, 1979).
R. N. Anthony, *Planning and Control Systems* (Cambridge: Harvard University Press, 1965).
P. Armstrong, 'Changing Management Control Strategies', *Accounting, Organizations and Society* (1985), pp. 129–48.

A. Briloff, *More Debits than Credits: the Burnt Investor's Guide to Financial Statements* (New York: Harper and Row, 1976).
R. Briston and R. Perks, 'The External Auditor: His Role and Cost to Society', *Accountancy* (Nov. 1977) pp. 48–52.
S. Burchell, S. Clubb and A. G. Hopwood, 'Accounting in its Social Context: a History of Value Added in the UK', *Accounting, Organizations and Society* (1985).
J. L. Carey, *The Rise of the Accounting Profession* (New York: AICPA, 1969).
A. M. Carr-Saunders and P. A. Wilson, *The Professions* (Oxford, 1933).
A. Cawson (ed.), *Organized Interests and the State: Studies in Meso-Corporatism* (London: Sage, 1985).
D. J. Cooper, A Political Economy of the UK Accounting Profession, unpublished manuscript, Department of Management Sciences, UMIST, Manchester (1984).
D. J. Cooper and M. Sherer, 'The Value of Corporate Accounting Reports: Arguments for a Political Economy of Accounting', *Accounting, Organizations and Society* (1984) pp. 207–32.
R. A. Dahl, *Dimensions of Pluralist Democracy: Autonomy versus Control* (New Haven: Yale University Press, 1982).
J. Dillard and K. Ferris, 'Sources of Professional Staff Turnover in Public Accounting Firms: Some Further Evidence', *Accounting, Organizations and Society* (1979) pp. 179–86.
F. Emery and Trist, 'The Causal Texture of Organizational Environments', *Human Relations* 18 (1965) pp. 21–32.
F. Frobel, Heinrichs and O. Kraye, *The New International Division of Labour* (Cambridge University Press, 1980).
J. Galbraith, *Organizational Design* (Addison-Wesley, 1973).
D. M. Gilling, 'Accounting and Social Change', *International Journal of Accounting*, 11, 2 (1976) pp. 59–71.
J. Habermas, *Towards a Rational Society* (London: Heinemann, 1971).
J. Habermas, *Theory and Practice* (London: Heinemann, 1973).
J. Habermas, *Legitimation Crisis* (London: Heinemann, 1976).
J. Habermas, *Knowledge and Human Interests* (London: Heinemann, 1978).
J. Habermas, *Communication and the Evolution of Society* (London: Heinemann, 1979).
D. Held, *Introduction to Critical Theory* (London: Hutchinson, 1980).
D. Held, 'Central Perspective on the Modern State' in G. McLennan, D. Held and S. Hall (eds) *The Idea of the Modern State* (Open University Press, 1984).
A. Hope and R. Gray, 'Power and Policy Making: the Development of an R&D Standard', *Journal of Business Finance and Accounting* (Winter 1982) pp. 531–58.
A. G. Hopwood, S. Burchell and C. Clubb, 'The Development of Accounting in its International Context: Past Concerns and Emergent Issues' in A. Roberts (ed.) *An Historical and Contemporary Review of the Development of International Accounting* (Georgia State University, 1979).
A. G. Hopwood, Accounting Research and Accounting Practice: the Ambiguous Relationship between the Two, unpublished, London Business School (1985).

A. G. Hopwood and C. Tomkins (eds), *Accounting in the Public Sector* (Deddington, Oxford: Philip Alan, 1984).
B. N. Horowitz and R. Kolodny, 'The Economic Effects of Involuntary Uniformity in the Financial Reporting of R&D Expenditures', *Journal of Accounting Research* (Supplement, 1980) pp. 38–74.
G. Ingham, *Capitalism Divided? The City and Industry in British Social Development* (London: Macmillan, 1984).
H. Jamous and B. Peloille, 'Professions or Self-Perpetuating Systems? Changes in the French University Hospital System' in J. A. Jackson (ed.) *Professions and Professionalisation* (Cambridge, 1970).
B. Jessop, *The Capitalist State* (Oxford: Martin Robertson, 1982).
T. Johnson, *Professions and Power* (London: Macmillan, 1972).
T. Johnson, 'What is to be Known: the Structural Determination of Social Class', *Economy and Society*, vol. 6 (1977).
T. Johnson, 'Work and Power' in G. Esland and G. Salaman (eds) *The Politics of Work and Occupations* (Milton Keynes: Open University Press, 1980).
T. Johnson, 'The State and the Professions: Peculiarities of the British' in G. Mackenzie and A. Giddens (eds) *Social Class and the Division of Labour* (Cambridge University Press, 1982).
E. Jones, *Accountancy and the British Economy 1840–1980: the Evolution of Ernst and Whinney* (London: Batsford, 1981).
L. Kelly, *Accounting Policy Making* (Addison-Wesley, 1980).
D. Knights and J. Roberts, 'The Power of Organization or the Organization of Power?', *Organizational Studies* (1982) pp. 47–63.
P. Lawrence and J. Lorsch, *Organization and Environment* (Harvard University Press, 1967).
C. Lehman and A. M. Tinker, A Semiotic Analysis of 'The Great Moving Right Show' Featuring the Accounting Profession, given at the Interdisciplinary Perspectives on Accounting Conference, Manchester (July 1985).
C. E. Lindblom, *Politics and Markets: The World's Political-Economic Systems* (New York: Basic Books, 1977).
E. A. Lowe and J. M. McInnes, 'Control of Socio-Economic Organizations: a Rationale for the Design of Management Control Systems' (Part 1) *Journal of Management Studies* vol. 8 (1971) pp. 213–27.
R. Miliband, *The State in Capitalist Society* (New York: Basic Books, 1969).
P. Montagna, *Certified Public Accounting: a Sociological View of a Profession in Change* (Scholars Book Co., 1974).
M. Neimark, The Social Construction of Annual Reports: A Radical Approach to Corporate Control, unpublished PhD thesis, New York University (1983).
M. Neimark and A. M. Tinker, 'The Social Construction of Management Control Systems', *Accounting, Organizations and Society* 11, 4/5 (1986) pp. 369–95.
J. O'Connor, *The Fiscal Crisis of the State* (New York: St. Martin's Press, 1973).
C. Offe, 'The Theory of the State and the Problem of Policy Formulation' in L. Lindberg, R. Alford, C. Crouch and C. Offe (eds) *Stress and Contradiction in Modern Capitalism* (Lexington, Mass: Lexington Books, 1975).

C. Offe, in J. Keane (ed.) *Contradictions of the Welfare State* (London: Hutchinson, 1984).

C. Offe and V. Ronge, 'Theses on the Theory of the State', *New German Critique* (Fall 1975) pp. 139–47.

L. Panitch, 'Recent Theorisations of Corporatism: Reflections on a Growth Industry', *British Journal of Sociology* (June 1980) pp. 159–87.

J. Pfeffer and G. Salancik, *The External Control of Organizations: A Resource Dependence Perspective* (New York: Harper and Row, 1978).

E. Rhenman, *Organization Theory for Long Range Planning* (Chichester: Wiley, 1974).

K. Robson and D. J. Cooper, 'Power and Management Control', this volume.

A. Sampson, *Changing Anatomy of Britain* (Coronet, 1983).

P. Schmitter, 'Modes of Interest Intermediation and Models of Societal Change in Western Europe', *Comparative Political Studies* (1977) pp. 7–38.

N. A. H. Stacey, *English Accountancy 1800–1954: A Study in Social and Economic History* (London: Gee and Co., 1954).

S. Strange, *Sterling and British Policy* (London: Royal Institute of International Affairs, 1971).

W. Streeck and P. Schmitter, *Private Interest Government and Public Policy* (London: Sage, 1985).

S. Terreberry, The Evolution of Organizational Environments, *Administrative Science Quarterly* March vol. 12, 4 (1968) pp. 540–613.

G. Therborn, *What does the Ruling Class do when it Rules?* (London: New Left Books, 1978).

A. M. Tinker, 'Theories of the State and the State of Accounting', *Journal of Accounting and Public Policy* (1984).

A. M. Tinker, *Paper Prophets* (London: Holt, Rinehart, Winston, 1985).

J. Tomlinson, 'Corporatism: A Further Sociologisation of Marxism', *Ideology and Consciousness*, 1981, pp. 1–11.

D. Tweedie and G. Whittington, *The Debate on Inflation Accounting* (Cambridge University Press, 1984).

H. Willmott, Serving the Public Interest: A Critical Examination of a Professional Claim, unpublished, University of Aston (1985).

UK Treasury, *Financial Management in Government Departments* (Cmnd 9058) (London, HMSO, 1983).

US Senate, Subcommittee on Reports, Accounting and Management of the Committee on Government Operations *The Accounting Establishment: A Staff Study* (Washington DC: US Government Printing Office, 1976).

13 Authority or Domination: Alternative Possibilities for the Practice of Control

John Roberts

INTRODUCTION

If management control simply concerned the actions of managers then it would probably be a fairly easy and uncomplicated subject to understand. In practice, however, management control involves managers seeking to control the actions of subordinates. Although the ideal of management control might be to reduce subordinates to mere passive extensions or instruments of their will, such a perfection of administration is impossible. By virtue of being self-conscious subjects subordinates will always retain both the ability and interest in exercising control over their actions. In any concrete relationship both manager and subordinate will be seeking to exercise control. Although individually both manager and subordinate may judge control in terms of their own individual intentions, effective control will in fact be the product of their relationship as it unfolds over time.

This paper sets out to explore the conditions and consequences of two different bases of the control relationship – authority or domination.

> 'Imperative control' (Herrschaft) is the probability that a command with a given specific content will be obeyed by a given group of persons.
> (Weber, 1968, p. 152)

> 'Domination' (Herrschaft) is the probability that a command with a given specific content will be obeyed by a given group of persons.
> (Weber, 1978, p. 53)

The above contrasting translations of Weber's use of the word 'Herrschaft' provide a convenient starting point for my present concern to explore the nature and relationship between authority and domination. Parsons' translation of Herrschaft as 'imperative control' reflects his interest in system integration and his consequent belief in the legitimacy of any power relations which contribute to such integration. Thus, Parsons defines power as:

> generalised capacity to secure the performance of binding obligations by units in a system of collective organisation when the obligations are legitimised with reference to their bearing on collective goals.
>
> (Parsons, 1965, p. 233)

As Giddens (1968) points out, Parsons in this way brings legitimation into the very definition of power and thereby excludes the possibility of non-legitimate power. In contrast to Parsons, Roth and Wittich argue that a 'Herrschaft' is simply a structure of superordination and subordination, which can be based upon a *variety* of motives and means of enforcement. From this perspective authority, in Weber's sense of belief in the legitimacy of the order to which one is subject, is only one possible basis for the order which is organisation.

At one level, these two contrasting translations of Weber can be seen as an instance of established divisions within the academic study of management control. Thus, there are those who, following Parsons, view managers and their activity as serving an exclusively integrative function within organisations. Since such integration is vital to the stability and survival of organisation the exercise power in the practice of management is viewed as being inherently legitimate. Against this background of assumed legitimacy, the study of management control can then concentrate its energies on helping managers devise the most efficient means of achieving integration. In other words the study of management control is reduced to a purely instrumental technical concern with devising the most efficient means for achieving the given ends of organisation.

Opposed to such 'managerial' studies is a whole body of work which has adopted a much more critical approach to the practice of control (for example, Braverman, 1974; Clegg, 1975, 1979; Clegg and Dunkerley, 1977, 1980; Edwards, 1979; Salaman, 1979). Control, such studies argue, cannot be viewed in purely neutral *technical* terms for a vital aspect of organisation is the control of some people by others. As such, the study and practice of control unavoidably involves *moral* issues of individual freedom, choice and responsibility which cannot be wished away simply by reference to collective goals (MacIntyre, 1981; Roberts, 1984). Whilst 'managerial' studies of control often implicitly assume that managers are acting in the interests of everyone because they are acting for the organisation 'as a whole', these more critical studies insist that organisations are made up of different groups of people with potentially conflicting interests.

Thus, whilst acknowledging the productive potential of cooperative relationships built around a complex division of labour (Durkheim, 1964) critical studies of control insist that we recognise the conflict of interests that stem from the particular way in which such cooperation is secured and its product distributed in capitalist organisations. Thus, critical studies of control typically align themselves with the interests of labour – with the interests of the controlled rather than the controllers – and seek to point to the way in which in practice managerial power is exercised not in the interests of all, but in the interests of shareholders (capital), and, as a happy complement to this, in the interests of managers' own careers and status.

One way to deal with these contrasting traditions in the study of control is to view them simply as competing ideologies between which the individual must merely choose. It is perhaps interesting to speculate about the consequences of such a choice. To choose the managerial perspective would perhaps lead one to devote energy to persuading employees of the necessity and therefore legitimacy of managerial power. To adopt a critical perspective would perhaps lead one to try to persuade employees that part of domination involves managers using resources to conceal their pursuit of sectional interest behind ideological claims that they are acting in the interests of all.

One way to inform such an ideological choice – an alternative which I intend to pursue in what follows – is to study the nature of power relations empirically. Whilst acknowledging both the importance of ideology as a power resource, as well as the destructive impact of competing ideologies on productive relationships, the root of these ideologies is perhaps ultimately to be found in the differential experience of individuals at work. Rather than simply make an a priori assumption that the power relations which constitute hierarchy are respectively either inherently legitimate, or grounded in domination, in what follows I want to explore the conditions for and consequences of authority and domination viewed as alternative and potentially conflicting bases of order in organisation. In particular, I want to examine authority and domination both as alternative conditions for the practice of control, and also as themselves the consequence of the different ways in which control is exercised.

Initially, I want to do this by means of a case study which describes the conditions and consequences of one woman's changing perceptions of the nature of the power relations in which she was involved. The study is drawn from a larger piece of empirical research[1] conducted in the North-west regional office of a national telephone sales organisation – PYT Ltd. Although the focus of the study is on one individual, the processes involved I believe are in many ways typical of, and are therefore of general relevance to, the understanding of the practice of control in contemporary economic organisations.

CASE STUDY

The extent of Clare's initial commitment to PYT Ltd. was implied in the following remark:

> Before all this happened my job was almost more important to me than my home life. I didn't want to go home in the evenings. Weekends were something to be got through till I could get back to work.

Part of this initial attraction lay in the numerous relationships that the job had allowed her to develop. She talked of there having been a 'great atmosphere' in the office before it had been reorganised, with everyone knowing each other and with frequent parties and socials outside office hours. Beyond these 'social' aspects the principal attraction of the job for Clare seemed to have been that it offered her a chance of doing well. She described herself as a 'great believer in competition' –

> I like to do well, but I also need to be seen to be doing well. That's the way I get my kicks. I like to be on top. I get a kick out of it.

The organisation of work at PYT Ltd, involved competition between offices, and between and within teams in each office, and had thus provided Clare with numerous opportunities to get her 'kicks' and indeed, to start with, she had done well in the competition, regularly 'smashing' her targets and earning herself a lot of commission. When the Area Sales Manager in the North West office, a man called Peter, started his own development programme, Clare was one of the six members of staff chosen to take part in it, and thus her immediate 'success' in the job was complemented by the possibility that it would lead to her having a successful career in the Company. Perhaps the pinnacle of Clare's 'success' at PYT Ltd came at the office Christmas Party which was held some two years after she joined the Company. Here she was seated next to the Sales Director, Paul Gamble, and she was presented by the Area Manager, with a gold pen for being the best Tele-Sales girl in the office. As Clare put it, 'I was doing so well; they sat me next to God and I got the pen.' Unfortunately, just after the party, things began 'to go bad' for Clare.

The Telephone Sales staff in the North West office were organised into three 'teams', each with its own telephone sales manager. The staff were further differentiated into Telephone Account Representatives (TARs) and Telephone Account Executives (TAEs). The Executives had a higher workload and received a higher basic salary than the Representatives. All the TAEs had been grouped together in one team under a manager called John. He had set very high work targets for his staff who were thereby having great difficulty in earning commission on their sales. At the time of my research there was a vacancy on the TAE section, but because of the higher workload of the TAEs and the difficulty of earning commission, despite the higher basic salary, none of the TARs wanted the job. Peter, however, contrived to use Clare's ambition to be a manager to get her to take the job. Clare's account of how he did this is worth quoting at length.

I didn't really want to be a TAE by then, no-one wanted the job, but Peter said to me, you can't be a manager unless you agree to be a TAE. Then one day Paul Gamble was up and called me into the office just so as to have a chat and get to know me better, and he talked about things like my relationship to my sister, and was I a spoilt child, and funny things like that. Then he said – 'Oh, I hear there's a TAE vacancy. You'll be putting in for it won't you?' He put me on the spot. There was no way I could say no. So I said, Oh, yes, yes, and I saw a grin come over Peter's face. The job wasn't mentioned again. Peter just said 'you are starting as a TAE on Monday', but after that the question of being a manager was completely dropped. They pushed me into being a TAE apparently for my development, and then dropped me. He said he was going to send me on the management development course at Head Office, but then in January he called me into his office and said 'I'm not sending you, I'm sending Mary Scale instead'. Up until then he'd been very friendly. Like at the Christmas do. He'd presented me and Roger with gold pens. I thought I was really going somewhere, but then after he dropped me, he never spoke to me.

The above serves as a good illustration of the way that managers used the promise of future promotion to get people to conform with their wishes. Whether or not the chat with the Sales Director was a deliberately conceived strategy on Peter's part I do not know, but it certainly achieved the objective of getting Clare to take the job. For Clare, I suspect, to have the Sales Director take a personal interest in her was itself a confirmation of how well she was doing, and in this context to have said no to his assumptive question about the TAE job would have been for her to appear both lacking in ambition and rejecting his advice. Moreover, although she did not actually want to be a TAE, in her own mind I suspect she was prepared to take the job because she had been encouraged to believe that it would only be a temporary thing on the way to her becoming a manager. This particular justification for doing the TAE job, however, disappeared when Peter dropped the idea that she was suitable for promotion.

Matters became even worse when Clare started work on the TAE section. As I described earlier, when the new manager took over the TAE team he set such high targets that they were impossible to reach. As Clare explained,

> The Mersey Campaign was really demoralising. I knew it wasn't our fault. It wasn't just me, it was Malcolm and Selina as well. John had set bad targets. It was all renewal work. There was no chance of making commission, so I was working harder than ever and wasn't getting my commission, and I wasn't getting my targets.

To add insult to injury at the end of the Mersey Campaign, Peter presented a bottle of champagne to one of Clare's old colleagues on the TAR team for having sold 300 per cent over target, but as Clare bitterly remarked – 'the thing was that I'd got more net gain than she had, it was just that I hadn't broken my target'. Thus, in the course of a couple of months, Clare had moved from being presented with a gold pen for being the best Tele-Sales girl, with the promise of a successful career in front of her, to being a TAE with neither promotion prospects, nor even the immediate satisfaction of breaking targets and earning commission, watching someone else receive a prize which could have been hers if she had not taken the TAE job.

I asked Clare about how she had felt at the time –

> I was really depressed. I always need a goal and all of a sudden I had nothing to aim for and there I was saddled with an enormous workload. Last year was very different. I was on the social committee; I used to help with training and things, and there I was stuck in the corner with too much work to have time to talk, and getting really, really down.

For Clare then, the job had lost all significance for it had lost the instrumental justification of letting her 'do well' and 'be seen to be doing well'. Significantly, however, despite her depression, the effect of having her ambition stopped or blocked in this way was that it forced her into a critical reappraisal of herself and her situation. Clare talked of having had 'a long, long think about what I was doing and what I wanted', and as a result of this period of reflection on what had happened to her, she claimed to have abandoned the pursuit of success. As she described –

> Up until then I never wanted a family. I just wanted a career. I'd always had to be top of the class at school. I don't know why. It was an ego thing, I suppose. Silly really, but I don't want anything to do with it now. What I want now is a family and a home life. I suppose it comes to most women at a certain stage. I'm twenty-five – it's the maternal urge. The career thing all seems a bit shallow. Always chasing things.

There was at least the implication in this that Clare was beginning to recognise the unrealisable character of the individualistic pursuit of 'being a success'.

At the same time that having her ambition blocked had led her to question her own projects and motives, it also led her to view managing in a new light. Again, as she described –

> When I came here I took getting on – going up into management – completely for granted. It was progress. It was the right thing to do. I never thought about what it actually entailed. I just naturally assumed it was a progression.

Clare, having questioned the value of chasing success, was now able to see the activity of managing outside this instrumental framework. Thus, Clare now viewed managing not in the context of the individualistic pursuit of success, but as a particular way of acting towards herself and others.

She recognised the way in which she would have had to have changed herself in order to be a manager and seemed pleased that this had not happened. As she put it –

> To be a manager here you've got to come out of a mould. I would have had to have completely changed my character which I don't really want to do. Probably in the long run Peter was doing me a favour though I lost a lot of faith in him.

Although she could see some positive value coming out of the frustration of her ambition, the way that this had happened had made her critical of the way she herself had been managed. Thus, the overwhelming sense that she communicated to me was a feeling of having been used, or more accurately, abused, by Peter and John. Of Peter she remarked –

> I don't think Peter was malicious – he was just very, very insincere. Like he'd come into the office and be all friendly and say he cared, and then he'd have the managers in the office and he'd be shouting at them and he didn't know we could hear, but he'd say – I don't give a damn about that girl, all I'm concerned about is my figures.

Thus, with Peter the contradictions embodied internally in what he had said in different situations, and between what he had said and done to her allowed her to recognise the instrumental intentions concealed behind his appearance of concern.

Even this use of her would have been acceptable to Clare had it been reciprocated, but as it was Peter had broken his promise of 'developing' her. Similarly, she was critical of John, her team manager, for having completely disregarded her wants.

> He was very, very ambitious, almost ruthlessly so. He didn't care who he trod on. . . . I feel he used us to further his career, which I don't resent in a way, but he didn't do anything for us back. He was very cold.

Again, in relation to John, Clare seemed to be drawing what for me was a highly significant distinction between used and, as she put it, being 'totally used'. It was quite acceptable to Clare for John to use her to further his career as long as, in doing this, he took account of her own wants and desires. What was seemingly unacceptable to Clare about John was that he had shown no concern for his staff, and had treated them *solely* as objects to be used, rather than as fellow subjects upon whose actions he depended.

In becoming critically aware of how others had managed her, Clare had also come to view the possibility of her being a manager in a new way. I asked Clare if she would still consider being a manager.

> No, not now. They use people. Though I suppose that's fair enough. That's what you're here for – to help make a profit. . . . I've been through this motivation bit now. It all seems a bit transparent. On the development course we learnt how to motivate people, but now you can see a pattern in things. I think a little knowledge is a dangerous thing. Like when they're training you, you can almost see them turning the pages of the book. Like, no matter how bad the first call is, you say that was fine – just to relax them. In a way it has made me cynical. I feel a person would see through it. Oh I don't know, I'm getting confused now. What's wrong with motivation? You get the person happy, they're earning lots, the Company makes a profit. What's wrong with that?

At one level then Clare's own experience of being managed had made her feel that she could not be a manager herself – she did not want to be involved in using people, but at another level she was confused about this.

Now I would argue that Clare's confusion here arose from the tension that existed between the ideology of modern management theories, like those of D. McGregor, which the area manager had embraced enthusiastically, and the practical use and application of these theories. In practice, they are used as techniques of control, and through Peter's development course Clare had come to recognise this. Now, when she was being trained, she took the appearance of personal concern and interest of her managers not at face value, but as the application of a technique that they had learnt on some course. Whilst Clare seemed to resent the deceit involved in the use of such techniques, she became confused when she judged the use of these techniques in terms of the ends they served; apparently they furthered the interests of both staff and the Company. Here, however, she was confusing the ideology of theorists like McGregor with the practical reality which she herself had experienced. Thus, whilst McGregor (1960) presents the possibility of non-coercive management/staff relationships based upon a reciprocal 'integration' of staff and Company 'needs', in practice this reciprocity was entirely lacking. Instead, as Clare had discovered through her own experience, the coercive basis of the employment relationship remained intact and management's interest in her 'needs' lasted only as long as it suited their instrumental purposes.

Whilst Clare's confusion can be explained in this way, it must itself be considered as a real feature of her understanding at the time I spoke to her. I have explained this particular confusion in terms of a tension between management ideology and practice, but a similar confusion seemed to run right through everything that Clare said to me, and this wider confusion can, I think, be explained in terms of a tension that existed for Clare between the practical understanding that she had gained through her own depressing experiences, and the weight of her own past understanding and the understanding of those around her. I asked her what interest she felt Peter had in her as a person. She replied –

> None – he just wanted me to be a TAE. Though I don't know – maybe I'm being a bit hard on him. No I'm not – he's a bastard. Well maybe I am being hard. Maybe I didn't have the right qualities for being a manager here. Maybe he was right not to put me forward. No, I think I do have the qualities.

Here Clare appeared to be completely torn between her own view of herself as having been used by Peter, and the way in which Peter himself might have explained and justified his actions towards her. From Peter's point of view, at the time he got her to take the TAE job, he might indeed have thought she was suitable for development, and only subsequently have decided that she did not have the right qualities. In viewing herself through Peter's eyes, Clare was again forced back into a competitive framework in which her lack of success appeared to be the consequence not of management instrumentality, but of her own personal inadequacy. From this perspective she could still view herself as a failure.

Partly, Clare was able to reject this view of herself by recognising that management themselves encouraged staff to feel inferior. As she argued:

> The thing is that management here is almost a clique. You start off on the shop floor, and they cream off people to join the elite, and what's left is the rubbish and I don't want to be the rubbish. I don't feel that as salespeople we're valued.

Here, in a sense, Clare seemed to be attempting to reject the whole notion that the value of self must be competitively based such that one person's value depends upon their being more or less successful than others. Despite this, however, Clare still seemed to feel herself to be captured by others' views of her – as she put it 'You do feel a failure. They think there's no credit attached to being a good salesperson.'

I have argued then that Clare's confusion arose from the tension between her own understanding born of practical experience, and the individualistic interpretations of her 'failure' that those round her presented. This confusion I think was highly significant. It pointed to the way in which, partially at least, Clare herself was still caught up in the individualistic attempt to secure herself in other's eyes. Thus, it can be suggested that behind her critical reappraisal of herself and her situation was the desire to protect herself from the image of herself as a failure. Since she believed that others saw her as a failure, the only way she could avoid accepting this label for herself was to reject the assumptions and actions of these others. Her criticisms were perhaps then merely a rationalisation of a deep felt sense of failure; they were the way in which she sought to protect her sense of value. Thus, whilst she could criticise the pursuit of 'success' as a 'shallow', 'silly ego thing', at a practical level, she herself can be seen to have been still caught up in the very individualism that she rejected in others. In my view this individualism did not invalidate the substance of Clare's criticisms of ambition and management. However, as I shall now attempt to describe, it did have a decisive impact on the actions that followed the collapse of her ambition.

As I have argued, in so far as Clare remained caught up in the prevailing ideology of competition then this served to turn her critical attention back on herself; it encouraged her to view her 'failure' in terms of her own personal inadequacies rather than as an inevitable feature of any competitive system. It was precisely this sense of personal inadequacy that I think led her into questioning the validity of the understanding she had gained through her experiences. Thus, the only other person apart from myself to whom she had voiced her criticism was her husband, James; presumably she herself half-believed and felt others would think that her criticisms were merely an attempt to explain away her failure. Rather than *act in the face* of these views, Clare adopted the individualistic solution of seeking to secure her sense of value *from* others. Initially, this took the form of seeking to physically distance herself from PYT Ltd; she started looking for other jobs. She went for one interview at a local newspaper, but although they offered her a job, it would have meant a substantial drop in salary, so as Clare described 'I thought well maybe it's not so bad here after all'.

Having decided to stay at PYT Ltd, Clare then sought to secure herself by redefining the significance of work. As I described earlier, in rejecting the pursuit of a career, Clare had said that her home and family life were now what was important to her. Starting a family, however, was not something that she could do immediately; as she explained, 'the money is important to us at the moment. We've been living with our parents for the last two years but we've just bought a house.' Thus, although she needed to continue working, home and family were now the focus of her personal life and plans. In this way she moved from a position where 'my job was almost more important to me than my home life' to being able to say, 'I shouldn't really worry, after all its only a job. My personal life's very happy.' Her work activity was now not something with which she personally identified. She had created a split between her 'work' self and her real self, by means of which she sought to discount the personal significance of what happened to her at work and thereby minimise her sense of personal failure.

Her new understanding still informed her actions at work, but now she was committed solely to the protection of herself. Her experiences had taught her the necessity of looking for the instrumental intentions behind managers' appearance of concern. Thus, of Tony, the manager who replaced John, she remarked, 'I'm suspicious of Tony just from personal experience. He seems enthusiastic and genuinely interested, but we'll see.' Clare would no longer trust what a manager said, but would wait for proof of his intentions in the way he acted. As a complement to this Clare was herself highly instrumental in her own commitment to work, viewing her own activity at work solely as the means of satisfying her material wants.

There was perhaps an apparent security to be had in such instrumentalism for unlike the intentions of others, within the realm of her own individual wants she could act with certainty. As she put it:

> I'm a capitalist at heart. I'd really like to have a lot of money. I've got expensive taste. I don't like worrying about money and I'd like to be able to buy what I want, but I realise I'll never be rich, and I know it's not the most important thing, but I'd like a house with grounds. I like privacy, I like to drink nice wine.

Property and privacy are perhaps obvious ideals for a person who is distrustful of others, for they hold out the promise of a sphere of action which is under one's own control and apparently secure from others. For Clare these ideals had apparently become a justification for her individualistic orientation to work, and yet I suggest they were ideals that would be difficult for her to realise.

Despite the mental split she sought to maintain between work and home, in practice the two spheres were inextricably interrelated. Thus, her 'failure' to get on at work would inevitably be reflected in the size of property, the degree of privacy, and the quality of wine that she could afford. This was one way in which a sense of failure might come to infect her personal life, and thus one way in which her individualistic pursuit of security both personal and material might be frustrated. As Sennett and Cobb write:

> The divided self is like most other kinds of conscious defences human beings erect for themselves; it stills the pain in the short run, but does not remove the conditions that made a defence necessary in the first place. If the defence fails finally to make men happy, or even reconciled the failure is.... a sign that

despite an extraordinarily subtle rebalancing of their feelings they cannot escape the influence of a destructive social order.

(1977, p. 219)

Within an individualistic perspective, mentally splitting herself in two was perhaps the only way in which Clare felt she could retain a sense of being in control of herself, for the social order that threatened her sense of value was perceived as being external to her and beyond her influence. However, the paradox of her individualism was that her mental distancing would not in practice yield the security it promised, and at the same time it blinded her to the creative possibilities of action; for the system that generated her insecurity, far from being something separate from her, was in fact reproduced and could potentially be altered only through her own and others' actions.

In her own experience, Clare seemed to have fallen foul of all the contradictions of both her own and others' individualism, and as a consequence of this experience at the level of what Giddens (1979) calls 'discursive consciousness' she had been able to penetrate many of these contradictions. Unfortunately, however, at the level of 'practical consciousness' she seemed to remain caught up in the individualistic pursuit of security, so that her 'new' understanding was used in yet a further attempt to secure herself in both thought and action. Rather than seeking to control her situation through interaction with others, she sought control more safely through mental distance; coming to view her work relationships in purely instrumental terms. Here, however, the circle of individualism was completed, for it was precisely staffs' instrumental attitude to work that, for managers like Peter, served as justification for their own coercive and manipulative actions towards staff. Once self interest becomes the basis for action, then a person will only recognise his interdependence with others to the extent that they can threaten or affect this self interest.

ANALYSIS

I began this paper by contrasting what I called managerial and critical perspectives on control. The managerial perspective, following Parsons, views the exercise of power by managers as inherently legitimate since it is oriented to securing the effectiveness of the operation as a whole. There is much of value in Parsons's attempt to move the study of power away from the narrow focus on the power of one person or group *over* another, and towards a more positive, enabling view of power. Power relations he argues are not necessarily of a zero-sum form in which one person's power is another's lack of power. Instead if viewed as a 'systems property' the total 'volume' of power can be increased; the interests of all can be enhanced through the realisation of collective goals.

The enormous economic surpluses generated by modern forms of commercial and industrial organisation lend support to such a systems view of power. The complex division of labour which characterises modern forms of organisation demonstrates that individuals are infinitely more productive when they work in concert with one another than they can ever be on their own. The activity of management can be viewed simply as part of this division of labour – the part concerned with the integration of individual effort, and can claim legitimacy precisely because such integration is imperative for the realisation of collective goals.

The problem with Parsons's analysis of power as a 'systems property', a problem reflected in the way power is typically viewed in organisations, is the reified view of systems upon which his analysis builds. The system is treated as if it were an entity with an existence and needs that are somehow independent of individuals, who are conceived of atomistically and merely slot into the system to fulfil particular roles. Interdependence is held to inhere in the system rather than between individuals. It is only through viewing the system and its needs as separate and superior to individual needs that Parsons can provide what is essentially an instrumental justification for domination. Managers must have certain resources with which to control individuals in order to secure the effectiveness of the system as a whole.

Against such a reified view of systems I would argue that systems can only be conceived as complex webs of interdependent practices between individuals and groups (Giddens, 1979; Wilden, 1980). Organisations do not exist as entities independent of the individuals who constitute them. Organisation is perhaps best viewed not as a noun but as an adjective describing the ordered or structured quality of relationships between people. The organisation as a system consists not of interdependent jobs or job holders but of the interdependent actions of people. If one adopts this view of systems, then power as a systems property can be seen to inhere in relationships *between* individuals and groups; the realisation of the productive potential of organised relationships depends upon the character and quality of these relationships.

The above case study was intended to be illustrative of these conflicting views of systems, and of the alternative understanding and practice of control that follows from adopting one or other view. Clare's managers appeared implicitly to adopt a Parsonian view of systems and power. Thus they could seek to legitimate their coercive and manipulative actions in relation to Clare in terms of their concern to secure the overall team or office objectives. In a similar way, throughout her experiences Clare remained 'a capitalist at heart' – committed to the material benefits of work. Both Clare and her managers, then, were able to find instrumental justifications for their immediate actions in relation to one another – the ends they were pursuing justified the means they employed. In terms of these ends, it could be argued that both Clare and her managers were successful in their exercise of control. Thus John and Peter, initially through encouraging Clare in her aspirations to be a success, and later through her simple need to have a job, were able to get her to do what they wanted. Likewise Clare managed to retain a sense of being in control albeit only through redefining what she wanted from work.

There is however an alternative way to understand and evaluate the exercise of control in the above case. If one abandons a reified view of organisational systems, and the instrumental legitimation for action that this provides, and instead views the power of organisation in terms of the quality of relations between Clare and her managers, then their reciprocal attempts at exercising control appear much less successful and more destructive. The problem with an exclusively instrumental orientation to action is that individuals judge the means they employ solely in terms of the ends they are pursuing, and in this way become blind or indifferent to the other, perhaps unintended, consequences of their actions. If however, one steps outside such an instrumental framework, and looks at these unintended consequences, then one can begin to view and evaluate control not in terms or managers *or* staff securing their objectives, but as an interactive social process *between* managers and staff. When viewed as a social process, it appears that the *way* in which individuals exercise control can often unintentionally generate consequences which work against the ends they are seeking to realise through their control. Such certainly appears to be the case if one views the actions of Clare and her managers not in terms of their individual objectives but as an interactive social process unfolding over time between them.

One way to read the above case study is as an account of the social process of domination. If one views organisational systems simply as interdependent practices then the contradiction embodied in domination as a form of practice of control in organisations, is that it seeks to deny or avoid this interdependence. Thus Clare's managers seemed to view Clare simply as a means to securing the team or office objectives, rather than as another self-conscious person with whom they were in a relationship of unavoidable interdependence. Consequently they did not view power as a property of their relationship with Clare the fulfilment of which required that they pay attention to Clare's beliefs concerning the legitimacy of their actions. Instead power was seemingly viewed in terms of resources, which they were authorised to use by senior management, and which enabled them to manipulate or coerce Clare into doing what they wanted. Having secured their objectives in terms of Clare's immediate overt behaviour they took no further interest in her. Yet, as the case vividly illustrates, the consequences of their actions continued to work on, first in Clare and ultimately back on management.

Although Clare's managers could seek to legitimate their actions towards her in terms of overall company objectives, if one looks to the actual effects of their manipulative and coercive actions on Clare then it is evident that they undermined her belief in their legitimacy. Thus Clare moved from a position of believing what they said, and trusting that they were acting with her best interests in mind, to believing that they had simply used her, and looking for the hidden intentions behind the appearance of interest. Parsons's analysis of systems builds on the assumption of a consensus of values underpinning social systems. Certainly Clare and her managers appeared to share a common commitment to the ends of organisation. However, these ends can be achieved by a variety of means, and indeed we attach value to means, for example democracy, independent of the ends secured by these means. Clare's disillusionment with her managers stemmed not from the objectives they were trying to achieve, but from *how* they sought to realise those objectives.

Part of the social process of domination, then, involves the undermining of belief in the legitimacy of power in those subject to it. Understandably perhaps Clare's managers appeared to ignore this consequence of their actions. Domination involves the elevation of one's own self interest above that of others, who are viewed solely as means or obstacles to one's private projects. Clare's managers saw her merely in terms of their wants of her, rather than as another selfconscious person. Having got her to do what they wanted, they had no interest in her beliefs about their actions. This lack of interest however can be seen to be misplaced.

The practice of domination as well as destroying trust actually teaches the values of distrust. Clare was taught that only she could be relied upon to defend her interests. She was taught by the way that others sought to control her, that the unitary appeal to a common interest in the Company's success, masked a conflict of interest in her immediate relationships. This for her was the lesson of her experience, and this was the lesson that in turn shaped her actions towards her managers. Domination both arises from the pursuit of self interest, and encourages in those subject to it a similarly individualistic defence and pursuit of self interest. Clare in her actions towards her managers in a sense merely sought to reciprocate what she saw as her manager's purely instrumental interest in her. The paradox of domination is that whilst it seeks to deny or avoid interdependence of self and other, in practice it does nothing to diminish this interdependence. What changes is merely the form of interdependence – the social process of power becomes one of opposition rather than cooperation; Clare and her managers began to work against rather than with each other.

Clare's first instincts for self defence were to look for another job. Staff turnover at PYT Ltd was very high, and in aggregate was recognised by management as a major problem. It involved high training costs and had a destructive impact on customer/company relationships. Yet neither Peter nor John appeared to think to relate this general problem with the particular way in which they exercised control. They preferred to explain turnover in terms of poor recruitment rather than as an unintended consequence of their own practices.

In the event Clare chose to stay on at PYT Ltd, but she now viewed the Company and its representatives in a highly distrustful and calculative manner. Work for her was now viewed merely as a means to her private life. Although management generally sought to harness this instrumentalism through incentive schemes, administering those schemes also raised major problems for them.

When the pursuit of self interest is no longer grounded in a recognition of the unavoidable interdependence of self and other then individuals no longer exercise any moral self restraint over the means employed to secure the ends they pursue. During my research at PYT Ltd, a major and widespread fraud concerning the incentive scheme was uncovered. Sales people had devised a relatively sophisticated way of being paid commission on bogus sales. Again management preferred to explain this away in terms of an essentially selfish human nature, rather than a human nature fashioned and shaped by experience – specifically by the experience of coercive and manipulative forms of management control. As well as the direct costs incurred, this fraud seemed to be illustrative of what one might call the vicious circle or process of domination at work. Control ceases to be about the coordination and integration of effort towards collective goals, and instead becomes a contest for control between individuals and groups within the Company. Such a contest increasingly diverts energy and resources away from the realisation of collective objectives, and consequently reduces the productive potential – the positive power – of organised relationships.

CONCLUSION

I have set out to argue that authority and domination are not simply two ways of viewing identical power relationships. Instead I have sought to illustrate how authority and domination when examined empirically should be seen as radically alternative conditions and consequences of the *way* that control is exercised in organisations. The case study focused on the social process of domination, and one woman's gradual withdrawal of belief in the legitimacy of the way others sought to exercise control. Coercive or manipulative forms of control destroy legitimacy, and in its place breed and reproduce a highly distrustful and self defensive instrumentalism. Domination therefore both expresses and reproduces individualism – a belief in the essential independence and opposition of self and other. It is this individualism which is so inappropriate and destructive in contemporary organisations, for the power of organisation (see Knights and Roberts, 1982) lies precisely in the interdependence of self and other. Domination by confusing *power* with having *power over* others, does not destroy the actual interdependence of action in organisation but merely transforms relationships into a struggle and contest between individual and groups (Fox, 1974).

Domination assumes that the only feasible form of control is the control of some people by others. There is however an alternative basis for order in organisation. Clare's early experience at PYT Ltd hints at such an alternative. Whilst she *believed* that her managers acknowledged her as another person, and acted with her interests in mind then she did not need to be actively controlled. Instead she was personally involved and committed to the rules of the Company, which were the standards in terms of which she exercised *self control*. Her managers were, for this time at least, free to act merely as advisers and integrators. Here is at least a glimpse of the alternative form which power relations can take when they are grounded in authority.

In the case of Clare and her managers this authority was shattered, since each granted legitimacy to the other for instrumental reasons; Clare so that she might be seen to be a success, her managers so that Clare might be more compliant. Authority in the sense of a shared commitment to an order cannot be exploited without destroying the trust that is the basis for this commitment. It is not something that can be possessed and used personally. Instead it is a quality of relationship that can only be created and maintained through a form of action that acknowledges others as people with whom one is in a relationship of unavoidable interdependence (Sennett, 1980). Managements' appeals for staff to acknowledge their common interest in the organisation will perhaps only be believed when individual managers acknowledge rather than deny this interdependence directly in the *way* in which they exercise control. The possibility for such a form of control is ever present at every level of organisation.

I am suggesting, then, that management control in the sense of managers achieving complete control over the actions of subordinates is an impossibility. Domination will always call out resistance, either covert or open, and the ensuing contest for individual or group control will actually weaken an organisation's collective ability to survive and grow. To avoid the damaging consequences of such struggles it is necessary for the rhetoric of appeals to the collective interest of all in the organisation, to be matched by the intentions expressed directly in the way that individual managers interact daily with their subordinates.

Note

1. For a full account of this research see J. D. Roberts, 'Power Authority and Identity at Work', Unpublished Doctoral Thesis, UMIST (1981).

References

H. Braverman, *Labour and Monopoly Capital* (Monthly Review Club, 1974).
S. Clegg, *Power, Rule and Domination* (Routledge and Kegan Paul, 1975).
S. Clegg, *The Theory of Power and Organisation* (Routledge and Kegan Paul, 1975).
S. Clegg and D. Dunkerley (eds), *Critical Issues in Organisations* (Routledge and Kegan Paul, 1977).
S. Clegg and D. Dunkerley, *Organisation, Class and Control* (Routledge and Kegan Paul, 1980).
E. Durkheim, *The Division of Labour* (New York Free Press, 1964).
R. Edwards, *Contested Terrain* (Heinemann, 1979).
A. Fox, *Beyond Contract: Work, Power and Trust Relationships* (Faber, 1974).
A. Giddens, 'Power in the Recent Writings of A. Giddens', *Sociology*, vol. 2 (1968) pp. 259–72.
A. Giddens, *Central Problems of Social Theory* (Macmillan, 1979).
D. Knights and J. Roberts, 'The Power of Organisation or the Organisation of Power', *Organisation Studies*, vol. 3, no. 1 (1982).
A. Macintyre, *After Virtue* (Duckworth, 1981).
D. McGregor, *The Human Side of Enterprise* (McGraw Hill, 1960).
T. Parsons, 'On the Concept of Political Power', Proceedings of the American Philosophical Society, vol. 107 (1963) pp. 232–62.
J. Roberts, 'The Moral Character of Management Practice', *Journal of Management Studies*, vol. 21, no. 3 (1984).
G. Salaman, *Work Organisations: Resistance and Controls* (Longman, 1979).
R. Sennett, *Authority* (Secker and Warburg, 1980).
M. Weber, *Economy and Society* (Bedminster Press, 1968).
M. Weber, *Economy and Society* (University of California Press, 1978).
A. Wilden, *System and Structure* (Tavistock, 1980).

14 Professional Authority and Resource Allocation: Treasurers and Politics in UK Local Governments

David Rosenberg

The rise to bureaucratic authority of elite professionals in UK local governments is part of the history of the transformation of the state in the nineteenth century. Under the old unreformed system the ruling aristocrats had 'no desire for a regulated, bureaucratic society: they had too great a stake in personal power'.[1] Furthermore, under what radicals called 'old corruption' municipal office was regarded as a form of property and a respect for such 'rights' acted as a barrier against bureaucratic reform. The absence of a history of the rise of elite professionals to bureaucratic authority in local governments has had a number of consequences. One, as emphasised by Rhodes, is that 'one of the major actors in the decision making process is noticeable primarily for his absence from studies of local politics'.[2]

Furthermore, this strange silence in the scholarly literature is in startling contrast to those relatively numerous studies of leading civil servants who place their stamp and values on much of nineteenth and twentieth century central government legislation. The historian Lambert, in a well known phrase, has stated that such civil servants 'acted as statesmen in disguise, using personal influences, public pressures, exploiting laconic discretion to achieve their ends. More importantly it marks the advent to power in government of a particular potent type of civil servant'.[3]

Before the rise of professional power in such bureaucratic structures, professionals, or rather the occupants of municipal office in local governments, possessed significant differences from those of the reformed system of late Victorian society. In the old unreformed system a Treasurer was allowed, and even expected, to hold a plurality of positions from which he drew revenue and income. As already suggested the position of the Treasurer was a type of property which could be passed down in specific families from father to son or even grandsons. In the rural counties where gentry had a strong dominance and in the towns where self-employed tradesmen and merchants dominated, these local notables often negotiated with the incumbents of the Treasurership over the amount of income to be drawn from such office holding. Keith-Lucas has noted that it was acceptable for those occupying Treasurers' roles in the counties to utilise the balances to make a personal profit by lending them out at interest. While the negotiated official's salary was often quite small, such control over funds was highly prized. Keith-Lucas documents a Surrey County Treasurer having a salary of only £150 a year, but being able to make another £450 by lending funds at interest. In Wiltshire, the Treasurer lent money to the Banks at 5 per cent per annum.[4] The power of office as property and the protection offered by traditional patron–client relationships underpinned such practices. Keith-Lucas quotes Cobbett in *Rural Rides* on the consequences of such a system. The Treasurer of Hampshire, 'a Mr. Hollis, who has for many years been under Sheriff as well as Treasurer of the County, and holds several other offices, and who has besides large pecuniary transactions with his bankers, has for years had his accounts so blended that he has not known how this money belonging to the County has stood. His own statement shows it was all a mass of confusion.'[5] Keith-Lucas further notes that the Treasurers of many different trusts came, not only from the self-employed professions, but also from the clergy, the peerage, members of Parliament, etc.

Garrard has noted that in the transition between the unreformed system and the beginnings of the new system, nineteenth century municipal officers were different from their successors. Corporate officials could become social leaders and even compete for local prestige with their employers. Indeed, some were successful local notables before acquiring their posts: the town clerk was often a leading solicitor and remained so after appointment.[6] To a certain extent, therefore, their influence was derived from the same source as that of the councillors and they could be seen as a legitimate part of the local elite of notables rather than its rivals. Party disputes often incorporated the professionals as patronage was dispersed through such mechanisms. In Liverpool the Treasurer was appointed at least as much for his significance as a liberal activist as for his financial skills. Fraser comments that 'attorneys naturally looked to clerkships and bankers to treasurerships'.[7] If these professionals were regarded as successful and influential in the municipalities, it was possible for them to transfer part of their social authority to their roles inside local governments. However, a too greater dependency on factional patron–client relationships could increase their vulnerability if the political wheel of fortune turned.

In contemporary times, it has been part of a 'conventional wisdom' that chief officers, the supposed mere servants of a council, have encroached on policy making to the point where they can, in fact, if not in theory, become the dominant force in the relationships to their political 'masters'. While, in an earlier period, folklore has given the impression of a golden age of the politician, a little king of a municipal castle, historical reality may be somewhat different. Waller argues that the boundary between professional advice and policy making in the late nineteenth century was admitted to be fluid in local government. 'Officers were expected to be creative figures, not simply agents obeying orders and executing routine work.' Waller gives evidence of the Town Clerks of Manchester and Liverpool, 'actively participating in council meetings: not just neutrally elucidating a complex point of law, but forcefully intervening to check councillors who in their view, advocated wanton or mistaken policies'.[8] Henneck quotes the American Lovell's 1908 book, that stresses that 'the excellence of municipal government was roughly proportionate to the amount of influence that the salaried officials were allowed to exercise'.[9] According to Lovell the main innovating force behind municipal government was to be found largely in these professionals, yet it would be a mistake to see the ostensible political masters as the mere dummies to the ventriloquism of their professional 'servants'. In the crucial area of finance, elected members could and did play a vital role. Henneck himself found that

> until 1853 the Leeds borough treasurer had been little more than a cashier receiving and paying out money as he was told, while the whole burden of drawing up estimates fell to the chairman of the finance committee. In Birmingham in the late 1860s it was the chairman of the finance committee who devised a new system of accounts as well as a cheaper method of raising loans ... for another generation powerful chairman of the finance committee,

drawn from the circles of big businessmen, continued to control the municipal finances in great detail.[10]

Other councils perhaps had less financial expertise at their disposal. Bolton in 1858, when the treasurer Wolfenden retired, elected him to the council and within three months he had taken over as chairman of the finance committee.[11] Two decades later, in spite of the respect paid in Bolton to financial expertise, the borough treasurer was blamed for the whole system of accounting which was 'defective in system and slovenly and inaccurate in execution'. In turn, the treasurer laid the responsibility on the finance committee.[12] Bolton at that time appeared to have a financial system that no one controlled; still less co-ordinated. Other councils have similar histories.

Not only were professional accounting systems crude and often non-existent in practice, but the audit in this period was equally defective. Even in the 1900s, the borough audit supported by central government was well known to be greatly defective. Waller quotes a one time city treasurer of Birmingham as stating

> borough auditor's reports were more spectacular than practical. Items which disclose any incidents of civic feasting or expenses paid to members of the council were emphasized, whilst important matters, such as the adequacy of reserves or depreciation allowances, are seldom dealt with.[13]

There are comparatively few studies of the modern institutional role of local government treasurers.[14] A number of political science-based studies throw some light on the political relationships of treasurers internal to their localities. In Liverpool, the Labour Party machine 'boss' Braddock combined the chairmanship of the Finance and General Purposes Committee with the leadership of the council. Elcock states the annual estimates were worked out by Braddock in collaboration with the city treasurer and the bulk of councillors had no effective part to play.[15] In a study of Cheshire county government before reorganisation, Lee noted the importance of the alliance between the County Treasurer and the Chairman of the Finance Committee. Rate fixing was a process of informal negotiations mainly between these two role occupants.[16] A later study of Cheshire between 1961 and 1974 inferred that the county treasurer was an influential chief officer who initiated financial policy and did not merely carry out a policy set by the politicians.[17] A recent study of Newcastle implies that the recommendations of the city treasurer and the finance committee varied in authority and acceptability. In one year a budget went through party and committee in a context where most councillors had little time to weigh up proposals or to obtain detailed information. This was in a period where the dominant party had an autocratic leadership in alliance with the treasurer. The next budget year an increase in financial information and the mobilisation of internal opposition among councillors produced significant modifications to budget patterns. Green's conclusions were that the influence of the Treasurer was considerable but was checked and balanced by new councillors 'learning the ropes' and in time gaining potential authority.[18]

A few further studies have commented on the socialisation of treasurers into the values of financial markets. Dunleavy has argued that the processes of borrowing money and servicing debt by treasurers and their advisers who normally are brokers, bankers, etc. socialise a treasurer and his staff in a specific manner. Dunleavy states the integration of local governments into the market via borrowing and investment must mean 'that such actors take on the role of market operators, participating in an acting on market signals and are likely to share the ideological outlook involved in such behaviour'. Dunleavy further suggests that this involvement in the financial markets 'notoriously variable, exaggerated and partisan view of the realities of the economic situation is likely to explain to some extent the irrationalities in local governments budgetary behaviour'.[19] Sbragia argues that an acceptance of market rationality by treasurers in capital expenditures was not particularly evident in other facets of local finance. Thus, Sbragia found that several strongly questioned the concept of 'value for money', a concept of least implicitly linked to market criteria in areas other than lending. She states however 'yet in the area of lending the market's criteria were accepted unquestioningly'.[20]

Greenwood, Hinings and Ranson have argued that any sociology of local government budgeting would have to be based 'upon the political features of organizational life, rather than upon the cognitive deficiences of decision makers'.[21] In this paper and others, they suggest that the Treasurer role is pivotal in the traditional precorporate planning budget system where the internal debates centred on resource inputs and neglected policy outputs. In these systems the built-in conflict between service chief officers and the role of treasurer is dominant and resource allocation is assumed to be highly incremental. Thus, they suggest in corporate systems the power of the treasurer goes down, and that of the majority party goes up. This is problematic and ignores perhaps the variety of relationships which create a diversity of power bases for a treasurer who has learnt political skills. From the evidence presented by Greenwood *et al.* it could be argued that the power of the treasurer is virtually unrelated to the commitment to corporate planning or even the power of a chief executive.

Danziger himself has commented that the institutional treasurer role has a more crucial impact on budget making than Greenwood *et al.* imply. He argues that a treasurer 'seems to have a power base that is not zero sum with that of the majority party or of corporate planning structures',[22] Danziger argues that he found in his own research that treasurers and their senior officers were often important actors in the budgetary process even when 'rational' techniques and corporate planning systems were instituted. Danziger implies that within these boundaries the allocation of resources was mainly influenced by the treasurer guided by policy advice from service chief officers and from the majority party leadership. Danziger insists in his study he found it was the Treasurer's role whose behaviour embodied corporate planning while making the necessary political concessions to the spending departments. He states 'it was not simply the case that the Treasurer would allocate incremental shares to all spending departments'. In the context of an alliance with the role of chief Executive the Treasurer would have a distinctive imprint into resource allocation. This would be 'contingent upon each Treasurer's reading of national policy, local decisions and his own assessment of local needs'. Hence, a system with a powerful Treasurer and few corporate management characteristics could produce a system of highly incremental budgetary outputs. Danziger, Greenwood, Hinings and Ranson stress that intra-organisational configurations of power have a significant input into resource allocation decisions. Danziger argues, correctly, the necessity of research to be 'sensitive to the continuing importance of the Treasurers' office and to the complex set of roles and alternative values that might be manifest in that office . . . ideally the . . . analytic framework needs to incorporate variables that measure the agenda and roles of the Treasurer most fully, so that the relationship between this important factor and budgetary outputs can be specified'.[23] Greenwood, Hinings and Ranson concede in replying to Danziger 'that the role of the Treasurer within alternative budgetary systems is more subtle and complex than is given credit'.[24] They also correctly argue on this point and others that 'Danziger himself fails to offer any alternative explanation' in his text 'Making Budgets'.

Authority and power in institutional roles should not be analysed merely as an extension of attributes of individuals who occupy roles but primarily as a product of structural relationships. The role of the treasurer in local governments should be usefully studied by an attempt to comprehend these relationships and the nuances which can develop from them. Otherwise, 'the absence of an adequate sociology of financial management and executive roles in local government literature allows a prescriptive formalism to exist in financial management textbooks'.[25]

This paper is a study of the mechanisms in resource allocation in which politicians and elite professionals bargain and negotiate over budgets. It is a tentative first step in the exploration of such relationships and the politics of the variety of professionalisms inside the bargaining process. The methodology utilised follows the path Danziger himself suggested in his important text *Making Budgets* though he himself did not adequately follow. He has argued

> configurative approaches at the individual level remain attractive because they provide a rich descriptive data from which to generate stories as explanations and because they capture more of the texture of politics than system level or organisational level approaches.[26]

The latter half of this paper reports on interviews with a sample of treasurers in district boroughs and non-metropolitan county councils. While most treasurers were merely interviewed, one treasurer allowed the researcher to gain access to confidential meetings of his authority's chief officers group. This was invaluable in working out the nuances and structural configurations inside budgetary roles.

A treasurer has strategic influence and indeed power in both an era of growth and an era of contraction. Nevertheless, fiscal contraction has the potential to accentuate a number of readjustments to the organisational cultures of local government. Stewart especially has speculated that the move from growth to standstill and actual decline radically shakes and alters the expectations around growth, which, while not written down, are written into the organisational procedures and alliances.[27] This world taken for granted in an era of expansion allowed a network of compromise understandings to exist between potentially competing professional interests inside local governments. Consensus politics were relatively easy for a treasurer and a chief executive to manage. It was not necessary, for example, for one alliance of officers and councillors based on a spending department to challenge all the bids of another spending department or for the administrative role of the treasurer to impose a regime of tight financial control with no possibility of movement on expenditure items. It is useful to see 'virement packages' which a treasurer would allow as forming part of an internal bargaining process. In such a context of growth present concessions by one spending department could be balanced and compensated in the future by gains made by another spending department.

Current fieldwork suggests that this era of easy consensus management has departed in many, if not most, local governments. One treasurer told the interviewer

> There is less co-operation than there has ever been simply because pressures are so great that each chief officer is obliged to defend his corner whether he wants to or not. The only corporate decision we are likely to get is the corporate decision on the distribution of the latest batch of unpleasantness. In practice, corporate decisions are no more than a collective agreement to protect a particular project. We never had these pressures on us quite like this. Politicians on committees are also clashing amongst themselves and dragging in Chief Officers or you could argue that Chief Officers are dragging them in.

A partial weakening of statutory legislation also creates new strains in role relationships as former sign posts for resources lose their meaning. A treasurer noted

> In the past two years central government has not given a single statement or indication of what its policies are apart from maximum support for law and order. It's a total retreat from a clear statement of policy which could commit resources. Things are becoming confused. On one hand DHSS continues to increase the amount of money available for joint finance and the Department of Environment is telling me to reduce expenditure in absolute terms. In the past we have sometimes gained from contradictory policies in central government as we used guidelines which were convenient and rejected those which were not. Nowadays we lose.

While it could be argued that a weakening of statutory legislation may allow formally more space in innovating specific programmes while cutting back others, in a standstill or contraction of resources era, other rationalities may develop. Treasurers especially, can develop mixed feelings about capital programmes they have been allocated by central government. They may even advise their politicians to tactfully reject them if such programmes implied a commitment at some later stage to assume direct financial responsibilities for such projects. In a past context where further growth was automatically assumed the basic assumption in such a situation was that the resources would be there, over time, to meet such commitments.

The Treasurership role seems to be closely linked to a defence of local government as a 'natural' relatively autonomous unit in central–local governmental relationships. Sbragia has noted that Treasurers who have 'entrepreneurial' attitudes 'saw themselves as leading the fight for local autonomy'. The retreat to a strong advocacy position has meant that earlier conception of central–local relations as a partnership has become significantly weakened. This can have an impact on role behaviour. In one local government where the leader of the council was a party leader of the same party in power in central government, and where the role of chief executive was occupied by an officer who was not able to strongly influence the leader the following situation was described by a treasurer.

> The leader was tight on financial resources. I thought too tight and we had some fairly strong arguments behind closed doors. I remember arguing a financial point which had considerable significance for the services. When we prepared the budget last year there was the question of the rate of inflation which was the key to a lot of problems. The government cash limits would indicate that next year we should only provide sixteen millions and my calculations indicated it should be nearer nineteen millions. The difference between those two assumptions in inflation was greater than the sum of all of those cuts we had made. I had three very prolonged meetings with the leader because in the report he wanted to follow the government line on inflation. I told him I could not agree. I'm the county Treasurer and I've got to advise the council what I think inflation would be and the impact on services. The government figures are too low but as a professional officer I can't accept it. In the end, after a lot of argument, we

struck a compromise and he went quite a long way towards my estimate.

In this local government it was the networks of party and government (the leader was recently awarded a knighthood) that allowed this council leader to subordinate the authority of fellow party councillors to his own. Other chief officers seemed to be unable to strongly resist his authority even when it conflicted with professional judgements. In such a context the expansions of influence of the Treasurers' roles had significance as the occupant was forced to take a strong advocacy position. The respect given to the 'non-political' professional as head of the major financial control system allowed him to be often, the informal spokesman for the suppressed collectivity of chief officers. The role of Chief Executive which is much more directly tied to political relationships and dependence seemed to be more vulnerable. The Treasurer noted,

> The budget of each committee would be determined in discussion. The Chief Executive used to sit in but it was mainly a dialogue between myself and the leader.... the main areas where we had problems were on the Community Leisure and Public Protection Committees. Community Leisure were given their allocation and it was up to the Chairman of that committee to decide whether it wanted to spend more on libraries and less on youth, etc. The Chairman was given the authority to decide what would be the allocation between departments. On the Public Protection Committee we had a number of small departments under one umbrella and for a number of years, the Chief Officers inside that committee wanted me to use my authority to give a sub-allocation within the total allocation to various departments. The Committee members also wanted me to do this. They thought I would be more objective than themselves. I refused and pointed out it would make less flexibility for the committee. They wanted me to take political decisions and I drew back and refused.

In the next local election the formerly dominant party and its leader lost control of the council. The Treasurer's role playing altered. Under the old regime he was a critic of local underspending policies and a spokesman for selective increased spending by service departments. His professional reluctance to accept Whitehall's estimation of the inflation rate was linked to a perception of Whitehall as a place to be circumvented when possible. Under the new regime which came to power on a programme to restore former cuts in expenditure and opposed the attempts to closely monitor local expenditure by central government the Treasurer re-learnt vital political skills. The new administration had no autocratic leader and indeed a number of influential councillors did not want such a leader. The new budget brought in by the new regime was seen by the Treasurer as less subject to his professional authority. He stated

> This year we have got what they call a continuation budget. In my view it's not working properly because it is an invitation to everyone to shove in as many bids on resources as they can. My Chairman of Finance who is an accountant can see the dangers of this. We discussed it and I said if we go for a continuation budget we will set down very clearly the rules for preparing the budget, because if we don't set down the rules, then the Committees and Chairmen will start crying 'foul' ... I was able to say to everyone this is what the Finance Committee has decided should be the rules we are playing by.

The Vice Chairman of the Finance Committee in this local government when interviewed admitted that some councillors of his party probably assumed that the Treasurer was antagonistic to their policies. The Treasurer's known influence in the last regime on the leader undercut the early development of a new 'trust' relationship based upon a supposed professional neutrality. The Treasurer's dislike of central government's new legislation to tighten controls on local governments helped to change councillors' perceptions. In addition, the treasurer was able to demonstrate his use as a loyal 'servant' of the council on financial grounds and policy grounds generally. The Vice Chairman of Finance stated

> The first thing was to establish at the outset that we wanted to prepare the budget on a continuation or no cuts basis. Politically it was very important to establish with the chief officers that that was going to be our starting point because we were not going to have cuts in any circumstances. The Treasurer's department were worried because a continuation budget allowed limited growth. What we want the Treasurer to do is ensure that financial regulations relating to virement and other things are very strictly adhered to because although we are allowing a modest expansion in parts

of our budget we have to make sure that certain rules and regulations are abided by. One important spending department was showing reluctance to conform to procedure and we supported the Treasurer in trying to get that chief officer to keep to the rules. The Treasurer's views are very similar to the Chairman of Finance on our policies but at the end of the day the overall budget was determined very firmly within our political group. The Chairman of Finance and perhaps the Treasurer did say that if we planned for an extra £12 million instead of £2 million that would be wrong but a majority of the group had already come to that conclusion.

It was in the professional interest of the Treasurer to establish the new rules of the financial game and to gain the support of the new regime in consolidating them. While in the old regime the Treasurer stressed his representational role on behalf of other chief officers, in the new regime a modification of role behaviour seemed to have occurred. A closer monitoring of financial deviations in the new situation where the heads of the service departments were allowed greater authority by the leader was one consequence. In a series of conflicts with other chief officers the Treasurer was seen to be not merely demonstrating a professional judgement as the principal finance officer but also claimed to be guardian of the new rules of the game. The Vice Chairman of Finance stated

> Recently the education department wanted a project and received the support of the education committee of which I am also a member. The Treasurer had informed the education department that as the project was not on the education budget virement must be found if it was needed. The Education budget is £200 million and the Chief Officer objected and said we can't find the money. At the education committee we had a very public and unseemly dispute between the representatives of the Treasurer and the Chief Officer. As Vice Chairman of Finance I supported the Treasurer as he was applying our regulations and rules. Inside the committee there was some argument between the Chairman and myself but we sorted it out and we are now united in feeling it was the education department and not the Treasurer who was at fault.

The new regime seemed to be interested in actually extending the authority of the Treasurer in those areas where overall financial policy seemed to be threatened by service departments, while resisting the Treasurer's advice when it contradicted party programmes. Other chief officers were dependent on the support of the Treasurer while attempting to lessen and check the authority of the Treasurer through collective pressure inside a corporate management system which was weak and formerly had been even weaker. Unlike the previous regime with its autocratic leader, decision making had to take into account the lack of automatic compliance with its policies on finance. The Vice Chairman of the Education Committee gave the following example

> We on the finance and education committees want joint financial reports between the education department and the Treasurer on projects. The education department seems to be resisting this. Perhaps they see the Treasurer as our arm and believe it will increase his department's influence over education, but we are worried about the education department financial planning and trust the Treasury.

The Treasurer perceived some of the differences in role performances as being structured by the differences between the two regimes in control of the council. In the old regime one of his major problems was the underspending politics of the budget and he attempted, as earlier described, to use his professional influence to correct this tendency by presenting a number of financial options. He saw the difficulties in this as follows:

> The leader of the last administration felt vulnerable if financial facts were put on the table as arguments because he felt his political opponents could pick these things up. That's what made giving professional advice so difficult. I had to insist that I was not happy with the government's estimates on inflation and cash limits and wanted the whole council to know it. What I was saying was choose the governments figures or mine or something in between but you should be clearly aware that choices have to be made.

The treasurer was extremely conscious of the problems posed by the elimination of possible strategic options from decision making by not according them legitimacy. Not allowing a range of options to be openly discussed as real possibilities in this context was seen by him as a threat to his conception of professionalism. However, even this Treasurer may not have accepted the legitimacy of economic of social policies in the extremes of political discourse, as part of the normality of local government decision making which is defined as being both pragmatic administration and 'non ideological'. The pressure on the Treasury role is not linked to any deep empathy with the new central government legislation – on the contrary. However, while 'creative accounting' to outwit central government is often seen as an integral part of the Treasurer's role the occupant still has to almost overplay the new possible penalties. The treasurer from the same local government described the situation.

> Whereas in the old days I would try to actually encourage the administration to spend and I disliked their underspending, nowadays, I'm faced with a new administration with a manifesto they want to implement. Basically they want no cuts in expenditure at all which I can understand but I'm worried about the County being penalised by the allocation given to us in the rate support grant. So now I play a different role. I don't know yet how the rate support grant will come out but I have to warn the administration that if they don't want to face an increase of x per cent in the rates you have to consider making selective reductions. The later the administration leaves the possibility of reductions the more difficult and expensive it may be to cut expenditures. I make sense to some of the councillors but others are resistant and I see their point of view. If I'm right of course I expect I will gain more influence when we discuss next year's budget.

Another interview with Treasurers emphasises the problems faced in an era of fiscal contraction where leading politicians resent the potential for decision making in Treasury roles. In one metropolitan city borough the leader, on the resignation of the Chief Executive, refused to appoint to refill the role. He himself was perceived as being a full time chief officer himself with the added strength provided by his political base. In addition he attempted to form new alliances which gave him access to organisational information and power. One chief officer stated

> The leader forms relationships with officers below chief officer level. For example, there is a talented officer at third tier level and he spends a great deal of time with him and he will cut out the chief officer and deputy. He has even done that in practice to

the Treasurer himself. By doing this he creates an atmosphere of uncertainty among the chief officers.

This leader was primarily responsible for recruiting ten more accountants to the Treasury. Their role was to increase the day-to-day financial monitoring of the service departments and to lessen the managerial autonomy of service department chief officers. The refusal to appoint a Chief Executive and the weakness of a corporate management structure did not significantly increase the role authority of this Treasurer though the Treasury personnel collectively grew in influence. The Treasurer himself while not insignificant, did not overshadow the collective influence of the staff who fed the leader information and power and in return were awarded status. One officer in the Treasury remarked:

> The leader is very involved in all the financial processes. He recruited ten extra accountants to tighten up the financial controls within the spending departments. He is not just interested in the overall budget but in the details. To give you some idea one of his tactics is to go through the budgets of departments, examining the provision in the original estimates for the current financial year, then he would go down line by line of the management budget and he would say how much have you spent on that. You've got £400 in there and you've only spent £150, we are in the seventh month of the year so I'm knocking you off £200 out of it.... He relies very much on the resources of the finance department.

The power to filter information as a power resource in organisational relationships is highly prized.[28] It would be misleading to infer that this leader did not offer chief officers the occasional carrot on budget issues. To form dependencies a certain degree of reciprocity had to be given. Also a leader can't afford to totally alienate a Treasurer by too much open encroachment on his work space. If such disputes are made public the oppositional parties could form conjunctural alliances with chief officers and even a strong leader's own internal political base may be shaken. To mollify service chief officers does not automatically help a Treasurer however, whose advice may not always be taken. However, a leader can increasingly take on the political skills of a Treasurer. In this local government

> The leader told the departments that if they co-operate with the accountants on their budget exercises any money which would be saved they can have back. He will not allow the Treasurer to claw it back. In effect he's saying you can build your own growth into the budget by exercising economies in areas where there is a surplus and utilising the money for developments in the service elsewhere. Of course it's too good an offer for them to turn down and say well we won't co-operate even if they resent the level of financial monitoring by the accountants.

Nevertheless, while it is possible for local politicians to tightly circumscribe individual Treasurers the overall picture from interviews is rather different. The emphasis on value for money, close financial monitoring, etc., have increased the potential in the role even if the occupant himself is reluctant to utilise such potential. The formal subordination of the role and the 'traditional' and 'constitutionalism' of the role hold in check the encroachment of the role on other political and organisational roles. Indeed a Treasurer can actually gain in the 'trust' awarded him by such careful distancing from open encroachment as it safeguards the diverse rules of the game which underpin the legitimacy of the system as a whole. One treasurer pointed out how his 'constitutionalism' affected other roles.

> It is most important to find an acceptable role for the Chief Executive starting from the assumption that the main points of a budget would be summarised and the document will be written by myself. I've consciously withdrawn from some, but not all of the longer range planning of money resources but I have held on very tightly to the actual summary of the budget. If I exercise my right to summarise all the financial issues arising from corporate planning then it's my experience that the councillors will always work to that document because it reduces the various options and problems to a series of relatively simple points.

Treasurers then value, even overvalue, the organisational culture in which they live, survive and flourish. The natural alliance between the roles of Chief Executive and Treasurer is also highly prized even by the supposed junior partner who is formally under the authority of the Chief Executive. Both roles act as the guardians of the existing balances, keeping back spending departments from openly overplaying their hands yet representing the spending department in contests with local politicians. Both roles are 'go betweens' with influence accumulated through such a multiplicity of representations. A Treasurer, interviewed, supported a statement of the formerly quoted Treasurer and displayed a similar political sensitivity to possible strains.

I deliberately do not come in too early into policy discussions. I leave the Chief Executive and the Chief Officers a lot of time to talk in non-financial terms abour policy issues. I don't draw out financial implications until that process has gone on for some time. I suspect many officers in fact would prefer me to get involved earlier. Some are glad of my support, others wary. Some feel they ought to be able to supply their own financial expertise and I have encouraged departments to be, in part, self-sufficient in financial personnel.

Treasurers can encourage service departments to hire accountants at fairly senior levels. Some of those interviewed who have done so have reported obvious organisational consequences. It enables a service department chief officer to make a 'fundamental' comment on finance at committee meetings on the basis of the briefing given by departmental senior accountants. To the extent he learns financial skills he can respond to the anxiety and worries of a Treasurer. The accountant in the employment of a service department can tighten up expenditure controls and lessen the vulnerability of a service department to external critics. Both a departmental manager and a Treasurer would welcome this new input. However, the potential of a service department to negotiate on more equal terms over such items as inflation rates, financial regulations and potential ambiguities are not always welcomed by Treasury personnel who can see a situation of a 'gamekeeper becoming a poacher'. A new power balance in negotiations could be then established and resistance to such a situation could make a Treasurer a semi-captive of the culture of his subordinates with a subsequent loss to the apparent autonomy of the Treasurer's role. In the interviews there was a variety of responses by Treasurers to such a situation.

It has already been argued that Treasurers can hold back from expanding the boundaries of role influence on decision making. This is especially true if the boundaries become blurred and politicians wish for greater protection. While unpopular decisions can never be popular politicians can present Treasurers with open political problems. When politicians of all parties have to make reductions of expenditure on services, it is a temptation for them not to attempt to manoeuvre the chief officers into presenting the cuts as being determined solely by non-political technical criteria as it strengthens the management of public discontent. The chief officers are normally aware of this and if they manage services they are placed in a difficult position as they don't want to abdicate from making decisions on what programmes the cuts shall fall and what areas will be given protection. The Treasurer's role as the chief accountant can become a smoke screen for highly political decisions which are taken as mere accounting technical decisions. A treasurer stated

> In the old administration because I am the Treasurer some councillors who wanted to cut expenditure seemed to expect me to take the initiative. They wanted me to say you have no alternative but to stop doing this. It would be implied I should have been tougher over expenditure. They wanted me to stand up in committee and say, in my opinion, this project or that project is most unwise and that would have been enough to influence the bulk of councillors. Some councillors implied it was my professional duty but I thought that type of hard advice is essentially political advice. In a sense they wanted to use me to justify their support for them following national government policies to cut expenditure. It's very helpful for them if the Treasurer comes along and says that government has said you must do this without looking closely at the small print, I've always taken the line that they must take their own decisions because they must be held responsible.

All the Treasurers interviewed realised that supposedly professional advice had strong political implications. In negotiations with central government over finance the Treasurer can sometimes be of crucial importance as on his professional competence in building a financial brief rests a significant part of the negotiations even if he personally does not conduct them at interface level. His technical ability as a manager, as a presenter of financial information are interlocked and his credibility can be of strategic importance. Authority in the Treasury role depends upon the ability to 'bring home the bacon'. The reputation and presumed ability of past occupants of the role are part of an invisible network of reference points in which he judges himself, and is judged by his professional peers in other local governments. The occupational community of Treasurers, while small, is very self conscious and integrated. Frequent meetings at regional and national level allow a consistent evaluation of each Treasurers' role performance. The work ideology is just as determined by such a national occupational culture as by the more obvious organisational culture of the local government in which he is based. This can complicate their advocacy role of local government against the dominance of central government. One Treasurer remarked

> CIPFA is interested in the defence of local government, but paradoxically they have agreed to help build a new audit system which will be the arm of central government. They don't expect to get professional control, but I think they hope they can influence it fairly substantially.

The organisational strength a Treasurer can draw from both intergovernmental relations and the national occupational culture can sometimes be translated, though not automatically, into increased authority inside the local government. However, it is possible for Treasurers, like other chief officers, to find the opposite. A great deal of time spent on national committees and affairs can even weaken a local political base. While Treasurers are not directly linked to Whitehall in the manner in which education and social services managers are and see themselves as the 'guardians' of local democracy the increased respect given to accounting evaluations by central government does benefit the status and centrality of the role and the national occupation community in general. However, the lack of direct contacts into the Whitehall 'village' networks allows them a possible greater credibility with local politicians. Unlike such local state professions as social services, housing, education, etc., accountants feel the lack of occupational representation in the governmental apparatuses. Sbragia rather convincingly notes in her sample from Scotland 'many officials saw the Treasury as filled with theoretically orientated economists and felt that both the Treasury and the DOE lacked accountants, professionals with the kind of background to which local finance officers could relate. They felt they had no-one to talk to.'[29] Data drawn from the English Treasurers tends to confirm this pattern. The lack of intimate contact of nearly all Treasurers with the Whitehall 'village' communities forces them to depend on CIPFA for representation and information. Yet CIPFA is at least a semi-corporatist institution with an interest in marginalising potential conflict areas between central and local government. In a situation where central government is unwilling to allow 'go betweens' too much negotiating power CIPFA is subject to opposing strains with a tendency to want to satisfy all parties and finding it difficult, if not impossible, to do so.

Differences in role perceptions as well as differences in value attitudes to specific aspects of local government were not uncommon. One metropolitan county Treasurer emphasised to a greater extent than others the accountability of politicians to the local electorate as a key and essential strength in local government. This Treasurer expressed strong concern that many of his fellow chief officers had a relatively blind belief in themselves as 'non-political' professionals and refused to scrutinise the recommendations on possible options they gave local politicians:

> In this local authority chief officers don't recognise the problems in the advice they sometimes give. Many don't realise that even when they discuss resource allocations their advice has a social edge to it. There have been suggestions that money should be spent in the Highways budget, and a certain balance worked at between road construction and support for the bus services. In fact I pointed out the highways construction programmes benefited some sectors more than others and public bus services benefited more than others. Chief officers attempted to present it as a totally professional decision and it was correctly recognised by members as a highly sensitive political issue. The chief officers concerned could not basically accept that. One of the reasons I'm negotiating with the bus companies at the moment is because there is a disagreement between the surveyors here, the bus company and the council and I'm acceptable as an honest broker.

It is very possible that another occupant of the role of Treasurer may not have decided to play out the role in this manner. It is also possible that another occupant could have decided to accept his fellow chief officer's self-definition of professionalism and not even consciously thought of challenging it. He could lose as well as gain by linking his role authority on these issues to the challenges made by councillors, after all. This Treasurer believed most councillors accepted the fact that he acted as an 'honest broker' and therefore occupied with their tacit consent, political space but they rationalised this by saying that the Treasurer 'can't really' be taking on political roles. In practice then because of the particular trust relationships established this Treasurer can seem to be allowed to float in the area which is artificially separated between politics and professionalism precisely because of the personal trust given as well as the institutional role trust in the Treasurer's advice as technical. While a Chief Executive draws his authority from representing service department to the politicians and vice versa (as well as balancing between the claims of different service departments) he can be more vulnerable than a Treasurer, precisely because his political relationships are integral to the authority in the role. The role strength of a Chief Executive is also its potential weakness. The strength of any competent and politically skilled Treasurer is that his institutional role allows him to effect policy construction without an automatic challenge by councillors that he is talking politics.

This Treasurer explained that he usually was able to decide the type of intervention he would make by examining the particular balances inside both chief officers and politicians in relationship to general long term goals. He gave the following example

> Immediately after the last local elections, the Minister made a perfectly clear threat that if we did not cut £10 million off our budget we would lose grant to the amount of £6.3 million. The new administration did not want to make these cuts but they did not want to be seen as taking an extreme stand based on an overt political philosophy. Initially I was brought into council discussions on the Minister's threat. I did not suggest they should make cuts merely suggested they consider what the effects of the cuts would be. My logic at that time was they were a new council and they had to play a public role of being reasonable and responsible and the most likely way of doing that was to actually examine the effects of cuts on services.

The Treasurer was interested in supporting the new council by the use of specific tactics of negotiating with the relevant central government departments and politicians and demonstrating that pragmatic administration was the dynamic of this local government. This sensitivity to the ideological level was coupled with a desire to win to the council's policies as much across the board support as possible in the local community as well as local and national newspaper support. The Treasurer stated:

We monitor our unit costs closely and the County has a good track record. We compare very well with other metropolitan counties who, on the whole, have the same problems. It was obvious that the exercise would lead to the realisation that cuts in expenditure would have fairly damaging effects on the services. The council were able to say to the Minister that they had considered. They were even supported by the local newspapers who normally dislike high spending on rates for obvious reasons.

The Treasurer considered that without the skilful use of public presentation of technical arguments this local government would have been forced to make severe cuts and the axe would have fallen on those departments with the weakest (in political relationships) chief officers. He saw his 'trust relationship' with councillors as having a strategic and important consequence in inter-departmental relationships and while often critical and opposing other chief officers' judgements on specific issues he also saw himself as the 'guardian' of spending departments in a context of an unstable environment. This 'natural' guardianship element to the role was linked to an ability to support councillors, at other times, against chief officers.

In another metropolitan city an exceptionally strong Chief Executive attempted after the reorganisation of local government to eliminate as far as possible external political inputs into the corporate process. In this city, perhaps more than any other, the possibility of increased rationality in a climate of financial contraction, should be taken as given. The Treasurer of this local authority was interviewed and stated he believed that chief officers would adhere to a strong corporate system only when it was in their interests and when the relative weakness of their political relationships forced them to compensate by increased dependency on the treasury and the Chief Executive. He stated:

> The weaker departments such as libraries, museums, recreation do better out of corporate management but the larger ones will support it only as far as they gain. If chief officers think they will be able to get political support for projects they will be less cooperative. The Director of Housing has now got a separate housing committee and that has increased his hand in making bids.

In this local authority it was common for the strong Chief Executive and his junior partner, the Treasurer, to dominate within limits the influential politicians in one of the major parties and to have considerable influence on a number of senior politicians in the other major parties. The coming to power of the Labour party on a manifesto of resistance to cuts in services made the Treasurer's input into policy more difficult as a significant minority of members wanted no cuts and many of the others were prepared to allow cuts to be made elsewhere than in particular departments they gave political priority. Forward planning according to this Treasurer had broken down as it was not possible to control the external resource environment over a number of years. He argued that he and other Treasurers, therefore, tended to operate more than ever before on a year-to-year basis while still attempting to make financial plans and recommendations. This Treasurer described last year's budget in a context when large cuts had to be discussed and agreed upon by the council.

> We decided to take £4.8 million from the education budget. It was possible politically to do this because the education budget has, after all, around seventy per cent of our resources and because the education department never learnt the necessary political skills to justify its keeping all its budget. He depended on the size and importance of his committee to get protection and his chairwoman was not very able in her political relationships. The Chief Executive and myself decided that they should learn a few lessons. So we did not intervene in their favour.

It is significant that this Treasurer was not automatically allied to the spending department with the largest budget. It is also significant that he saw a learning process as integral to the management of a budget with penalties being inflicted as well as rewards. This particular Treasurer expected to be able to have a definite influence on party policy and perhaps had less doubts about openly attempting to narrow the policy options presented to council members than other Treasurers. He believed that the local authority had a tradition of openly strong officers and the council members would be lost if they failed to get definite advice. A presentation of all options would not in every issue be justified and would lessen administrative efficiency. He saw his role behaviour as legitimately crossing the grey boundaries of professionalism and politics and sanctified by the local 'rules of the game'.

I wrote the budget speech for the last leader. With the change in power on the council I have just written a speech which condemned the budget. Its just professionalism. Budgets are electoral devices. I do intervene when I feel it necessary. The new administration started off with a target of 20 per cent rate increase and at the end ended up with 13.2 per cent. I had a head on collision with the deputy leader. He said I had too much in contingencies. I had £2¼ million and he said we are going to reduce that by a penny in the rates. I said in my professional judgement that contingencies were likely to be under-provided rather than over. He eventually accepted that. It was too, by £2 million.

All the Treasurers interviewed expected to be consulted and to have a significant influence on council policy over the rates. It is rare for a Treasurer to be able to step back on this issue from maximising his role authority as the issue is so intimately related to the current debates on local government employment initiatives, etc., and closely entwined to expectations to a Treasurer's inputs held by politicians and chief officers. Furthermore, as already argued on finance issues the Treasurer is the only chief officer who can give financial advice which translates from a technical professionalism without feeling exposed to a political attack by members on his role legitimacy. On these issues the Chief Executive and other chief officers can find that their alliance with the Treasurer is then at times potentially unstable. A Treasurer argued that he had to professionally balance, in his policy calculations on rates, between his personal perceptions of what local industrialists and self employed would stand without public outcry and also against the felt needs of service departments and their political allies. He suggested it was also possible that in his local authority several councillors adopted on the Finance Committees or their equivalents, an advocate role as far as local firms and enterprises are concerned and this is especially important in policy terms in regimes based on the Liberal or the Conservative party. If they are also on service department committees such councillors could also experience various degrees of role conflict as they saw their role in local government politics as primarily to reduce expenditure, and loyalty to service department committees was relatively nominal rather than otherwise, though if central government funding would increase, this could change. He pointed out that the CBI were encouraging their membership to enter the local political arena as councillors and mentioned one councillor on the Finance Committee in his local authority who was, in his opinion, the 'CBI's representative'. The Treasurer, he thought, cannot afford not to register such pressures and allow them a legitimate weight in his calculations. However, whether or not they determine his professional advice rests upon such variables as his professional influence in the politics of the council as a whole, the 'trust' relationships built up around his role and his estimation of the balances in the political forces at a particular conjuncture. Advice from a Treasurer can be seen as reasonable by councillors in one conjuncture and rejected in another. It is part of the Treasurer's role to recognise that between parties and even inside parties in local government there may be a significant variation among councillors on their attitudes to rates and this variation can lead to differential inputs into negotiations between councillors before a consensus is created on what the public want or will stand, on the rate level. Treasurers can tell councillors what the services need and tell the services what the politicians think the public will accept without a political backlash automatically taking place.

Another Treasurer had some doubts about the too clear advocacy of a rates policy. He thought it important not to be over precise.

> I have influence because of the way I put things over. For example, to get them to see sense on the rate levy I told the elected member, about a local large mail order firm who had already publically stated that they were going to reduce their employment by 1000. This company at the moment had to pay £505 000 in rates. If the rates went up by the figures the politicians wanted, they would pay £625 000. If they were asked to pay an additional £125 000 they may increase the numbers they could make redundant. I won my case.

This Treasurer in his financial calculations was heavily affected by what he thought could be the direct result of a political desire to raise rates. Whether or not he had a personal intimate knowledge through his Finance Committee of the local self-employeds' attitudes and the attitudes of large and small firms to increases on the rates he, in effect, became their advocate rather than the advocate of the spending departments in the corporate process. This area of role authority of the Treasurer could potentially be translated into a significant political capital to be used according to professional and personal judgements. As the 'go-between', the broker, the mediator of resource bids on the budget by spending departments and their committees, the 'neutrality' of the Treasurer role offers significant political and organisational power. If he sees himself as a spokesman for an 'invisible' constituency of rate payers, a Treasurer can, in some circumstances, play a more significant role in the context of financial policy than even a Chief Executive. The last role while also a broker role is set by the necessity to be closely attuned to building consensus agreements inside a local authority. A chief Executive would normally find it difficult, if not·impossible, to advocate in isolation from the Treasurer, controversial positions on finance. Interviews with both a sample of Treasurers and Chairman of Finance and Policy and Resources Committees present a picture whereby those who have a 'localist' ideology favour the general grant system, which in 1958 replaced grants specifically tied to expenditure on individual local services as it both increased the space of discretion and also strengthened the local internal allocation system. Such actors on the local stage now face Whitehall departments and politicians who desire to transform the Rate Support Grant so it becomes weighted in the direction of an aggregate of specific grants strongly tied to particular services. Their perceptions are in striking contrast to other important actors on the local government stage. In contrast to Treasurers the Chief Officers of spending departments such as education may value to some degree the semi-autonomy of local government, yet not be automatically hostile to attempts by central government to tie more strongly services to specific areas of grant. Thus, they do not feel always (it does depend on the value and perceptions of each Director of Education) the same straightforward antagonism as their committee politicians and Treasurers to these changes which may reduce the level of internal competition. The natural alliance between politicians on an education committee who gain from the semi-autonomy of local governments and chief officers who do not gain in the same way as heads of spending departments is strained by such nuances. The lack of such ambiguity among Treasurers was in contrast to that of Education chief officers. One County Treasurer stated:

> Quite a lot of our professionals I believe would be reasonably happy to be an extended arm of Whitehall. Their professional perception of their work is comparatively clear and I think they could accept the disappearance of the local political input into policy making with almost complete equanimity as they have

always distrusted it. They are less concerned with local government as a system than they are with their own particular service. Treasurers on the other hand have felt a certain politicisation of their role and an increased consciousness of the need to defend local government as a system. Treasurers like myself feel that our alliances are inside local government nowadays and in no way can we gain in a comparable sense by allowing it to go under.

Stewart, Stanyer and other writers have insisted that local governments are local political systems and show a range of diversities in the cultures which bind and bond the actors inside them.[30] The Treasurer role is significant in every local government as its technical core is a common base line of influence and authority. The degree to which additional factors become important in expanding or contradicting the influence of the formal role depends upon such factors as the values of the occupant, the balances inside the 'interests' both party political and professional in the local government system, and the ability of the Treasurer to function as a political 'non-political' accountant. A bookkeeper in the formal role may find himself rejected if he attempts to deny the politician in the role while overstressing the accountant. Thus the role is not above or below politics. It is shaped by politics and in turn shapes the politics in which it is located. All the Treasurers interviewed acknowledged this as a fact of organisational life. Unfortunately, such facts of life are not easily accepted in the existing body of normative prescriptive literature.

Notes

1. See R. Porter, *English Society in the Eighteenth Century* (Penguin, 1982), p. 308. Also Perkins comments that the ruling aristocrats 'least of all would they entrust the state ... with a local bureaucratic civil service through which to outflank their territorial power', H. Perkins, *The Origins of Modern English Society 1780–1880* (Routledge, 1969), p. 67.
2. See R. Rhodes, 'The Lost World of British Local Politics', in *Local Government Studies*, vol. 1, no. 3, July 1973.
3. See R. Lambert, 'A Victorian National Health Service,' in the *Historical Journal*, no. 1, 1962, p. 16.
4. See B. Keith-Lucas, *The Unreformed Local Government Systems* (Croom Helm, 1980), pp. 61–3 and W. D. Rubinstein, 'The end of old corruption in Britain 1780–1860', *Past and Present*, no. 101, Nov. 1983.

5. See also Doig comments on the unreformed municipal corporation of Ipswich. 'The treasurers did not produce accounts, public monies passed through private accounts.' 'I do not know by whom or for what purpose,' said one treasurer when £1500 was found in the bank under his name 'A. Doig', *Corruption and Misconduct in Contemporary British Politics* (Penguin, 1984), p. 62.
6. See J. Gerrard, *Leadership and Power in Victorian Industrial Towns 1830–1880*, Manchester University Press, 1983, p. 81. Also A. Briggs noted that in Birmingham from 1869, 'there was a tradition that the town clerk carried on his private business as a solicitor as well', in A. Briggs, *Victorian Cities* (Penguin, 1968), p. 238.
7. See D. Fraser, *Urban Politics in Victorian England* (Macmillan, 1979), p. 148.
8. See P. J. Waller, *Town, City and Nation England 1850–1914* (Oxford University Press, 1983), pp. 282–3.
9. See E. P. Henneck, *Fit and Proper Persons* (Edward Arnold, 1973), p. 7.
10. Ibid., p. 113
11. See J. Garrard, Leadership and Power in Victorian Industrial Towns 1830–1880 (Manchester University Press, 1983), p. 73.
12. Ibid.
13. See P. J. Waller, *Town, City and Nation England 1850–1914* (Oxford University Press, 1983), p. 308.
14. See comments by D. Rosenberg, 'The politics of role in local government', in *Local Government Studies*, January/February, 1984.
15. See H. Elcock, 'Tradition and change in Labour Party politics', in *Political Studies*, vol. XXIX, no. 1, March 1981.
16. See J. M. Lee, *Social Leaders and Public Persons* (Oxford University Press, 1963), pp. 145–6.
17. See J. M. Lee, B. Wood, B. W. Solomon, P. Walters, *The Scope of Local Initiative* (Martin Robertson, 1974), p. 4.
18. See D. E. Green, *Power and Party in an English City* (Allen and Unwin, 1981).
19. See P. Dunleavy, *Urban Political Analysis* (Macmillan, 1980), pp. 126–7.
20. See A. Sbragia, *Capital Markets and Central-Local Politics in Britain: The Double Game. Centre for the Study of Public Policy* (University of Strathclyde, 1983), pp. 314–15.
21. See R. Greenwood, C. R. Hinings and S. Ranson, 'The Politics of the Budgetary Process in English Local Governments', in *Political Studies* 25, 1977, p. 27.
22. See J. N. Danziger, 'A comment on the politics of budgetary process', in *Political Studies*, vol. XXVI, 1978, p. 112.
23. See ibid., p. 113.
24. See R. Greenwood, C. R. Hinings and S. Ranson, 'A Rejoinder to Danziger's Comment', in *Political Studies*, vol. XXIV, no. 1, 1976, p. 117.
25. See D. Rosenberg, 'The Politics of Role in Local Government', in *Local Government Studies*, January/February 1984.

26. See J. M. Danziger, *Making Budgets* (Sage Publications, 1978), p. 205.
27. See J. Stewart, 'From Growth to Standstill', in M. Wright (ed.), *Public Spending Decisions* (Allen and Unwin, 1980).
28. See A. Pettigrew, *Information Control as a Power Resource in Sociology*, vol. 6, no. 2, May 1982.
29. See A. Sbragia, *Capital Markets and Central-Local Politics in Britain: the double game* (Graduate School of Business Administration, Harvard University, 1983), p. 38.
30. See J. Stanyer, *Understanding Local Government* (Fontana-Collins, 1976); J. Stewart, *Local Government: the Conditions of local choice* (Allen and Unwin, 1983).

Part III
Autocritiques

15 Autocritique I
Keith Maunders

Once upon a time life for the management accounting academic was simple. Static versus flexible budgets; controllable versus uncontrollable costs; significant versus insignificant variances. Prescriptions about accounting control systems could be confidently founded on a consensus of textbook authorities. It is easy to choose a straw man from amongst such authorities to illustrate the degree to which 'problems' in control were, in the relatively recent past, primarily identified as technical accounting issues (like the choices in the second sentence above). But such a selection is perhaps unfair – just as economists insist 'it's all in Keynes', future researchers in accounting history will no doubt be able to uncover the roots of current wisdom in temptingly vulnerable texts such as Anthony and Dearden (*pace* Lowe and Puxty).

By 'current wisdom' I mean in part the breadth of perspective adopted by authors in the present text and its precursor. For although the writings in these two books can by no stretch of the imagination be labelled '*conventional* wisdom', the wider view of control which they all espouse seems to be an idea whose day has arrived. Thus, textbooks and syllabi on control from an accounting perspective has successively digested 'behavioural aspects', and '(hard and soft) systems views' as well as incorporated analytical and empirical research results from psychology; social psychology and organisational studies/sociology to the point where prescriptions, if ventured at all, are heavily qualified, 'contingent' or simply made 'dependent upon organisational circumstances'.

What has been gained in this kind of development might be variously termed insight, understanding or *verstehen*. But what has been lost? In place of a clear set of prescriptions as to how to 'improve' accounting control systems has come a reluctance to make any kind of prescription at all. In place of empirically testable 'models' which can form the basis of predictions has come a questioning of whether the variables involved in control can ever be captured for such purposes. The management consultant/analyst, selling a suck-it-and-see, participative and/or action-research approach can probably still make a living under such conditions; but what about the itinerant management accounting specialist?

It is plausible to believe that the 'market for excuses' (Watts and Zimmerman) probably still exists in relation to accounting control systems. In this case, from whatever motives, individual and groups will still want to 'sell' changes in systems which are desirable to them on the basis of theoretical rationales. And simple prescriptive models, preferably empirically validated, are likely to be more effective for this purpose than complex or contingent ones. So, one omission from the current collection of readings appears to be a meta-theory which can handle the problem of how to conduct (participative or action-) research or achieve change (in any predictable direction) in such a setting.

Such a criticism could itself be criticised as too glib. It is after all always theoretically possible to criticise a set of systemic approaches as being too narrow from the perspective of a higher level system. Nevertheless, it seems to me that a system which explicitly embraces organisational policy makers is one particularly appropriate level of analysis for those seeking *verstehen*.

Of course, the papers in this volume do not neglect the broad perspective – as already stated, this is probably one of the outstanding characteristics of this and the previous book. Hopwood, for instance, rightly points to the insights to be gained from looking at accounting (control systems) from a societal perspective, whilst others of the authors (e.g. Black and Neathey) illustrate the significance of social controls at the action level of organisational control systems choice.

Another perhaps unfair line of criticism could be one based on implicit and explicit contradictions between papers – for example the class-based analysis (historical materialism) outlined in Cooper and Robson contrasts with the apparently crucial role played in practice by individuals (history men?) in local government finance (Rosenberg). As well as possibly misrepresenting the individual authors' richer expositions, such selectivities would also miss the point that the volume is intended to make a contribution to understanding precisely through such juxtapositioning. Presumably the reader who has reached this far is sufficiently tolerant of ambiguity (semi-confusing information systems?) to agree.

For the reader who employs the dialectic method, however, opposing views should presumably be offered on all major dimensions of a topic of enquiry. In this respect, it is understandable that the title of the book 'Critical Perspectives in Management Control' limits the extent to which arguments in favour of the traditional (accounting textbook) unitarist approach to control systems are covered as does the 'critique' based approach (see Introduction). Less obvious is the rationale for omission of modern economic theories of organisational control, either based on the 'organisational failures framework'/'markets and hierarchies' literature (e.g. Williamson, Ouchi) or agency theory (e.g. Baiman). Fundamental flaws in the behavioural bases of such analyses have been identified (e.g. in Cooper and Robson), but it is perhaps regrettable that space could not be found for their advocacy also.

Given freedom to select dimensions a priori it is clearly always possible to claim 'significant' viewpoints on management control are inadequately covered in the text. Thus, from a pluralistic viewpoint, whilst a number of the contributions herein are clearly sympathetic to the interests of the 'controlled' versus the 'controllers' (e.g. Roberts), no extensive consideration is given to empirical characteristics of labour-controlled organisations (reference to potentials of self-managed firms (Berry) notwithstanding). Maybe the inclusion of 'management control' in the title again dictated this limitation.

In part, the title of the book reflects the collective affiliation of the authors – as members of the Management Control Workshop Group (now Management Control Association). In this respect it is to be noted that all the authors are academics and the book, like the Group, possibly suffers from a lack of direct contributions from practising managers.

In the absence of practitioner volunteers, however, there appears to be little the editors could have done to remedy this. It does, nevertheless, mean that if there are alternative viewpoints on control ranged along a practitioner–non-practitioner dimension, then only one end of the spectrum is directly reflected herein.

Another possibly relevant set of dimensions is suggested by Burrell and Morgan: subjective versus objective; and radical versus regulative – based on their synthesis of approaches to organisational analysis. Whilst there is considerable attention given to the inevitable dependence between control research and ideology (e.g. Puxty and Chua), I doubt if any of the current contributions would be accepted as espousing a politically radical approach to control as represented, for example, by the Institute for Workers Control or anarchists. Despite this, a majority of the papers are concerned with explaining possibilities for changes within organisations which if achieved could have implications at the national socio-political level also. As Lowe points out, however, understanding might be better served if such social implications are themselves modelled and made explicit. Suppression, whether intentional or not, of foreseeable possible consequences of policy recommendations may be an effective tactic in multi-person decision processes, but does not necessarily contribute to academic debate, particularly from the point of view of dialectic method.

On Burrell and Morgan's second dimension, objective–subjective, the papers almost all implicitly adopt an objectivist approach. Thus while the relevance of such factors as 'power' (Cooper and Robson), 'culture' (Berry), 'personality' (Rosenberg), 'value systems' (Puxty and Chua), and 'group membership influences' (Chua) to 'control' are discussed and illustrated, it appears to be assumed that all could, where necessary, be empirically identified and measured. A subjectivist author would, of course, take an opposing view on ontological grounds. Again, this may be unfair to current contributors. Otley's suggestion for a grounded theory approach does not necessarily preclude subjectivist methodology, though illustrations from his own research appear to be firmly grounded on objectivist assumptions.

It may be objected that, although the way to subjectivist research in accounting has been signposted (Tomkins and Groves), few, if any, have yet essayed it. One explanation for this is probably a lack of comparative advantage on the part of contemporary accounting researchers as opposed to some sociologists etc. But isn't there the danger here that like the apocryphal drunkard we shall all end up looking for our lost coins under a lamp-post?

SUMMARY

According to the aims of this book (see Introduction) the function of this autocritique is to expose the substantive contents of the book to specific criticism. What has been written above has to be read in this light and not viewed as a destructive approach to the individual authors' contributions.

It will be noted, in fact, that the points made here relate principally to possible 'sins of omission' rather than commission. If the identification of these is agreed, then the reader might note that in this respect the text is on the whole fairly reflective of the current state of the art of control systems research (at least as far as management accounting is concerned). This autocritique itself therefore reinforces a theme taken up by most of the other contributors – that there is a need for broader based research in control systems to inform policy makers in the management accounting field. Specific suggestions for the direction such research might usefully take and the methodologies which could be employed are to be found throughout the text. It is in terms of the impact of these that the contributions herein must ultimately be critiqued.

References

All references are to papers within the current volume, except as follows:

R. N. Anthony and J. Dearden, *Management Control Systems*, 3rd ed. (Irwin, 1976).

S. Baiman, 'Agency Research in Managerial Accounting: A Survey', *Journal of Accounting Literature*, vol. 1 (1982), pp. 154–213.

G. Burrell and G. Morgan, *Sociological Paradigms and Organizational Analysis* (Heinemann, 1979).

W. G. Ouchi, 'A Conceptual Framework for the Design of Organizational Control Mechanisms', *Management Science*. vol 25, no. 9 (1979), pp. 833–48.

C. R. Tomkins and R. E. V. Groves, 'The Everyday Accountant and Researching his Reality', *Accounting Organizations and Society*, vol. 8, no. 4 (1983), pp. 361–74.

R. Watts and G. Zimmerman, 'The Demand for and Supply of Accounting Theories: The Market for Excuses', *Accounting Review*, vol. 65, no. 2 (1979), pp. 273–305.

O. E. Williamson, *Markets and Hierarchies* (Free Press, 1975).

16 Autocritique II
Hugh Willmott

A key question for contributors to a collection of critical studies is: what is meant by critical? In response, it can be said with confidence only that what is intended and recognised as 'critical' takes shape and is interpreted within discourses that differ fundamentally in their conception of its purpose and meaning. This being the case, it may be helpful, for both didactic and polemical purposes, to draw a distinction between two ideal-typical notions of critical analysis.

The *first* recognises as critical any form of study that extends the boundaries of conventional wisdom – for example, by showing how a significant variable has been overlooked or misinterpreted in previous research. Typically, such studies attend to their topic (e.g. management control) as a given, reified object and treat it as if it exists independently of its investigators. In which case, the material and symbolic resources applied by both actors and researchers in the production of their topic are not addressed reflexively as conditions of possibility for the topic's identification and analysis. To use Habermas' (1972) terminology, the cognitive interest guiding this mode of critical analysis lies in developing better predictive models by producing more accurate empirical-analytic knowledge of human behaviour. Accordingly, the reality of the social world is studied and represented as if it is devoid of political intent and significance. Even in its most sophisticated form, this mode of critical analysis favours a process of mutual rational criticism amongst the community of researchers which, in Popper's words, recognises that 'all observations are theory-impregnated' and enables the scientist to 'break through the barriers of normality' (Popper, 1976, pp. 299, 295). This latter phrase sounds fruitful for a more radical conception of criticism. However, the penetration of the barriers of normality does not extend to an exposure of the relations of power, as articulated in political economy and ideology, that organise the reality of phenomena, such as management control. Indeed, forms of knowledge that *are* guided by such a concern are viewed as value-laden or politically biased, and therefore lacking in (scientific) authority. A conservative or liberal politics is thereby accommodated and concealed within an objectivistic epistemology that either denies or seeks to bracket the 'interested' nature of scientific engagement (Habermas, 1976; Willmott, 1983; Jackson and Willmott, 1986).

In contrast, the *second* ideal-typical conception of 'critical' analysis is informed by the understanding that knowledge is *inseparably* fused with cognitive interests which have *unavoidable* political conditions and consequences (Habermas, 1972). In commenting upon the self-deception that lies at the heart of a Popperian philosophy of (social) science, Habermas (1976, pp. 203-4, emphasis added) has observed how it

> wants to sublate the *origins* of theories, namely, observations, thought and tradition alike, in favour of the method of testing which is to be the only way of measuring empirical validity.

Habermas continues:

> It would instead be more meaningful to attempt a basic analysis of the connection between the theories of the empirical sciences and the so-called facts. For in this way, we would apprehend the framework of a prior interpretation of experience. At this level of perception it would seem obvious, to apply the term 'facts' only to the class of what can be experienced, a class which has been antecedently organized to test scientific theories. Then one would conceive of the facts as that which they are: namely, produced. One would thus recognize the concept of 'facts' . . . as a fetish which merely grants to the mediated the illusion of immediacy.

Critique does not engage in the generation of more refined predictive models of a depoliticised object-world, nor does it seek the 'improved' functioning of existing, oppressive institutions. Instead, it assigns to reason a partisan position in facilitating emancipation from social relations and ideologies that involve or legitimise socially unnecessary suffering (Knights and Willmott, 1982). Accordingly, the butt of its criticism is not imperfect knowledge in the *abstract*. Rather, it is critical of the concrete manifestations of ignorance and irrationality as expressed in the needless deprivations, dogmatism and distorted communication of everyday life.

It is the second conception of 'critical' that informs this critique. Historically, the term is associated with the efforts of radical thinkers of the Enlightenment who mounted an intellectual challenge to the oppression and dogmatism of despots and priests. In the Western world, much of the unnecessary suffering occasioned by the powers of feudalism has been exposed and negated. The target of critique today has changed to the reactionary presence of capitalism and the materialist domination of technical, 'scientific' reason. Substituting 'the ideology of science and technology' for 'religion', Marx's critique of the latter can be rephrased:

> The abolition of the ideology of science and technology as the *illusory* happiness of the people is the demand for their real happiness. To call upon them to give up their illusions about their condition is to *call on them to give up a condition that requires illusions*. The criticism of the ideology of science and technology is therefore in *embryo* the *criticism of that veil of tears* of which the ideology of science and technology is the *halo*.
> (Marx, 1975, p. 244, original emphasis)

In modern society, the technically-rational search for ever more efficient 'means' has tended to displace democratic debate over their appropriateness for identifying and realising human 'ends'. As a result, 'the development of the social system *seems* to be determined by the logic of scientific-technical progress' (Habermas, 1971, p. 105), and political debate tends to be confined to argument over the relative effectiveness of alternative means for facilitating the progress of this logic.

Today's 'veil of tears' is the unnecessary manipulation and oppression associated with sustaining a capitalist world economy that is distinguished by an intensity of discipline and surveillance 'previously only approached in isolated sectors' of other modes of production (Giddens, 1981, p. 9). In seeking to both reproduce and legitimise these conditions, managerial action is preoccupied with easing and containing their dysfunctions by introducing or reviving ever more sophisticated, insidious and coercive forms of technocratic control. Central to an analysis of management control, therefore, is an appreciation of how, within the labour process, for example, Capital continues to sustain and extend its expropriation of control over their means of production. In this process, 'scientific' knowledge about management can be seen to play a key role: since employers do not directly possess the means of violence, it is through power/ knowledge relations (Foucault), for example, in the 'sciences' of management and administration, that Capital secures, naturalises and legitimises its control over Labour.

By connecting knowledge and interest, critique challenges the legitimacy of theory and practice that has the effect, if not the intent, of naturalising and legitimising relations that are unnecessarily manipulative and oppressive in their effects. To be clear, the target of critique is not technical reason per se. Rather it is the one-sided universalisation and absolutisation of technical reason, resulting in mankind becoming servants, not masters, of technical reason. As Habermas (1974, p. 281) acknowledges, 'science as a productive force can work in a salutary way when it is suffused by science as an emancipatory force'. But, in the same work, he also cautions that science

> becomes disastrous as soon as it subjects the domain of praxis, which is outside the sphere of technical disposition, to its *exclusive* control. The demythification which does not break the mythic spell but merely seeks to evade it will only bring forth new witch doctors. The enlightenment which does not break the spell dialectically, but instead winds the veil of a halfway rationalisation only more tightly around us, makes the world divested of deities itself into a myth.

For this reason, it is essential to distinguish between two types of rationalisation associated with the two ideal-typical modes of critical research. Insofar as the focus of the first mode is exclusively upon the improvement of means, it either overlooks the determination of ends and/or treats them as irrational and subjective; it also disregards the (often unintended) effects of technical reason upon the identification and attainment of ends. In contrast, the second mode of enquiry focuses upon the conditions, both material and ideal, that are discerned to support exploitation and domination, thereby distorting communication and constraining personal autonomy. In distinguishing between these two forms of enquiry and their contribution to the two dimensions of rationalisation, the challenge for contemporary critique is to expose and disarm the forces that impede their *emancipatory fusion*.

In the light of the previous discussion, chapters in this collection can be divided into three groups. The first consists of papers whose analysis is critical in the first sense of the two ideal types outlined above. That is to say, their criticism of the understanding and practice of management control does not directly draw upon, nor contribute to, the contemporary tradition of critique. Papers in the second group present or reflect some elements that are central to this second mode of analysis. Finally, in the third group, there are a number of papers which directly enrich empirically, or augment theoretically, a critique of management control.

The chapters in the first group are continuous with the central thrust of contributions to the earlier volume *New Perspectives on Management Control*. A distinguishing feature is their concern to develop or reform orthodox perspectives and practices. For example, Otley recommends an approach that acknowledges and combines the insights of functionalist and action theoretic paradigms of research. Implicit within his proposal is a correspondence theory of truth in which the generation of knowledge is assumed to be removable from the articulation of interests. Berry's focus, in contrast, is upon practice. Having explored a range of proposals and experiments for group control in organisations, he outlines an alternative model. Absent from its discussion, however, is a sustained analysis of both the politico-economic and the moral conditions that currently are unsupportive of self-management. Not surprisingly, Berry's conclusion consists of a listing of the unanswered questions that are begged by his uncritically idealist proposal. Finally, in the piece by Lowe and Puxty the widespread presence of reification in the orthodox literature on management control is exposed. But their discussion does not examine reification in relation to its role in the reproduction of asymmetrical relations of power in organisations and society. Nor is their critique of reification connected with the wider issue of the domination of technical rationality and the scientisation of political economy.

In the second group, the chapter by Chua and Puxty highlights the limitations of conventional discussions of rationality by drawing upon Habermas's distinction between technical and practical reason. Perhaps the chief limitation of this otherwise valuable paper resides in its assumption that management control processes are solely technical in intent and effect – a misapprehension that is compounded by an appeal to the existence of an apparently unmediated 'objective reality' as grounds for exposing their ideological character. The study by Chua of the rise of the 'nurse-expert' well illustrates how the ideology of science and technology has permeated the discourse and practice of modern nursing. In particular, it explores how, under the domination of technical reason, nursing has increasingly become medicalised, standardised and mechanised, with the result that 'the qualitative, physical delivery of care is transformed into a production process'. This study also insightfully reveals how nurses as an occupational group have actively colluded in the construction, promotion and legitimation of these developments as a means of securing and advancing their position in the market for skilled 'caring' labour. Lacking in her analysis, however, is a sustained examination of the impact of central government pressures and initiatives in developing (technocratic) structures and controls that are only rhetorically concerned with facilitating a qualitative improvement in patient care.

In the third group, the chapters by Black and Neathey and Cooper and Robson both explore the contribution historically materialist forms of analysis to the study of management control. Drawing upon the initial phase of the post-Braverman debate on the labour process, Black and Neathey's case study of management control in the cut-glass industry shows how craft and managerial ideologies serve to mediate and institutionalise the conflict between Labour and Capital. However, in revealing how the continuation of the structure of capitalist social relations is practically accomplished at the point of production, they tend to divorce this analysis from the wider processes of social reproduction. This limitation is something that Cooper and Robson seek to correct in their chapter. Like Black and Neathey, they favour an approach in which the content, diversity and development of management control systems is studied in relation to their (functional) contribution to the reproduction of the class structure of capitalist political economy. Drawing upon the work of Althusser, they argue that the appearance, reform and decay of control systems is most adequately theorised as a reflection of struggles over capital realisation and allocation and over the reproduction of the ideological and repressive apparatuses that preserve the conditions for accumulation, a recommendation that echoes recent calls to situate the form and dynamics of management control within the complete circuit of capital (cf. Kelly, 1985; Storey, 1985). However, they then go on to suggest the relevance of Foucault's work for exploring the specific discourses and technologies associated with the 'the everyday exercise of power', something which the heady abstractions of structuralist Marxism tend to overlook.

Specifically, Cooper and Robson emphasise the significance of Foucault's formulation of the (contradictory) relationship between power and knowledge for appreciating how social science, including 'management science' has been empowered by the necessity of disciplining Labour to work for Capital. However, while their discussion of Foucault highlights the need for a more penetrating investigation of the discourses and technologies of control, it offers comparatively little of substance in understanding how processes of control (and resistance) are practically accomplished. So, while it is acknowledged that there are 'silences' between the frameworks of Althusser or Braverman and Foucault, there is conspicuously little by way of a clarification of what these silences are, or a revelation of how Foucault's work on concrete disciplinary practices may complement, rather than displace or replace, the abstractions of structuralist Marxism.

The chapter by Roberts provides a penetrating analysis of the concrete practices and contradictory consequences of individualistic, instrumental forms of management control and worker resistance. Despite its exclusion of the contextual conditions of control, his detailed case analysis reveals how a mutual denial of the essential, *practical* interdependence of relations has the effect of sustaining and legitimising a manipulative mode of interaction between management and staff in which each regarded the other primarily as an *impersonal* means of securing reified individual and organisational objectives. In attempting to resist control, staff are shown to reciprocate the instrumentalism of management – an effort which, in turn, provokes the introduction of additional impersonal mechanisms of coercive, instrumental control. The unintended consequence of these instrumental relations, Roberts shows, is to increase distrust, erode legitimacy, divert energy from collaborative to oppositional activity and thereby undermine both the personal and productive potential of organised, interdependent relations.

To those who insist upon a traditional Marxist historical materialist basis to critique, Roberts' exclusive focus upon the micro-politics of power may appear prone to the very psychologisation of social practices that it seeks to expose and transcend. However, without denying its limited field of vision, such a dismissive assessment would seem to reflect an unfortunate impatience and insensitivity in respect of the complexities and consequences of oppressive relations of production, especially in regard to the influence of existential preoccupations in the attraction and development of (contradictory) strategies of resistance (Knights and Willmott, 1985).

This is an impatience picked up in the contribution by Hopwood who is attentive to the problematic, constructed nature of interests. His piece is particularly critical of studies (e.g. Johnson, 1980) that assume that accounting controls function in the service of interests that are 'defined prior to and outside of the context of the specific organisational and social arenas in which they intervene'. This central message of Hopwood's paper resonnates both with the studies by Black and Neathey and Roberts and, more generally, with some of the more recent theoretical and empirical contributions to the labour process debate (e.g. Knights and Willmott, 1985a). More generally, the challenge for future studies seeking to advance a critique of management control is to examine contemporary processes of nationalisation in the light of a perspective capable of penetrating the existential as well as the historical dimensions of the social practices through which relations or production and distribution in advanced capitalist society are organised and controlled (Knights and Willmott, 1983).

Future contributions to the critique of management control must develop and integrate elements of a 'dialectical' analysis contained in this volume and elsewhere (e.g. Giddens, 1982; Storey, 1983; Willmott, 1985). Their concern will be to expose the oppressive conditions and consequences of management control. It is to be hoped that they will also reveal how contradictions within the organisation of labour processes present opportunities for demonstrating the rational basis and potential for promoting a movement away from the further extension of forms of technocratic control towards social relations that express a commitment to the removal, and eventual elimination, of the unnecessary experiences of exploitation and domination that inhere within the institutions of advanced capitalist societies. At the core of such studies will be an appreciation of the crucial difference between technical and practico-emancipatory modes of rationalisation. For, as McCarthy (1978, p. 23) has observed,

> Political emancipation cannot be identified with technological progress. While rationalisation in the dimension of instrumental action signifies the growth of productive forces and extension of technological control, rationalisation in the dimension of social interaction signifies the extension of communication free from domination.

References

T. W. Adorno, H. Albert, R. Dahrendorf, J. Habermas, H. Pilot and K. R. Popper, *The Positivist Dispute in German Sociology*, trans. G. Adey and D. Frisby (London: Heinemann, 1976).

A. Giddens, *A Contemporary Critique of Historical Materialism* (London: Macmillan, 1981).

A. Giddens, 'Power, the dialectic of control and class structuration', in A. Giddens and G. Mackenzie (eds), *Social Class and the Division of Labour* (Cambridge University Press, 1982).

J. Habermas, *Toward a Rational Society*, trans. J. Shapiro (London: Heinemann, 1971).

J. Habermas, *Knowledge and Human Interests*, trans. J. Shapiro (London: Heinemann, 1972).

J. Habermas, *Theory and Practice*, trans. J. Viertel (London: Heinemann, 1974).

J. Habermas, 'A Positivistically Bisected Rationalism', in Adorno *et al.* (1976).

N. Jackson and H. C. Willmott, 'Beyond Epistemology and Reflective Conversation – Towards Human Relations', *Human Relations*, 40, 6, pp. 361–80.

T. Johnson, 'Work and Power', in G. Esland and G. Salaman (eds), *The Politics of Work and Occupations* (Milton Keynes: Open University Press, 1980).

J. Kelly, 'Management's Redesign of Work: Labour Process, Labour Markets and Product Markets', in D. Knights *et al.* (1985a).

D. Knights and H. C. Willmott, 'The Problem of Freedom: Fromm's Contribution to a Critical Theory of Work Organisation', *Praxis International*, 2, 2 (1982) pp. 204–25.

D. Knights and H. C. Willmott, 'Dualism and Domination', *Australian and New Zealand Journal of Sociology*, 19, 1 (1983) pp. 33–49.

D. Knights and H. C. Willmott, 'Power and Identity in Theory and Practice', *Sociological Review*, 33, 1 (1985) pp. 22–46.

D. Knights, H. C. Willmott and D. Collinson (eds), *Job Redesign* (Aldershot: Gower, 1985a).

D. Knights and H. C. Willmott (eds), *Managing the Labour Process* (Aldershot: Gower, 1986).

K. Marx, *Early Writings*, trans. R. Livingstone and G. Benton (Harmondsworth: Penguin, 1976).

T. McCarthy, *The Critical Theory of Jurgen Habermas* (London: Hutchinson, 1978).

K. R. Popper, 'Reason or Revolution?' in T. Adorno *et al.* (1976).

J. Storey, *Managerial Prerogative and the Question of Control* (London: Routledge and Kegan Paul, 1983).

J. Storey, 'The Means of Management Control', *Sociology*, 19, 2 (1985) pp. 193–212.

H. C. Willmott, 'Paradigms for Accounting Research', *Accounting, Organizations and Society*, 8, 44 (1983) pp. 389–405.

H. C. Willmott, 'Dialectical Analysis, Labour Process and the State', paper delivered at the 3rd Annual Aston/UMIST Organisation and Control of the Labour Process Conference, Owens Park, Manchester (1985).

H. C. Willmott, 'Unconscious Sources of Motivation in the Theory of the Subject', *Journal for the Theory of Social Behaviour*, 16, 1 (1986) pp. 105–22.

Index

accountability 229, 231–7
accountancy profession 248–52, 263–7
accountants 154
accounting and interests 141–57
accounting defined 50–2, 56–9
accounting – service activity 47
accounting, social analysis of 141–57
accounting – social science 47–50, 52–5
accounting standards 255–6, 263–6
accounting standards (steering) committee 263–6
accounting systems 229–31, 241–2
  use by managers 232–6
accounting – technical activity 47
agency of individuals 219–20
ambiguity *see* uncertainty
analytics of relations of power 100–7
authority 63, 64, 272
authority and anarchy 66
authority and the self 76

barriers to entry 198
budget systems 10
budgetary control 36
budgeting 293–319

capital 333, 336
causation 39
central government 154
Christian 71, 73
Christian socialist 69
class 250–2, 259–62, 267
class barriers 195
class position of managers 239
conflict 273
contingency approach 24
contingency theory of management accounting 30
contingency theory of organisations 34
contradiction 237–9, 260–6
control 65
control, imperative 271
control and anxiety 67
control and co-operation 69, 70
conventional wisdom 325, 331
corporatism 246, 252–8
cost accounting 154
craft consciousness 163
credentialling 192
crisis 246, 261, 264–7
critical analysis 331–2
critique 3, 4
culture 317–19, 226–9
cybernetics 4, 11, 12, 17
cybernetics – feedback and control 19
cybernetics – relevance to control 12

deductive approach 29
dependency 65
determinism 220
dialectic method 326, 328
dialectical analysis 338
dialectics 229, 235
direct control 161
discipline 101–3
discourse 146
domination 4, 271–2, 287–90, 335
  see also power

economics 10
elitism 82–3
emancipatory knowledge 332, 334
enlightenment 332, 334
environment 16–18, 20, 245–6
environment – relevance to management control 16–18, 20, 22

epistemology 332
evolution 152-3
experts 189

feedback 19
foreign currency translation 256
fractions of capital 257, 266-7
free markets 72, 74, 76
future research 329

'garbage-can' model 123-4
general systems theory 17
goals 22-3, 120-2, 127
government *see* state
grounded theory 27, 29, 31, 36

Herrschaft 271-2
hierarchy 13, 63ff
hierarchy, alternatives to 68, 69
historical materialism 91-9

ideology 3, 115-16, 126-30, 134-7, 168
ideology of science and technology 331-3
incorporation 163
inductive approach 29
inflation accounting 246, 255, 263-7
informal information systems 225-6
information filtering 307
institutionalisation 182
instrumental 56
instrumental control 280, 286
instrumentalism 337
integration 272, 285
integrationist 87-91
interdependence 337
interests 257-8
interests, knowledge-constitutive 130-2
interpretive sociology 218-19, 222

labour 336
labour process 338
language *see* signification
legitimacy 168, 182

legitimation 226-9, 232-3, 235, 253, 261-6
legitimation of power 272

management 333
management control 79-114, 333-4
 definition 12, 15-17, 20-1
 history 9-10
 interdisciplinary character 9-11
 predictive function 21
managerial power 163
market for excuses 326
meaning *see* signification
monopolisation 192, 197, 199, 201-2
morality 193, 195, 227
motivation 10
mutual accountability 75, 76
myths 125

National Coal Board (NCB) 222-41
 accounting systems 229-31, 241-2
 accountability systems 231-7
 contradictions in management 237-9
 culture of management 226-9
 management information systems 224-6
 mining engineers and management 222-3

omissions 328, 329
optimism in budgets 39
organisational goals 145
organisational structure 23-4
overtraining 201

phenomenological tradition 33
planning 224, 315
pluralism 81-2, 258-9
political economy 331
positivism 5, 332
power 4, 79-114, 219, 221-3, 234-235, 247-8, 272, 273-4, 285
power base 298
power, personal 293
practical reason 334, 337

Index

practitioners 327
product market 178
productive potential 337
professional accounting bodies 254, 256–7, 263
professionalism 191
professions 245–6, 248–52

radicalism 83–4
rationality 115–16, 118–20, 125–7, 134–7, 234–6
regulator 19
reification 22, 335
reification, alternative view to 285
research and development 255–6
resistance 154
responsibility centre 13
retrospective rationality 121–3, 135
rituals 234

scandals 48
scientific authority 331
scientific progress 333
scientism 132
self-managing 69, 73, 74
signification 224–6, 232–3, 238
skew distributions 40
skill, survival 163
slack, organisational 230, 236
smoothing of accounting data 224–5, 235–6
social psychology 10, 11, 14
socialisation 297
socio-technical systems 33

standard costing 223
state 246, 248, 252–67
  and use of accounting data 241–2
strategic planning 12, 15–17, 19–21
structural invariance 23–4
structural Marxism 336–7
structuration theory 217–22
  and accounting 229–39
structure, social 219–20
style of budget use 37–9
subjectivism 80–7, 328
symbols 124
systematic dependence 71
systems, social 220
systems theory 33

task control 12, 15–17
technical control 3
technical rationality 206–7, 332–4, 335
theoretical sensitivity 31–2
theory 52
theory generation 36
theory verification 36
training 194

uncertainty 224, 230–1, 233, 236
Utopianism 66, 76

value added 154
Verstehen 33, 325, 326

work 72, 73

GPSR Compliance

The European Union's (EU) General Product Safety Regulation (GPSR) is a set of rules that requires consumer products to be safe and our obligations to ensure this.

If you have any concerns about our products, you can contact us on

ProductSafety@springernature.com

In case Publisher is established outside the EU, the EU authorized representative is:

Springer Nature Customer Service Center GmbH
Europaplatz 3
69115 Heidelberg, Germany

www.ingramcontent.com/pod-product-compliance
Lightning Source LLC
Chambersburg PA
CBHW031808110426
42873CB00040B/1